MW00616974

Be Still My Soul

A Collection of Essays about Finding Hope and Encouragement in the Face of Suffering and Trials

Luci Partain

Gospel Armory
PUBLISHING

Be Still My Soul: A Collection of Essays about Finding Hope and Encouragement in the Face of Suffering and Trials
Copyright © 2020 by Luci Partain

All Rights Reserved. No portion of this book may be reproduced in any form without the written permission of the publisher, except in the case of brief excerpts to be used in a review.

Published by:
Gospel Armory Publishing
Bowling Green, Kentucky
www.GospelArmory.com

Printed in the United States of America

ISBN: 978-1-942036-67-8

Table of Contents

Preface

As Jesus bore His cross to Calvary, a great many mourned and wept. Jesus said, "Daughters of Jerusalem, do not weep for me, but weep for yourselves and your children." Then as a footnote He said, "For if they do these things when the wood is green, what will happen when it is dry."

The year 2020 has been the year of the tear, a trial for all of us, not just the disruptions of the pandemic of our work and business, but the sickness and dying. I never dreamed that in my lifetime I would see the church doors closed on Sundays.

The trials have our nerves on edge and there seems to be no end in sight. It is a test that many are failing. It is bringing out the worst even in some of the saints of God. It can still get a lot worse. The wood is still green. When the wood is dry, what will we do? How will we bear up to the rigors of the test?

Luci has put together a number of Bible studies over the years that address many of these issues. It is the fruit of her own trials, beginning perhaps with the death of her mother. That loss came at a time when one of our children was critically ill. She has broken her arm in a fall while being a good mother playing with her children, then after the memory of that nightmare was fading, she stepped into a hole and broke one leg and badly sprained the other ankle. In that condition with her leg in a cast and unable to walk she received a phone call that her father had had a heart attack 600 miles away and was near death. Luci is married to an evangelist who happened to be in Mexico at the time and unable to help her get to her father's side. Seven years later last june, the pandemic was strong in Miami when her dad reached the end of his days. Luci sat at his side for six days as he slowly slipped away. She could not leave his side because the rules of the hospital would not allow her to return. On the way home we all began to suffer the Covid19 virus ourselves. Luci's sister nearly died, her cousin actually did die. When we were tested well and could get back to normal, my mother departed this life and we journeyed to Odessa to join the family in God's kind comfort. Add to such experiences, all of the other special crises that come to the wife of a preacher, and you can see that she has had a rich field of experiences that one after the other have driven her to seek refuge in the wisdom and counsel of our loving Savior. Her writing has been therapeutic for her heart.

God has given Luci special gifts that help her dig into the Sacred Word and search for the answers that God provides His children for these perplexing times. Questions such as, "Why is this happening to me?" and "What does God want me to do? How does He want me to deal with these things?"

Let me encourage you to take full advantage of these studies. Take your time and read them at your leisure. You will find that the hand of God is strong to help you and give you the peace of God, which surpasses all understanding.

Terry Partain

Does Jesus Care?

"Casting all your anxieties on him, because he cares for you." 1 Peter 5:7

The past two months have been challenging and painful for us. This is the year of the tear. In less than two months, we have painfully come face to face with the loss of three loved ones, my father, my mother-in-law, and my cousin, who was like a brother to me. The song *"Does Jesus Care"* hits home because it expresses our Lord's care for us during our times of pain, heavy burdens, and cares.

"For as we share abundantly in Christ's sufferings, so through Christ we share abundantly in comfort too." (2 Corinthians 1:5)

In times of sadness, heartache, darkness, and the loss of loved ones, we can rest in the assurance that our Lord Jesus cares for us. He loves and cares for us His children and asks us to cast our burdens on Him.

"Cast your burden on the LORD, and he will sustain you; he will never permit the righteous to be moved." (Psa. 55:22)

He has promised us that He will give us rest from the cares of this life, and we must believe and trust Him (Matt. 11:28-30). When our hearts are filled with pain, we can confidently look to God for comfort (2 Cor. 1:5). Thus, the question is, *Does Jesus care?*

Our Lord Jesus also manifests His care toward us during our times of dread and fear. And though we may walk through the valley of the shadow of death, we have nothing to fear because He is with us (Psa. 23:4). God has given us the spirit of power, not of fear (2 Tim. 1:7). We need not live in fear, for perfect love casts out fear (1 Jn. 4:18).

> *"For God gave us a spirit not of fear but of power and love and self-control."* (2 Tim. 1:7)

> *"There is no fear in love, but perfect love casts out fear. For fear has to do with punishment, and whoever fears has not been perfected in love."* (1 John 4:18)

Our Lord and Savior also cares for us amid our times of temptation and grief. Although no one can say we have no sin, we indeed fail at times to resist some temptation strong.

> *"If we say we have no sin, we deceive ourselves, and the truth is not in us."* (1 John 1:8)

Nevertheless, we must have a tender heart and be compelled to grieve or mourn for our sins.

> *"Blessed are those who mourn, for they shall be comforted."* (Matt. 5:4)

We must weep with godly sorrow every time we fail our Lord and sin against Him. Our sin must cause our tears to flow all night long.

> *"O LORD, rebuke me not in your anger, nor discipline me in your wrath. Be gracious to me, O LORD, for I am languishing; heal me, O LORD, for my bones are troubled. My soul also is greatly troubled. But you, O LORD—how long? Turn, O*

> *LORD, deliver my life; save me for the sake of your steadfast love. For in death there is no remembrance of you; in Sheol who will give you praise? I am weary with my moaning; every night I flood my bed with tears; I drench my couch with my weeping."* (Psalm 6:1-6)

Since our Lord Jesus experienced sadness at the loss of a dear and beloved friend, He understands and cares for us during those dark times (John 11:32-35). His words found in the Scriptures can comfort and encourage us in such circumstances.

> *"But we do not want you to be uninformed, brothers, about those who are asleep, that you may not grieve as others do who have no hope. For since we believe that Jesus died and rose again, even so, through Jesus, God will bring with him those who have fallen asleep. For this we declare to you by a word from the Lord, that we who are alive, who are left until the coming of the Lord, will not precede those who have fallen asleep. For the Lord himself will descend from heaven with a cry of command, with the voice of an archangel, and with the sound of the trumpet of God. And the dead in Christ will rise first. Then we who are alive, who are left, will be caught up together with them in the clouds to meet the Lord in the air, and so we will always be with the Lord. Therefore encourage one another with these words."* (1 Thes. 4:13-18)

Since He suffered death, He is able to be our merciful and faithful High Priest to help us be free from the fear of death, bringing the comfort of hope into our lives.

> *"Since therefore the children share in flesh and blood, he himself likewise partook of the same things, that through death he might*

destroy the one who has the power of death, that is, the devil, 15 and deliver all those who through fear of death were subject to lifelong slavery. 16 For surely it is not angels that he helps, but he helps the offspring of Abraham. 17 Therefore he had to be made like his brothers in every respect, so that he might become a merciful and faithful high priest in the service of God, to make propitiation for the sins of the people. 18 For because he himself has suffered when tempted, he is able to help those who are being tempted." Heb. 2:14-18

CONCLUSION:

Our Lord cares during our times of pain, burdens, cares, dread and fear, temptation and grief, sadness, heartache, and the loss of loved ones.

> *"O yes, He cares, I know He cares; His heart is touched with my grief;*
> *When the days are weary, the long nights dreary, I know my Savior cares."*

Jesus not only demonstrated that He cares for us through His death but also that He continues to care for us. Thus, in times of darkness and sorrow, we can rest in the confident assurance that He cares and is willing to help us.

When life's storms besiege our soul, God is always near us to prove that He cares for us. He is our Anchor. Our faith in God can help us bear the fiery furnace of our trials, keeping us from being burned. Our Lord gives us quiet and sweet rest when we are weary because of persecution, affliction, suffering, difficulties, adversities, and Satan's buffeting. In Christ, we have such an abundance of precious promises that all things shall work together for good, in blessedness. He is our great Rock that shelters and sweetly refreshes us in our time of need.

Indeed, our most in-depth spiritual lessons come from trials, pain, and suffering. The deep waters, the hot fire, and the dark valleys teach us to walk the path of faith.

> *"When you pass through the waters, I will be with you; and through the rivers, they shall not overwhelm you; when you walk through fire you shall not be burned, and the flame shall not consume you."* (Isaiah 43:2)

God walks with us through our darkest valleys, troubled waters, and hot fires. He never breaks His promises. Every time that we walk through the deep waters of difficulty and suffering, He is there with us to provide refuge and rest. And no matter how many fierce storms, challenges, and suffering come our way, God will be our refuge and the solid and sure anchor that we can hold on to. He is our source of protection or shield and rest during life's storms. But we must learn to hide ourselves in Him alone.

> *"You are my hiding place and my shield; I wait for Your word."* (Psalm 119:114)

> *"For in the day of trouble He will conceal me in His tabernacle; In the secret place of His tent He will hide me; He will lift me up on a rock."* (Psalm 27:5)

> *"Deliver me, O LORD, from my enemies; I take refuge in You."* (Psalm 143:9)

He is our place of shelter and safety. He will carry us with loving and tender care in our times of fear and sorrow.

> *"God is our refuge and strength, a very present help in trouble. Therefore we will not fear though the earth gives way, though the mountains be moved into the heart of the sea, though its waters roar and*

foam, though the mountains tremble at its swelling. There is a river whose streams make glad the city of God, the holy habitation of the Most High. God is in the midst of her; she shall not be moved; God will help her when morning dawns. The nations rage, the kingdoms totter; he utters his voice, the earth melts. The LORD of hosts is with us; the God of Jacob is our fortress. Come, behold the works of the LORD, how he has brought desolations on the earth. He makes wars cease to the end of the earth; he breaks the bow and shatters the spear; he burns the chariots with fire. 'Be still, and know that I am God. I will be exalted among the nations, I will be exalted in the earth!' The LORD of hosts is with us; the God of Jacob is our fortress.'" (Psalm 46)

Our God shelters us like the wings of care and protection of a protective mother bird. In our times of trouble and sorrow, our merciful and loving God spreads His wings to guard His children so that no harm will overtake them.

"Be merciful to me, O God, be merciful to me, for in you my soul takes refuge; in the shadow of your wings I will take refuge, till the storms of destruction pass by." (Psalm 57:1)

"He will cover you with his pinions, and under his wings you will find refuge; his faithfulness is a shield and buckler." (Psalm 91:4)

"No evil shall be allowed to befall you, no plague come near your tent." (Psalm 91:10)

"O Jerusalem, Jerusalem, the city that kills the prophets and stones those who are sent to it! How often would I have gathered your children together

as a hen gathers her brood under her wings, and you were not willing!" (Matthew 23:37)

May we all come to our place of refuge, strength, and defense, in our Lord and Savior, Jesus Christ. May we find rest and quiet solitude in His arms where we can just drown out this world's cares. May we find hope and healing in Him alone amid our burdens and distress, for He cares and is touched by our sorrows and trials.

I hope the words of this lovely song stir your soul the way they do mine.

"Does Jesus Care?"

"Does Jesus care when my heart is pained Too
    deeply for mirth and song,
As the burdens press, and the cares distress,
    And the way grows weary and long?"

"Does Jesus care when the way is dark With a
    nameless dread and fear?
As the daylight fades into deep night shades,
    Does He care enough to be near?"

"Does Jesus care when I've tried and failed To
    resist some temptation strong,
When for my deep grief I find no relief, Though
    my tears flow all the night long?"

Does Jesus care when I've said 'good-by' To the
    dearest on earth to me,
And my sad heart aches till it nearly breaks–Is
    it aught to Him, does He see?

Chorus,

"O yes, He cares, I know He cares; His heart is touched with my grief; When the days are weary, the long nights dreary, I know my Savior cares."

Be Still My Soul: Embracing God's Provision in Our Trials

"Be still, and know that I am God. I will be exalted among the nations, I will be exalted in the earth!" The Lord of hosts is with us; the God of Jacob is our fortress.'" Psalm 46:10-11

Most of us spend our lives in quiet desperation, wondering when the next calamity or disaster will strike us. We imagine that we are alone. In this context, the song *Be Still My Soul* has touched me and moved me to enter a very encouraging study of God's counsel for us in our trials. I invite you to join me as we ponder this life-transforming Bible message.

Psalm 46:10-11 was the inspiration for Katharina Von Schlegel's hymn, *"Be Still My Soul."*

In the Bible, *"be still"* means more than just being quiet. Rather it projects the idea of total relaxation, which produces that assurance that comes from our Lord since He is our refuge. Under His mighty hands, we are held firm. He watches carefully over us.

In this beautiful song, the author describes all the challenges or problems that cause us to be anxious. Indeed, when our lives are filled with chaos, pain, loss, and tribulations, we find it difficult to relax. In the song, she gives us many reasons why we should be still since our God is on our side. He faithfully will remain. The song is very dear to my heart because it encourages and reminds me of God's precious assurances as found in His Word, that reassure me I have a supreme, omniscient, omnipresent, wise and magnificent God who loves, cares, and provides for me. He sympathizes with me and is trustworthy. He protects us. That is why I have great hope in Him.

I hope you will find great encouragement, assurance, and peace in the study, knowing that God is our refuge in time of need.

The winds of difficulty and suffering often threaten and render us weak. Such winds are usually cold and merciless, knocking us down. When they blow into our lives, they carry us away with a storm of questions, doubts, fears, discouragement, and disillusionment. At that moment, we must realize that we need the strength of God, secure and unmovable, to keep us from being swept away.

The Word of God warns us that *"evil days"* will come (Ecclesiastes 12:1; Matthew 6:34; Ephesians 5:16). Job observed, *"Man born of woman is of few days and full of trouble"* (Job 14:1; cf. Psalm 73:14, 21). Sometimes events, situations, diagnoses, tragedies, and conditions in our lives do not make sense. The Psalmist pondered aloud, *"Why standest thou afar off, O LORD? Why hidest thou thyself in times of trouble?"* (Psalm 10:1).

One of the most troublesome areas in our walk with the Lord is life's trials and tribulations. All those who want to live godly will suffer persecution from our persecutor, Satan. Satan is the author of much of our sufferings, tragedies, sickness, hurt and eventually death.

In Acts 14:22, Paul states:

> "*Strengthening the souls of the disciples, encouraging them to continue in the faith, and saying that* **through many tribulations we must enter the kingdom of God.**"

Indeed, in this life, trouble is unavoidable:

> "*Man, that is born of a woman, is of few days, and* **full of trouble.**" (Job 14:1)

> "*When the righteous cry for help,* **the Lord hears and delivers them out of all their troubles.** *The Lord is near to the brokenhearted and saves the crushed in spirit. Many are the afflictions of the righteous, but the Lord delivers him out of them all.*" (Psalm 34:17-19)

> "*For it has been granted to you that for the sake of Christ you should not only believe in him but also* **suffer for his sake.**" (Philippians 1:29)

> "*Indeed, all who desire to* **live a godly life in Christ Jesus will be persecuted.**" (2 Timothy 3:12)

> "*And after* **you have suffered a little while,** *the God of all grace, who has called you to his eternal glory in Christ, will himself restore, confirm, strengthen, and establish you.*" (1 Peter 5:10)

Let us consider God's point of view when He sees us suffering and how He expects us to respond:

I. GOD'S PERSPECTIVE AND PURPOSE IN SUFFERING:

REJOICING WHILE SUFFERING:

We live in a culture that ignores the suffering or sorrow that other societies before us had to undergo. As one reads their journals, he can obviously see that they understood the problem of suffering. They were never surprised by suffering. Amazingly, we are a culture that seems to be surprised by life's path of suffering. In the Bible, we can read from cover to cover of those who had to endure suffering. Notice what the apostle Paul said to the Christians of his day:

> *"Therefore we do not lose heart, but though our outer man is decaying, yet our inner man is being renewed day by day. For momentary, light affliction is producing for us an eternal weight of glory far beyond all comparison, while we look not at the things which are seen, but at the things which are not seen; for the things which are seen are temporal, but the things which are not seen are eternal."* (2 Corinthians 4:16-18)

Paul speaks of suffering as a reality. Our bodies, as Paul said, are wearing away. Our bodies are like wind-up clocks that are just ticking away. We cannot stop our physical body from wearing out. Our relationships wear away also. *Isn't it something that time and circumstances pull us apart from each other?* Our skills and talents wear away. Our families are wearing away, dying off one by one. The truth is that everything is like a wave in the sand that cannot be pinned down because it recedes from us.

The apostle Paul wrote to the Corinthians about *"wasting away."* Some brethren may have suggested that he could not be trusted, and that God was not with him because of all his sufferings and difficulties. Consider what Paul said about all the tragedies and challenges he had to experience.

> "*Five times I received at the hands of the Jews the forty lashes less one. Three times I was beaten with rods. Once I was stoned. Three times I was shipwrecked; a night and a day I was adrift at sea; on frequent journeys, in danger from rivers, danger from robbers, danger from my own people, danger from Gentiles, danger in the city, danger in the wilderness, danger at sea, danger from false brothers; in toil and hardship, through many a sleepless night, in hunger and thirst, often without food, in cold and exposure. And, apart from other things, there is the daily pressure on me of my anxiety for all the churches.*" (2 Cor. 11:24-28)

Paul responded by saying that all his suffering and hardship were a confirmation of the glorious Gospel of Christ rather than a denial. Therefore, he writes:

> "*We are afflicted in every way, but not crushed; perplexed, but not driven to despair; persecuted, but not forsaken; struck down, but not destroyed; always carrying in the body the death of Jesus, so that the life of Jesus may also be manifested in our bodies. For we who live are always being given over to death for Jesus' sake, so that the life of Jesus also may be manifested in our mortal flesh. So death is at work in us, but life in you.*" (2 Cor. 4:8-12)

In these verses, Paul is speaking of the courage and long-suffering of the apostles. The apostles were great sufferers for preaching the Truth of the Gospel of Christ. They acknowledged how the Gospel helped and sustained them amid afflictions. Paul stated that just as Jesus' suffering and death led to a greater life, he can experience the same thing in his life. All his sufferings led to a more excellent life as they heard the Gospel and experienced abundant life in Christ. When one chooses to die to self, he finds out that his death leads to a greater life for those around us.

Death to self can be accomplished only through suffering and trials. You see, when one dies to self, he can bear much fruit, *"Truly, truly, I say to you, unless a grain of wheat falls into the earth and dies, it remains alone; but if it dies, it bears much fruit."* (John 12:24) Suffering leads to life, but that seed of grain must fall to the ground and die to bear life.

In Romans 5:3-5, Paul goes on to say:

> *"Not only that, but we rejoice in our sufferings, knowing that suffering produces endurance, and endurance produces character, and character produces hope, and hope does not put us to shame, because God's love has been poured into our hearts through the Holy Spirit who has been given to us."*

So, what is Paul trying to say here exactly? He is saying that his suffering not only leads to greater life in those around him but also to himself as well. The basis for Paul's rejoicing was faith. Not only does our faith justify us, but it gives us peace with God. By faith, we can have access to God's grace. But we must believe that God exists before we can believe in Him, Hebrews 11:6. There is no purpose in rejoicing while suffering if one removes God from the picture. Sadly, many keep God out of the picture when they suffer, assuming that God is not there. The truth is that without God, our suffering is meaningless and fruitless, causing us to despair. In Hebrews 11:6, we are told that God will reward those who diligently seek Him. This ties in well with Matthew 6:33.

Faith in God's Plan for our Suffering:

Therefore, to rejoice while suffering, one must believe in the God who can provide and reward us if we seek Him and His kingdom of righteousness. Likewise, we must have strong faith, believing that He will not allow us to suffer beyond what we can handle. We must believe that He, by His grace, will provide a way of escape (I Cor. 10:13). We must believe that His discipline will train us and perfect our faith if we let Him. And finally, we must believe that He is with us no matter what we suffer (Hebrews 13:5).

We must believe firmly that He is working in us to accomplish His will (Phil. 2:12-13). Therefore, we can say with confidence that we can do all things through Him (Phil. 4:13). *Do you believe in that awesome God and all His promises?* You must believe that you might be able to rejoice when things are bad and ugly. You must believe in the God of Abraham, Jacob, Joseph, Moses, David, Job, and Daniel. These are all witnesses who suffered but survived because of their faith in God. *More than surviving, they were rewarded!* (Hebrews 12:1-2).

Romans 4:12 speaks of walking in the footsteps of faith. Our God wants us to live our faith by our actions (James 2:18), only doing what He ordains. God's ways work. So, if we want to rejoice while suffering, we must start having faith, believe in Him, and surrender our lives to Him alone (Galatians 2:20).

Looking Forward to God's Goal in our Suffering:

To understand our suffering, we must fix our eyes on Jesus. In the darkest hour of sorrow, one must reflect on the Truth. One's foundation of joy in suffering is based on his looking forward to God's goal. Suffering has a very particular place in God's plan. Without suffering, no one can go to heaven. Take for example, what Acts 14:22 has to say about tribulations getting us to the kingdom of God.

"Strengthening the souls of the disciples, encouraging them to continue in the faith, and saying that through many tribulations we must enter the kingdom of God."

God allows suffering so that we can learn to be merciful to others. Romans 5:3-5 teaches us that suffering produces endurance, longsuffering, steadfastness, or perseverance. Patience helps us to make it through suffering. In other words, without suffering, we cannot learn endurance. It is weight training. Those who lift weights, push themselves. They challenge themselves, building themselves up. They have learned that if they only lift the easier weights, they will never develop the strength to lift the heavier ones. They push themselves beyond their limits, straining and struggling with much heavier weights, increasing the burden and pushing their muscles to their limits. By doing this, the fibers in their muscles rip and tear. The good news is that the healing process is what builds up those muscles that have been compromised, allowing them to handle more and more weight. The same process heals our souls. Our other burdens help us to endure the heavier loads. It is being pushed to our limits in our suffering that we learn strength and endurance. It allows us to remain faithful despite the wiles of Satan to stop us. Tolerance is our goal. The character of endurance or patience is priceless! God tests our faith so that we might build the quality of character in our lives. *"The more tests we pass, the tougher we become."*

Our suffering produces proven character. Our endurance matures us and shapes us into the image of Christ (Ephesians 4:11-13; Romans 8:28-29). It is in suffering that our God develops in us a godly and Christlike character so that we may bear good fruit, John 15:1-2.

The word that is translated "character" in Romans 5:4 is also found in I Peter 1:6-7. Peter speaks of the "genuineness" of our faith and how we ought to rejoice even in suffering because we know that trials test and prove our faith. Today many easily misunderstand this concept since they view the testing as an issue of pass or fail. They think testing is to see how faithful we are. The fact is that God does not allow us to suffer just to see how much faith we have. Rather the real picture of suffering and trials is that of gold being tested under fire. I am not going to deny that the testing can show how pure gold is. However, the testing causes the impurities to float on top of the molten rock so that it can be skimmed off in the process of purification.

Without suffering and tribulations, we might deceive ourselves thinking that we have strength when, in fact, we don't. The truth is that we gain strength by suffering. *Why do I say that?* Because it is the only way that we can see the weaknesses and work our hardest to remove them. *Do you know that we cannot enter the kingdom of God without suffering?* Suffering is permitted so that we can see our weaknesses and rely on the Lord to help us strengthen them. Suffering strengthens us by providing endurance. And as our tolerance increases, it helps us to remove our weaknesses as the suffering brings them to the surface. But that is not the end. Paul states that our proven character gives us hope. The hope the Bible speaks about is not wishful thinking like the hope of those who are not in Christ. True Bible hope is the hope of the glory of God (Romans 5:2). This is parallel with the hope mentioned in Romans 8:18-19 that is going to be revealed to us in eternity: *"For I consider that the sufferings of this present time are not worth comparing with the glory that is to be revealed to us. For the creation waits with eager longing for the revealing of the sons of God."*

A few verses later in verse 24, Paul says that *"in this hope we were saved. Now hope that is seen is not hope. For who hopes for what he sees?"* You see, when we endure suffering, we gain greater endurance, and our testing helps us remove the dross from our lives. Therefore, we have the hope of glory through

God in eternity. Our salvation is, therefore, the end and goal of suffering.

Faith is vital to rejoice amid our sufferings. It is through suffering that we will enter the kingdom of heaven. In 2 Corinthians 12:7-10, we read of Paul's thorn in the flesh. Paul acknowledged that he needed to rely more on God. Such discipline helped keep Paul from becoming conceited and kept him on his path to heaven. This is precisely what God wants for us.

We Must Look Back to God's Love:

We tend to put our hope in things that disappoint and put us to shame. Our hope is in earthly things. We fail to acknowledge that our hope comes to us because of God's love that has been poured into our hearts as revealed to us by the Spirit (Romans 5:5). This is not in any way a miraculous operation of the Spirit working in our hearts. Rather, God's love is poured into our hearts because of Jesus' sacrifice.

In Romans 5:11, Paul states that *"we also rejoice in God through our Lord Jesus Christ, through whom we have now received reconciliation."* So, when we are suffering and tempted to believe that God has forsaken us, *why not look back to God's love that He has poured out into our hearts through His Son's death for our sins?* **What an amazing love that is!** To send His only begotten Son to die for our sins that we might be saved even though we were not worthy of such love and sacrifice. After all, *"one will scarcely die for a righteous person—though perhaps for a good person one would dare even to die"* (Romans 5:7). And though we were sinners, unrighteous, unholy, and not worthy of such love, He sent our Lord Jesus to die for us. *That is hard for me to fathom!*

Therefore, we must realize whatever the trials, they have all been resolved at the cross. God loved us so much that He took our sins away through His Son. Our faith and His love ought to help us to overcome any suffering, whether it is persecution, sickness, financial crisis, national crisis, or whatever we are going through. We must know in our heart that in the end, this shall pass, and that God's love will never fail us. In the end, if we remain faithful, we will be saved and go to heaven.

If God has loved us enough to reconcile us to Himself through His Son, then He will still love us enough to help us get through whatever suffering or trials that we may face if we hang on to our faith. *You can be sure of that!* You must believe in His promises. He said He will not allow us to endure more than we are able (1 Corinthians 10:13). *What a great and loving God we serve!*

THE BLESSINGS OF SUFFERING AND PAIN:

> *"For I consider that the sufferings of this present time are not worth comparing with the glory that is to be revealed to us... For we know that the whole creation has been groaning together in the pains of childbirth until now."* (Romans 8:18, 22)

Pain is usually defined as "unpleasantness." Just as physical pain is an early warning system to the brain, so it is a warning system to our souls. Pain reminds us that something is wrong. But pain itself, the hurt of pain, is a blessing. There are so many lessons we can learn from suffering. It is vital to experience pain that we may learn the blessings that spring out of it. So often, we miss out on such blessings because we do not learn the spiritual lessons it can bring us. Sadly, pain drives many away from their faith. Pain causes many to blame God for allowing misery. On the other hand, it turns others to God alone.

Many times, when pain strikes us, we get upset, angry, and frustrated. Most of us have been there! But it is faith in our God that has always brought us back to the fact that He is still in control and holds the future and that we must trust in Him. He has many times brought me down from the clouds with trying times. I have learned to trust Him. Prayer, God's Word, and singing songs of praise have helped me find my way back to hope and faith even when I could not see a way out. In all these, I have seen God's beauty. I thank Him for being faithful and lifting me when I am struggling. I am determined to see the good in it and the blessings God is bestowing upon me through pain. He has shown me over and over how much He is mindful of me. So, I have purposed in my heart to keep my eyes open to see the blessings He has provided for me. I want to put on my blessing lens that I may see His hand and mindfulness in my troubled times.

Consider the following ways in which pain or suffering help our Christian walk with our Lord and Savior:

It draws us closer to Christ:

When we experience pain, whether it is inflicted or afflicted, we are forced to choose whether we are going to run away so the pain will subside or cling to Jesus tightly. It is so much easier to run away from pain. But we must choose to hang tightly to Him and draw all the strength we need from Him to face our suffering. Whatever pain we go through; it is very present. Pain is good for us Christians because the more we learn how to draw strength from our Lord Jesus Christ, the higher our tolerance for pain and its challenges. Yes, this is where we can be blessed, learning tolerance under any circumstance.

It helps us focus on what is truly important:

Pain and suffering teach us that although we experience them at many different levels, our Lord gives us a tremendous opportunity to recommit ourselves to our walk with Him and know the value of such a walk. There is victory in all this. It boils down to our perspective. The choice is ours to allow ourselves to refocus on what is truly important, the healing. We must remember that this world with all its suffering and ugliness is not our home. We are pilgrims and sojourners. We await something better, heaven (I Peter 2:11; He-brews 13:14). The Word of God is crystal clear on this. We long for our home in heaven and the new body that will never have to suffer or die again. *Such beautiful and comforting promises!*

Without suffering, who would want to leave this our temporary tabernacle? Who would desire heaven as our eternal home? Therefore, we must prepare ourselves to go there. Yes, suffering keeps this world from becoming too attractive to us.

It strengthens our character:

Our faith is always stretched to the limits. So, what do you do when troubles, trials, and tribulations come your way? Consider James' exhortation:

> *"Count it all joy, my brothers, when you meet trials of various kinds, for you know that the testing of your faith produces steadfastness."* (James 1:2-3)

It is so much easier to give up and run away when we are in pain and suffering. Losing our faith is easy. But it is here that we must rely on our Lord Jesus to carry us through our clouds and challenges. It is here that our character is strengthened.

It deepens our Faith:

We must force ourselves to open our Bibles, pray fervently, and sing songs of praise when we find ourselves amid pain and suffering. In doing all these things, we will find rest for our souls, trust God and His promises to be with us, and provide for our needs. It is here that we must believe in Him, go back to Him, and wait on Him. It will be great gain, and victory, the highest prize.

It purifies us:

> *"Behold, I have refined you, but not as silver; I have tried you in the furnace of affliction."* (Isaiah 48:10)

> *"And I will put this third into the fire, and refine them as one refines silver, and test them as gold is tested. They will call upon my name, and I will answer them. I will say, 'They are my people'; and they will say, 'The Lord is my God.'"* (Zechariah 13:9)

> *"He will sit as a refiner and purifier of silver, and he will purify the sons of Levi and refine them like gold and silver, and they will bring offerings in righteousness to the Lord."* (Malachi 3:3)

We are all aware of Job's fiery trials and how he was put through the fire of such trials but remained faithful, trusting, and hoping in God. He humbly accepted that all his trials had a purpose. Job did not give up even when his wife rejected him, and his friends discouraged him. He did not give up even in the greatest weaknesses! He knew well his furnace of affliction would be good for him. He was aware that he would be refined as pure gold after being tested and tried by fire. We need to have Job's attitude of heart.

> *"But He knows the way I take; when He has tried me, I shall come forth as gold."* (Job 23:10)

Like Job, we all go through our valleys of trials, tears, sorrows, and afflictions. We must trust in God and the beautiful work He is doing in us. *It is all for our good!*

God has told us that He will take us through the fire so that we might be refined like silver. He does this to purify us like gold! Being the Creator of these precious metals, He knows that such metals must be heated to extremely high temperatures before being molded and shaped. He also knows that the heart of man is stubborn and hard to change. Yet, as a loving Father, He desires to guide us through that fire so that we may be modified. In like manner, the goldsmith or silversmith never leaves his crucible once it is on fire. Our loving God sits as a refiner and purifier of silver. He has His eye on us and will keep watching over us until He sees His image in us (Romans 8:29; 1 Peter 1:6-7). *Thank God for the furnace!*

It teaches us compassion:

Is it not something that the people who have suffered the most are usually the most compassionate ones? The more struggles, sufferings, and challenges a person has had to endure, the more efficient they become in being compassionate toward others. The more they uplift, encourage, and help those who are struggling. They seem to have a heart for others and feel their pain.

It makes us supportive:

Pain teaches us to support those who need relief from their pain and suffering. Compassion is the fruit of pain, and it is manifested when we lift and help those in pain.

It gives us understanding:

It is a fact that no one can understand pain better than someone who has already been through it. Understanding is such a great blessing to those who struggle with either chronic illness, invisible illness, or any other source of pain, spiritual or emotional. This understanding of those who are struggling with pain is priceless.

It makes us good servants:

Pain teaches us to be more compassionate, supportive, and understanding in helping others bear their pain. Those who have gone through pain have learned to be hospitable and attentive servants even when they are in pain. They bestow blessings upon others who are suffering and struggling with life's toil, difficulties, and storms.

It helps us to be more sympathetic toward others:

Pain and suffering teach us to say the right words in a spirit of sympathy, which is so necessary for those who are struggling and suffering. Because we have experienced pain and suffering, we can sympathize and understand the hurts of others. When one has experienced pain, it makes him more likely to *"weep with those who weep"* (Romans 12:15). Moreover, it enables us better to comfort others when they are suffering. Personally, I did not know this until I experienced the loss of a loved one, my mother.

It teaches us empathy:

Empathy is a more robust support than sympathy. It is a blessing to know someone who has been through the exact struggle you have been through, who can share with you and help you to understand. It is more than a blessing. It is a blessing to be a blessing to others. To return blessings for blessings.

It teaches us to appreciate and be more grateful:

Pain and suffering teach us to appreciate the little things. There is so much joy in seeing God's beauty amid our suffering. It is this appreciation for God's beauty that gives us hope and more hope. We are learning to be grateful to God and grateful to others for their help in getting us through the tough times. We learn the depths of sorrow. Managing to be grateful helps us to find joy even during much pain and suffering.

Pain teaches us to be warriors:

It deepens our faith and strengthens our character. It draws us closer to God with hope and joy. Pain teaches us perseverance, tolerance, and longsuffering, which are necessary to have victory in our walk with Christ.

It helps to appreciate and pay more attention to what really matters:

I have learned some good lessons through pain and failure. *Isn't it something, that so many times we don't learn the value of something until we lose it?!* Suffering helps us change our ways. *It gets our attention like nothing else!* "It is good for me that I was afflicted, that I might learn your statutes" (Psalm 119:71). "Blows that wound cleanse away evil; strokes make clean the innermost parts" (Proverbs 20:30).

FAITH TRIED AND PROVED:

The Potter and the Clay:

> "The word that came to Jeremiah from the Lord:'Arise, and go down to the potter's house, and there I will let you hear my words." So I went down to the potter's house, and there he was working at his wheel. And the vessel he was making of clay was spoiled in the potter's hand, and he reworked it into another vessel, as it seemed good to the potter to do.

Then the word of the Lord came to me:"O house of Israel, can I not do with you as this potter has done? declares the Lord. Behold, like the clay in the potter's hand, so are you in my hand, O house of Israel." (Jeremiah 18:1-6)

Have you ever seen a potter at his wheel? After the clay is molded and worked on the potter's wheel, a vessel takes shape as the potter's hands mold and direct the upward flow of clay. When the vessel meets with the potter's approval (allowing the potter to redesign and reshaped its flaws perhaps because of bubbles in the clay), the final product is beautiful, usable, and designed by the potter. The potter's purpose is to make a perfect work, a masterpiece. He is not trying to destroy his work. In the same way, God has promised us a place of rich fulfillment and abundant living only after He has led us, guided us, shaped us, fashioned us, and changed us into something more beautiful and more functional for His purposes. The following is one of my all-time favorite verses:

"But now, O Lord, you are our Father; we are the clay, and you are our potter; we are all the work of your hand" (Isaiah 64:8).

God, like the Potter with the clay, is at work in our lives. He is shaping and making us into His image that we might glorify Him and be of great use in His kingdom of righteousness. But He will use many things such as pain and suffering to shape and mature us.

After all, it is God's riches that are worth fighting for and pursuing in this life. They lead us to eternal life, peace, refinement and shaping that only our loving God can do. In the end, it is that trial by fire that gives us richness and abundance and ultimately, eternal life.

As Christians, we need the rod. Our faith must be proved under trial. It is more precious than gold which perishes, though it is tried by fire. Our faith endures the fire and is kept by God's power when we cling to Him alone. Our trials and sufferings are like fire. They burn up nothing in us but the dross. It makes gold much purer. It does the same thing to our faith.

Choosing to Trust in God:

"In God I trust; I shall not be afraid" (Psalm 56:11)

David wrote this beautiful Psalm when the Philistines seized him in Gath (I Samuel 21:12). In David's Psalms, we see David's great determination to trust His God Jehovah. He chose to trust Him despite all his sufferings or circumstances. He always trusted God (Psalm 23:4; Psalm 16:8). We must learn to trust God and depend on Him to help us through His Word and prayer (Psalm 34:4). We must trust God in times of adversity. Trusting in God is a powerful weapon. It will help us to lay hold on His promises and cling to them despite our troubles that so often overwhelm us. Trust is the mark of a Christian's maturity. *"When I am afraid, I will trust in You."*

We can trust God in the dark. Someone once said, *"When a train goes through a tunnel, and it gets dark, you don't throw away the ticket and jump off. You sit still and trust the engineer."* So, it is in life. We can trust God farther than we can "see." Solomon wrote, *"Trust in the LORD with all thine heart and lean not unto thine own understanding; in all thy ways acknowledge Him, and He will make thy paths straight"* (Proverbs 3:5-6).

When we hurt, and life does not make any sense, we have only two choices:

1. We can hurt with God, or
2. We can hurt without Him.

When we are suffering, we need God more than ever before. Losing faith will not remove our pain. It rather adds a second problem as a greater consequence, "unfaithfulness."

In the Old Testament, we read of a great man named Job who was righteous and feared God. A man who trusted in God despite much suffering. When all his children died, he lost all his possessions, and resources. He simply said, *"Naked I came from my mother's womb, and naked shall I return. The Lord gave, and the Lord has taken away; blessed be the name of the Lord"* (Job 1:21). He soon also lost his health and suffered months of agony. He remained unfazed: *"Though he slay me, I will hope in him"* (Job 13:15). *Such powerful words of hope and trust came from the suffering Job!*

Suffering makes us depend on God more, hope, and trust in Him more. It makes us more desperate for Him and His Word to find rest, confidence, joy, strength, faith, and perseverance. Everything we need! In our weaknesses, God's power is made perfect. Christ is with us to comfort us in our darkest moments (Psalm 23:4). He has been with me, providing everything I needed. He has also been my solid foundation amid the storms of suffering and sorrow. Unless we are convinced that the Bible is true and we can trust its message, there is nowhere to go for any meaningful resolution. We will fall into the devil's trap of doubt. I hope that He will provide all you need to shape your thinking and still your soul.

When we don't know the answers to our why's, why not trust God, Who knows why:

When everything that you have worked so hard for is gone: your family, house, car, savings, health, everything. When you are just barely hanging onto life. In those moments, when we are bitter, we ask the question: *God, why is this happening to me?*

When we look at the enormous problem of pain and suffering, we are compelled to ask the question: *Where is God when it hurts, and that hurt does not stop?* The Bible gives us ample information, but we must search for the answers. God does not always explain the why. It is a fact that God allows suffering for various reasons, maybe as a warning or perhaps as a chance calamity that is a part of life here on the earth. Of course, sometimes, Satan is the author of our sufferings.

Suffering is the most severe trial of faith that a Christian must face. It raises many sharp, insistent, and damaging questions that test our faith. *Can faith bear the pain and still trust in God? Can we trust God, acknowledging that He cares for us and knows best? Or will our pain be so massive as to endure our judgments? Can we catch a glimpse of God's glorious ways and allow ourselves to draw true conclusions about what He is doing and why? Would it not be a good idea to resist jumping to the wrong conclusions which might misrepresent God and sow doubt? Can we not say in our heart, "Father, I do not understand, but I trust You?"* Failing to grasp that will keep us from trusting God.

The test of our suffering reveals our "knowing why" since our conviction is grounded in the Word of God. It shows that our faith is resting on solid ground rather than sand. When we ask the "why's" (*Where is God? Why is He avoiding us? Why won't He answer? Why, if He is all-powerful, doesn't He remove all suffering from this world?*), we are assuming that He hasn't done anything at all. The truth is that He has, is, and will. Jesus our Lord, as man, came into this world of pain, sorrow, and lawlessness and He lived here. Our Savior was well acquainted with suffering. He knew poverty, thirst, hunger, injustice, physical abuse, heartbreak, and ultimately betrayal. *He died a cruel death of excruciating pain!*

So, if anyone truly understands pain, it is our God. He understands our condition. Our Lord personally experienced it, Isaiah 52:14. It is amazing to me that Jesus would leave heaven and choose to suffer for us. The fact that God sent His only begotten Son to die that cruel death for our sins is enough proof that our God cares about our suffering and pain. *Don't ever forget that!*

Our Lord as High Priest can hear each one of our prayers. He is also grieved by everything bad that happens to us. So, for us to clearly see the picture of pain and sufferings the way it must be, we have to hear the whole story of Jesus. *Remember that our suffering is just temporary. It will come to an end!* (2 Cor. 4:16-18; Revelation 2:14).

"Though he slay me, I will hope in him." (Job 13:15)

Such powerful words of hope!

Job's Suffering:

Throughout history, God has used pain and suffering to correct, discipline, and perfect our faith. In Job's case, Satan was the one responsible for what happened to Job, and God allowed it to happen. Job did not understand the whys of his sufferings and complained to God about it (Job 10:1-3):

> *"I loathe my life; I will give free utterance to my complaint; I will speak in the bitterness of my soul. I will say to God, **Do not condemn me; let me know why you contend against me**. Does it seem good to you to oppress to despise the work of your hands and favor the designs of the wicked?"*

> *"Your hands fashioned and made me, **and now you have destroyed me altogether**"* (Job 10:8).

"Why did you bring me out from the womb? **Would that I had died before any eye had seen me"** (Job 10:18).

Consider some of the crucial lessons we can learn from the book of Job. These lessons are priceless and worthy of reflection. They are God's truths that will help us to reflect on Him and His faithfulness to remain faithful to Him. Though we understand many of these points, it is easier to forget them as we are suffering. I hope you find them helpful and encouraging.

God cares about each of one of us and is involved in our lives:

We often forget or refuse to believe this truth when we are suffering. When God told Satan, *"Have you considered my servant Job, that there is none like him on the earth, a blameless and upright man, who fears God and turns away from evil?"* He knew there was none like Job since he knew Job, and He still knows all mankind. We see God's caring and compassionate interest in the soul of mankind in 2 Peter 3:9: *"The Lord is not slow to fulfill his promise as some count slowness, but is patient toward you, not wishing that any should perish, but that all should reach repentance."* Our God desires all men (human beings) to be saved (1 Tim. 2:4). *Yes, He is interested in you!* Even when it seems that the whole world is collapsing all around you. *What an awesome God we serve!*

God is worthy of all praise because of Who He is, apart from all the blessings He imparts to us:

Indeed, this was a lesson Satan needed to learn.

"Then Satan answered the Lord and said, "Does Job fear God for no reason? Have you not put a hedge around him and his house and all that he has, on

every side? You have blessed the work of his hands, and his possessions have increased in the land. But stretch out your hand and touch all that he has, and he will curse you to your face" (Job 1:9-11).

You see, Satan was mistaken! After Job had lost everything, wealth, and family, he *"arose and tore his robe and shaved his head and fell on the ground and worshiped. And he said, 'Naked I came from my mother's womb, and naked shall I return. The Lord gave, and the Lord has taken away; blessed be the name of the Lord'"* (Job 1:20-21). Job likewise had to remind his wife of this big truth when she tried to discourage him saying he should curse God and die. But he said to her, *"'You speak as one of the foolish women would speak. Shall we receive good from God, and shall we not receive evil?' In all this Job did not sin with his lips"* (Job 2:10). Notice what the Lord commands us to do even during difficulties and adversities when blessings seem to be few: *"Rejoice in the Lord always; again I will say, rejoice"* (Philippians 4:4). Our God in heaven is worthy of worship and praise, even amid our valleys of suffering.

The temporal things of this world (money, possessions, food, clothing, houses, health, etc.) do not really matter, and we should not be concerned about them:

This is a truthful statement connected to my 2nd point. It leads me to this question: *Do we praise our God for Who He is only for the physical blessings He bestows on us?* Remember what Job declared *"Naked I came from my mother's womb, and naked shall I return."* He acknowledged how we all would end our lives. Accepting this great truth will help us to minimize or avoid our so-called "attachment" to the things of this world as well as our sorrow that so often is a consequence of it. You see, Job's wife did not recognize this truth. Why? Because if she did, she wouldn't have encouraged her husband to sin against God.

Throughout the New Testament, we are exhorted about the emptiness and fruitlessness of material riches or possessions. Jesus warned us about this in Matthew 6:19-24. Notice what John says:

> *"Do not love the world or the things in the world. If anyone loves the world, the love of the Father is not in him"* (1 John 2:15).

Paul also said,

> *"for we brought nothing into the world, and we cannot take anything out of the world... As for the rich in this present age, charge them not to be haughty, nor to set their hopes on the uncertainty of riches, but on God, who richly provides us with everything to enjoy"* (1 Timothy 6:7, 17).

Since everything will be destroyed on the Day of Judgment, every physical thing (2 Peter 3:10-13), except God (as Job did), then one must realize that having God is all we need! The temporal things of this life don't really matter after all.

God is to be trusted even when we don't understand the whys of our questions:

Even when we yearn for and wish to have all the answers to our whys, we must trust God. Job understood this well. God has the absolute right to give and take away (Job 1:21). Job even worshiped God when his heart ached with pain, and he lacked understanding. His words were: "Though he slay me, I will hope (trust) in him" (Job 13:15). You see, Job did not lean on his own understanding. Instead, he acknowledged His Creator in all his ways, allowing His LORD to direct his paths. Therefore, we must trust Him as well as His Word, regardless of our circumstances.

Suffering is not always the result of personal sin:

This was a typical theology of Job's days as well as in the days of Jesus and for many today. Suffering is not always the consequence of personal sins. Many talk that way incorrectly. Consider the life of Jesus, who indeed was sinless, yet He suffered greatly (1 Peter 2:21-24).

Suffering is no excuse to commit sin:

Job endured all his calamities without sinning. He maintained his integrity all the way to the end (Job 1:22; 2:10; 42:7-9). We must remember the promises made in 1 Cor. 10:13 that God will not allow us to be tempted beyond what we can endure. Indeed, suffering is one of the biggest tools in Satan's toolbox to pull us away from the Truth. Alas, we have all seen this happen! Satan is persistent and will try at all costs to lead us away. Don't be deceived when one falls into sin. Adversities are not the cause. It is still our fault when we sin.

Suffering will either be a stumbling block or a stepping-stone in our spiritual walk:

Job's wife evidently found a stumbling block when they lost their wealth and children. Instead, Job responded differently to his tragedy. He stepped up and allowed it to grow him spiritually. Like Job, we must acknowledge that our faith will be tested by fire (1 Peter 1:6-9). Will we pass the test or fail like Job's wife?! We must approach our problems and sufferings with a positive attitude of heart, realizing that many great things will result from them. But we must focus on maturing and pleasing our Creator, no matter how bad we think our circumstances are. Let us take refuge in the example of the apostles who used suffering as a steppingstone to grow (Acts 5:40-42). They refused to let it become a stumbling block.

It is absurd to think that one can live godly and not experience suffering:

Yes! We should not be surprised when suffering knocks on our door (Job 2:10). We are reminded of this in 2 Timothy 3:12. Another reminder is found in Romans 8:18 that tells us that the sufferings of the present world are not worthy of being compared with the glory which shall be revealed in us. *Indeed, we will suffer!* It is just an ugly truth of when and why, and we must embrace it (1 Peter 2:20). Remember that Christ our Savior suffered, the apostles suffered, Job suffered, Joseph suffered, Jacob suffered and many other faithful ones. This is a reality, no matter how terrible the circumstances. So, who are we, to think for a second that we are exempt from suffering and that we will avoid it as well (John 15:18-20)? As long as we are in this earthly tabernacle, suffering is inevitable. We must remain faithful no matter our adversity or pain.

Though Satan uses suffering to tempt us to sin against God, his power is limited by God and by us as well:

The fact that Satan must have permission from God to afflict us, like in the case of Job, it should comfort us. It implies that Satan is not all-powerful. He is allowed to do only what God permits him to do. That is, God is in control (Job 1:12;2:6)! He will flee from us when we resist him and submit to God (James 4:7). And though he is very crafty, we can defeat him victoriously when we put on the whole armor of God against him (Eph. 6:11). *You can be sure of that!*

Silence is often better than words:

Don't we all need to learn this? Job's wife and his friends needed to learn this as well. They like us would do much better to say less. *Alas, how often are we guilty of saying too much, too many words?* We must learn to cherish silence and measure our words with caution when we speak. In Ecclesiastes 5:2 we have a warning: *"Be not rash with your mouth, nor let your heart be hasty to utter a word before God, for God is in heaven, and you are on earth. Therefore let your words be few."* Again in Matthew 12:36-37: *"I tell you, on the day of judgment people will give account for every careless word they speak, for by your words you will be justified, and by your words, you will be condemned."* *"When words are many, transgression is not lacking, but whoever restrains his lips is prudent"* (Proverbs 10:19). Consider other passages concerning the power of our words (James 3:5-8; Proverbs 18:21; Matthew 12:33:35; Ephesians 4:29; Proverbs 12:18; Proverbs 13:3). We will be condemned or justified by our words. Likewise, we will give an account of each idle word we speak. *Let us develop better listening skills!*

Man needs God; man alone is not enough:

Job acknowledged this great truth in Job 10:12. Paul also affirmed this truth in 2 Corinthians 3:5. *"Our sufficiency is from God."* We are what we are through God's grace (1 Cor. 15:10). When we become aware of our own weaknesses, ignorance, flaws, etc., it will be much easier to acknowledge God and submit to His will.

Our friends may disappoint us, but our God will never forsake us:

Job called his friends *"miserable comforters"* (Job 16:2). They evidently had let him down; did more harm than good to him. But such is never the case with our God. He will never leave us nor forsake us when we need Him (Hebrews 13:5-6). *He is faithful! Let this sink deeply into your hearts!*

Prosperity is not a sign of spiritual standing:

Job addresses this well for us in chapter 21. Jesus acknowledge that also. *"It is hard for a rich man to enter the kingdom of heaven"* (Matthew 19:23). Therefore, we must pray harder, work harder, and trust God more than ever despite how much or little we have been blessed physically.

We must be concerned for the well-being of others:

Even though Job's friends were so cruel to him, he prayed for them in chapter 42:10. Moreover, the apostle Paul commanded us in Philippians 2:3-4 to *"Let nothing be done through selfish ambition or conceit, but in lowliness of mind let each esteem others better than himself. Let each of you look out not only for his own interests, but also for the interests of others."* Such powerful exhortation!

Learn from Job who showed great care for those who abused him with their words (Gal. 6:10; Matt. 7:12).

Finally, all things work together for good for those who remain faithful to God and develop longsuffering amid their fiery trials:

Toward the end of the book of Job, this is well demonstrated (Job 42:10-17). Job was blessed again physically. Romans 8:28 is a great reminder: *"And we know that for those who love God all things work together for good, for those who are called according to his purpose."* Remember that although each day we live is not filled with rainbows and sunshine or free of adversity, God will bless those who love Him and do His will, even when it seems difficult to grasp the many blessings.

My fervent prayer is that you may be encouraged with these lessons from Job amid your sufferings.

II. GOD'S PROVISION IN OUR SUFFERINGS:

"Beloved, do not be surprised at the fiery trial when it comes upon you to test you, as though something strange were happening to you. But rejoice insofar

as you share Christ's sufferings, that you may also rejoice and be glad when his glory is revealed. If you are insulted for the name of Christ, you are blessed, because the Spirit of glory and of God rests upon you" (1 Peter 4:12-14).

DARK VALLEYS

Our Father in heaven knows well when we are going to need His strength and provision. He will supply the strength we so desperately need, just in time. David acknowledged that though he walked through the valley of the shadow of death, he will fear no evil (Psalm 23:4). He knew what it was like to be in the dark valley of mourning. For many of us, the darkest valley of all is the one we dread the most to cross. David describes this valley as one of deep darkness. It speaks of our dark experiences in life.

In Psalm 23, David speaks of his world as not being ideal, but rather one full of dark valleys (verse 4); with the presence of evil enemies (verse 5). David did not feel safe in this environment. He feels marred, spiritually scarred, and in danger. And although he had struggled through many difficulties, he remained faithful and confident that God was going to be with him in the many shadows of darkness. David applied the Word of God in his own life. *Did you know the words "The LORD is my Shepherd" were spoken by Jacob first?* Toward the end of his life, Jacob gives his patriarchal blessing to Joseph's sons, Ephraim, and Manasseh, saying:

> *"The God before whom my fathers Abraham and Isaac walked, the God who has been my shepherd all my life long to this day, the angel who has redeemed me from all evil, bless the boys; and in them let my name be carried on, and the name of my fathers Abraham and Isaac; and let them grow into a multitude in the midst of the earth"* (Genesis 48:15-16).

Indeed, Jacob was a man who walked through many dark valleys, both morally, spiritually, emotionally, and physically. He was brought up in a family where there was favoritism (Isaac loved Esau and Rebekah loved Jacob more, Genesis 25:28). He likewise had plotted with his mother to cheat his foolish brother Esau of his birthright (Genesis 25:29-34). He deceived his father (Genesis 27). In a similar twist, he found himself betrayed by his uncle, Laban. He found himself married to the wrong woman, Leah, rather than Rachel, the one he loved (Genesis 29:15-30). David had known fear and loneliness, but God's grace met him at Jabbok, where he wrestled with Him and whom God fashioned and modeled into a great man, a prince (Gen. 32:22-32; Hos. 12:4).

Though God had fashioned Jacob into a great man when He was broken, Jacob still made mistakes later in his life. Mistakes he apparently imitated from his own parents: *"Now Israel (Jacob) loved Joseph more than any other of his sons, because he was the son of his old age. And he made him a robe of many colors"* (Genesis 37:3).

Jacob had struggled with God and with men (Genesis 32:28). But toward the end of his life, Jacob could look back and rejoice that His Jehovah God had been his Shepherd, seeking him like a lost sheep, rescuing him, healing him, and providing for him. *It is beautiful beyond words!*

Like Jacob, David shared the same experiences. He, too, wandered in the darkness. He also discovered that *"the LORD is my Shepherd. I shall not be in want."* God had been with him and was still with him. David acknowledged that God shepherded him through the darkest valleys of his life with His presence and strength and that all was sufficient to keep him strong and firm. God's presence and power can free us from our fears: *"For you are with me; your rod and your staff, they comfort me."* Such *precious words of comfort!* Our Shepherd uses the staff of His hand to work with us, His sheep. He directs, retrieves, and disciplines us. His rod or cudgel hangs from His belt and is ready to defend us when the enemy attacks. We, the sheep, look on these things to remind ourselves that the Shepherd will protect us well.

David experienced God's presence in his life as He shepherded, protected, and saved him. Yet David's view of God cannot compare with the revelation of the Lord as our Shepherd:

> *"I am the good shepherd. The good shepherd lays down his life for the sheep."* (John 10:11)

> *"Now may the God of peace who brought again from the dead our Lord Jesus, the great shepherd of the sheep, by the blood of the eternal covenant, equip you with everything good that you may do his will, working in us that which is pleasing in his sight, through Jesus Christ, to whom be glory forever and ever. Amen"* (Hebrews 13:20-21).

> *"For the Lamb in the midst of the throne will be their shepherd, and he will guide them to springs of living water, and God will wipe away every tear from their eyes."* (Revelation 7:17)

We Christians have enough reasons to rejoice. *Why?*

1. Because Christ is our Shepherd, who died for our sins.
2. Our Shepherd became our sacrificial Lamb, accepted by God that we may be made alive (Luke 24:46; 1 Cor. 15:20-22; Romans 6:3-4; Gal. 3:13).
3. Our Shepherd brought peace and reconciliation to God by taking the guilt of sin away.
4. We, Christians, have been raised from death because of sin to newness of life in the Spirit of Christ.

In Christ, we have abundant life, which He shares with His flock (John 10:10).

5. Our Shepherd came to this world that we may go to heaven. What an incredible hope! Deity left heaven and came to this ugly world so that mankind might have the chance to go to heaven. This is beyond our comprehension! This beautiful story of redemption shows God's love for us (1 Timothy 1:15). *"The saying is trustworthy and deserving of full acceptance, that Christ Jesus came into the world to save sinners, of whom I am the foremost."* Jesus, our Lord, was born of a woman that we may be born of God (Galatians 4:4-5; Isaiah 7:14; 1 John 5:4; John 3:3-5; 2 Cor. 5:17; 1 John 3:1).

6. Jesus was rejected as our Shepherd that we might be accepted of God (John 1:11-12). We know that Jesus was despised by men during His ministry here on earth. So much so, that He was nailed to a cross! According to God, the Father's plan (Colossians 1:19-21; Acts 10:35).

7. Jesus, our Shepherd, became the Man of sorrows that we might rejoice and be glad (Isaiah 53:3).

8. Our Shepherd accepted sorrow and sadness that we might have a reason to rejoice. We have so much to be thankful for! We were like lost sheep without a Shepherd. Let us keep in mind that His sorrow and grief make our joy and gladness possible.

9. Our Shepherd accepted poverty that we might enjoy riches in heaven (2 Cor. 8:9; Luke 9:58; Eph. 2:6-7). *Jesus became poor so that we might be able to inherit eternal riches!*

10. Jesus, our Shepherd, made sin for us that we might be the righteousness of God, meaning that He became the sacrifice for our sins (2 Cor. 5:21, Isa. 53:6; 1 Peter 2:22-24). Jesus suffered great pain and suffering because of our sins, He "bore" our "iniquities" in that sense. As Jehovah was pained because

of the sins of His people, so was Jesus also pained in that same way. He bore the burden, suffering both in soul and body (Matthew 23:37). It does not mean our sins, guilt, penalty, or punishment were transferred to Him, that is, imputed to Him. Through His blood, we are justified and made righteous.

Like David, we must realize that our God is with us at every stage of our life, in every circumstance, there and then, in glory, but also here and now. His "goodness and love" will follow us throughout our lives.

GOD'S PROMISES WILL SUSTAIN US:

God's children live by the promises He has made to us. Promises that will sustain us when life does not make sense. We have the assurance of His presence. God has never promised us a life free of problems or a bed of roses. But He did promise us that He will be with us, His children (Matthew 28:20; Hebrews 13:5; Psalm 46:5-7). God was with David in the valley of the shadow of death (Psalm 23). He was with the three Hebrew men in the fiery furnace (Daniel 3) and with Daniel in the lion's den (Daniel 6). God sent an angel to the garden to strengthen Jesus (Luke 22:43). God is not a disinterested spectator in our lives. He is neither distant nor disengaged. He does care (1 Peter 5:7). Even when we are afraid, through faith, we can sing, "What a fellowship, what a joy divine, safe and secure from all alarms."

Our God in His infinite lovingkindness has given us the assurance of His peace (John 14:27; 16:33; 20:19-21; Ephesians 2:12-14; 1 Peter 5:14). The assurance of His providence (Romans 8:28). So rather than asking, "Where is God?" or "Why me?" why not ask, "What can I learn from this?" and "Who can I help because of this?" (2 Corinthians 1:3-4). Life's problems and sufferings are not easy, but they qualify us to serve in ways we never could otherwise.

GOD'S POWER IN OUR WEAKNESSES:

As we humble ourselves in our weaknesses, we experience the fullness of God's strength. God draws near to us when we humbly draw near to Him. He is near to those who run to Him for refuge and strength. When God is our refuge, we are free from fear. As we grow in our love for Him and His love for us, this mature love casts our fear, 1 John 4:18.

In 2 Corinthians 12:9, we read. *"But he said to me, 'My grace is sufficient for you, for my power is made perfect in weakness.' Therefore I will boast all the more gladly of my weaknesses so that the power of Christ may rest upon me.'"* So what are the weaknesses Paul is talking about in these verses? Insults, hardships, persecutions, and calamities (distresses, difficulties, troubles). Our weaknesses are our circumstances, situations, experiences, and wounds.

- If we were strong, we might return insults.
- If we were strong, we might turn back the emerging hardship and change our circumstances that they might go away and not give us discomfort.
- If we were strong, we might turn back persecution.
- If we were strong, we might take charge of our calamity or distress as fast as possible to minimize its pressure.

Weaknesses are not sins but rather experiences, situations, circumstances, and wounds that are hard to bear and remove because they are beyond our control. Our love demands that we not return evil for evil but good, that is, blessings.

So, what is the source of our weaknesses? Do they come from Satan or God? Or both? Paul calls it a "messenger of Satan," verse 7. It was given to Paul to harass him. Satan afflicts God's children through his angels or messengers. His goal is to destroy us! But Satan is not the only one at work either. God is at work too. Paul's thorn in the flesh was not just the work of Satan to destroy him. It was the work of God to save him. We know this because Paul describes the purpose of his thorn in terms of pride. But Satan's goal is to produce pride rather than preventing it. That is how he destroys us, either with pride or despair. God uses Satan's hostile intentions for our good and our holiness. Satan wanted to turn Paul away from the faith and his ministry, perhaps because of the value of his visions revealed to him. God wanted Paul to humble himself and turn away from self-exaltation. So, God assigned Satan's thorn for salvation.

Just like it was with Job, God allows Satan to afflict his righteous servants. He turns the affliction for His good purposes (Luke 22:31-32). So, the answer to the second question is that the source of our weaknesses may sometimes be Satan to destroy us, or perhaps our weaknesses are turned by God for our good, to perfect us.

- *So, what is the purpose of our weaknesses (insults, hardships, persecutions, calamities, troubles)?*
- *Why can't I find a job?*
- *Why am I trapped in this awful marriage?*
- *Why did my loved one die?*
- *Why can't I have children?*
- *Why do I feel so lonesome and have no friends?*
- *Why is nothing working in my life?*
- *Why, why-why?*

Paul briefly gives us answers to these questions:

Satan's purpose is to buffet or harass us, verse 7: Here is where we must pray fervently for God's help. Paul did that.

God does not delight in our sufferings. *Satan does! Satan must be resisted!*

God's overriding purpose for Satan's harassment is our humility. God took steps to keep Paul humble when he was in danger of pride. Humility is of greater value to God than comfort. Humility is more important than freedom from pain. God will give us mountain tops to climb and then bring us down through pain or suffering, lest we think we have risen above the need of total dependence on His grace. So, God's purpose in our weaknesses is humility, lowliness, and complete reliance on Him (2 Cor. 1:9; 4:7).

Finally, God's purpose in our weaknesses is to glorify Him: This is the focal point of 2 Corinthians 12:9-10. *"But he said to me, 'My grace is sufficient for you, for my power is made perfect in weakness."* God wants to exhibit His Son's power, not by freeing us from our weaknesses but rather by giving us the strength necessary to endure and rejoice in tribulations. God shows His Son's power in our weaknesses, not necessarily to help us escape from our weaknesses. Hebrews 11 is a perfect example. It speaks of the faith of God's heroes who by faith escaped the edge of the sword (verse 34); by faith, some were killed (verse 37); by faith, some stopped the mouths of lions; by faith, some were sawn asunder; by faith, some were mighty warriors; and by faith, some suffered chains and imprisonment (Phil. 4:11-13).

So, God's ultimate purpose in our weaknesses is to glorify His Son, who went to the cross through love until His work of love was done. Paul said that Christ crucified was foolishness to the Greeks, a stumbling block to the Jews, but to us who are called, it is the power and wisdom of God (1 Cor. 1:23). Therefore, the purpose of our weaknesses, insults, hardships, persecutions, and calamities is to glorify our Lord.

WE MUST SUFFER AS CHRIST DID:

> *"When he was reviled, he did not revile in return;*
> *when he suffered, he did not threaten, but continued*
> *entrusting himself to him who judges justly"* (1 Pe-
> ter 2:23).

Our Lord and Savior has left us a perfect example of long-suffering under intense suffering like no other in the world. The Son of God suffered in the most undignified, humiliating manner, extreme torture, pain, and anguish in both body and soul. Something intolerable to any human being. And He did this for us, knowing that He was innocent but condemned for us, sinners. He suffered for the sins of strangers. *"WHO COMMITTED NO SIN, NOR WAS ANY DECEIT FOUND IN HIS MOUTH."*

Then why did the Jews persecute and crucify Him and put Him to death? Because of envy and evil hatred. Christ was under no obligation to endure disgrace and ill-treatment (being disgracefully hung up nude between two murderers, being lifted up as unworthy to touch the earth and live among men). *Yet, He did not hate the Jews!* Even in His sufferings upon the cross, He prayed for His enemies with mercy. He had all authority on earth and in heaven. He had all power and would have been justified. He could have had revenge on His enemies, cursed them, and reproved them as they deserved. *But He did none of these things!* Even in His pinnacle of anguish, He willingly interceded for them to His Father in heaven (Isaiah 53). Jesus, our Lord, is our perfect example of calm and endurance. *Let us imitate His example!*

The Son of God bore patiently and submissively and much more, He even prayed for those who were causing Him so much agony. Instead of being angry, reviling, and hating when suspended from the cross, He endured the most shameful slanders and defamation. He prayed with strong cries and tears, "Father forgive them." It was indeed an act of unfathomable love amid severe suffering. *He had compassion on His persecutors and blessed them in great measure. It moves me! So, what did our Lord do instead?* He "*committed himself to him that judgeth righteously.*"

Peter declares that Christ committed the matter to God, Who judges righteously. So as Christ did, so should we conduct ourselves in our sufferings. *If Christ, my Lord, suffered with meekness and patience for me, how much more do I have to submit to suffering?! What harm can come to me if I suffer when I know it is for my own good or perhaps God's will? Would I be willing to suffer, knowing that it is going to perfect and mature me or because He died and suffered for me? Let this sink deeply into your hearts!* The exercise of faith in what Christ endured is the only way to bring contentment in our suffering and pain.

REFUGE AND REST IN CHRIST:

> "*Each will be like a hiding place from the wind, a shelter from the storm, like streams of water in a dry place, like the shade of a great rock in a weary land*" (Isaiah 32:2).

Our Lord gives quiet and sweet rest to us when we are weary because of persecution, affliction, difficulties, adversities, and the buffeting of Satan. In Christ, we have such an abundance of precious promises that all things shall work together for good, in blessedness. He is the great Rock that shelters and sweetly refreshes us in our time of need.

Our God in His infinite mercy has provided His children something stable, solid, and secure, "*an anchor of the soul*" to hold on to. Such an anchor sustains us and gives us rest and hope so that we might not be blown down by the powerful winds that threaten us. Such hope set before us can fasten us securely to God's promises.

> *"Wherein God, being minded to show more abundantly unto the heirs of the promise the immutability of his counsel, interposed with an oath; that by two immutable things, in which it is impossible for God to lie, we may have a strong encouragement, who have fled for refuge to lay hold of the hope set before us: which we have as an anchor of the soul, a hope both sure and stedfast and entering into that which is within the veil."* (Hebrews 6:17-19)

When our souls fly to Jesus, our Rock, they find rest. He will come to our rescue. He has promised it, and we must believe it. So, let us resort unto Jesus for refuge and rest. The purpose of our struggles is to teach us not to trust in ourselves but in God alone. The good news is that God provides us a special shelter. May we all come to our place of refuge, strength, and defense, in our Lord and Savior, Jesus Christ.

Truly, our most in-depth spiritual lessons come from trials, pain, and suffering. The deep waters, the hot fire, and the dark valleys teach us to walk the path of faith (Isaiah 43:2). God has been with me through the darkest valleys, troubled waters, and hot fires. He has never broken His promises. God has been there for me, every time I have walked through the deep waters of difficulty and suffering. I know in my heart that no matter how many fierce storms, challenges, and suffering come our way, God will be our refuge and our solid and sure anchor that we can hold on to. He is our foundation of comfort, Psalm 46. He is our source of protection, shield, and rest amid life's storms. But we must learn to hide ourselves in Him alone (Psalm 143:9).

CONCLUSION:

Times of crisis prove our friendship with God and declare the authenticity of our faith. *Do we love God because He provides gifts? Do we love those gifts more than we love the Giver?* This was

Satan's accusation against Job (Job 1:8-12; cf. 1 Peter 1:6-9). All the things we cling to in this world will eventually disappear. But the One, who gives them all to us, is the One that will ultimately remain.

We must learn to seek strength, peace, and rest in God and His promises. Even as our souls are wrestling with pain and hurt deep inside. Our merciful God is the only One who can meet our deepest needs. In His Word, He has taught us through His promises to trust Him. God will nurture us if we trust Him through life's trials. He is our place of shelter and safety. He will carry us with loving and tender care in our times of fear and sorrow. *You may rest assured!* (Psalm 46). Our God shelters us like the wings of care and protection of a protective mother bird. In our times of trouble and sorrow, our merciful and loving God spreads His wings to guard us so that no harm will overtake us (Psalm 57:1; 91:4; 91:10; Matthew 23:37).

As children of God, we must sink the teeth of our faith into God's faithfulness when we are undergoing trials, pain, and suffering. He is utterly faithful to His promises (Hebrews 6:17-20). Our hope, even amid intense suffering, is in our Lord's ceaseless loving kindness. In His never-failing ways, there is new compassion.

We have a cloud of witnesses who had to endure a tsunami of insults, hardships, persecutions, and calamities (distresses, difficulties, troubles) and yet remained faithful and rejoiced while they suffered. *We have the example of the apostles who had to suffer significantly but were thrilled that they were able to suffer for doing what was right!* They were thrilled to be able to endure hardship for the cause of Christ. *What an example of true faith and love for the Lord!* An excellent attitude to have and worthy of our imitation. True faith does not cower in fear or fall apart when challenged and attacked. It maintains a joyful attitude and continues doing what is right and good regardless of our circumstances. It requires a pleasant disposition. Suffering and pain did not deter them. They continued sharing the Gospel of Christ both publicly and privately.

When life is difficult and filled with pain, let us resolve in our hearts not to quit or go any other way than God's ways, even when it hurts deeply. *Can your faith remain steadfast and unyielding? What better way to refresh our frame of mind or attitude and strength than to go to Gethsemane and Calvary as portrayed in Matthew 26 & 27?* Those events unfolded almost 2,000 years ago. Our Lord and Savior suffered enormously and voluntarily on our behalf. He agonized in the garden as His hour was approaching. Not wanting to die but knowing it was His Father's will for mankind to be redeemed by His shed blood at Calvary. Therefore, let us strengthen our weak hearts and run with endurance the race that is set before us.

> *"Therefore, since we are surrounded by so great a cloud of witnesses, let us also lay aside every weight, and sin which clings so closely, and let us run with endurance the race that is set before us, looking to Jesus, the founder and perfecter of our faith, who for the joy that was set before him endured the cross, despising the shame, and is seated at the right hand of the throne of God"* (Hebrews 12:1-2).

Our God is aware of our sufferings and permits it to happen that we might serve Him better. Take, for example, Job, who had to endure intense suffering but grew through them and turned out to be better in the end. As James says, *"Count it all joy, my brothers, when you meet trials of various kinds, for you know that the testing of your faith produces steadfastness"* (James 1:2-3). Our sufferings are sometimes because of our poor choices, and other times for no reason that we might understand.

As in Job's case, he did not understand, at the time of his suffering, the reason behind it but learned a great lesson that we all must learn. He learned that God's ways and thoughts are beyond our own (Isaiah 55:8-9). Thus, let us trust our God and believe that He will work things out for our good, for those who love Him (Romans 8:28). Job's story reminds us that there are no easy answers to the questions about why God allows bad things to happen to us, losses, and even pain. Job's example reveals that this kind of questions miss the point of what truly is going on. Of course, when we find ourselves amid our long-term suffering, we tend to react this way, missing out on the importance of our suffering. Job did not need to learn any lesson when he was chosen to suffer, though he surely learned some valuable lessons along the way. God was not trying to correct any flaw or sin, leading Job to repent. It was God's testimony about His heavenly rule. It was about silencing Satan.

If God allows Satan to tempt us, all that Satan does will be calculated for our own good, Rom. 8:28. It will work out for our good. We must learn like Job our own insignificance compared to God, the Great I AM. Remember, God never answers Job's questions. Instead, He questions Job. But Job does not complain. He repents. Job admits his failure in speaking of things he could not know. In the same way, we must acknowledge that God is God, and we are not. We must learn with God's help that we cannot fathom all His ways, but we can trust Him, even when nothing makes sense.

Finally, Paul reminds us that we must learn to rejoice even while we suffer. So, if you find yourself going through persecution, rejection, suffering, pain, hurt, financial struggles, family struggles, illness, loss of a loved one, *why not look up in faith to God, to His purpose for your sufferings, looking back in memory of His love? Why not pray fervently to the God of compassion and mercy? Why not pour out your heart to Him, asking Him for His help and strength (1 Peter 5:6-7, Phil. 4:6-7)?*

He understands well what we are going through: our sufferings, grief, anxiety, pain, everything. He was well acquainted with sorrow and grief. He knows better than anyone how to heal us. *Why not renew your faith in God and His promises? We can do all through Christ who strengthens us! Paul believed this great truth, and so should we!* God is working all things out in our best interest. *But we must trust Him!* Read and reflect upon His precious Word during your most difficult times. God is in control and loves us. *Don't ever forget that!* Moreover, seek encouragement and fellowship from other Christians, our brethren of the same precious faith, to help you bear your suffering and hardship. God expects us to support one another (1 Thess. 5:11; Heb. 3:13; 10:24-25).

May we trust in our Lord with all our heart, mind, and soul who loves us enough to let us face our challenges so that we may grow and enter His kingdom. May we find rest and quiet solitude in His arms where we can just drown out the cares of this world. May we find refreshment and fresh perspective for our weariness. May we find hope and healing in Him alone. May we turn our afflictions into mercies and darkness into light. And finally, may we find contentment, acting out our faith in all the pains and sufferings that Jesus our Lord suffered.

I leave you with the beautiful words of this poem, written from the Lord's perspective:

"The Savior's Words"

If you never felt pain, how would you know
I'm a healer?

If you never experienced difficulty, how would
you know I'm a deliverer?

If you never endured a trial, how could you be
one who overcomes?

If you never felt sadness, how would you know
I 'm a comforter?

If you never made a mistake, how would you
know I'm forgiving?

If you never were in trouble, how would you
know I came to rescue you?

If you never were broken, how would you
know I can make you whole?

If you never had a problem, how would you
know I can solve them?

If you never had any suffering, how would you
know what I went through?

If you never went through the fire, how would
you know you become pure?

If I gave you all things, how would you appreciate them?

If I never corrected you, how would you know I
love you?

If you had all power, how would you learn to
depend on Me?

If your life was perfect, what would you need
Me for?

Though He Slay Me

"Though He slay me, I will hope in Him." Job 13:15

"Though He slay me, I will hope in Him." What powerful words Job speaks! Who would hope so much and still proclaim such trust after thinking that God had stabbed him? This is what Job models for us. This is exactly what God has instructed us to do through His Word. He wants us to trust Him even when we think He has stabbed us in the back. He wants us to receive our trials and suffering with faith and hope. *There are so many blessings in our sufferings!* Suffering perfects our faith.

> *"In this you greatly rejoice, even though now for a little while, if necessary, you have been distressed by various trials, so that the proof of your faith, being more precious than gold which is perishable, even though tested by fire, may be found to result in praise and glory and honor at the revelation of Jesus Christ; and though you have not seen Him, you love Him, and though you do not see Him now, but believe in Him, you greatly rejoice with joy inexpressible and full of glory, obtaining as the outcome of your faith the salvation of your souls"* (I Peter 1:6-9).

So often, we question ourselves, but then others also doubt us when they see us suffering as in the case of Job. They wonder why this is happening to us. *We are overwhelmed with many questions! Why won't God let me get pregnant? Why won't God heal my child? Why did my loved one die? Why did my spouse leave me for someone else? Why did my friend marry so much better than I did? Why am I lingering in so much loneliness and pain? What is wrong with me? Is it disobedience in me or some hidden sin that I need to repent of? Is there a lesson I need to learn?* The questions are numerous. Job's example reveals to us that these kinds of questions miss the point of what truly is going on. Of course, when we find ourselves amid our long-term suffering, we tend to react this way, missing out on the importance of our suffering.

Job did not need to learn any lesson when he was chosen to suffer, though he surely learned some valuable lessons along the way. God was not trying to correct any flaw or sin leading Job to repent. It was God's testimony about His heavenly rule. It was about silencing Satan.

I. GOD'S PURPOSE IN OUR SUFFERINGS:

Job's suffering seems a bit unfair, maybe even wrong. For God to let Satan stretch out his hand against all that belonged to Job does not seem right. But we must remember that God restrains Satan in what he might do in our lives. We must see Satan's limitations. Although it may seem that God was unfair to Job, there are many things that we do not understand. Nevertheless, we must cling to the God of all Scripture. He is good, righteous, loving, longsuffering, steadfast. We must always remember God's ways are not our ways. If God allows Satan to tempt us, all Satan does will be calculated for our own good. It will work out for our good.

> *"And we know that for those who love God all things work together for good, for those who are called according to his purpose"* (Romans 8:28).

We must learn like Job to know our own insignificance compared to God, the Great I AM. Remember, God never answers Job's questions. Instead, He questions Job. But Job does not complain. He repents. Job admits his failure in speaking of things he could not know or understand. In the same way, we must acknowledge and accept that God is God, and we are not. *We must learn with God's help that we cannot fathom all His ways, but we can trust Him!*

Consider God's purposes in our sufferings:

- Suffering increases our consciousness of the power, sovereignty, and sustenance of our Almighty God, Psalm 68:10.
- Suffering is used by God for our refining, perfection, strength, and to keep us from falling, Psa. 66:8-9; Heb. 2:10.
- Suffering allows Jesus to be manifested in our mortal flesh, 2 Cor. 4:7-11.
- Suffering weakens us, making us dependent upon God, 2 Cor. 12:9.
- Suffering teaches us humility, 2 Cor. 12:7.
- Suffering makes known to us the mind of Christ, Philippians 2:1-11.
- Suffering teaches us character and Christlikeness, Rom. 5:3-4; Heb. 12:10-11; 2 Cor. 4:8-10; Rom. 8:28-29.
- Suffering teaches God's discipline for us, for our good, so that we may share in His holiness, Hebrews 12:1-11.
- Suffering can help us learn obedience and self-control, Heb. 5:8; Ps. 119-67; Rom. 5:1-5; James 1:2-8; Phil. 3:10.
- Suffering for others can demonstrate the abundance of joy and love, 2 Cor. 8:1-2,9.
- Suffering is part of the struggle against evil men, Psalm 27:12; 37:14-15.
- Suffering is part of being worthy of the kingdom of God, 2 Thes. 1:4-5.

- Suffering is the struggle against injustice, I Peter 2:19.
- Suffering is sharing in the sufferings of Christ, 2 Cor. 15; I Peter 4:12-13.
- Suffering teaches us endurance so that we may win our crown, eternal life, 2 Cor. 4:17; 2 Tim. 2:12.
- Suffering binds Christians in sharing with the needs of the saints with a common purpose, Philippians 4:12-15.
- Suffering teaches us God's statutes and brings us back to the way of God when we go astray, Psalm 119:66-67,71.
- Though we suffer for our sins, our broken and contrite spirit pleases God, Psalm 51:16-17.
- Suffering helps us to focus on our hope, the salvation of our souls, the grace that will be brought to us when Jesus is revealed, I Peter 1:6, 13.
- Suffering produces humility in us, I Peter 5:6-7.
- Suffering helps us to number our days, Psalm 90:7-12.
- Suffering is necessary to win the lost, 2 Tim. 2:8-10; 4:5-6.
- Suffering strengthens us by allowing us to comfort others, 2 Cor. 1:3-11.
- Suffering is nothing compared to the value of knowing Christ, Phil. 3:8.
- Through suffering, we can know God's Truth, Psalm 51:6; 119:17.
- Suffering is part of proclaiming the Gospel of Jesus, 2 Tim. 1:7-8, 4:16-18.
- Suffering teaches us thanksgiving and joy, I Thes. 5:18; 2 Cor. 1:11.
- Suffering gives us hope, Jeremiah. 29:11; Job 13:14-15.
- Suffering reveals God's care for us, Psalm 56:8.

With all these lessons learned from suffering, let us never forget that Jesus, the Man of sorrows, was very acquainted with grief and suffering. Our Lord Jesus modeled for us endurance in suffering. Most importantly, His perfect suffering made it possible for us to have redemption through Him. He endured the cross and the curse for us. For the joy that was set before him, Jesus despised the shame, but He sat down at the right hand of the throne of God, Hebrews 12:2. So we must share in His sufferings, Matt. 26:36-46. Jesus trusted His Father in the garden of Gethsemane. He had to finish and face His worst fears becoming the Man of sorrows for our souls' salvation. Let us purpose in our heart, soul, mind, and strength to walk like Jesus and Job, who trusted completely in God in times of deep suffering and despair.

It is remarkable to me that although Job was stripped of everything in this life, he still trusted in God. *Job held unto his faith! He put his hope only in God! God gives, and God takes away. Blessed be the name of God!* Anyone who has had to endure deep suffering like Job and Jesus can recognize these moments in their journey.

Though He slay me, yet will I trust Him!

May our Lord help us to meditate with wisdom on God's purpose in our sufferings and various trials. May we consider them all joy, knowing that the testing of our faith produces endurance to be complete, lacking in nothing. May our Lord help us to persevere under sufferings and trials. May we be approved of God and receive our reward in heaven, our crown of life, which our Lord has promised to those who love, believe, trust, and obey Him. To Him be the glory. Amen

Wait for the LORD!

"The LORD is my light and my salvation —
whom should I fear?
The LORD is the stronghold of my life —
of whom should I be afraid?
2 When evildoers came against me to devour my
flesh,
my foes and my enemies stumbled and fell.
3 Though an army deploys against me,
my heart is not afraid;
though a war breaks out against me,
still I am confident.
4 I have asked one thing from the LORD;
it is what I desire:
to dwell in the house of the LORD
all the days of my life,
gazing on the beauty of the LORD
and seeking Him in His temple.
5 For He will conceal me in His shelter
in the day of adversity;
He will hide me under the cover of His tent;
He will set me high on a rock.
6 Then my head will be high
above my enemies around me;
I will offer sacrifices in His tent with shouts of joy.
I will sing and make music to the LORD.
7 LORD, hear my voice when I call;
be gracious to me and answer me.
8 My heart says this about You,
'You are to seek My face.'

LORD, I will seek Your face.
9 Do not hide Your face from me;
do not turn Your servant away in anger.
You have been my helper;
do not leave me or abandon me,
God of my salvation.
10 Even if my father and mother abandon me,
the LORD cares for me.
11 Because of my adversaries,
show me Your way, LORD,
and lead me on a level path.
12 Do not give me over to the will of my foes,
for false witnesses rise up against me,
breathing violence.
13 I am certain that I will see the LORD's goodness
in the land of the living.
14 Wait for the LORD;
be strong and courageous.
Wait for the LORD!"

Psalm 27

All Scripture inspired by God is profitable. Many of us deny ourselves the great help that God has placed in the sacred Psalms. A great example is the 27th Psalm. Jesus and the apostles of the New Testament cry out to us that we must believe in the LORD. They give us much detail, but the 27th Psalm dramatically shows us some of what is involved in waiting for the LORD. Let us give careful thought to David's beautiful song of real faith in our Almighty God.

I love the Psalms so much because they are rooted in God's Word to strengthen and help me remain steadfast when life's storms and difficulties seem to blow my faith away. It is then that I look to the Psalms for help. They help me to plant my feet firmly in God's Truth. Indeed, they transform my heart and mind as I read, and study God's riches found in them.

They instruct, comfort, encourage and guide me when I need it the most. It is my life's manual that I must put into practice daily. In the Psalms, I find Jesus our Lord. The truths of God found in the Psalms help me to find freedom, peace, confidence, assurance, and joy. Through the Psalms, I build my faith up as I worship Him in a deep and intimate way. They teach me to seek God with all my heart, that I may pour out my heart to Him and tell Him everything. They help me to worship Him for who He is and not for what He is doing for me. They help me to accept my trials as victories. They also help me to examine my heart, that I might repent and receive God's gracious forgiveness. In a few words, they help me in my pilgrim journey here on earth as they deepen my faith and commit me to obedience and discipline toward God and His Son.

The Psalms show me the beauty of walking intimately with my God when I meditate on them. They strengthen my prayers as they help me express what I want to say to God with the right words that, at times, I struggle with. *How wonderful it is to have such communion with our God through our prayers!* They also help me to acknowledge that my ways are not God's way and that I must wait on Him when life is difficult. They teach me to hold on to God alone, even when it seems that He is not holding on to me. They help me to trust in God as I plead with Him for deliverance. They remind me that my walk with God is based upon trust, faith, and not sight. They help me to praise Him in all situations, for He is trustworthy and faithful. They help me to see His presence and glory all around us as I read and study them. They help me to accept the truth that I must fear God and keep His commands, for He will bring every act to judgment (Eccl. 12:13-14). Since the Psalms help us to see God for who He is, we must resolve to trust in Him, obey Him, be faithful to Him, and pray to Him to commune with Him.

Psalm 27 is very dear to my heart because it deepens my faith and my trust in God as it helps me face my fears. This Psalm was written by David himself concerning his life, circumstances, and trust in the LORD. Through this Psalm, we learn that the antidote for fear is God. It was written during David's low and difficult times when he fled from his enemies. David chooses to trust in God as he waits for Him with confidence. This Psalm begins and ends with faith in God and David's determination to wait in faith for the LORD. Notice that David is uttering a prayer to God to remind Him of his circumstances. Psalm 27 reminds us that our LORD is our Light, our salvation, the stronghold of our life, our Deliverer, and our guidance when we draw near Him and walk with Him faithfully. We can rest assured with complete confidence that He will be there for us in our time of need.

I. THE LORD IS OUR DEFENSE (STRONGHOLD) AND STRENGTH:

David expresses his confidence in the LORD in verses 1-6.

> *"The LORD is my light and my salvation—whom should I fear? The LORD is the stronghold of my life —of whom should I be afraid? When evildoers came against me to devour my flesh, my foes and my enemies stumbled and fell. Though an army deploys against me, my heart is not afraid; though a war breaks out against me, **still I am confident. I have asked one thing from the LORD; it is what I desire: to dwell in the house of the LORD all the days of my life, gazing on the beauty of the LORD and seeking Him in His temple. For He will conceal me in His shelter in the day of adversity; He will hide me under the cover of His tent; He will set me high on a rock.** Then my head will be high above my enemies around me; I*

will offer sacrifices in His tent with shouts of joy. I will sing and make music to the LORD."

The LORD Is My Light:

In this Psalm, David describes how God impacts our lives spiritually and as a physical defense against our enemies (verse 1). David recognizes that in the end, God will help us win over our fears. He begins this beautiful Psalm with an amazing picture of encouragement. He says, "The LORD is my light and my salvation." David recognizes that God is his "light" (understanding) and "salvation" (deliverance). In the Old and New Testament, the word "light" has a significant meaning since it refers to God as "light." In Genesis 1:3, God said, "'Let there be light,' and there was light. And God saw that the light was good. And God separated the light from the darkness. God called the light Day, and the darkness he called Night. And there was evening and there was morning, the first day." You see, light was the first element of the creation that God spoke into existence. God Himself is called the Light (Ps. 4:6; Is. 10:17; Mic. 7:8, 1 Jn. 1:5). Jesus declared that He is the Light. God removes the darkness of ignorance and sin through His Light. We are commanded to walk in the Light just as He is in the Light. Moreover, light means walking with God and having His favor.

In Lamentations 3:1-3, we see an illustration of this: *"I am the man who has seen affliction by the rod of His wrath. He has driven me away and made me walk in darkness rather than light; indeed, he has turned his hand against me again and again, all day long."* You see, God's people lost that fellowship with Him and thus were destroyed because they were walking in darkness. Micah 7:8-9 describes the same sentiment: *"Do not gloat over me, my enemy! Though I have fallen, I will rise. Though I sit in darkness, the Lord will be my light. Because I have sinned against Him, I will bear the Lord's wrath, until he pleads my case and establishes my right. He will bring me out into the light; I will see His righteousness."* The prophet Micah declared that because the nation of Israel had sinned, they would have to bear the LORD'S wrath upon them. They were "sitting in darkness" and *"bearing the LORD'S wrath."* However, God showed mercy and brought them *"out into the light."*

In Psalm 27:1-6 David described his relationship with God as he communed and walked with Him. He was confident he had nothing to fear. *Isn't it beautiful to have such confidence in our God no matter what may come our way!*

The LORD Is My Salvation:

Besides God being David's "light," He was also his "salvation." God was David's source of deliverance from all the severe and violent circumstances in which he found himself. He could say with confidence, *"The LORD is the stronghold of my life—of whom should I be afraid? When evildoers came against me to devour my flesh, my foes and my enemies stumbled and fell"* (Verse 2). David remembers that the LORD has been, is, and will be his only "defense" or "stronghold." God brought hope and encouragement to David as He replaced the gloom of his doubts with His glorious presence. David had no reason to tremble in fear since he knew that the Almighty God was his salvation. He knew that God would fight his battles, defend him against his enemies, and sustain him during his most troublesome and dangerous times. David was confident that God was his light, his salvation, and his deliverance since He has the power to deliver us from our enemies, our sins, and the power of Satan. No matter what we go through, our God can help us through them.

In verses 2-3, we can see David dealing with his enemies who are fighting violently against him. In verse 2, David goes back to remember his walk with God. His life had not been free of toil and difficulties, for his enemies would come to him to devour him like the wild beasts, who pounce on their prey to rip it up and consume it. However, his enemies failed because God was with him as His Savior. His victories came from God and not from any military forces. The LORD was faithful to him as He dealt with his foes, his enemies. He caused them to stumble and fall. *I am amazed beyond words! I must remind myself of this always!*

In verse 3 David exults saying, *"Though an army deploys against me, my heart is not afraid; though a war breaks out against me, still I am confident."* You see, faith will give us confidence, the trust to face whatever comes our way, even our enemies. Our faith (our trust and confidence) helps us to see God as the One who shields and protects us from all evil forces. In David's case, the LORD stood before him to help and keep him secure. Thus, in faith, he says, *"Though a war breaks out against me, still I am confident."* His victories gave David confidence to believe, have faith, even amid war and enemies. He acknowledges that God would fight for him and protect him. *Our God also fights for us Christians today!* Paul recognized this when he said, *"No, in all these things we are more than victorious through Him who loved us"* (Romans 8:37). *Such comforting words enlighten our souls!*

Throughout the Scriptures, we see God's power as He took care of His nation. Take, for instance, what God told Abraham in a vision. *"Fear not, Abram, I am your shield; your reward shall be very great."* God reassured Abraham that he need not fear because He would make him a great nation even though he was without a son (Genesis 15). God also told Jacob not to fear moving him and his family down to Egypt because He would take care of them and make them a great nation. God said, *"I myself will go down with you to Egypt, and I will also bring you up again, and Joseph's hand shall close your eyes"* (Genesis 46:3-4). God also told Joshua repeatedly to take courage and not be afraid because He was with him (Joshua 1:9; 8:1; 10:25; 11:6). God told Jeremiah not to be afraid to speak to the nation (Jeremiah 1:6-8). He also told Ezekiel to speak to the nation of

Israel when they were rebelling against Him. God said, "*And you, son of man, be not afraid of them, nor be afraid of their words, though briers and thorns are with you and you sit on scorpions. Be not afraid of their words, nor be dismayed at their looks, for they are a rebellious house. And you shall speak my words to them, whether they hear or refuse to hear, for they are a rebellious house*" (Ezekiel 2:6-7). God told the people of Israel before conquering the land of Canaan, "*Be strong and courageous. Do not be afraid or terrified because of them, for the Lord your God goes with you; He will never leave you nor forsake you*" (Deuteronomy 31:6).

God not only made these promises in the Old Testament but throughout the New Testament as quoted in Hebrews, "*I will never leave you, I will never forsake you. So we say with confidence, 'The Lord is my helper, I will not be afraid. What can man do to me?'*" (Hebrews 13:5-6). In Matthew 10:28-31, Jesus said, "*And do not fear those who kill the body but cannot kill the soul. Rather fear him who can destroy both soul and body in hell. Are not two sparrows sold for a penny? And not one of them will fall to the ground apart from your Father. But even the hairs of your head are all numbered. Fear not, therefore; you are of more value than many sparrows.*" Therefore, we have nothing to fear except being outside of the Light of God, for if God is not our Light, then there is much to fear. But if God is our Light, then there is nothing to fear, for He is with us and is our deliverance.

II. THE LORD IS OUR STRENGTH:

> "*I have asked one thing from the LORD; it is what I desire: to dwell in the house of the LORD all the days of my life, gazing on the beauty of the LORD and seeking Him in His temple. For He will conceal me in His shelter in the day of adversity; He will hide me under the cover of His tent; He will set me high on a rock. Then my head will be high above my enemies around me; I will offer sacrifices in His tent*

with shouts of joy. I will sing and make music to the LORD" (Psalm 27:4-6).

The Stronghold of Our Life:

Our God is a mighty stronghold, the anchor of our lives, when there is turmoil, storms of doubt, discouragement, despair, defeat, and when we face the waves and winds of temptation, the trials, and the sorrows that tear at our sails. When we are faithful followers of Christ, we have the confidence that no matter how bad things might appear, we need not worry, for God is on our side. Our God brings us inner peace, a calm spirit. The LORD is our peace because He is our Light. Death itself has no hold over us. Death is what every person fears, but as Christians, we must not fear death since it is merely a transition into eternal life and paradise with God. The Scriptures repeatedly reassure us saying, *"And we know that in all things God works for the good of those who love Him, who have been called according to His purpose"* (Romans 8:28). Our God is our strength and joy. *Isn't that marvelous!*

David's earnest desire was to seek after God that he might dwell in His House (verses 4-6). David wanted to be in God's presence more than anything else he desired. He wanted *"to dwell in the house of the LORD all the days of my life."* It was David's chief yearning, and it must be ours too. Verses 4-6 are captivating to me because of David's earnest desire to seek after God and dwell in His house. And though the Temple was not completed yet when David wrote this Psalm (Solomon his son finished building the Temple after David's death), David was not speaking literally about dwelling in the Tabernacle (only the priests could enter it). David was speaking of the close and intimate relationship he had with his LORD. The word "house" does not refer to a physical one. It is a figurative "house," which refers to God's presence, where God is, and he wants to be. David wanted to be where God dwelt and see Him in all His infinite beauty. He wanted to behold the beauty of the LORD and meditate in His presence, His temple. God's glory and presence gave him joy continually. He gazed upon God's kindness and goodness all the time. He would come to inquire in God's temple to know His will more perfectly. His chief desire was to be in God's presence in his actions, love, growth, and the understanding of God's will. *It is beautiful beyond description!*

David knew that although life is full of troubles and trials, God would be his Helper to shield him with His strength. He says, *"For He will conceal me in His shelter in the day of adversity; He will hide me under the cover of His tent; He will set me high on a rock."* You see, God is our protection (a tabernacle or tent), and a rock. As our tabernacle or tent, our God is our security to hide us in His presence. As our rock, He sets us on high to keep us far from the arrows and slingshots of our enemies. David tells us that God will put us in the hollow of His mighty hand to protect us with His presence and strength from all harm. As we walk with God in true communion, we can rest assured that He will help us handle life's difficulties and give us strength to endure them. God will provide for us in times of danger. He will lift our head in victory over our enemies and those who want to harm us. *When I think of what God has done in my life and how He has met His promises to me, I can't help but shout of joy and sing praises to Him!*

Therefore, like David, we must desire earnestly to draw near God. We must want to be with Him and seek Him in all His glory and beauty, as David did. Our greatest desire in life must be to have an intimate relationship with our Creator and walk with Him as friends. We must yearn to see Him face to face as our God and Creator like Enoch, Abraham, and Moses did. David longed for the LORD only and nothing else. Therefore, our God must be our only focal point and nothing else in our lives.

III. HEAR MY CRY (VOICE): David's Earnest Prayer to God: (27:7-10)

> *"LORD, hear my voice when I call; be gracious to me and answer me. My heart says this about You, "You are to seek My face." LORD, I will seek Your face. Do not hide Your face from me; do not turn Your servant away in anger. You have been my helper; do not leave me or abandon me, God of my salvation. Even if my father and mother abandon me, the LORD cares for me."*

David Needs to be Heard:

In verse 7, David cries out saying, *"LORD, hear my voice when I call; be gracious to me and answer me."* As a helpless and needy servant, David seeks God's face. He earnestly petitions God to come to his rescue. He puts his faith in God, asking Him to place His protective arms around him, and that is exactly what we must do. He remembers who God is and what He has done for him. Thus, he begs God to come to his defense against his enemies. Indeed, God hears when we cry out to Him, and He is never too busy to listen to us. Yet, He is the last person we want to talk to. *How is He going to listen to us if we don't even bother to approach His throne of mercy?* God is the only one on whom we can confidently lay our heavy burdens, to find relief and rest for our weary souls. We must believe and trust Him, for He will indeed listen to us. He is a faithful and perfect Father who longs to hear us when we cry out to Him. *Can there be a better or more perfect listener than our Father in heaven who wants to hear us?* No one, for there is no better listener who can help us with our cries like our God! No one can assist us and grant us that inner peace that we so desperately need in our times of turmoil except our Father in heaven. We must always remind ourselves of all His promises. Jesus, our Lord, promised us that if we *"keep asking, and it will be given to you. Keep searching, and you will find. Keep knocking, and the door will be opened to you"* (Matthew 7:7). *Such faithful promises are too much for me to fathom! So, I will trust in Him with all my heart and soul!*

David Needs Acceptance:

"My heart says this about You, 'You are to seek My face.' LORD, I will seek Your face." God has asked His children to seek His "face." The word "face" regarding God represents that intimate or unique communion, God's favor, we have with Him. God wants us to have close fellowship with Him. God invites us to seek Him. David accepts God's invitation to seek Him, so he begins praying to Him fervently.

In verse 9, David prays to God saying, *"Do not hide Your face from me; do not turn Your servant away in anger. You have been my helper; do not leave me or abandon me, God of my salvation."* In his prayer, he cries out and begs God to answer him. He is aware that his prayer is an emergency that demands urgency, for he is indeed in deep despair and trouble. He needs immediate assistance. So, he pleads with God to hear him and respond with mercy and kindness. As he prays to God, his eyes move from the clouds of conflict and doubt. David fervently expresses his need for acceptance and for God to come to rescue him. *Don't we all want to be accepted when we struggle with rejection?* At times, we experience such rejection perhaps from our family, or maybe our spouse, friends, co-workers, brethren, and those we encounter in our everyday tasks in life.

"Even if my father and mother abandon me, the LORD cares for me." Verse 10 captivates my heart because of its beauty. David felt as if the world had discarded him, for even his dearest friends had turned against him. Indeed, there was a blanket of loneliness upon him. But he is confident, because of his faith, that God will take better care of him than anyone else he has met in life. And even though others have failed him in the past, he is confident that God will not forsake him but instead

be with him all the way. David's faith found refuge and strength in God. He found consolation in Him as God shielded him and strengthened him when troubles surrounded him.

And though at times we feel as if the world has cast us away, God will not abandon us, for He cares for us. *Such mighty comfort and confidence in our God Almighty!* David acknowledged God's immense love for him, and so must we. Thus, in verse 9, David exclaims, *"Do not hide Your face from me; do not turn Your servant away in anger. You have been my helper; do not leave me or abandon me, God of my salvation."* God had been David's help when he most needed it in his life. God did not abandon David. God's help and approval is all that must matter in our lives. Even when the world rejects us, God is faithful to us. He will not reject and abandon us. Therefore, like David, we must seek the LORD for true acceptance and not the world. Without God's acceptance, we will starve and run the risk of seeking the acceptance of this world.

IV. GOD IS OUR GUIDANCE: (27:11-14)

> *"Because of my adversaries, show me Your way, LORD, and lead me on a level path. Do not give me over to the will of my foes, for false witnesses rise up against me, breathing violence. I am certain that I will see the LORD's goodness in the land of the living. Wait for the LORD; be strong and courageous. Wait for the LORD!"*

David also pled with God for guidance. He said, *"Because of my adversaries, show me Your way, LORD, and lead me on a level path."* Our faith casts away our fears through God's guidance as found in His Word. God's faithful followers want to know the ways of God better. They want to be led by God to a "level path." God guides our steps in His path of righteousness. Like David, we must want to walk a level path of obedience. When we stand on God's stable path, we can face our enemies. God protects us from evil and danger, and He will care for us as His precious children. As His beloved children, we must allow God to teach us. Since God loves and cares for us, we can confidently turn to Him for guidance. Because we are often stubborn and reject our Father's guidance and wisdom, we find ourselves in trouble. We deceive ourselves, thinking that we are wiser and have more knowledge than Him, but the truth is that without God as our Helper, we are completely lost. We must learn to humble ourselves and turn to God Almighty for His hand of mercy and help. Let us not harden our hearts and retreat into our weaknesses and the delusions of sin that ensnare us. Let us surrender our will to God's will, that He may lead us in the path of righteousness, the only perfect path.

David Needs God's Protection:

> "Do not give me over to the will of my foes, for false witnesses rise up against me, breathing violence" (Verse 12)

In verse 12, David makes a special plea to God for protection. Evil and slanderous men are speaking evil against him. Violent men are trying to ensnare him. They are breathing violence and seek to harm him. He feels overcome.

David prays to God for protection amid so much darkness and turmoil. As we read this Psalm, it is evident that David had many enemies (in verses 2, 3, 11, 12). God is our Provider, for He alone, provides for our needs. Sadly, we often try to fill these voids in other ways that are not God's ways. Yet, our heavenly Father cares enough for us that He is willing to meet our needs when we allow His Light to guide and protect us. When we walk in the Light as He is in the Light, we can confidently trust in Him and not be afraid.

David's Reminders Amid His Trials and Turmoil: (27:13-14)

"I am certain that I will see the LORD's goodness in the land of the living. Wait for the LORD; be strong and courageous. Wait for the LORD!"

Wait for the LORD!

"Wait for the LORD" is one of my all-time favorite phrases in the Bible. Verse 13 manifests David's immense confidence in God in moments of much turmoil. Were it not for God's goodness, David would have given up in despair. He declares, *"I am certain that I will see the LORD's goodness in the land of the living."* His enormous hope in God sustained him. His faith allowed him to see God's goodness, His kindness. Our God will come to our rescue and keep us in the *"land of the living"* because of His *"goodness"* toward us. *Such precious hope is marvelous beyond words!*

In verse 14, David exclaimed, *"Wait for the LORD; be strong and courageous. Wait for the LORD!"* David knew that God would answer his prayer because he knew God keeps His promises. God's promises are faithful and not false. So, David prayed, knowing that God would answer his prayer as he patiently walked with Him. David waited for the LORD's goodness because he had faith. He acknowledged that God was with him in whatever state he found himself. He did not give into his doubts and fears. He was determined to have courage. He believed God would extend His hand of mercy and goodness to him. He chose to be patient until God could give him victory over his trials. So, David had two reminders: First, to wait for the LORD, and second, God's timing is not our timing. Thus, David chose to pray and wait for the LORD. He knew God would not delay in coming to spare him from all his troubles. We must learn patience. We must learn to wait for the LORD to help us. Let us keep these two reminders and not get discouraged when fear assails our door. David states these reminders at the beginning and the end of verse 14 as his farewell words.

So, are you waiting for the LORD with confidence and patience? In Proverbs 20:22 we are reminded of God's justice, *"Don't say, 'I will avenge this evil!' Wait on the LORD, and He will rescue you.'"* Sadly, because of our bad habits, we demand answers and solutions to our problems immediately. We refuse to wait for the LORD. We cannot wait to see how things might turn out. We delude ourselves, thinking that we know all the answers. We think we already know the best solution to our problems. We demand that things be done according to our folly, knowledge, and desires, rather than trusting in the faithfulness of God's promises. *But what does this lack of trust in our LORD portray?* Merely a lack of faith in Him. When we behave in such a manner, we are telling God we do not trust Him. *How often do we wait for the LORD? Very little!* We choose to complain about Him for not hearing our prayers. We complain that He has let us down and refuses to help us. *Such whiners and complainers we are! Where is our patience and trust in God? We must wait for Him!*

We Must Be Courageous:

God commanded Abraham, the nation of Israel, Joshua, Jeremiah, and Ezekiel, to be courageous and wait upon Him. We must be courageous in the LORD. We must be flexible and depend on the LORD more. We must not concede when obstacles come our way. Indeed, God's people find an infinite number of obstacles as they walk the narrow way on the way to heaven. However, our LORD repeatedly demands that we believe and trust Him with all our might.

God is with us and will be with us to the gates of heaven. He has promised that He will come to our aid to help us overcome all of life's obstacles and the darkness in our path, only if we will faithfully trust in Him to deliver us. He has promised us that if we have faith in Him, we will overcome everything. We must trust in Him to meet whatever challenges that might come our way. He has promised us that He will strengthen our minds and hearts to do whatever it is that He requires us to do. We must not act foolishly and demand that everything be done our way. We must not complain, but instead cry out to Him with all our heart, for He cares for us. Therefore, let us resolve to be strong in the LORD, and in His power to help us overcome. Let us learn this attitude of heart to endure our many trials victoriously. Let the heroes of Hebrews 11 be our motivators. They trusted and waited for the LORD in the face of adversity. *Are you willing to wait for the LORD as your only deliverer and stronghold? Are you willing to stand for the LORD and His kingdom of righteousness while facing your needs and trials?* Remember, many of these heroes came through victoriously. Their faith grew stronger because of their courage to remain faithful to God in the face of hardship. *Will you hold on to your faith in your times of turmoil and suffering? Will you stand for the LORD and wait for Him no matter the price? Or will you give up and accept defeat? The choice is yours!* I choose always to wait and stand for the LORD in whatever circumstances I am.

CONCLUSION:

Our faith in God will win over fear and doubt, for He is our defense, strength, and guidance. He surrounds us with His Almighty arms of protection against our circumstances and enemies. God helps us to bear the fiery furnace of our trials, that we might not be burned. We must walk by faith and not by fear. God is our Light, who brings us out of the darkness of sin into His glorious Light of righteousness. God provides guidance to life's problems through His Truth. He is our salvation, for He delivers us with His strong hand. He is also our defense when we put our trust in Him as faithful servants. He puts us on a high rock to keep us from harm and danger, for He loves us and cares for us. *May our God be praised for His marvelous Light, salvation, and defense!* Our God is not only a God of love but also of Truth. He keeps His promises, and there is no falsehood in Him. Therefore, we must trust Him with an unwavering faith to face each trial that comes our way.

Our heart's yearning must be to seek after God and dwell with Him, walking with Him as His companions and members of His family. We must behold God's beauty with purity and love that His magnificence might surround us. Like David, we must desire to know God's Truth and have His mind to do all things His way. To do this, we must have a yearning to study, learn, and do His will. God will deliver us when we submit our will to His will in all things. In doing this, we can rest assured that He will give us spiritual victories over our difficulties. God's goodness compels us to rejoice amid our trials. His presence, love, and victory are enough to walk our journey here on earth. He has provided all that we need through His Son to accomplish His Will. Therefore, we must offer living sacrifices of joy and praise to Him with a heart of gratitude. We demonstrate our gratitude to Him by our godly and holy living, and by the way we live out His Word.

So, when trouble comes your way, don't lose heart but choose to be strong and wait on the LORD. Believe with all your heart that you will see God's goodness in the land of the living. Trust in His goodness and faithfulness. And though waiting is hard, it is necessary. Remain faithful to Him and keep praying. Wait on Him and remain faithful. Seek God's face by drawing nearer to Him in prayer. Approach His throne with confidence and cry out to Him. God will hear your deep feelings, even your broken and distressing ones. Put yourself in God's hands and let Him guide you into His level path of righteousness. Remember to be patient and wait on the LORD. He will lead you to a safe and secure place. *What an awesome Father we have in heaven!*

Is God the Light in your life? Is He your deliverance, your salvation, and your stronghold? If you are not walking the level path of righteousness with God as you draw near Him, it will be hard to have that confidence, faith, and trust I have mentioned in my study. Don't lose God's great blessings by turning away from Him and living in the sinful desires of the flesh. *Why not draw near to Him and His ways that lead us to the path of righteousness? Why not pray and talk to Him more in prayer? Why not choose to be in His presence by studying and meditating on His Word? Why not choose to walk with Him that He might be your Friend to listen to you, protect you, and guide you?* He will not let you down and will not forsake you. *You can be sure of that!* Let us wait for the LORD to provide all that we need. *When you find yourself in the pit, look up to God in prayer!*

May we have an unwavering faith, waiting, and trusting in God when we feel lost, without hope and mercy. May we always turn to our Light that He may give us strength and victory over our fears, our enemies, and evildoers who rise against us. May we stand firm and rooted in His Word that we may have confidence in Him. May we always seek His face and worship Him with songs of praise as we walk His level path of righteousness. May we learn to wait for Him steadfastly by praying and by keeping watch. May we focus on God as our shelter and hiding place. May we seek the LORD while He may be found and call upon Him while He is near. May all men return to the LORD, that He may have compassion on them, for He will abundantly pardon.

The following song was my motivation to write this study.

THE LORD IS MY LIGHT
Written By C.E. Couchman

The LORD is my light and my salvation.
Whom shall I fear?
And He is my strength, the defense of my life.
Whom shall I fear?
Have mercy, O LORD, and answer my cry.
Turn not away.
For You are my help, the God of salvation.
Turn not away.

O LORD lead me now in Your path straight and
    even.
Teach me Your way.
I will not despair; Your goodness sustains me.
Teach me Your way.
To dwell in His house all the days of my life:
This shall I seek.
And oh, to behold the LORD in His beauty!
This shall I seek.

[Chorus]
Wait, wait, O wait on the LORD.
Be strong and take courage!
Wait on the LORD.
Wait, wait, O wait on the LORD.
Be strong and take courage!
Yes, wait on the LORD.

Jehovah God, Shine Forth!

"O Jehovah, thou God to whom vengeance belongeth,
Thou God to whom vengeance belongeth, shine forth.
Lift up thyself, thou judge of the earth: Render to the
proud their desert. Jehovah, how long shall the wicked,
How long shall the wicked triumph?" Psalm 94:1-3

Our Creator is a good and righteous God. Because He made us in such a way that we may choose to love Him and do what is right and good or ignore Him and do otherwise, our world is filled with wicked men and women who hurt and destroy the good that God wants. Our job as His faithful servants is to trust His ways and purposes when we cannot see the ultimate justice that He is bringing about. The day will come when all the righteous children of God will cry out, *"Righteous and true are all your judgments!"* Psalm 94 presents our God in this light.

It is not easy to truly believe in God. Of course, it is easy to believe that God exists and that He is almighty and all-wise. The evidence is overwhelming in the Creation and the marvelous things that He has made. What makes it hard to truly believe is that we often see injustice that is not in harmony with the character of the God that we believe in. When the wicked afflict the righteous, we become impatient and wonder, *"Can we truly trust our God?"* That kind of doubt encourages us to disobey our Lord.

Psalm 94 focuses on the persecution of the faithful. The wicked are selfish and proud. They despise the way of Truth and those who pursue it. One thing that struck me about this Psalm is that no matter how much wickedness, oppression, enemies, and evildoers cloud our lives, we have the assurance that our Jehovah God will triumph and shine forth. The wicked will not defeat us if we genuinely call on God to deliver us. Our Jehovah God will bless His people and punish evildoers.

In this Psalm, we see a God of grace and love who upholds His faithful servants in any trial and who assumes the role of vengeance. God's faithful children can rest assured that God will comfort and sustain them in their difficult times. God is not deaf or blind to unjust acts. God knows everything: the ungodly acts of the unjust. God calls them fools, for they cannot fool Him. He sees and knows everything. He knows how worthless they are. The unjust, the evildoers, and those who defy God, and His principles of righteousness will not escape His righteous judgments and punishment. They will not destroy God's righteous ones. He will rise up and not forsake them. And though our God is a God of love and mercy, He is also a God of vengeance. A God who will rise up and act, bringing justice, and vengeance. God notices and really cares. *What confidence, comfort, and hope!*

The Psalmist is especially calling for God to judge the proud to receive what they deserve. It must not cause us any trouble or concern to ask God in prayer to give evildoers what is due to them, for He is a God of justice (vengeance). *When the righteous cry out to the LORD to shine forth, the wicked will not triumph!* I hope to persuade you with the following words of encouragement when persecution, affliction, trouble, trials, and difficulties come your way. I hope that you will hide yourself in the LORD our God and let Him sustain you, for He is our refuge and fortress. *He will always be our only sure protection against anything or anyone that could possibly harm us! I certainly*

*need these words of encouragement and assurance as much as you
do!*

I. SHINE FORTH, GOD OF VENGEANCE! (94:1-7)

> *"O Lord, God of vengeance, O God of vengeance,
> shine forth! Rise up, O judge of the earth; repay to
> the proud what they deserve! O Lord, how long shall
> the wicked, how long shall the wicked exult? They
> pour out their arrogant words; all the evildoers
> boast. They crush your people, O Lord, and afflict
> your heritage. They kill the widow and the sojourner,
> and murder the fatherless; and they say, "The Lord
> does not see; the God of Jacob does not perceive."*

The Psalmist begins by describing God, not as a God of
love and mercy but as a God of vengeance. His appeal for
judgment starts with a complaint, for He is calling upon God
to take His seat on His throne of glory and give the proud and
wicked their just punishment. The word "vengeance" is from
the Hebrew plural word, נְקָמָה (neqamoth), that speaks of full
judgment. He appeals to God in the urgency of his heart. He
pours out his feelings to God. He calls on Him for three reasons: to shine forth, to lift Himself up, and to render punishment. *Why?*

1. Because God's judicial infliction of righteousness is
   His revenge.
2. Because God is the One who handles all vengeance.
3. Because God shines forth in the darkness, and as
   the Psalmist had cried out, darkness had taken over.

And though God is righteous, He will, according to His
divine wisdom, bring the wicked, the evildoers, into judgment. The Psalmist is petitioning God to lift Himself up or to
rise because it appeared to him that God was sleeping, for the
wicked went free. He wanted God to act and not be indifferent

but to punish the wicked. He called on Him to carry out His vengeance and to deliver him from the hands of evildoers. He felt surrounded by them with no way out. *Does this sound familiar to you?* The Psalmist expressed his desire for the wicked to be stopped and not go free in triumph. And since He knew that vengeance belongs to God alone, he wanted God to act by punishing the wicked. The Psalmist cried out, *"Jehovah, how long shall the wicked, How long shall the wicked triumph?"* The wicked around him were proud, so He asked God, the Supreme Judge, to bring them before Him and demand that they give an account for their evil works. The wicked around him were boasting about what they were doing. The wicked were arrogant, selfish, and vain. They were destroying the Lord's nation. *"They crush your people, O Lord, and afflict your heritage."*

Have you noticed how often criminals and evildoers seem to have more rights than you? If you agree, then this is your Psalm to read as you pray for God's deliverance. *Isn't it outrageous that the atheist questions our God's goodness and existence for allowing evildoers to get away with evil?* But there is one big difference between the one who believes in God and the atheist. Although the Psalmist wondered when God was going to rise up and act, he knew quite well that God exists and is working on our behalf. Because he acknowledged this truth, he pledged with God to do the right thing and not hold back.

In verses 4-7, the Psalmist appears to be pleading with God to not allow the wicked to shine in their wickedness. The wicked often appear to do evil freely or do as they please without any restraint. In their freedom, they speak against God and His Divine Word. Not only are they free to do as they please by insulting their Creator and His statutes, but seem to find delight in oppressing, crushing, destroying, and breaking God's children. They are a hindrance to God's children. They think that God does not care or notice and is not looking at what they are doing. *Isn't it something that so many think this way when they sin?* In verse 6, the wicked lack compassion. *"They kill the widow and the sojourner, and murder the fatherless."* They afflict the widow, the stranger, and the fatherless by taking advantage of them. They can do that because the weak cannot defend themselves. In verse 7, they say, *"The Lord does not see; the God of Jacob does not perceive." How cruel can they be? Do they not have any consciences? How can they tolerate such actions? Do they not know that they will have to answer to God, their Creator?* They believe that God does not see the wicked things they are doing. They recklessly say that God does not consider or understand what they are doing. The wicked become persecutors, oppressors, murderers, proud, and boastful. In today's society, the wicked will even teach our children that God does not exist, misusing and perverting science to affirm evolution with no other purpose than to deny their Creator and His creation. We see this happening in our public schools and our universities. *We wonder why our children curse and deny their Creator!* What they do is cruel. *It exceeds their wickedness!*

II. THE LORD SEES! (94:8-11)

> *"Understand, O dullest of the people! Fools, when will you be wise? He who planted the ear, does he not hear? He who formed the eye, does he not see? He who disciplines the nations, does he not rebuke? He who teaches man knowledge—the Lord—knows the thoughts of man, that they are but a breath."*

In verses 8-11, the Psalmist charges the wicked saying, *"Understand, O dullest of the people! Fools, when will you be wise?"* He is urging the wicked to shine in understanding and wisdom. The wicked do not understand because they do not care to know God. He tells the wicked to be wise in their understanding because they appear to be unaware that He is the Creator. The Psalmist voices three rhetorical questions which demand affirmative answers.

1. *"He who planted the ear, does he not hear?"* Since God created the ear, He can hear what they say. *The One who made our ears can hear the wicked things they say and do! So, is God not also a God who hears and understands what happens in this world? Do we not expect Him to have the same abilities with which He has made us?*

2. *"He who formed the eye, does he not see?"* Is it that hard to understand that the same God who made the *"eye"* for us to see, perceive, and make judgments is the God who also sees, notices, discerns, and judges? Likewise, since He created the eye, He is certainly able to see the wickedness that they do.

3. *"He who disciplines the nations, does he not rebuke?"* Are we not aware that the One who is the true Teacher of mankind, will also judge His people? Indeed, God disciplines, corrects, and judges His own children when they need it. *The God who judges others, will He not also judge His own children?* In like manner, our God teaches all men His knowledge, for He is the God of all knowledge and knows everything that is happening on earth. *"The Lord—knows the thoughts of man, that they are but a breath."*

Therefore, He has all power and authority to rebuke everyone and correct the wicked. He assures us that He can punish the wicked and all their lawlessness. Lest we forget, He Who created man, the ear, the eye, and everything can with certainty know and search the heart of man and all his intentions. He knows with certainty our thoughts. He knows that man's thoughts are vain and fruitless. He measures the thoughts of the wicked and finds them worthless and like a vapor. Man's empty thoughts disappear quickly as does his breath. *God knows everything!* Not only does He know everything, but He judges the thoughts, intentions, and actions of men. We can rest assured that wickedness will not triumph. *It will fail!* Those who dispute with God will fail, for righteousness will eventually triumph over lawlessness. And although in their barren vanity, the wicked think in their heart that they will get away with their wickedness or lawlessness, *God is still in control, and He will chastise them!* And though God's judgment is not immediate, no one will escape it, for God will bring justice at the proper time.

III. THE BLESSING OF GOD'S DISCIPLINE: (94:12-15)

> *"Blessed is the man whom you discipline, O Lord, and whom you teach out of your law, to give him rest from days of trouble, until a pit is dug for the wicked. For the Lord will not forsake his people; he will not abandon his heritage; for justice will return to the righteous, and all the upright in heart will follow it."*

Blessings in Adversity:

In verses 12-17, the Psalmist stresses the need for the righteous to find blessings in life's difficulties. He points out that blessings arise from hardship. *"Blessed is the man whom you discipline, O Lord, and whom you teach out of your law."* The word *"discipline"* or *"chasten"* in other translations includes all of life's discipline that leads us toward maturity. In this Scripture, the word "chastening" or "discipline," implies the teaching of God's Law. The writer of Hebrews stresses the value of hard times, calling it discipline (Hebrews 12:3-13). The Psalmist is also stating that God blesses men by teaching them His Law so that they can meditate on it with a willing and humble heart. In doing this, they can learn from Him Who created the heavens and the earth and knows all our thoughts. *Can there be a better or more eminent Teacher?* Imagine all the knowledge He is willing to give us from His written Word. *It is too much for me to fathom!* All that He has revealed to us from that same Word to obtain knowledge and wisdom and not perish. Therefore, we must know the importance of that Word and be determined to read and study it with a humble heart. God's Law is His instrument of instruction and method of teaching. In our times of oppression and suffering, we learn from them as we endure them. *There are many hidden blessings when we choose to learn from our ordeals!*

In verse 13, the Psalmist prays to God to allow the sufferer to find some rest from the days of hardship as he patiently awaits God's judgment of the wicked. He pleads, *"to give him rest from days of trouble, until a pit is dug for the wicked."* He prays for a time of quiet rest and undisturbed peace. God's purpose in revealing His Word to us is to instruct us to live righteously and godly. It will give us rest and peace in the days of adversity. Judgment will arrest the wicked when God puts them in the pit. We can rest assured that God will deal with the wicked at the time He deems best. The *"pit"* here is the wicked man who eventually receives the judgment of his wickedness. Indeed, God provides relief from troubled times, and we are never crushed beyond hope (1 Corinthians 10:13). God will make sure to give us rest in the days of trouble. He will get us back on our feet before the next challenge comes. God will punish the wicked, for a time will come when a pit is dug for them and will be ensnared for their sins. *We can rest assured that justice will come!*

The LORD Keeps His Own:

In verse 14, the righteous look at persecution and hardship through the eyes of reassurance, for they know that God will not forsake them. *"For the Lord will not forsake his people; he will not abandon his heritage." God has promised to take care of us, His inheritance, His chosen people, and we must believe that!* God will not reject His own people, for He will not abandon His special possession. And though at times it seems as if deliverance is delayed, and times are difficult, God will not abandon us. So, when you find yourself wondering, frustrated, and discouraged about God's apparent lack of judgment on the wicked, you must go back and read His revealed Word to know Him better. It is the only way to know with certainty that He will give you rest. *How do I know that?* Because He will not forsake or abandon those who do His will. He will not forsake us, for we are His inheritance. *Such promise of assurance and rest! Have you ever felt the way that the Psalmist did when he thought that God had abandoned him? I have!* It is at such times that I must force myself to think of all His precious promises; promises that reassure and strengthen our faith because we are His inheritance. He has promised not to abandon us in the days of adversity, anxieties, cares, and trials. And I believe with all my heart that He will never break His promises. *This ought to motivate us to walk by faith and not by sight!*

In verse 15, God's righteousness demands that justice returns to the righteous and that they always seek it. *"For justice will return to the righteous, and all the upright in heart will follow it."* The Hebrew literally says, *"Because unto righteousness judgment returns and after it are the upright of heart."* Vindication will always come to the righteous, and the upright of heart can indeed depend on such a promise. *The faithful do not have to fear God's judgments, but rather rejoice, for His judgments will bring glory and honor to them!* The faithful can rely on God's faithfulness toward them. *The righteous can trust in God's ultimate victory in the end!* In time you and I will truly see judgment rendered for righteousness. The upright in heart will follow righteousness. Their righteousness makes them just, upright and honorable. The word upright refers to posture or position. *How would the righteous, the guiltless, and unashamed stand up?* They stand upright in spirit and heart. *Righteousness and justice will triumph!* We must not be shaken when justice and righteousness are delayed. The righteous know they will triumph if they persist in doing righteousness. *What about the unrighteous, the guilty, and the ashamed? They can't stand upright!*

IV. GOD, OUR RESCUER: (94:16-19)

> *"Who rises up for me against the wicked? Who stands up for me against evildoers? If the Lord had not been my help, my soul would soon have lived in the land of silence. When I thought, 'My foot slips,' your steadfast love, O Lord, held me up. When the cares of my heart are many, your consolations cheer my soul."*

In verse 16, the Psalmist reminds us that although at times, it seems as if we are standing alone, we are not alone. *"Who rises up for me against the wicked? Who stands up for me against evildoers?"* God will indeed stand up for us. He will be our companion when others (our closest friends) forsake us and are not standing with us. Only our God is faithful enough to walk beside us to help us as we walk through the deepest valleys of trials. Only He will sustain us, for He is our Rescuer. He is the only One who will protect us from the wicked and will stand up against our enemies. *There is no better Deliverer than our God!* We can confidently rely on Him. *Without His help, we can do nothing!* He is our Comforter, who loves us with unfailing love. A love that will support us during our most difficult and trying times. And though His disciples may falter during the hours of crisis and ordeal, He has promised that He will not abandon us. When Paul was in prison, he said that all had abandoned him and that no one came to his defense and stood by his side, except the Lord, who stood by him and strengthened him (2 Tim. 4:16-17). *Oh, such words of comfort!*

Indeed, verse 16 contains some excellent rhetorical questions:

1. *Who will protect us from the wicked?*
2. *Who will stand up against our evildoers?*

The resounding answer is no one, except our God, for He is our only Deliverer on whom we can confidently rely. We would be nothing if our God did not help us, for He is the God of comfort. He will be there to provide for us and deliver us with His unfailing love. His unfailing love can indeed support us through our difficulties and ordeals. The Psalmist surely knows the answer and expects us to know it as well. *Who will rise up for us? Surely, Our God will rise up for us!* No other god will help but the True God.

In verses 17-19, the righteous of the LORD acknowledge that had it not been for God, they would have gone under. *"If the Lord had not been my help, my soul would soon have lived in the land of silence."* Had the LORD not held him up or helped him, he would have died. The Psalmist refers to the grave as *"the land of silence."* It is a metaphor that underlines the absence of any communication from the dead. When the righteous suffer, they are confident that God is with them and is watching over them because of their faith and walk with Him. *"When I thought, 'My foot slips,' your steadfast love, O Lord, held me up."* God manifests His providential care to His servant by making his journey a safe one. When he feels that his foot is slipping, he is confident he can count on the LORD to rescue him, for he trusts that God's lovingkindness will supply his need. The slipping foot here portrays those difficulties that could easily end in tragedy, were it not for God's intervention. God will hold us up or keeps us standing upright when we find ourselves amid slippery places, finding it difficult to stand firm.

We clearly see that our God shines. He is rising and standing up against the wicked and their lawlessness. He is our Ebenezer that Samuel spoke of in I Samuel 7. In Samuel's days, we see Israel during the darkest times of her history. In those days, one of Israel's fiercest enemies, the Philistines, drew up in battle array against them, near Ebenezer. As the battle spread, Israel was defeated, and about four thousand men were killed on the battlefield (I Samuel 4:2). The Israelites could not understand what was going on. They did not understand that the nation's spiritual decline was forfeiting the protection and victory of their Jehovah God. When the elders sent for the Ark of the Covenant at Shiloh and saw it coming into the camp, they shouted with joy. But there was a problem. They were placing their trust in the magic of the Ark and not in their Almighty God Who dwelt above the Ark. This time, they lost 30,000 and the Ark (I Samuel 4:5-11). God had given them conditional promises. They had not obeyed those conditions which were part of that covenant. They had broken the covenant. Since they had broken the covenant, God was not obligated to answer their prayers.

In 1 Samuel 7:3-14, we read that Samuel tells Israel:

- To return to God with all their heart.
- To remove their foreign gods from among them.
- To direct their hearts to God, confessing their sins.
- To serve God alone.

All these things are part of repentance. Repentance requires a broken and contrite spirit. Samuel promised them deliverance if they had a heart of true repentance. So, they met those conditions for deliverance. Amid all that, Samuel assembled all Israel at Mizpah to pray for them. They had pled for Samuel to pray for them since they feared another attack of the Philistines. He offered a whole burnt offering in worship, and he cried to the LORD for Israel, and He answered him. As Samuel offered the sacrifice, crying out to God for Israel, the Philistines were getting ready to attack Israel. *God fought for Israel that day!*

> *"Now while Samuel was offering up the burnt offering, the Philistines were gathering together to battle against Israel. But God fought for Israel that day. He thundered against them and confused them on the*

battlefield, so that they were badly beaten before Israel."

The LORD answered Samuel's prayer. Let us consider God's answer to his prayer and what Samuel did while he prayed to God for deliverance:

*"Now when the Philistines heard that the sons of Israel had gathered to Mizpah, the lords of the Philistines went up against Israel. And when the sons of Israel heard it, they were afraid of the Philistines. Then the sons of Israel said to Samuel, 'Do not cease to cry to the Lord our God for us, that He may save us from the hand of the Philistines.' Samuel took a suckling lamb and offered it for a whole burnt offering to the Lord; and Samuel cried to the Lord for Israel and the Lord answered him. Now Samuel was offering up the burnt offering, and the Philistines drew near to battle against Israel. But the Lord thundered with a great thunder on that day against the Philistines and confused them, so that they were routed before Israel. The men of Israel went out of Mizpah and pursued the Philistines, and struck them down as far as below Beth-car. Then Samuel took a stone and set it between Mizpah and Shen, and named it **Ebenezer**, saying, 'Thus far the Lord has helped us.' So the Philistines were subdued and they did not come anymore within the border of Israel. And the hand of the Lord was against the Philistines all the days of Samuel. The cities which the Philistines had taken from Israel were restored to Israel, from Ekron even to Gath; and Israel delivered their territory from the hand of the Philistines. So there was peace between Israel and the Amorites." (I Samuel 7:10-12)*

God answered Samuel's prayer and helped the Israelites because:

- They had repented of their sin.
- They confessed their sin.
- They rededicated themselves to the LORD.
- They humbly asked for prayer.
- They wanted the LORD to fight for them, acting on their behalf.
- They behaved in a manner of repentance, acting for Him.

Going back to the Psalmist's words, *"If the Lord had not been my help, my soul would soon have lived in the land of silence. When I thought, 'My foot slips,' your steadfast love, O Lord, held me up. When the cares of my heart are many, your consolations cheer my soul."*

If the LORD does not help us, our souls will dwell in deep dark silence. *We will be hopeless!* It is disturbing to see so many lost people who do not know the LORD's rest and deliverance. When life hurls wickedness at them, they are overwhelmed with life's adversities and anxieties. They seem to have no hope, rest, joy, or deliverance. *It is sad! Why?* Because they are sinking into an irreversible silence and darkness. However, the good news for those who love their LORD, know Him, and have learned from Him from the Sacred Text is that they have their LORD as their Ebenezer, their Helper. His mercies are new every morning. Indeed, His mercies carry and hold us up when our foot slips. And although we might have a multitude of anxieties and cares, we find delight, comfort, refuge, peace, and strength in the LORD. *How does He comfort us amid our anxieties, trials, and cares?* By putting delight and joy into our hearts because we know and are confident that He will judge righteously. We know that He rules.

V. THE LORD IS OUR FORTRESS AND REFUGE: (94:20-23)

"Can wicked rulers be allied with you, those who frame injustice by statute? They band together against the life of the righteous and condemn the innocent to death. But the Lord has become my stronghold, and my God the rock of my refuge. He will bring back on them their iniquity and wipe them out for their wickedness; the Lord our God will wipe them out."

The final stanza of this Psalm takes us back to the beginning. In verses 20-23, the LORD shines for the upright in heart and against the wicked one. The Psalmist tries to reason with God's heart and thinking. In verse 20, the Psalmist asks, *"Can wicked rulers be allied with you, those who frame injustice by statute?"* The word "throne" in our context implies a group of people or nations who are ruled by evil and bound to accomplish their wickedness at any cost. Wickedness is described as having been put upon a throne, given honor, a platform to exercise a destructive influence. The Psalmists asks, *Will God allow the wicked to build an evil strategy into the form of command or a statute? Will God then approve the wicked when he pursues it as a national commitment or personal resolve? Will He unite and work with such a strategy?* The Psalmist obviously implies that He will not. *He declares that God's righteousness will prohibit Him from doing it!*

His holiness will not permit it and be compromised. His holy and righteous nature will not compromise with evil. He will not and cannot have fellowship with wickedness or lawlessness. It is against His righteous nature (1 John 1:5-6). In other translations, *"the devices of evil by law,"* which would imply that His throne has fellowship with wickedness. The Psalmist knew God would not go for that. So, the question is, *what evil were they conceiving by law?* The evil was in the laws they had made against the life of the righteous. They condemned the innocent to death. *So, will God approve any law that advocates and legalizes a sinful way of living? Of course not!* Why? Because the righteous acknowledge that when human laws conflict with the laws of God, they must follow the laws of God (Acts 5:29).

Verse 21, states that the righteous are often trampled under the heels of the wicked, because of their faithfulness to God and His divine order of life. The righteous are usually attacked by others who oppose their righteous living. The Psalmist says, *"They band together against the life of the righteous and condemn the innocent to death."* The wicked condemn the innocent to death. They come against the righteous, seeking to destroy their life. In verses 22-23, we notice the confidence the Psalmist has in the LORD, in His work. He is confident that God will defend the cause of the righteous. He is the Rock of our refuge, and we are safe in His providential care. Not only will He protect us, but with confidence, we can say that He will cause the wicked to reap as they have sown. He will cut them off in their wickedness. *How do the righteous respond when they are persecuted?* They respond by trusting in God and hiding themselves in Him, for He is our safe refuge from the storms that rise up against us. Regardless of the severity of the storm, the righteous can rest assured that God will be their refuge. *"But the Lord has become my stronghold, and my God the rock of my refuge." Such powerful words of hope! So why despair?* Our God is indeed our best "stronghold," and a cliff-like "rock" of "refuge." God's righteous children can confidently put themselves in God's hands, for He is an invisible wall against all forces of destruction.

In verse 23, God's justice will uncover the sins of evildoers and bring them down upon their heads. *"He will bring back on them their iniquity and wipe them out for their wickedness; the Lord, our God, will wipe them out."* We can rest assured that God will turn or bring back the sins on the heads of the wicked. *He will destroy them!* You see, sin metes out its own punishment, for when we sow to the flesh, we must also reap what we have sown (Gal. 6:7-8). *Evildoers will be punished for their sins perhaps on earth but certainly will be punished for their sins in eternity!* The lawless and the wicked must pass through two judgments: the judgment of sin and the judgment of God's throne. *God's righteousness and moral law demand it!* A law He has built into this world and from which there is no escape. And though one might escape from the law of gravity, it is not the same with God's Law or moral retribution. The law, *"whatever one sows that will he also reap"* (Gal. 6:7b), applies to more than personal giving.

Truly, the destruction of the wicked derives from two sources. First, their sins will return to them, because what they intended to do to others will usually come back to them. The destructive powers of evil (working through their own sins) will batter and destroy them. Second, God will judge them in eternity. God not only administers due punishment through His universal moral laws, but also through His jurisdiction and lordship. Justice will eventually come. God will give us relief from our sorrows and evildoers who afflict us, for He will turn their sins upon themselves. This leads us back to the beginning of this Psalm with the question: *"O Lord, how long shall the wicked, how long shall the wicked exult? They pour out their arrogant words; all the evildoers boast."* The answer is that God will bring all humanity before His throne of righteousness and holiness to give account for their sins. God will repay them for their sins and will punish them for their wickedness or lawlessness. *He is the most righteous and just Judge!* We can confidently say, *"Jehovah is on my side; I will not fear: What can man do unto me?"* (Psalm 118:6). *What hope and confidence!*

CONCLUSION:

The Psalms are undeniably beautiful! They represent a rich tapestry of prayer and praise. Some reflect a texture of deep despair. They glow with a deep peace and strength provided by God. They exalt the Most High God. They express a range of human emotion and experience. They teach us how to improve our prayers to reach out to God from every imaginable experience. They help us to find peace amid turmoil. Most of all, they help us to grow deeper in our walk with God. The Psalms are my prayer book, for they help me to love my God better, strengthen my faith, and share my deepest fears and emotions with Him when I struggle to express them. *For me, the study of Psalms is an excellent way to enter God's world of inspired and inspiring poetry!*

Psalm 94 is a vivid portrait of the wicked, their attitudes and actions against God's righteous children. This Psalm is a reminder of God's care and protection toward the righteous. God sees His children as His own possession or inheritance (94:5). God regards those who seek first His kingdom and His righteousness as His responsibility. If, we, His children remain within the circle of His will and fellowship, God will guide, protect, and provide for us. *We can rest assured that He will!* God will not abandon the upright in heart, the righteous, for they are His inheritance. He will vindicate the ways of the righteous. He is a continual refuge and fortress to them. He will take a stand against lawlessness or wickedness. He is a shield for the righteous against all harm and wickedness. His faithful children can rest assured that no evil will harm them. God offers peace, comfort, and encouragement to the troubled heart. Our God is like a caring and loving parent, for He extends His gracious hand to His children and covers them with His lovingkindness to sustain and keep them through their difficult times. God provides His children times of rest from adversity. God's goodness is amazing, for it is full, concrete, and well balanced. *He is our Shepherd, who covers all our needs!*

Psalm 94 teaches us that blessings are found in God's chastisement or discipline. When we respond well to God's discipline, we demonstrate our good hearts as true children of God (Hebrews 12:6). God's discipline helps us to face our trials so that we might learn, mature, and grow as we should. Discipline has a humbling and softening effect, for it conditions our soul to heed the teachings of God. Our soul is being refined, polished, and nourished for service to God's kingdom through adversity. Our thorns make us more humble and cause us to look more consistently to God for strength. Spiritual growth comes through the school of adversity. When the school is over, and we graduate, we learn to be thankful for being chosen to be part of it. We Christians must learn to rejoice and be glad through all life experiences: pleasant and unpleasant. They build up a Christ-like spirit within us.

Psalm 94 is like a book about us, for it asks the question: *"He who planted the ear, does he not hear? He who formed the eye, does he not see?"* If one should ask, *what is God like?* He would simply turn to his body for the answer. You see, our hands, eyes, ears, and minds talk to us and teach us about the God who made us. *That same awesome God who made us and gave us our abilities can see all that is going on in this world in which we live!* He can hear our prayers. He can speak to us and communicate His will through His revealed Word. God has revealed in His Word an outline about what He wants us to do to accomplish His purpose. The more we study about Him through His Word, the more we learn about what God is like. We can reach out to God through His Word and His creation.

The godly can rest assured that persecution will come to them. And though they might not be asked to die for their faith, they will at least be attacked for believing in God (2 Tim. 3:12; Phil. 1:29). Paul described persecution as an extension to Christ's sufferings (Col. 1:24). Psalm 94 gives us the answers to how we must respond to persecution and adversity. The righteous must remember the following.

- God will not abandon them in their time of trial.
- To look at the bright side, the blessings that come from our trials, persecution, and adversity.

- To call on the LORD to carry out His justice and bring the wicked to judgment.
- To commit to reading and studying God's Word to know Him better and find strength from it.
- To keep following all righteousness with an upright heart.
- Suffering, persecution, and trying circumstances are God's training tools.
- Everyone will be repaid, and no one gets away with anything. The wicked will be judged, and the righteous will be vindicated.
- They can take comfort in God's consolation that He makes available for them.
- When afflictions come, it is good to remember that God will never side with evil. Our righteous God will always be opposed to evil or lawlessness and will always stand with us against it.
- Vengeance belongs to the LORD.
- Evil comes back to haunt and punish those who commit it (Rom. 6:23).
- God our Creator will sustain us, for He is a refuge to the righteous and a fortress to the faithful.
- He will always be our sure protection from anything that could possibly harm us.
- Christ has told us that life in His kingdom must involve handling persecution and that we must go through fiery trials as citizens of God's kingdom.
- God is glorified when we endure hardship.
- He knows the intentions of our hearts and thoughts.
- He is our Teacher and Master.
- He will give us rest.
- He will not abandon us.
- He will help us and hold us up.
- He can carry us through.
- Hard times help us to learn the Way of the LORD.

- The righteous find blessings in life's difficulties and thorns.
- Hard times, challenges, and thorns will make us more reliant upon God.
- Hard times teach us to be more diligent about following God's instructions.
- God will cut off the wicked and their lawlessness.
- And finally, the Father will honor the righteous saying, *"Blessed are you when others revile you and persecute you and utter all kinds of evil against you falsely on my account. 12 Rejoice and be glad, for your reward is great in heaven, for so they persecuted the prophets who were before you."* (Matthew 5:11-12)

Those who invest their life defying God, and His principles of righteousness will not escape His punishment. *God will not allow the wicked to destroy the righteous!* We must remember that vengeance belongs to the LORD. The Psalmist speaks of the LORD who sent His only begotten Son to die for our sins. He used His Son's death and His blood to save us from His judgment coming for the wicked. The beauty of all this is that He has provided rest for our dying souls. Moreover, He has promised to give us rest from our days of anxiety when they seem to overwhelm our hearts. *Why not take advantage of His death and blood? Why be cast off and be judged by the Judge of all? Why not admit that you have sinned and are in desperate need of a Savior to rescue you?*

May the LORD rise and shine on us in our time of need that we may not lose heart. May we trust Him patiently, waiting until we see the fulfillment of His good and wise purposes. And may we always remember that vengeance belongs to the LORD and not to us.

Lamentations:
Grief, Comfort, and Hope

"I am the man who has seen affliction under the rod of his wrath; he has driven and brought me into darkness without any light... my soul is bereft of peace; I have forgotten what happiness is; so I say, 'My endurance has perished; so has my hope from the LORD.' Remember my affliction and my wanderings, the wormwood and the gall! My soul continually remembers it and is bowed down within me. But this I call to mind, and therefore I have hope: The steadfast love of the LORD never ceases; his mercies never come to an end; they are new every morning; great is your faithfulness. 'The LORD is my portion,' says my soul, 'therefore I will hope in him. The LORD is good to those who wait for him, to the soul who seeks him. It is good that one should wait quietly for the salvation of the LORD. The LORD is good to those who wait for him, to the soul who seeks him. It is good that one should wait quietly for the salvation of the LORD." Lamentations 3:1-26

The LORD Jehovah had to tread the winepress of His wrath in Jerusalem. He had crushed them as grapes are crushed to give up their lifeblood. *Was this the end for the people of God?* Most of them were dead with their bodies strewn about as carrion for the vultures to devour. Jeremiah grieved not just for their loss, but because he knew they deserved it.

God was righteous. He was vindicated. But, Jeremiah knew something else about God: He is a God of mercy and grace. The prophet's job now was to comfort the survivors and their children who would return someday. They had to know there was hope so that they might endure the harsh trials and humiliation of their exile. Let us examine the short message of the Lamentations of Jeremiah.

The Book of Lamentations is God's book about pain, despair, and grief. It is a book about the lament (a cry) uttered when life is falling apart. The book is composed of five poems. The first poem of The Lamentations of Jeremiah is a cry to the LORD for comfort, for there was no comfort. The second poem of Lamentations shows a dramatic shift in Jeremiah's message to God's people. The intensity of this poem reveals the anger (wrath) of the LORD. But it also reassures us that we can wail with a broken heart to God. So, there is no need to restrain our emotions, for we may speak with raw honesty to God. The third poem affirms that we can trust the LORD amid our pain and distress because of God's faithfulness. God's mercies are new every day, and with each new day, there is another opportunity for God's refreshing to carry us through. We can rest assured that He will get us through today. The fourth poem teaches us to reflect on what is happening. The only way we can *"count it all joy"* and *"be gold refined amid our fires of pain and despair"* is by reflecting on what has happened, choosing to learn from our difficult times.

Hardship transforms our lives and keeps us faithful to God. Finally, in the fifth poem, we learn that we can pray for restoration, knowing that God keeps His word to forgive us of our sins, placing us back into a relationship with Him. Christ is the fulfillment of God's Word to save the world and give us what we need to avoid the wrath of God.

I. COMFORT FROM THE BOOK OF LAMENTATIONS:
(Lamentations 1)

Lack of Comfort, Grief, and Hope:

The first poem of The Lamentations of Jeremiah is a cry to the LORD for comfort, for there was no comfort.

1. *"She has none to comfort her"* (1:2).
2. *"She has no comforter"* (1:9).
3. *"My eyes flow with tears for a comforter is far from me"* (1:16).
4. *"Zion stretches out her hands but there is none to comfort her"* (1:17).
5. *"They heard my groaning, yet there is no one to comfort me"* (1:21).

Jeremiah declares the lack of comfort for the city of Jerusalem and its inhabitants three times (1:2,9,17). However, he refers to himself (notice the switch to the first person) and his own lack of comforters in his grief (1:16, 21). The word *"groaning,"* which occurs five times in this poem, is closely tied to it (1:4,8, 11, 21, 22). The city, its people, and of course, Jeremiah are groaning. These words of groaning and lack of comfort ring like the gong of a funeral bell throughout the poem.

> *"Jerusalem remembers in the days of her affliction and wandering all the precious things that were hers from days of old. When her people fell into the hand of the foe, and there was none to help her, her foes gloated over her; they mocked at her downfall"* (Lamentations 1:7).

Verse 7 depicts complete helplessness and hopelessness. The city is in profound misery, sorrow, and despair. All that is left is a memory of the former days of happiness. Disaster and despair do the same thing in our own lives. Our grief, fear, despair, and pain become so overwhelming that life seems helpless and hopeless. All that is left for us to do is to remember the good days in the past. We lose hope for the future because it seems that the good days are gone and will never come back. *It is hard to find hope for the future!*

> *"Is it nothing to you, all you who pass by? Look and see if there is any sorrow like my sorrow, which was brought upon me, which the Lord inflicted on the day of his fierce anger"* (Lamentations 1:12).

Verse 12 continues this thought with the cry.

> *"Look and see if there is any sorrow like my sorrow."*

This mindset intensifies our grief and despair. We often deceive ourselves feeling like no one else has gone through what we are going through. We say, *"No one is sorrowful like me! No one is sorrowful like us!"* We wonder why we are in agony while trying to be righteous when we look and see the joy of the wicked. So, we are frustrated and say there is no one to comfort. It is indeed a sign of grief and pain. As much as we enjoy the sympathy of others, when we get down to it, it is not comfort. It does not matter how wonderful it is that we have many friends and family to care for us; we still feel like there is nothing that a person can do for us. Indeed, when we are going through pain and grief, there are no words that can help. There are no quick fixes. There is no comfort.

> *"She has none to comfort her."* (1:2)

Jerusalem had many who were supposed to be her allies and supporters, yet they turned their backs on her. When we put our hope in people instead of God, our hope is a false one. *Why?* Because many people are going to let us down. They cannot be our comforters. They do not have the power to comfort us as we need to be comforted. They cannot help. They are just as helpless as we are. So, we must turn to God amid our pain, grief, and despair, for He is always faithful.

Jeremiah describes his pain and the pain of those who lived in Jerusalem. *Their physical grief and despair is intense and overwhelming!*

> *"From on high he sent fire; into my bones he made it descend; he spread a net for my feet; he turned me back; he has left me stunned, faint all the day long"* (Lamentations 1:13).

In verse 13, he describes the pain as fire in his bones. The intensity of his grief caused his body to ache all over. He was stunned and faint.

> *"For these things I weep; my eyes flow with tears; for a comforter is far from me, one to revive my spirit; my children are desolate, for the enemy has prevailed"* (Lamentations 1:16).

In verse 16, he is crying, and his eyes are flowing with tears. *When I see despair and pain around me, my pain is so great that my eyes just overflow with tears! Have you been afflicted with pain so great that your eyes just overflow with tears?* Sleepless nights filled with tears. Jeremiah's body hurt with the grief he was enduring.

> *"Look, O LORD, for I am in distress; my stomach churns; my heart is wrung within me, because I have been very rebellious. In the street the sword bereaves; in the house it is like death"* (Lamentations 1:20).

In verse 20, he says that his stomach churns because of his distress, and his heart is wrung within him. He feels like his insides have been twisted and turned over. When we are enduring grief and distress, we often begin to think that God has done something wrong. We must never forget that God is always in the right, whatever happens to us. We are the ones who are not in the right. Jeremiah is so disturbed and distressed that in his pain, he asked God, *"How could God do this?"* But we also see him declaring, *"The LORD is in the right."* And though at times, like Jeremiah, we do not understand the purpose of our suffering and pain, there is one thing we must know: our God is always right in all that He does. So, we must hold on to this truth amid our pain, despair, and grief.

> *"O LORD, behold my affliction!"* (1:9)

> *"Look, O LORD, and see."* (1:11)

> *"Look, O LORD, for I am in distress."* (1:20)

In times of grief and distress, our first response must be to cry to God in prayer, knowing that only He can comfort us even when we don't find the words to express our need.

Grief is physically painful. Grief hurts. Jeremiah declares a truth that is his first anchor in his grief.

> *"The LORD is in the right"* (1:18).

God is always in the right. Deuteronomy 32:4 declares this truth.

> *"The Rock, his work is perfect, for all his ways are justice. A God of faithfulness and without iniquity, just and upright is he."*

II. GOD'S ANGER REVEALED: (Lamentations 2:1-10)

> *"How the LORD in his anger has set the daughter of Zion under a cloud! He has cast down from heaven*

to earth the splendor of Israel; he has not remembered his footstool in the day of his anger. The LORD has swallowed up without mercy all the habitations of Jacob; in his wrath he has broken down the strongholds of the daughter of Judah; he has brought down to the ground in dishonor the kingdom and its rulers. He has cut down in fierce anger all the might of Israel; he has withdrawn from them his right hand in the face of the enemy; he has burned like a flaming fire in Jacob, consuming all around. He has bent his bow like an enemy, with his right hand set like a foe; and he has killed all who were delightful in our eyes in the tent of the daughter of Zion; he has poured out his fury like fire. The LORD has become like an enemy; he has swallowed up Israel; he has swallowed up all its palaces; he has laid in ruins its strongholds, and he has multiplied in the daughter of Judah mourning and lamentation. He has laid waste his booth like a garden, laid in ruins his meeting place; the LORD has made Zion forget festival and Sabbath, and in his fierce indignation has spurned king and priest. The LORD has scorned his altar, disowned his sanctuary; he has delivered into the hand of the enemy the walls of her palaces; they raised a clamor in the house of the LORD as on the day of festival. The LORD determined to lay in ruins the wall of the daughter of Zion; he stretched out the measuring line; he did not restrain his hand from destroying; he caused rampart and wall to lament; they languished together. Her gates have sunk into the ground; he has ruined and broken her bars; her king and princes are among the nations; the law is no more, and her prophets find no vision from the LORD. The elders of the daughter of Zion sit on the ground in silence; they have thrown dust on their heads and put on sackcloth; the young women of Jerusalem have bowed their heads to the ground."

The second poem of Lamentations shows a dramatic shift in Jeremiah's message to God's people. The intensity of this poem reveals the anger (wrath) of the LORD.

> "How the LORD in his anger has set the daughter of Zion under a cloud!" (2:1).

> "He has not remembered his footstool in the day of his anger" (2:1).

> "In his wrath he has broken down the strongholds of the daughter of Judah" (2:2).

> "He has poured out his fury like fire" (2:4).

> "In his fierce indignation has spurned king and priest" (2:6).

> "You have killed them in the day of your anger, slaughtering without pity" (2:21).

> "On the day the anger of the LORD no one escaped or survived" (2:22).

God's Wrath and Judgment Against Sin:

> "How the LORD in his anger has set the daughter of Zion under a cloud! He has cast down from heaven to earth the splendor of Israel; he has not remembered his footstool in the day of his anger. The LORD has swallowed up without mercy all the habitations of Jacob; in his wrath he has broken down the strongholds of the daughter of Judah; he has brought down to the ground in dishonor the kingdom and its rulers." (Lamentations 2:1-2)

Verses 1-2 declare God's anger toward the nation and His devastating judgment. Verse 1 begins declaring that they are no longer in the privileged presence of the LORD. Israel's splendor has been cast down from heaven to earth. This is a reference to the Temple of God and the Ark of the Covenant that was contained inside (Isaiah 64:11; Psalm 78:60-61). The Ark of the Covenant was also called God's footstool (1 Chronicles 28:2). The Temple had not been the key to their deliverance. When Solomon completed the Temple, the dedication declared that God would hear the people's prayers for forgiveness if they turned their faces to the Temple with repentant hearts. But now the Temple is gone, and the sense of doom is great. The city and people are under a dark cloud (2:1).

> *"He has laid waste his booth like a garden, laid in ruins his meeting place; the LORD has made Zion forget festival and Sabbath, and in his fierce indignation has spurned king and priest. The LORD has scorned his altar, disowned his sanctuary; he has delivered into the hand of the enemy the walls of her palaces; they raised a clamor in the house of the LORD as on the day of festival"* (Lamentations 2:6-7).

Verses 6-7 carry the idea further. God has spurned king and priest (2:6), scorned the altar, and disowned the sanctuary (2:7). Spurning king and priest is very serious, for the king was of the Davidic dynasty, and the priest was the legitimate heir of Aaron. It looks like all hope for forgiveness is completely gone. They are spurned, scorned, and disowned. God's people did this first to Him, for they spurned, scorned, and disowned Him.

> *"And when you tell this people all these words, and they say to you, 'Why has the LORD pronounced all this great evil against us? What is our iniquity?*

What is the sin that we have committed against the Lord our God?' then you shall say to them: 'Because your fathers have forsaken me, declares the LORD, and have gone after other gods and have served and worshiped them, and have forsaken me and have not kept my law, and because you have done worse than your fathers, for behold, every one of you follows his stubborn, evil will, refusing to listen to me. Therefore I will hurl you out of this land into a land that neither you nor your fathers have known, and there you shall serve other gods day and night, for I will show you no favor" (Jeremiah 16:10-13).

They thought that because they had the Temple, they were safe. Jeremiah records what they were saying.

"Thus says the LORD of hosts, the God of Israel: Amend your ways and your deeds, and I will let you dwell in this place. Do not trust in these deceptive words: 'This is the temple of the LORD, the temple of the LORD, the temple of the LORD'" (Jeremiah 7:3-4).

"Behold, you trust in deceptive words to no avail. Will you steal, murder, commit adultery, swear falsely, make offerings to Baal, and go after other gods that you have not known, and then come and stand before me in this house, which is called by my name, and say, 'We are delivered!'—only to go on doing all these abominations?"' (Jeremiah 7:8-10).

They deceived themselves, thinking that because they had the Temple, their sinful behavior was acceptable. They thought God was with them, and thus God was fine with their sins and lawlessness. *But they forgot that sin and rebellion (disobedience) provokes God to wrath!*

> *"Whoever believes in the Son has eternal life; whoever does not obey the Son shall not see life, but the wrath of God remains on him"* (John 3:36).

> *"For you may be sure of this, that everyone who is sexually immoral or impure, or who is covetous (that is, an idolater), has no inheritance in the kingdom of Christ and God. Let no one deceive you with empty words, for because of these things the wrath of God comes upon the sons of disobedience"* (Ephesians 5:5-6).

We must be careful and not make the same mistakes they did.

1. We must not deceive ourselves, believing that because we were baptized and forgiven of our sins and go to church, we can live as we please.
2. We must avoid the wrath of God. Just because we are the people of God does not mean that the wrath of God will not affect us. We must carefully learn from the nation of Israel.
3. God's anger is never explosive, unreasonable, or unexplained.
4. We do not begin to understand the restraint and the longsuffering of God.
5. God's wrath is His firm expression of real displeasure because of our sins, lawlessness.
6. And though we experience the benefits of God's patience (which is not to be confused with apathy or complete indifference), His longsuffering or restraint will finally end when we refuse to change our ways, that is, unless we repent.
7. This is the point the writer of Hebrews made to the Christians.
8. *"For if we go on sinning deliberately after receiving the knowledge of the truth, there no longer remains a sacri-*

fice for sins, but a fearful expectation of judgment, and a fury of fire that will consume the adversaries" (Hebrews 10:26-27).

When we refuse to change our ways, there is no more forgiveness but the fearful expectation of judgment, God's wrath. As Israel was seeing, God carries out His Word.

"The LORD has done what he purposed; he has carried out his word, which he commanded long ago" (Lamentations 2:17).

God has declared He would bring judgment for this behavior back in the book of Deuteronomy. But His people rejected His warnings. Listen to what they were saying in the days of Jeremiah.

"Now, therefore, say to the men of Judah and the inhabitants of Jerusalem: 'Thus says the LORD, Behold, I am shaping disaster against you and devising a plan against you. Return, every one from his evil way, and amend your ways and your deeds.' 'But they say, 'That is in vain! We will follow our own plans, and will every one act according to the stubbornness of his evil heart'" (Jeremiah 18:11-12).

God said disaster was coming! The people said there was no point in changing their ways. They would follow their own plans and stubborn hearts. We must never think that God will not execute judgment.

"But because of your hard and impenitent heart you are storing up wrath for yourself on the day of wrath when God's righteous judgment will be revealed" (Romans 2:5).

"But by the same word the heavens and earth that now exist are stored up for fire, being kept until the day of judgment and destruction of the ungodly" (2 Peter 3:7).

"For we must all appear before the judgment seat of Christ, so that each one may receive what is due for what he has done in the body, whether good or evil" (2 Corinthians 5:10).

When we insist on being stubborn and unrepentant, God will judge our sins. Thus, we must turn our hearts back to God. His judgment is to bring us to our knees in our sorrow and brokenness of heart for our sins and the things we have done. Jeremiah understood that what had happened was because God is right and just, and they deserved it. They had sinned and committed lawlessness.

Hope in Grief and Despair:

So, what are we to do?

"Their heart cried to the LORD. O wall of the daughter of Zion, let tears stream down like a torrent day and night! Give yourself no rest, your eyes no respite! 19 'Arise, cry out in the night, at the beginning of the night watches! Pour out your heart like water before the presence of the LORD! Lift your hands to him for the lives of your children, who faint for hunger at the head of every street'" (Lamentations 2:18-19).

Like Jeremiah, we must let our tears flow. We must exhaust every effort to plead with God. We must rise and cry out to Him in the night. We must lift our hands to Him in prayer. We must plead to God.

*"My eyes fail with tears, My heart is troubled; My
bile is poured on the ground because of the destruction of the daughter of my people, because the children and the infants faint in the streets of the
city"* (Lam. 2:11).

In verse 11, Jeremiah declares that he has cried until the
tears no longer come. His heart is broken. And this is exactly
what God wants, even in our sins. Whatever the cause for our
grief, let our tears flow to God. Let our pleas rise to God. *How
wonderful it is that we can articulate our sorrows and grief to God!*
Not only are we privileged to do this, but we are commanded
to do it.

*"Humble yourselves, therefore, under the mighty
hand of God so that at the proper time he may exalt
you, casting all your anxieties on him, because he
cares for you"* (1 Peter 5:6-7).

"Because he cares for you."

We must listen to those words in our grief and distress.
God cares for us. Even when we are disobedient, God cares for
us.

*"Will the Lord spurn forever, and never again be
favorable? Has his steadfast love forever ceased? Are
his promises at an end for all time? Has God forgotten to be gracious? Has he in anger shut up his
compassion?"* (Psalm 77:7-9).

*No, God is still compassionate even though His anger is right
and due upon us!* Jeremiah exclaims the final words of this
poem in verses 20-22.

*"Look, O LORD, and see! With whom have you
dealt thus? Should women eat the fruit of their*

womb, the children of their tender care? Should priest and prophet be killed in the sanctuary of the LORD? In the dust of the streets lie the young and the old; my young women and my young men have fallen by the sword; you have killed them in the day of your anger, slaughtering without pity. You summoned as if to a festival day my terrors on every side, and on the day of the anger of the LORD no one escaped or survived; those whom I held and raised my enemy destroyed."

Look and see what has happened. He wants God to see it, for he wants God's compassion to look on them with mercy and steadfast love. So, pour out your heart like water to God when you are in trouble, pain, despair, and grief (2:19). Be persistent in prayer. *Jesus called for us to continue in prayer and not lose heart (Luke 18:1)! Why not pray in your grief and despair without stopping? Why not tell God what is happening and distressing your heart?* God is a God of compassion who loves His children. *So why not turn your heart to Him?*

III. GREAT IS YOUR FAITHFULNESS: (Lamentations 3)

Hope Lost: (Lamentations 3:1-20)

"I am the man who has seen affliction under the rod of his wrath; he has driven and brought me into darkness without any light; surely against me he turns his hand again and again the whole day long. He has made my flesh and my skin waste away; he has broken my bones; he has besieged and enveloped me with bitterness and tribulation; he has made me dwell in darkness like the dead of long ago. He has walled me about so that I cannot escape; he has made my chains heavy; though I call and cry for help, he shuts out my prayer; he has blocked my ways with blocks of stones; he has made my paths crooked. He is

a bear lying in wait for me, a lion in hiding; he turned aside my steps and tore me to pieces; he has made me desolate; he bent his bow and set me as a target for his arrow. He drove into my kidneys the arrows of his quiver; I have become the laughing-stock of all peoples, the object of their taunts all day long. He has filled me with bitterness; he has sated me with wormwood. He has made my teeth grind on gravel, and made me cower in ashes; my soul is bereft of peace; I have forgotten what happiness is; so I say, 'My endurance has perished; so has my hope from the LORD.' Remember my affliction and my wanderings, the wormwood and the gall! My soul continually remembers it and is bowed down within me.'"

The third poem in Lamentations is the pinnacle of this book. In the first 20 verses of this poem, we see the intensity of the author's pain. His grief is so great that he is physically ill and in physical pain.

"He has made my flesh and my skin waste away; he has broken my bones" (3:4).

Now his flesh was not literally falling off him, nor were his bones literally broken, for he is using a metaphor to describe the physical anguish he felt because of the pain he was experiencing. Broken bones picture loss of hope in the future. In the Old Testament, the bones of the righteous are not broken; that is, they have hope in God for the future and what He will do (cf. Psalm 34:20; contrast Isaiah 38:13). Further, the writer Jeremiah is swallowed up in bitterness (3:5). He feels walled in, chained down, and blocked off (3:7-8). He felt as if God had shot arrows through his body, even into his bowels, crushing his emotions (3:10-13). His pain is so great that he says, *"I have forgotten what happiness is"* (3:17). The crowning statement is in verse 18.

> *"So I say, 'My endurance has perished; so has my hope from the LORD.'"* (3:18)

Has life ever made you feel this way? Often, when we go through much turmoil, our grief and sorrow seem to destroy us from within. We tend to forget what happiness is. The darkness that surrounds us takes away our hope. So, our strength and endurance perish, and our hope is gone. As we read this book, we can see the devastation that Jeremiah is feeling. His grief is boundless, his strength is gone, and his hope is lost. But this is not the end of the poem, nor is this the end of the book. Too many times, people are consumed by grief and wallow in their pain and sorrow. But we must not stop and wallow in our circumstances. And even though our days might seem to be filled with bitterness and tears, we must not end our day on this note. We must learn from Jeremiah, who though he found himself amid great pain and devastation, did not allow his emotions and feelings to rule him but chose to put his hope in God alone.

Hope Renewed: (Lamentations 3:21-24)

> *"But this I call to mind, and therefore I have hope: The steadfast love of the LORD never ceases; his mercies never come to an end; they are new every morning; great is your faithfulness. 'The LORD is my portion,' says my soul, 'therefore I will hope in him.'"*

Verse 21 helps us to handle our times of deep despair and grief.

"But this I call to mind, and therefore I have hope."

Jeremiah did not give up in hopeless despair amid his pain and distress. He chose to hope or trust in God (verses 22-24). He reminded himself of God's steadfast love that never ceases, for His mercies never come to an end. They are new and fresh every morning. *Great is God's faithfulness!* Thus, he said,

> "The steadfast love of the LORD never ceases; his mercies never come to an end; they are new every morning; great is your faithfulness. 'The LORD is my portion,' says my soul, 'therefore I will hope in him.'"

The first thing Jeremiah did was to remind himself of God's steadfast love that never ends, and so must we. God's faithfulness never stops. His compassion and His mercies never come to an end. They never fail. Jeremiah recalls God's multiple proofs of His steadfast and faithful love. He calls to mind how God's love never ends. *When I think about God's faithfulness to me and how good He has been to me over and over in the past, I cannot stop thanking Him with all my heart and soul for His unfailing love!* His love never fails. So, we must remind ourselves of His steadfast love and His faithfulness toward us in our times of grief, uncertainty, and despair.

The steadfast love and mercies of God are renewed every morning. *Every day brings a new set of opportunities and a new fresh outpouring of God's great love and compassion!* Because of God's compassion, each day offers new hope to our lives. While the future might seem dark and hopeless, each day God gives us is another day to see His steadfast love. Therefore, we must learn to live one day at a time and appreciate God's mercy for today. Choose not to worry about tomorrow's difficulties, concerns or problems. *Why not live in the compassion and mercy of God today? Great is the faithfulness of God!* He will get us through our storms of doubt, despair, and difficulty today, for we are only promised today. *God is faithful to us each and every day! Don't forget that!*

Jeremiah reminds himself in verse 24, saying,

"The LORD is my portion."

A portion implies the land allotted by God to each Israelite. Jeremiah declares his dependence on God for his provisions and survival. He is acknowledging and reminding himself that God will take care of him, and so must we. Thus, his conclusion is:

"Therefore I will hope in him."

There is a saying, *"Hope springs eternal."* When our focus is God, our hope will spring eternally. As we focus on God, it will give us the hope and the courage that we need so much in our times of pain, fear, doubt, and grief.

Hope Proclaimed: (Lamentations 3:25-39)

"The LORD is good to those who wait for him, to the soul who seeks him. It is good that one should wait quietly for the salvation of the LORD. *It is good for a man that he bear the yoke in his youth. Let him sit alone in silence when it is laid on him; let him put his mouth in the dust— there may yet be hope; let him give his cheek to the one who strikes, and let him be filled with insults. For the LORD will not cast off forever, but, though he cause grief, he will have compassion according to the abundance of his steadfast love; for he does not afflict from his heart or grieve the children of men. To crush underfoot all the prisoners of the earth, to deny a man justice in the presence of the Most High, to subvert a man in his lawsuit, the LORD does not approve.* **Who has spoken and it came to pass, unless the LORD has commanded it? Is it not from the mouth of the Most High that good and bad come? Why should a living man complain, a man, about the punishment of his sins?"**

Jeremiah takes his hope in God and proclaims it to those who are in grief, pain, and despair.

> *"The LORD is good to those who wait for him, to the soul who seeks him. It is good that one should wait quietly for the salvation of the LORD."*

Verses 25-26 urge us to wait for the LORD and seek Him. Wait for His deliverance and salvation. For God to help us, we must seek Him and wait for Him.

> *"It is good for a man that he bear the yoke in his youth. Let him sit alone in silence when it is laid on him; let him put his mouth in the dust— there may yet be hope; let him give his cheek to the one who strikes, and let him be filled with insults."*

In verses 27-30, Jeremiah is declaring that the yoke of suffering and pain is instructive and helpful. The earlier we learn this yoke, the more valuable it will be for us later in life. So, we must accept God's will and refuse to complain (3:28). We must humbly bow before God in heart and mouth (3:29). As we humbly submit to God as His servants (3:30), the more hope we will have to endure life's difficulties.

Jeremiah's message is to build our faith (verse 31-32).

> *"For the LORD will not cast off forever, 32 but, though he cause grief, he will have compassion according to the abundance of his steadfast love."*

Even in grief and distress, God will have compassion on us because of His abundant steadfast love. *Such a thought is beautiful beyond words!*

> *"Who is a God like you, pardoning iniquity and passing over transgression for the remnant of his*

inheritance? He does not retain his anger forever, because he delights in steadfast love. He will again have compassion on us; he will tread our iniquities underfoot. You will cast all our sins into the depths of the sea" (Micah 7:18-19).

What an amazingly beautiful picture of the character of God!

"For he does not afflict from his heart or grieve the children of men" (3:33).

God's punishment for our sins is not willingly from His heart. And though He does not want to judge us, He must because He is just and righteous.

"To crush underfoot all the prisoners of the earth, to deny a man justice in the presence of the Most High, to subvert a man in his lawsuit, the LORD does not approve."

Verses 34-36 stress this for us. God is just and does not approve of our sinful ways. God is always right.

Who are we to complain against God? (verses 37-39).

"Who has spoken and it came to pass, unless the LORD has commanded it? Is it not from the mouth of the Most High that good and bad come? Why should a living man complain, a man, about the punishment of his sins?"

We are full of sins! God is righteous and just. God is pure and holy. We receive what we rightfully deserve. In fact, we are not receiving what we deserve for our sins because of the steadfast love of God toward us. We must maintain the right frame of mind. It must keep us humble and lowly in heart (humility). *Why?* Because we deserve nothing and everything that we have in life comes from God's Grace poured out on us.

Hope in Prayer! *(Lamentations 3:40-51)*

> *"Let us test and examine our ways, and return to the LORD! Let us lift up our hearts and hands to God in heaven: 'We have transgressed and rebelled, and you have not forgiven. 'You have wrapped yourself with anger and pursued us, killing without pity; you have wrapped yourself with a cloud so that no prayer can pass through. You have made us scum and garbage among the peoples. 'All our enemies open their mouths against us; panic and pitfall have come upon us, devastation and destruction; my eyes flow with rivers of tears because of the destruction of the daughter of my people. 'My eyes will flow without ceasing, without respite, until the LORD from heaven looks down and sees; my eyes cause me grief at the fate of all the daughters of my city.'"*

Jeremiah, inspired by God, urges us to honestly examine our ways and ourselves, and pray to the LORD. Every time we examine our lives and ourselves with a sincere and honest heart, we must be compelled to pray. *Why?* Because as we do this, we become aware that we have woefully fallen short of God's glory. So, we must turn to God, tearing our hearts before Him (cf. Joel 2:13). We must continue to pour out our tears and prayers to God until He looks down and sees us from heaven. Remember, this must always be our cry to God. We must unite our voices with Jeremiah saying,

"Look, O LORD."

We can rest assured that by doing this, we will continue to pray, having hope in the steadfast love of the LORD whose mercies are new each morning.

Hope for Restoration: (Lamentations 3:52-66)

> "I have been hunted like a bird by those who were
> my enemies without cause; they flung me alive into
> the pit and cast stones on me; water closed over my
> head; I said, 'I am lost." 'I called on your name,
> O LORD, from the depths of the pit; you heard
> my plea, 'Do not close your ear to my cry for
> help!' You came near when I called on you; you
> said, 'Do not fear!' 'You have taken up my
> cause, O LORD; you have redeemed my life.
> You have seen the wrong done to me, O LORD;
> judge my cause. You have seen all their vengeance,
> all their plots against me. 'You have heard their
> taunts, O LORD, all their plots against me. The lips
> and thoughts of my assailants are against me all the
> day long. Behold their sitting and their rising; I am
> the object of their taunts. 'You will repay them, O
> LORD, according to the work of their hands. You
> will give them dullness of heart; your curse will be
> on them. You will pursue them in anger and destroy
> them from under your heavens, O LORD."

In Lamentations 3:52-66, we cannot help but observe Jeremiah's feelings of despair, springing out of his broken heart. His despair is so great that it is as if he is drowning because water has closed over his head. He says that he is lost. But amid his deep despair, he cries to God, and He hears his plea, his supplication (3:55-57). God came near when he cried out to Him. The LORD gave him the hope and courage he needed. Hope comes from calling on the name of the LORD, turning to Him in prayer without ceasing. *God sees and cares when His children cry out to Him! God sees the evil of those who afflict us!* (3:58-63). *His steadfast love for us is mind-blowing!*

Here is Jeremiah's hope:

1. God will repay (3:64-66).
2. God will take care of all our suffering, pain, and grief one day.
3. Because God is just, faithful, and compassionate toward those who wait for Him and seek Him, He will act faithfully against those who bring pain and distress to us, as in the case of Jeremiah.

IV. TIME TO REFLECT: (Lamentations 4)

The fourth poem of Lamentations brings us back to a crashing and painful truth even though chapter 3 gives us hope and assurance. Indeed, the book of Lamentations is not a book of sunshine and rainbows. It is a book about real pain and despair and how it invades the life of God's children. In the fourth poem, things are not better at all. Though Jeremiah hopes in God, his anguish and despair are real because of the devastation of his beloved city of Jerusalem and her people.

God's Wrath Poured Out: (Lam. 4:1-11)

"How the gold has grown dim, how the pure gold is changed! The holy stones lie scattered at the head of every street. The precious sons of Zion, worth their weight in fine gold, how they are regarded as earthen pots, the work of a potter's hands! Even jackals offer the breast; they nurse their young; but the daughter of my people has become cruel, like the ostriches in the wilderness. The tongue of the nursing infant sticks to the roof of its mouth for thirst; the children beg for food, but no one gives to them. Those who once feasted on delicacies perish in the streets; those who were brought up in purple embrace ash heaps. For the chastisement of the daughter of my people has been greater than the punishment of Sodom, which was overthrown in a

moment, and no hands were wrung for her. Her princes were purer than snow, whiter than milk; their bodies were more ruddy than coral, the beauty of their form was like sapphire. Now their face is blacker than soot; they are not recognized in the streets; their skin has shriveled on their bones; it has become as dry as wood. **Happier were the victims of the sword than the victims of hunger, who wasted away, pierced by lack of the fruits of the field. The hands of compassionate women have boiled their own children; they became their food during the destruction of the daughter of my people. The LORD gave full vent to his wrath; he poured out his hot anger, and he kindled a fire in Zion that consumed its foundations."**

As I read the description of the destruction of God's people, it is almost too much for me to bear. *Can you imagine witnessing such devastation as this prophet did?* The whole population has been discarded as broken pottery is tossed to the ground by the potter. Verse 3 describes the abandonment as ostriches that abandon their eggs.

"Even jackals offer the breast; they nurse their young; but the daughter of my people has become cruel, like the ostriches in the wilderness."

The infants and children are starving and thirsting in the streets (4:4).

"The tongue of the nursing infant sticks to the roof of its mouth for thirst; the children beg for food, but no one gives to them."

The rich are now perishing in the streets (4:5).

"Those who once feasted on delicacies perish in the streets; those who were brought up in purple embrace ash heaps."

Their punishment is greater than Sodom (4:6).

"For the chastisement of the daughter of my people has been greater than the punishment of Sodom, which was overthrown in a moment, and no hands were wrung for her."

Many are left to suffer in the streets of Jerusalem until they die (4:6, 9).

"Happier were the victims of the sword than the victims of hunger, who wasted away, pierced by lack of the fruits of the field."

Their bodies are blackened, and their skin has shriveled to their bones (4:7-8).

"Her princes were purer than snow, whiter than milk; their bodies were more ruddy than coral, the beauty of their form was like sapphire. Now their face is blacker than soot; they are not recognized in the streets; their skin has shriveled on their bones; it has become as dry as wood."

The distressed women are eating their own children because the situation is so awful (4:10).

"The hands of compassionate women have boiled their own children; they became their food during the destruction of the daughter of my people."

God has indeed poured out His full wrath against His own people (4:11). *Perish the thought that such a thing might ever happen to us!*

> *"The LORD gave full vent to his wrath; he poured out his hot anger, and he kindled a fire in Zion that consumed its foundations."*

Reflecting on Our Pain: (Lam. 4:12-20)

> *"The kings of the earth did not believe, nor any of the inhabitants of the world, that foe or enemy could enter the gates of Jerusalem.* **This was for the sins of her prophets and the iniquities of her priests, who shed in the midst of her the blood of the righteous. They wandered, blind, through the streets; they were so defiled with blood that no one was able to touch their garments. 'Away! Unclean!' people cried at them. 'Away! Away! Do not touch!' So they became fugitives and wanderers; people said among the nations, 'They shall stay with us no longer.' The LORD himsel has scattered them; he will regard them no more; no honor was shown to the priests, no favor to the elders.** *Our eyes failed, ever watching vainly for help; in our watching we watched for a nation which could not save. They dogged our steps so that we could not walk in our streets; our end drew near; our days were numbered, for our end had come. Our pursuers were swifter than the eagles in the heavens; they chased us on the mountains; they lay in wait for us in the wilderness. The breath of our nostrils, the LORD'S anointed, was captured in their pits, of whom we said, 'Under his shadow we shall live among the nations.'"*

Verse 13 is the focal point of this lament.

> *"This was for the sins of her prophets and the iniquities of her priests, who shed in the midst of her the blood of the righteous."*

Jeremiah is reflecting on all that is happening and the reasons why. He says, *"This was for the sins of her prophets and the iniquities of her priests."* The reason for this disaster and tragedy is the sins of the people. As he acknowledges the reasons, he can now express his deep emotions to God in prayer and learn from them. Pain, grief, and suffering affords us an occasion to look at our own life circumstances and learn from them. *There are so many blessings disguised in our trying and difficult times!* We can learn more about God and our relationship with Him. James expresses this thought.

> *"Count it all joy, my brothers, when you meet trials of various kinds, for you know that the testing of your faith produces steadfastness. And let steadfastness have its full effect, that you may be perfect and complete, lacking in nothing."* (James 1:2-4)

There must be a time of reflection to count our trials as joy. Reflection on what has happened in our trials can produce steadfastness and maturity. As we accept what has happened to us, we can learn and grow and be transformed spiritually. In Jeremiah's case, he acknowledges that the disaster and tragedy that has fallen upon them is the wrath of God because of their sins.

> *"This was for the sins of her prophets and the iniquities of her priests, who shed in the midst of her the blood of the righteous."* (Lamentations 4:13)

The sins of the priests and the prophets who shed the blood of the righteous were the supreme problem. Those who were the teachers and proclaimers of God's Laws were the worst violators. Instead of proclaiming and teaching the ways of God, they were soft-pedaling God's message in the way that the people wanted to hear (cf. Jeremiah 2:8; 5:4-5; 6:13; 8:8-12; 23:11-36; 26:7-24; 28:1-17). You see, inadequate spiritual leadership leads to doom. Sadly, they had not learned this lesson when Jesus came. Jesus rebuked the leaders of His day.

> *"Then the disciples came and said to him, 'Do you know that the Pharisees were offended when they heard this saying?' He answered, 'Every plant that my heavenly Father has not planted will be rooted up. Let them alone; they are blind guides. And if the blind lead the blind, both will fall into a pit.'"* (Matthew 15:12-14)

The Pharisees and scribes criticized Jesus because His disciples did not wash their hands according to the traditions of the elders. Jesus called them hypocrites whose hearts were far from God. Jesus called them blind guides, for they caused the spiritual ruin of others. God has charged the spiritual leaders with the critical task of proclaiming the pure, clear Word of God, not what people want to hear. God's Word is what we need to hear to get us back to walking in His light again. These priests and prophets were blind and unclean, for they had corrupted themselves. They were supposed to be examples of purity. *We must revere the Word of God and trust it and nothing else!*

Their sins had made them worthless and unprofitable before God, like broken pots cast aside (4:2). And since their value to God was tarnished, judgment had to come.

Sins Will Be Punished: (Lam. 4:21-22)

> *"Rejoice and be glad, O daughter of Edom, you who dwell in the land of Uz; but to you also the cup shall pass; you shall become drunk and strip yourself bare.*

The punishment of your iniquity, O daughter of Zion, is accomplished; he will keep you in exile no longer; but your iniquity, O daughter of Edom, he will punish; he will uncover your sins."

You can rest assured God's wrath, and judgment will come because of our sins! We will not get away with our sins. No one will escape! This is precisely the message of verses 21-22. Edom is sitting on the sidelines with glee over the fall of Jerusalem. But verses 21-22 declare that the cup of wrath will come to them also. In verse 22, God will uncover their sins and punish them. *God is just and will judge us for our sins!* Thus, we must reflect on this truth. The apostle Paul said:

"For the wrath of God is revealed from heaven against all ungodliness and unrighteousness of men, who by their unrighteousness suppress the truth." (Romans 1:18)

The wrath of God has been revealed against all ungodliness. But many try to suppress this truth in their own unrighteousness. They do not want to reflect on the wrath of God, so they ignore and suppress that Truth. When we use carnal tactics, we suppress the Truth and are doomed because of our sins.

"Our eyes failed, ever watching vainly for help; in our watching we watched for a nation which could not save." (Lamentations 4:17)

No one can save us. We cannot save ourselves. Others cannot save us. Only God can save us. God is the only one who can deliver us from the wrath we deserve because of our sinful ways. Our sins are uncovered before God, for nothing is hidden from His sight. We cannot escape them. Therefore, we must cry out to God, reflecting on our sinfulness and lawlessness. We must learn from our sins and turn our hearts to God, crying out for mercy. *This is what adorns the Gospel!*

> *"For while we were still helpless, at the right time*
> *Christ died for the ungodly."* (Romans 5:6)

Christ, in our helplessness and hopelessness, came and died for us to spare us the wrath of God. A wrath that is rightly appointed to us because of our sins. Christ is our hope. In the days of Jeremiah, we see how their earthly kings failed and destroyed their hope of God's blessing because of their unrighteousness (Lamentations 4:20). Jesus, our perfect and sinless King of righteousness, restores our hope and makes us a blessing to the nations. He comforts and restores us to God. So, while we were helpless in our sins, at the perfect time appointed by God, the Father sent Jesus to die for us. Through Jesus, atonement is made for our sins. Our sins are uncovered before God. But in Christ, we have atonement, that is, our sins are covered, forgiven.

> *"Blessed are those whose lawless deeds are forgiven,*
> *and whose sins are covered."* (Romans 4:7)

Thus, let us reflect and learn in our times of grief, distress, and pain and count our trials as joy. Let us reflect on what God has done to carry us through, knowing that our sins are covered in Christ, which will carry us through our times of difficulty and distress.

V. TIME TO PRAY: (Lamentations 5)

This excellent book of Lamentations describes the people of Jerusalem and their suffering during the fall of the city and Temple. Their suffering and pain was an opportunity to reflect and examine their hearts. It was a time to acknowledge that their unwillingness to obey the truth of God's messengers caused God's judgment on them. Sadly, the teachers of God's message (the prophets and priests) were committing sins and shedding the blood of the righteous in the streets. Lamentations 4:17 states that there was no one to help deliver and save them but God. Since the prophets, priests (4:13), and kings (4:20) had failed the people, they were looking for true prophets, priests, and kings to save them.

This reflection leads Jeremiah to pray to God because of their grief and pain. No one can help and comfort except God.

Remember: (Lam. 5:1-18)

> "**Remember, O LORD, what has befallen us; look, and see our disgrace!** Our inheritance has been turned over to strangers, our homes to foreigners. We have become orphans, fatherless; our mothers are like widows. We must pay for the water we drink; the wood we get must be bought. Our pursuers are at our necks; we are weary; we are given no rest. We have given the hand to Egypt, and to Assyria, to get bread enough. **Our fathers sinned, and are no more; and we bear their iniquities. Slaves rule over us; there is none to deliver us from their hand.** We get our bread at the peril of our lives, because of the sword in the wilderness. Our skin is hot as an oven with the burning heat of famine. Women are raped in Zion, young women in the towns of Judah. Princes are hung up by their hands; no respect is shown to the elders. Young men are compelled to grind at the mill, and boys stagger under loads of wood. The old men have left the city gate, the young men their music. **The joy of our hearts has ceased; our dancing has been turned to mourning. The crown has fallen from our head; woe to us, for we have sinned! For this our heart has become sick, for these things our**

> *eyes have grown dim, for Mount Zion which
> lies desolate; jackals prowl over it."*

"Remember, O LORD, what has befallen us; look, and see our disgrace!" (5:1)

Jeremiah acknowledges that God knows what is happening and has not forgotten. He reminds God of His covenant promises that He made to them as a nation. He wants God to act on those promises, for he knows that God is faithful and keeps His promises. God had made a fundamental promise to David in 2 Samuel 7:13-16.

> *"He shall build a house for my name, and I will establish the throne of his kingdom forever. I will be to him a father, and he shall be to me a son. When he commits iniquity, I will discipline him with the rod of men, with the stripes of the sons of men, but my steadfast love will not depart from him, as I took it from Saul, whom I put away from before you. And your house and your kingdom shall be made sure forever before me. Your throne shall be established forever."*

God said that the throne of his kingdom would be forever. He also said that His steadfast love would never depart even though he would commit sins. God said the house (which is the Temple) and the kingdom would be sure and established forever. But now there is no throne, the Temple is destroyed, and the people are ruined. Jeremiah reminds God of His promises and urges Him to take notice of what has happened to them. Jeremiah is invoking in his prayer the faithfulness of God to keep His word. In Lamentations 5:7, Jeremiah acknowledges that the ax of judgment should have fallen long ago when their fathers sinned.

> *"Our fathers sinned, and are no more; and we bear their iniquities."*

He often declared that they had sinned (5:16).

> *"Woe to us, for we have sinned!"*

The only appeal that we can make before a righteous God is to be merciful in His Grace to us, the sinners (Luke 18:13).

The LORD Reigns: (Lam. 5:19-22)

> *"But you, O LORD, reign forever; your throne endures to all generations. Why do you forget us forever, why do you forsake us for so many days? Restore us to yourself, O LORD, that we may be restored! Renew our days as of old—unless you have utterly rejected us, and you remain exceedingly angry with us."*

Verse 19 is the key to Jeremiah's prayer.

> *"But you, O LORD, reign forever; your throne endures to all generations."*

He acknowledges that we all are in His hands, for He reigns and exercises sovereign control. He still reigns and is in control, even in desolation. The book of Revelation conveys the same message. And though Christians are killed for the cause of Christ, yet the book of Revelation opens with the Lord on the throne (Revelation 4) and ends with Jesus riding on a white horse, destroying His enemies (Revelation 19). *God reigns and is in control!* Thus, Jeremiah cries out to God, asking why He has forgotten them, and His covenant promises to them. So, he asks God to restore them to Himself (5:21).

"Why do you forget us forever, why do you forsake us for so many days? Restore us to yourself, O LORD, that we may be restored! Renew our days as of old."

What a privilege it is to have access to God's throne in heaven! Through His beloved Son, we receive mercy and find grace in time of need (Heb. 4:16). *How wonderful it is that we can go to God in prayer and make our requests known to Him, holding on to His faithful promises!* In Philippians 4, we are urged not to be anxious about anything but instead, make our requests known to God. The purpose of God's promises is to give us an anchor through life's difficulties, pain, and grief. Thus, we must hold on to God's faithful promises.

"The effective prayer of a righteous man can accomplish much."

Do you believe in the power of a righteous man's prayer? You should! To pray fervently means to petition God repeatedly, pleading before Him, begging Him for help! Do we all do this in our prayers? God is attentive to the prayers of His faithful children (Psa. 35:15). He has given us the promise that He will hear the supplications of His faithful. *Do you sincerely believe God's promise that He will listen to our prayers? We must!* We have been given every assurance, so there is no need to doubt. The prayer of God's righteous children avails much (James 5:16-18). God is able to do exceedingly more than we think or ask (Eph. 3:20-21; Matt. 21:20). Thus, we must pray with faith and depend on God's promises to be accomplished according to His will.

CONCLUSION:

The book of Lamentations was written under distressing and painful circumstances. It describes the fall of Jerusalem and its Temple in 586 BC. During the Babylonians' final siege, about 80% of the towns and villages of Judah were destroyed and abandoned. Their destruction was massive. Jeremiah 52 records Judah's destruction during the 18-month siege. Those who survived the starvation and slaughter went on a 1,000-mile journey by foot into exile, leaving only a few poor survivors scattered throughout the land. The Temple of God was defiled, looted, and burned. It is hard to grasp the severity of this event since we have never experienced anything like this in history.

And though we have experienced perhaps a time of great sorrow in our nation's history, yet nothing can compare to the painful fall of the Temple of God. *Why?* Because the capital of Judah was destroyed, the freedom of the nation was lost completely, a vast number of their people were slaughtered or removed from the land, and the Temple was destroyed. After many warnings through God's prophets, His people did not repent and heed His words. So, God in His wrath appeared to have forsaken His people and was no longer with them. *God's people were impacted immeasurably!*

Although God is all-merciful and His steadfast love endures forever, He had allowed His people to be conquered and killed by their enemies because of their rebellious and stubborn hearts (Lamentations 2:20-22). Consider the words of Jeremiah, the prophet, about these horrible events.

> *"Look, O LORD, and see! With whom have you dealt thus? Should women eat the fruit of their womb, the children of their tender care? Should priest and prophet be killed in the sanctuary of the LORD? In the dust of the streets lie the young and the old; my young women and my young men have fallen by the sword; you have killed them in the day of your anger, slaughtering without pity. You summoned as if to a festival day my terrors on every side, and on the day of the anger of the LORD no*

> *one escaped or survived; those whom I held and*
> *raised my enemy destroyed."*

The book of Lamentations is God's book about pain, despair, and grief. It is a book about the lament (a cry) uttered when life is falling apart. The Psalms are also filled with laments, that is, cries and prayers to God. You see, the people of Judah were distressed and in great despair. *Can we relate to this? Have you ever felt in great despair? Have you ever felt like everything is falling apart in your life? Have you had times of grief and despair?* This book helps us to handle pain and despair.

God wants our pain, despair, and hopelessness directed toward Him. *Does a parent want to hear the pain his child is experiencing? Of course!* We want to know when our children are hurting. We also want to know the reason for their pain and despair and how they are coping with it. Though we might think that suffering and despair lead us into a deeper relationship with God, to the contrary, it often pulls many away from Him. But grief and despair, according to this book, can bring us closer to God, for where there is pain, despair, and hurt, there is God.

Jeremiah suffered extreme loss when Jerusalem fell, friends and family died, and his beloved city was burned. Hope was gone. God had left. *So, what must we do when we go through grief and despair?* We must pray and place our focus on the faithfulness of God to wipe our tears from our eyes (cf. Revelation 21:4). Only in God can we find true comfort. Only in God can we truly find help. Only in God can we find all the answers to our cries.

The main message of Lamentations is that God's children must recognize that their lives are not determined by some cold, impersonal fate, or destiny. Our lives are in the hands of the living God. *A God who is good, merciful, and compassionate, who hears our cries and will act on our behalf! Thus, we must be hopeful and motivated!* Our God is good and is faithful, and His goodness is intrinsic to His glory (cf. Exodus 34:6-7; Mark 10:18). We must acknowledge in our grief and despair God's compassion for us. His compassion portrays His steadfast love, the depth, and tenderness of His feelings toward His children when they are in need. God's faithfulness and great mercies, which are new every day, are our hope. This hope must motivate us, even when we feel hopeless and lost.

> *"Let us hold fast the confession of our hope without wavering, for He who promised is faithful."* (Hebrews 10:23)

May we always remember that He Who has promised is faithful to all those who seek, wait, obey, and trust in Him. May we acknowledge that our lives are in the hands of the living God. May we find comfort and peace in God amid our grief and despair, knowing that He is good, merciful, and compassionate. May we always remember that God hears our cries and will act on our behalf. And finally, may we draw near to the throne of grace and receive mercy and find grace to help us in our time of need.

Great Is Thy Faithfulness

*"Remember mine affliction and my misery, the wormwood and the gall. My soul hath them still in remembrance, and is bowed down within me. **This I recall to my mind; therefore have I hope. It is of Jehovah's lovingkindnesses that we are not consumed, because his compassions fail not. They are new every morning; great is thy faithfulness. Jehovah is my portion, saith my soul; therefore will I hope in him.** Jehovah is good unto them that wait for him, to the soul that seeketh him. It is good that a man should hope and quietly wait for the salvation of Jehovah."* Lamentations 3:19-26

We have recently elected a new set of leaders for our country, who have made many promises. *Will they keep their word or falter like so many before them?* I don't know about these men, but I do know that our Lord Jesus will not fail us. This is a good time to remember the beloved words of Jeremiah.

As strange as it is to find a beautiful flower on a desert cactus, it is likewise strange to see such beautiful hope amid such ugliness and despair in the Book of Lamentations. Lamentations 3:19-26 is one of my favorite passages of the Bible because it underlines some precious and powerful principles about the God we serve and the life He gives us to live. These verses teach us about God's steadfast faithfulness, love, mercy, and forgiveness. The song, *"Great is Thy Faithfulness"* is one of my all-time favorites. It is dear to my heart because of its message about our Jehovah God's faithfulness toward us day in and day out, no matter our circumstances. All He asks is that we be faithful to Him as well. God gives us the chance to prove His faithfulness. *The providential care of our God is amazing!*

The author of this beautiful song wrote,

> Great is Thy faithfulness, oh God my Father;
> There is no shadow of turning with Thee;
> Thou changest not, Thy compassions, they fail
>   not;
> As Thou hast been, Thou forever wilt be.

> Chorus:
> Great is Thy faithfulness! Great is Thy faithful-
>   ness!
> Morning by morning new mercies I see.
> All I have needed Thy hand hath provided;
> Great is Thy faithfulness, Lord, unto me!

> Summer and winter and springtime and har-
>   vest,
> Sun, moon, and stars in their courses above
> Join with all nature in manifold witness
> to Thy great faithfulness, mercy and love.

> Pardon for sin and a peace that endureth
> Thine own dear presence to cheer and to guide;
> Strength for today and bright hope for tomor-
>   row,
> Blessings all mine, with ten thousand beside!

When we think of faithfulness, we think of one who is firm in his faith, committed to obeying God, steadfast and reliable.

In the Bible, when we think people who represented faithfulness, the Prophet Jeremiah quickly comes to mind.

Jeremiah is the author of the Book of Lamentations. He is referred to as the "weeping prophet." The Book of Lamentations was written during the time of the Babylonian invasion and the destruction of Jerusalem. The book portrays an unending sadness and profound depression. It speaks of Jeremiah's sorrows amidst the tragedy in the city of Jerusalem and the nation of Judah. These were times of mourning, despair, and weeping. As we read through this book's pages, we observe the terrible sufferings that the people of God had to endure in the hands of their enemies, the Babylonians and King Nebuchadnezzar. Yet, amid so much chaos, despair, and mourning, Jehovah God called on Jeremiah, His Prophet, to record all the events and bring honor to His name. He, Jeremiah, knew that God was a God of mercy and compassion. He stood in the gap for his people and urged them to repent and return to God. Jeremiah knew what God would do for His people and himself. He was aware that God was faithful and that He would do what He said He would do.

In Jeremiah 1: 5-6, God told the prophet,

> *"Before I formed thee in the belly I knew thee, and before thou camest forth out of the womb I sanctified thee; I have appointed thee a prophet unto the nations. Then said I, Ah, Lord Jehovah! behold, I know not how to speak; for I am a child."*

Isn't it something that God's Word calls on us to do things that are difficult, impossible without His help? However, it is then that we learn that what is impossible for men is possible with God's help. *For with God, all things are possible!*

It is precisely here in Lamentations that the Prophet remembered that though he is a man of constant sorrows and afflictions because of God's rod of wrath, there is still hope. Jeremiah knew that God was his portion. Therefore, he had hope. He knew that God was faithful and merciful. He knew that God was still God.

Let us consider some of this precious man's background:

1. The northern kingdom (Israel) had fallen because of their lawlessness (apostasy, idolatry).
2. Jeremiah's message to the Southern Kingdom (Judah) was that they, too, were going to fall for the same reasons and should submit to the Babylonians as slaves.
3. God strengthened Jeremiah for this painful labor. He told Jeremiah, *"I make you this day a fortified city, an iron pillar, and bronze walls, against the whole land, against the kings of Judah, its officials, its priests, and the people of the land."* (Jeremiah 1:18)
4. God put him over nations and kingdoms *"to pluck up and to break down, to destroy and to overthrow, to build and to plant"* (Jeremiah 1:10, see chapters 46-51).
5. Though God appointed Jeremiah to the nations, he did not want to minister (Jeremiah 1:5-6)
6. He was called to preach nothing but the Judgment of God over the nations (Jeremiah 1:9-10).
7. He reminded them of God's rules and pleaded with the people to repent of their wickedness, but they refused to believe him and repent (Jeremiah 2:13,32;8:7, 18, 9:1; 11:3-5).
8. They trusted in the Temple. They would say peace, peace when there was no peace (Jeremiah 7:4; 8:11).
9. They trusted in men rather than God, turning away from Him (Jeremiah 17:5).
10. The people fought and plotted against Jeremiah, but the LORD was with him to protect him (Jeremiah 1:19).

11. They would say, *"Come, let us make plots against Jeremiah, for the law shall not perish from the priest, nor counsel from the wise, nor the word from the prophet. Come, let us strike him with the tongue, and let us not pay attention to any of his words"* (Jeremiah 18:18; Mat. 5:11; James 3:9).

12. They would accuse him of being a bigot like so many do to us today when we take a stand for righteousness.

13. His so-called friends were his enemies (Jeremiah 9:3-5; 11:19; 20:10).

14. His once-trusted friends mocked him, throwing his own words back at him, saying, *"Terror is on every side! "Denounce him! Let us denounce him!"* (Jeremiah 20:10).

15. He was beaten and put in stocks (Jeremiah 20:2; 37:15-16).

16. He was forbidden to have a wife for himself or have any children because the sons and daughters born in that place were going to die of diseases, and they were told not to lament their deaths (Jeremiah 16:1-13; 17). As a result of this, he became familiar with loneliness.

17. He was a man of deep sorrow. He wept and mourned openly about the sins of his people (Jeremiah 9:1).

18. Because of his severe message of God's Judgment toward his people, he endured depression. His people would not take heed to his message. He was so weary and frustrated that he tried to escape the burden of it (Jeremiah 20:9). It must be hard and discouraging to proclaim the Truth and Judgments of God and have no one to pay attention to them. In Jeremiah's case, he preached for 50 years and failed to save his people from the wrath of God. He suffered unmerciful injustice and imprisonment at the hands of King Zedekiah. The king did not approve

of Jeremiah's preaching (Jeremiah 32:5). This poor man of God was still suffering in a dungeon when the Babylonians invaded the city. Notice that he had already prophesied this (Jeremiah 32:2).

19. Despite all this, he would compassionately exhort his people (Jeremiah 8:18; 9:1).
20. Indeed, he was a tenderhearted man like Elijah. He is an example of how Christians ought to be.
21. After Jerusalem fell, and many of his people were killed or taken captive into exile, he did not rejoice saying, *"I told you so."* He instead was broken in heart and deep despair, mourning with the remnant that was left behind. He fell into deep lament and sorrow with them (Lamentations 1-5). *It moves me deeply!*

Indeed, this precious man of God endured a life of turmoil, desolation, despair, and sorrow. The Prophet Jeremiah was overwhelmed with discouragement and affliction. He began to curse the day he was born and wondered why he did not die before birth inside his mother's womb. He said, *"Why did I ever come forth from the womb to look on trouble and sorrow so that my days have been spent in shame?"* (Jeremiah 20:18). *Do you think this is an exaggeration? Not at all!* We read in chapter 20 that the chief officer had him beaten then placed him in stocks. He may have been tortured with such a device that caused his body to bend double.

Imagine this happening after he was beaten! Why did he suffer all this? Was he guilty of any crime? Absolutely not! He had simply declared the Word of God. He did what was right, but in return, he received punishment. *That hurt him, no?* His prayers were full of loneliness and complaints: *"O LORD, Thou hast deceived me and I was deceived; Thou hast overcome me and prevailed. I have become a laughingstock all day long; everyone mocks me.... for me the word of the LORD has resulted in reproach and derision all day long"* (Jeremiah 20:7-8).

His constant loneliness and rejection caused him to be discouraged. He felt alone, useless, hopeless, and depressed (Jeremiah 15:19). Jeremiah was emotionally spent, confused, even to the point of doubting God (Jeremiah 15:18), but God was not done with him.

From his life, we can find comfort in knowing that even great prophets of God, like Jeremiah, experienced rejection, discouragement, and disappointment as they walked with God. It is a normal part of growing spiritually.

We can see a discouraged man in despair and anguish. *Have you ever felt this way when you were tried, tested, and low, feeling as low as you can get, sunk in the mud?* Yet, Jeremiah obeyed even when he could not understand the purpose of God's commandment. He obeyed because of his great faith, humility, compassion, courage, and perseverance (Jeremiah 20:9,11). He remained faithful even when he stood alone (like Noah, Joseph, Daniel, and many others) amid so much turmoil. *He rose above discouragement and despair!*

Imagine living a life of rejection, hatred, mockery, imprisonment, indifference, and profound sorrow after seeing his beloved city, Jerusalem, being plundered, desecrated, and destroyed into nothing. Imagine experiencing the horrible results of war, the brutality of the invading enemies, and the pangs of hunger. Still, Jeremiah stood tall amid the debris of the city and the dead bodies, while the city burned, lifting his voice in praise to Jehovah God for His great, unfailing faithfulness toward His people. *It is very moving!*

How was this possible? How could Jeremiah still hope in His Jehovah God? In the faithfulness of his great God? The answer is not complicated. Jeremiah knew Who God was. He knew that God would still be merciful and faithful to those who seek Him and wait for Him (Lamentations 3:21).

Like Jeremiah, we all go through turbulent times when things are difficult, hopeless, and filled with despair. Everything seems to fall apart. During these trying and difficult times, we must remember that blessed assurance of God's faithfulness toward us. The word "faithfulness" of verse 23 means "firmness, fidelity, steadiness, steadfastness." The word "faithfulness" portrays a God on Whom we can completely depend. I am sure that no matter what storms, trials, and valleys we might face, God will be there to prove His faithfulness and steadfastness to you and me. *We can count on Him!*

Jeremiah acknowledged that true contentment is found in walking God's old paths. *"Stand by the roads, and look, and ask for the **ancient paths, where the good way is; and walk in it, and find rest for your souls**. But they said, 'We will not walk in it'"* (Jeremiah 6:16). The old path was, of course, the Mosaic Law. For us today, the old path is the New Testament, the Law of Christ, which was delivered to us nearly 2000 years ago. Indeed, true contentment is to live in submission to God (Matt. 11:28-30). Most of God's promises are conditional (Jeremiah 18:7-10). They are conditioned upon one's obedience to God's commandments (Deut. 28).

Let us examine in more depth Lamentations 3:22-26 and understand why Jeremiah was able to proclaim: *Great is Thy faithfulness!* Though God's people went into captivity and punishment, it was temporary since there would be a restoration. God is always faithful to His faithful children. This ought to be our great motivator of hope. Let us consider the precious words of Lamentations 3:22-26 that teach us about the great, unfailing, and faithful God we serve.

GOD IS FAITHFUL IN HIS GRACE:

"It is of Jehovah's lovingkindnesses that we are not consumed." (Lamentations 3:22a)

Notice that the word "lovingkindness" is mentioned over 30 times in the Old Testament. It is a significant word that carries the idea of love, grace, mercy, faithfulness, goodness, and devotion. This word portrays God as the Divine lover of all men. In the New Testament, it is found as an equivalent to God's love and grace.

Jeremiah seems always to remember that it was by God's Grace that He brought Israel out of Egyptian slavery. Likewise, it was also God's Grace that had kept them a redeemed nation despite their failures and wanderings.

Let us consider some amazing thoughts about God's Grace:

- God's Grace saves us from the penalty of sin: It was only through His grace that we were made alive since we were dead because of sin, and His wrath was upon us (Ephesians 2:1-4). But God being rich in mercy and grace, sent His only begotten Son, our Lord, and Savior to be our guilt offering, dying that cruel death on the cross. Our Lord came in the Person of the Lord Jesus to die for our sins (Phil. 2:5-8). He came to draw us to God that we might be saved (John 16:7-11, John 6:44). Jesus, our Lord, came to seek and save that which was lost (Luke 19:10). He came to offer salvation (I Timothy 1:15, I Thess. 5:8-9). It is God's grace, His mercy that saves us from His wrath, the second death (Rev. 20). God does not want that for us. He wants us to be saved from sin through His Son. Our merciful God offers salvation through His Son Jesus under His Gospel (Romans 5:9-10; James 5:19-20; 2 Timothy 1:10; Heb. 2:2-3; Titus 2:13-14; Rom. 6:23; Luke 1:77).
- God's Grace is Conditional: We must meet all the conditions of the Gospel our of Lord to be forgiven of our sins. Jesus is the author of eternal salvation

to all those who obey Him (Heb. 5:9). We must work out our own salvation with fear and trembling (Phil. 2:12). Our merciful God indeed offers salvation through our Lord Jesus Christ to all, but men must meet those requirements to receive salvation. There is no room for disobedience; otherwise, we will not be saved (James 2:14-26). The conditions we must meet are: a) hear the Gospel (Acts 11:14; I Cor. 1:18-21; 15:2; 2 Timothy 3:15; 2 Peter 2:20); b) believe the Gospel (Romans 1:16; Mark 16:15-16; Romans 10:9-10; Acts 16:31; Ephesians 2:8-9); c) repent of sins (Acts 5:31; 2 Cor. 7:10); d) confess Jesus as Lord (Romans 10:9-10); e) be baptized for forgiveness of sins (Mark 16:15,16; I Peter 3:21; Romans 6:3 and Acts 2:38) and finally f) live a faithful life unto death (Matthew 10:22; Acts 2:47; Eph. 1:13; 5:23,25; 2 Thess. 2:10,13; Heb. 10:39; I Cor. 1:21; 15:2; I Tim. 4:16; Tit. 3:5; Mark 8:35; Luke 9:24; 8:11-12). His grace will be secured if we obey and meet all His requirements or conditions. *Thanks be to God for His indescribable Grace!*

GOD IS FAITHFUL IN ALL HIS GIFTS:

"Because his compassions fail not. They are new every morning; great is thy faithfulness." (Lamentations 3:22b-23)

The word "compassion" literally means "womb." It means *"to be moved in the heart out of love for another."* It means that God's grace gives us the strength through counsel of His Word and His answers to our prayers. It is actively working in our lives because we walk in the Light as He is in the light, and we have fellowship with one another. It is through life's storms that His grace is carrying us. He bears us through the dark valleys of sorrow and struggle. *We are not alone!* God's Grace give us all that we need for the journey. Consider how great God' gifts are:

- His gifts are faithful: God never promised us a bed of roses. He promised that His grace would be sufficient for the need (2 Cor. 12:9).

The word "grace" is not just "the unmerited love and favor of God toward sinners." It means so much more than that. It is "the strength of God through His Word and prayer to face all of life's battles and to bear up under times of difficulty."

We can surely be confident that God will give us the necessary strength to face the trying and rugged valleys in our life no matter what life sends our way. *Yes, we can trust Him!* Our God is greater, by far than any problem we might have to face. He will take care of us. We must always remember that *"Now to Him who is able to do far more abundantly beyond all that we ask or think, according to the power that works within us"* (Eph. 3:20). Our God gives us the gift of His provision. He wants to meet the needs of those who seek Him (Phil. 4:19; Matt. 6:25; Psalm 37:25). He also gives us the gift of His Person and presence. What that means is that He is always reliable and present (Heb. 13:8; Mal. 3:6; Heb. 13:5; Matt. 28:20).

GOD IS FAITHFUL IN HIS GOODNESS:

> *"Jehovah is my portion, saith my soul; therefore will I hope in him. Jehovah is good unto them that wait for him, to the soul that seeketh him. It is good that a man should hope and quietly wait for the salvation of Jehovah."* (Lamentations 3:24-26)

The word "good" gives the idea of being pleasant, agreeable, and excellent. It refers to the character of God.

- God is our Satisfier (verse 24a). He is described as our soul's portion. The word "portion" means "share" or "booty." It also refers to the spoils of war. Here, Jeremiah is saying, *"In the battle of life, God is my reward, my share, and my portion. He is what our soul needs to be satisfied"* (Psa. 103:5; Psa. 107:9; Rom. 8:28).

- He is our Sustainer (verses 24b-25). Our God would never fail those who seek, obey, and place their trust in Him (Isa. 49:23; Rom. 10:11; Matt. 5:18; Psa. 119-89-90; Isa. 40:8).

- He is our Savior (verse 26). In this context, Jeremiah is saying, *"Those who wait upon the Lord will see Him bring them out of their troubles and trials. He will not fail His children, but, in His time, He will deliver them from all their valleys."* God offers salvation through Jesus' sacrifice to all sinners. God is our ultimate Savior. A Savior that wants to rescue or deliver all from peril or hardship. God can deliver us from all our problems that no one else can solve. When we find ourselves powerless, hopeless, and helpless, we need a Savior. He and no one else has the solution to our greatest needs: a) The Lord fed the 5,000 (Matt. 14:30); b) saved Hezekiah (II Chron. 32:22); c) saved Israel when they cried out to Him by sending saviors (Nehemiah 9:27); d) saved Daniel from the lions (Daniel 6:27); e) saved Israel from their enemies (Numbers 10:9); f) saved Israel from the Philistines at Ebenezer and again at Beth-Aven (I Samuel 7:8; 14:23); g) saved Jerusalem from the Assyrians (II Kings 19:34); h) promised to save the Israelites from assault if they stood before the Temple (II Chr. 20:9); i) saved Noah (Heb. 11:7; 2 Peter 2:5).

CONCLUSION:

In the Lamentations of Jeremiah, we see that there is hope despite life's heartbreaking experiences. Though Jeremiah is known as the weeping prophet, we notice that his bitter tears did not blind him but rather strengthened him with hope, love, and confidence that reminded him of the steadfastness and faithfulness of God toward His people even amid horrible circumstances. God continued to extend His mercy in the lives of His people even after their destruction caused by their fault and rebellion. Just as God's steadfast love and mercy never cease toward His children, so it must be among us Christians. Love and mercy (compassion) must never come to an end. *They must be new every morning!*

The message of the book of Lamentations is that although Judah's people had defied God, rebelling against Him for generations, He still was not through with them. The candle had not yet burned out. The door had not yet closed. God was still reaching out to His people. Notice what Jeremiah said in Lamentations 3:19-26 as hope reigned because of God's mercy.

> *"Remember mine affliction and my misery, the wormwood and the gall. My soul hath them still in remembrance, and is bowed down within me. **This I recall to my mind; therefore have I hope. It is of Jehovah's lovingkindnesses that we are not consumed, because his compassions fail not. They are new every morning; great is thy faithfulness. Jehovah is my portion, saith my soul; therefore will I hope in him.** Jehovah is good unto them that wait for him, to the soul that seeketh him. It is good that a man should hope and quietly wait for the salvation of Jehovah."*

These precious words remind us of three things about the faithfulness of God:

1. God's love will never change (*"It is of Jehovah's lov-ingkindnesses that we are not consumed"*). Even when we don't deserve to be loved, God keeps loving us. Often what we claim to be love is conditional and temporary. For some, "I'll love you forever" means, "I'll love you until you disappoint me ... I'll love you until it becomes inconvenient ... I'll love you until it's easier not to love you anymore." Instead, God's love is unwavering. His love is permanent, forever. Take, for instance, the people of Judah. They didn't deserve to be loved by God. They were ungrateful and rebellious. But God in His infinite mercy provided for them again and again. *What did they do instead?* They turned their backs on Him over and over. Today is no different. Today God shows His steadfast love and mercy through the Gospel of Christ. *"But God shows his love for us in that while we were still sinners, Christ died for us"* (Romans 5:8).

2. God will be merciful to us (*"because his compassions, mercies fail not"*). God is merciful to us and expects us to show mercy to others. Jesus said, *"Blessed are the merciful, for they shall receive mercy"* (Matthew 5:7). To show and maintain a steadfast love for others that never ceases even when they sin against us, we keep in mind what James said on this subject:

> *"Speak and act as those who are going to be judged by the law that gives freedom, because judgment without mercy will be shown to anyone who has not been merciful."*

Mercy triumphs over judgment. If we want God's mercy, we must show mercy to others. Our hope is the mercy of God extended to us through His Son, Jesus Christ.

3. Every day is a new beginning (*"They are new every morning; great is thy faithfulness. Jehovah is my portion, saith my soul; therefore will I hope in him."*). Our hope is renewed every morning. It doesn't matter what happened yesterday. There is noth-

ing we can do to change it. *It's gone!* Even though we messed up yesterday, we can say with confidence, *"that part of my life is over, today I'm going to strive to do better."* It will be wise to remind ourselves as much as possible that today we are starting with a clean slate and unlimited possibilities. But, we must refuse to hang on to the past. We must let old habits die. We must break all connection to yesterday. It does no good to wallow in the regrets of yesterday or coward in the fear of tomorrow. *Today is all that matters! Thank God because we have today! And with God by our side, every day is a new day with unlimited possibilities!*

God will always love us, and nothing will ever change that. He will always forgive us if we repent from the heart. He will always pick us up when we fall if we humbly let Him. He will always give us a second chance to get right with Him if we humbly surrender to Him. Every day He gives us is a new day, a new life, a new possibility, or opportunity to be all that He wants us to be: to do all that we are capable of doing. So, when you find yourself struggling to stay on your course, keep your commitments, discouraged by negative results despite your efforts, *why not move forward and remember Lamentations 3:19-26?* These are very comforting verses. *Why not follow Jeremiah's example of great faith amid the wreckage of life?* He praised God amid this wreckage. *Why not imitate his example of hope?* Let us never forget that we are His little children, His little lambs and that He can sustain us faithfully during our times of battles, struggles, valleys, storms, and trials. He can carry us safely through.

> *"Jehovah is good unto them that wait for him, to the soul that seeketh him. It is good that a man should hope and quietly wait for the salvation of Jehovah"* (Lamentations 3:25-26).

I hope that we all may say, as Jeremiah did, *"Great is Thy faithfulness."*

"Let us hold fast the confession of our hope without wavering, for He who promised is faithful" (Hebrews 10:23)

May we always remember that He Who has promised is faithful to all those who seek, wait, obey, and trust in Him.

Soaring Like Eagles to the Heights of God

Have you not known? Have you not heard? The Lord is the everlasting God, the Creator of the ends of the earth. He does not faint or grow weary; his understanding is unsearchable. He gives power to the faint, and to him who has no might he increases strength. Even youths shall faint and be weary, and young men shall fall exhausted; but they who wait for the Lord shall renew their strength; they shall mount up with wings like eagles; they shall run and not be weary; they shall walk and not faint." Isaiah 40:28-31

Who hasn't dreamed of flying like an eagle, high above all of the dangers on earth below, high above all of our worries and concerns? Our God invites us to think like eagles in our waking hours. Let us listen to His words that challenge us to let Him lift us high, soaring as on the wings of eagles.

In Isaiah 40:28-31, God is prophesying to the remnant who would be languishing in Babylonian captivity for 70 turbulent years. The prophet Isaiah had predicted about 150 years before the captivity, that the remnant would return home to restore and rebuild the Jewish nation. They would soar on the heights of joy in anticipation of the long-awaited journey home. Their journey was going to be long, difficult, and dangerous before they could finally see their homeland again. It was a journey of about 600 miles on foot. Their efforts traveling that road were going to be hard even to their strong and vigorous youths. Yet, God promised them that they could trust in Him alone, rise above the journey's many obstacles, and soar on the wings of faith.

> *"'For I know the plans that I have for you,' declares the LORD, 'plans for welfare and not for calamity to give you a future and a hope.'"* (Jer. 29:11; cf. 29:10-14).

God's children would be like eagles. Like these birds, they would be strong, confident, and majestic. Eagles depend on the thermal currents of the air to soar gracefully and spread their God-given wings to soar high and efficiently in the air despite the dangerous storms. When the eagles rest, they dwell in the high, rocky clefts, for they trust in them for protection. God has made us to soar enormous heights while we walk our journey here on earth. Nevertheless, our life's journey may be long, tiring. Our faith may grow tired and our hope dim. Thus, we must trust in God to help us not become weary or feel defeated. Our faith will help us to look up to God and His Word for guidance and hope.

> *"And without faith it is impossible to please Him, for he who comes to God must believe that He is and that He is a rewarder of those who seek Him"* (Heb. 11:6).

Our God dwells above the clouds where the sun is always shining, in the calm light of eternity. He can lift us up above our shadows and sorrows with His joyous Light. Our steadfast faith will help us reach our home (Romans 10:17). God is able to keep us from stumbling so that we might be able to stand in His glorious presence (Jude 24-25).

We live in times when most people seem to be running in circles aimlessly and desperately, seeking a false fulfillment and purpose. Meanwhile, our Creator is waiting patiently, stretching out His hands, calling us to come to Him. *But what do people do instead? They long for the things of this world, rejecting God and His remedy. How sad it is for them to refuse God and turn to Him instead of their own understanding to find rest for their weary souls!* There is a common saying, *"It's hard to soar with eagles when you are running with the turkeys."* With God, we "turkeys" can soar like eagles and fly above the mountains of life's confusion, disappointments, weariness, and obstacles. *Indeed, our life's journey is hard and exhausting!* We have to rest regularly to regain our strength. We get up and move again. *And though it is not easy to get up and keep moving, we must!* We must come to God to give us enough strength (Isa. 40:28-31). God can provide strength and encouragement to the weary, for He never tires. Even vigorous young men tire and stumble (Isa. 40:40). *Yet, men place much emphasis on the physical body, worshiping fitness, and youth!* They refuse to acknowledge that we will wear out even when we are in our best physical condition. Sadly, this is the way the world thinks. Today it is disturbing to see so many, young and old, battling depression, anger, discouragement, lacking motivation, and purpose in life. *Why?* Because sin has taken them captive and made them very weak, though they strive to worship fitness and youth.

They reject what Jesus said,

> *"Come to Me, all who labor and are heavy laden, and I will give you rest. Take my yoke upon you, and learn from Me, for I am gentle and lowly in heart, and you will find rest for your souls. For My yoke is easy, and My burden is light"* (Matt. 11:28-30).

Hebrews 4:1-3 urges us saying,

> *"Therefore, let us fear lest, while a promise remains of entering His rest, any one of you should seem to have come short of it. For indeed we have had good*

news preached to us, just as they also; but the word they heard did not profit them, because it was not united by faith in those who heard. For we who have believed enter that rest."

So, are you willing to enter the rest that God is offering you at no cost? It is a rest that can renew and strengthen us spiritually so that we can mount up with wings like an eagle, and soar God's heights in this life instead of trudging onward from one day to the next. God warns us repeatedly not to look to the pleasures of this world, for they will never lead us to righteousness and His ways. God wants all men to seek Him diligently, searching His Word and His Ways to find rest in Him and soar His heavenly heights. *Are you resting in the Lord so that you can soar with Him?*

There is a lot that we can learn from the eagle. God wants us to soar on wings like an eagle. So, let us learn something from this majestic creature. Consider how the eagle is made.

I. TRAITS OF THE EAGLE AND OUR CHRISTIAN WALK:

An Analogy of The Eagle:

In Isaiah 40:31, God has given us a specific analogy of the eagle. God wants us to study the eagles' traits that we might learn something about our walk with Him. *Did you know that eagles can soar without flapping their wings?* They spread their wings straight out and soar with perfect ease on the wind currents.

An Eagle Has to be Born an Eagle:

Eagles are born with big and heavy wings. Part of the survival mechanism they are born with is that they must learn how to fly without flapping their big wings. They have to learn to do this to conserve energy. They may die if they waste too much energy flapping their wings while flying instead of soaring without flapping their wings. Eagles must learn this ability at an early age to be able to soar without flapping their wings. They learn to wait for wind thermals to come upon them. A wind thermal is a big gust of wind that rises in the atmosphere. Sometimes eagles remain perched for days before they encounter a good and strong wind thermal, on which they can launch and combine flapping and soaring on that strong wind thermal to ride them where they want to go. God compares us to eagles. The wings of the eagles represent our faith in God. Just like the eagle must learn to fly on the wind thermals, we must be born again of a different Father. We can never become children of God unless we have a new birth. *Crows and canaries will never become eagles!*

In John 3:3-5 Jesus declared,

> *"Truly, truly, I say to you, unless one is born again he cannot see the kingdom of God.' Nicodemus said to him, 'How can a man be born when he is old? Can he enter a second time into his mother's womb and be born?' Jesus answered, 'Truly, truly, I say to you, unless one is born of water and the Spirit, he cannot enter the kingdom of God.'"*

Ezekiel 36:25-27,

> *"I will sprinkle clean water on you, and you shall be clean from all your uncleannesses, and from all your idols I will cleanse you. And I will give you a new heart, and a new spirit I will put within you. And I will remove the heart of stone from your flesh and give you a heart of flesh. And I will put my Spirit within you, and cause you to walk in my statutes and be careful to obey my rules."*

1 Peter 1:23,

> *"Since you have been born again, not of perishable seed but of imperishable, through the living and abiding word of God."*

Just like the eagle that must learn how to catch the wind thermal to survive in this world, we must be born of water and the Spirit to enter God's kingdom and accomplish everything that He wants us to do for Him in this life. And as the eagle must learn how to ride and navigate on those wind thermals once they launch onto them, we must learn how to walk according to God's will. When we learn to walk by the Spirit, we can go where God wants us to go, for He will lead us into His paths of righteousness, but we must be born again (John 3:3-5). We must have faith to be born of the water and the Spirit to take flight and serve God. The eagle must take that big leap off the edge of the cliff to fly and soar on the wind. If the eagle does not take flight on the thermal updraft when it comes upon him, he will forever stay perched, and he will starve to death perched on the cliff. In the same way, if we refuse to be born again to be part of God's kingdom and righteousness, we will perish and die eternally without the hope of salvation. And just as the wings of the eagle are the only thing that will allow them to soar, in the same way, the only thing that will enable us to fly the heights of God is our steadfast faith in the Lord. Faith is vital for God to guide us and give us the strength to reach His heights of salvation.

Eagles Are Master Fliers:

Eagles are master fliers because they have learned to fly on strong wind thermals. They can soar to heights that no other bird can. They can fly as high as airplanes! *Their ability and skill to ride on these strong wind thermals and fly high is amazing!* Similarly, we Christians must learn through God's Word how to be master fliers daily. Just as eagles depend on these strong winds to lift them to heights that no other bird can reach, so we Christians must diligently seek after God through His Word, that He may take us to heights that we may have never dreamed possible. *Just think how much abundant fruit we could produce and the works that we may accomplish for the Lord if we just study His Word, allowing that same Word to lead our steps unto righteousness daily!* But we must be humble and willing to be taught by God to walk in righteousness. The Word of God is powerful and can fully equip us unto every good work that we may accomplish what God wants us to do.

Eagles Are Master Fishermen:

Eagles are also considered master fishermen. They are very skilled in locking in on their prey and swooping down to catch them. Eagles can swoop down on the water to pick up fish with ease and accuracy. They are masters at hunting down their prey. And just as eagles are master fishermen in the way they catch their fish, Jesus has made us "fishers of men." Jesus has commissioned us to make disciples of all the nations. God has commanded that we be fisherman of souls to save them and help them enter the gates of God's kingdom.

Eagles Fly Alone:

Though eagles mate for life, they fly alone for the most part. As Christians, we are all part of the body of Christ, where the little finger is just as important as the big toe. David was alone when he fought Goliath, for there was none who would step onto the battlefield with him to fight that giant. Peter was alone when he stepped out of the boat to walk on water. The rest of the apostles were too scared to try. Moses was alone for 40 years in the desert before God called him out to deliver the Israelites from Egypt. David was hiding out in caves from Saul for several years before he was finally called out to become the greatest king of Israel. At times we Christians feel very much alone, and everything seems to be dark and difficult, but we must keep pressing on toward our goal and fly alone like the eagles. God will be with us as we soar above the earth, giving us the strength and courage to win and accomplish the tasks that He has given us.

Eagles Live on Higher Ground:

Eagles live on higher ground for the most part. As Christians, we live on higher ground because of who we are in Christ compared to the world lost in darkness. We are born-again children of the Most High God. We are now kings and priests of the Lord. We have the Word of God to help us walk in righteousness and holiness. And though we live in this world, we are not of this world, for we must keep ourselves separate from the corruption, lawlessness, pollution, vices, and sins of this world so God can commune with us and we with Him. We live on higher ground because of what Jesus did for us and because we have obeyed His Gospel.

Eagles Are Extremely Bold, Courageous, and Powerful:

Another compelling trait of the eagle is its boldness, courage, and strength. God commands Christians to be His Son's mighty soldiers. He wants us to put on His armor to engage in our spiritual war. Just like the eagle who has no fear of any man, beast, or snake, we Christians must have no fear of anything or anyone, for we have God on our side fighting for us. *Greater is He that is in us than he who is in the world!* David perfectly proved this when he fought Goliath and won. So, we must learn from the eagles, for they are the most powerful and feared. We Christians must be mighty and courageous soldiers of Christ to fight for Him and His kingdom.

Eagles Are Majestic:

Eagles are majestic and invincible because of the way they look and act. They have the look of royalty. In the same way, we Christians have the look of royalty since we are kings and priests of the Lord when we obey the Gospel. This majestic royalty that we now have comes from being partakers of God's divine nature through Jesus. It all comes to us because of Jesus dying on the cross for our sins. Through Jesus' blood, we are forgiven of our sins and made kings and priests in God's Kingdom of righteousness.

Eagles Are Faithful For Life:

Eagles are true and loyal to their mates for life. In the same way, God wants us to stay true, loyal, and faithful to the vows and commitments that we made to our Lord at the wedding altar. God takes marriage and the vows that come with it very, very seriously, and it is nothing to be trifled with or taken for granted when we hit minor bumps in marriage. God can help us through His Word and heal any hurts or misgivings that may have occurred in our marriages or whatever it is that is broken in our lives. *Yes, He can heal us and mend our lives!*

Eagles Are Very Patient:

Another remarkably interesting trait of the eagles is their patience. Take, for instance, how eagles spot rabbits to target as prey. Once the rabbit senses danger, he will sometimes hide in a hole for as long as an hour or two before he finally comes back out. The eagle will wait for that long until the rabbit finally comes back out again. Once he does, the eagle will swoop down and catch him within a few seconds. The eagle is rewarded with a big fat meal because of its patience. Similarly, we Christians must be patient and longsuffering in doing good, doing the will of our Father here on earth to be rewarded with heaven. Longsuffering or patience is one of the nine fruits of the Holy Spirit that we must put into practice to enter the kingdom of heaven and receive our heavenly reward. We also need this patience to weather the storms of life and not be defeated.

Eagles Can Anticipate When A Storm Is Approaching:

Did you know that an eagle can anticipate when a storm is approaching long before it happens? The eagle will fly to some high spot to wait for the winds to come. When the storm hits, it sets its wings so that the wind will pick it up and lift it above the storm. *Isn't that remarkable?* While the storm rages below, the eagle is soaring above. It does not escape the storm but simply uses the storm to lift it higher. *It rises on the winds that bring the storm! What an extraordinary way to deal with adversity! What a wonderful lesson for us, God's children, to learn! There is so much that we can learn from the eagle about how to approach a storm!* The way that the eagle rises above the storm teaches us that we must rise above the storms of life when they come upon us fiercely. With God's help, we can lift ourselves above adversity by setting our minds and our hearts toward God and His kingdom of righteousness. The storms of life must not overcome us any more than they overcome the eagle. We can allow God's power and strength to lift us above them.

Our storms or trials of life can help us in our walk of faith. Our faith is strengthened, refined, and built up when it goes through the fire. *It is for our good, and we must accept the storms of life!* The apostle Paul reassured the Corinthians, *"For our light affliction, which is but for a moment, is working for us a far more exceeding and eternal weight of glory"* (2 Corinthians 4:17). *Amen to that!* When the eagle soars above the storm, he is overcoming and enduring it. He uses the strength of the storm to soar above it. *Isn't that remarkable!* Our God wants us to do the same thing when adversity strikes, for we can use adversity or hardship for gain. But we must learn to fly to the heights of God when we fall into trials, that we may grow and become better Christians (James 1:2-3). God has promised to help us "escape" our trials (1 Corinthians 10:13). He urges us to flee when we can (Matthew 10:23). Trials must be confronted and endured (2 Thessalonians 1:4; 2 Timothy 4:5; Hebrews 12:7). We must face everything that challenges our faith and be determined to grow in virtue. *God is looking for overcomers!* He has promised us saying, *"To him who overcomes I will grant to sit with Me on My throne, as I also overcame and sat down with My Father on His throne"* (Revelation 3:21).

The Eagle Has Two Sets of Eyes:

Another very fascinating trait of the eagles is that they have two sets of eyes. The first set is their natural eye, which they have when they are in a resting mode. However, when they start taking flight on these strong thermal winds, they have a second eye that comes into service. This second eye enables them to fly on these winds without damaging their original eye. This second eye is also used when they are flying through actual storm clouds. The heavy winds from a storm cloud can easily damage their natural eye. Thus, this second eye gives them a protective covering as they navigate through heavy storm clouds. *Did you know that eagles can see fish swimming from several hundred feet above the water?* Eagles, like all birds, have color vision. Their eyes are as large as humans, but their sharpness is at least four times greater than that of a human being with perfect vision. The eagle can identify a rabbit moving almost a mile away. That means that an eagle flying at an altitude 1,000 feet above could spot prey over an area of nearly 3 square miles from a fixed position. *How amazing is the vision of an eagle!* As Christians, we also have two sets of eyes. The first set is our normal natural eye, which we use to see the natural world in which we live. However, we also have a second set of eyes, which is God's eyes, to see things from His perspective. As we draw closer to Him, wanting to do His will, we can see the things of God revealed in His Word. We start loving and seeing God's Truth for what it is and start applying it in every compartment of our lives. By doing this, we see things through God's eyes, His point of view and perspective. By seeing things through God's eyes, we begin to love the Truth and allow it to set us free from sin. So, we must diligently seek to have the eyes of God's Truth to lead us to newness of life and live. Just as the eagle needs two sets of eyes to survive and live in this world, we also need our God-given eyes and His eyes of righteousness to obey Him and do His will to be saved.

The Nests of Eagles Are Built in the Wilderness:

The mother eagle builds her nest away from everything to raise her newborns in the wilderness when the eagles are first hatched. She does this to protect them from harm. In the same way, the Lord will sometimes build up His eagles in a wilderness type setting. Take, for instance, Moses, who lived in the desert for 40 years before God called him out to complete the greatest deliverance mission of all time. David was in the wilderness caves for many years, possibly for 13-15 years, before he was called out by God to become the greatest king that Israel ever had. *What about us Christians?* The Lord calls us to be set apart from the world, some kind of spiritual wilderness, to raise us up, and allow us to grow up, that we might be devoted to Him and serve Him. Often, in these wilderness type settings, our God helps us to grow spiritually and walk upright.

Eagles Have Contrasting Color Patterns – Noticeable From a Distance:

God's creatures have been created with different color patterns that blend in with their natural surroundings to protect them from other predators. However, this is not the case with the eagles. For instance, the American bald eagle has dark brown feathers with a white-colored head. As a result of this contrasting color pattern, they can easily be seen from quite a distance. Similarly, we Christians are called to be the light and salt of this earth to be noticeable from a distance, the world. The world must see the Light in us, Christ radiating in our lives. As we walk closely with God, doing His will, being renewed, and transformed, people will see the Gospel working in our lives. Our faith and works will stand out because of walking God's ways of righteousness. And just as the eagle stands out in its environment because of its might, ability, and contrasting color pattern in the animal kingdom, we must also stand out in a world of darkness, radiating with His Light to show His beauty living in us. Jesus is our Light, and He shines through us to shine all the time, and not hide our light under a cover. *We must let His light shine through us so we can reach those lost in darkness because of sin with His Gospel Message of salvation!*

The Mother Eagle Disciplines Her Eaglets:

A mother eagle builds her nest on the face of a cliff and puts it in a safe place for her eaglets to be nurtured. She makes her nest with great skill and care. Her nest must be large enough for her eaglets. She builds it with branches that must be intertwined to make it strong. Once the branches are woven, she lines it with feathers and grass to make it soft. Once she lays and hatches her eggs, she has an endless task of going off on delivery missions to feed her baby birds. She goes back and forth to perch on the edge of the nest and feed the eaglets, one by one. The mother eagle always knows which eaglet was fed last. She feeds the one that has waited for the longest without food even when they're moved around. She feeds and nourishes them continually. But there is something different that she must do to help her baby birds learn to fly. She hovers about 3 feet above the nest instead of resting on the side of her nest. *Did you know that eagles can hover like hummingbirds?* She shows her eaglets that they must learn to use their wings to move around. After hovering for a time, she moves down into her nest and starts teaching her little eaglets how to fly. She snuggles up against her little ones and begins to lightly nudge them to the edge of the nest. She keeps nudging them to the edge until they fall out of their nest. They seem to be going down to their destruction, but as quick as a flash, this mother eagle swoops down to catch them on her back. She brings them safely back to their nest. *Did you know that this process must be done with each eaglet? Why would the mother eagle do that? Do you suppose she doesn't love her eaglets? Not at all! And though the mother eagle wants her babies to feel secure and comfortable, she must go through this process to help them learn how to fly, for they were made to fly and it is their nature!*

God does the same thing to us, for He must discipline us for our good (Hebrews 12). You see, when the mother eagle sees that her eaglets don't fly yet after this first stage, she moves into the next one and starts making her eaglets' life miserable. She starts taking away the soft lining of the nest and continues to pull the nest apart. *Now, don't you think that it must be uncomfortable for her baby birds to be in that nest? But she must continue until there is nothing left of the nest!*

In Deuteronomy 32:11-12 we read, *"Like an eagle that stirs up its nest, that flutters over its young, spreading out its wings, catching them, bearing them on its pinions, the Lord alone guided him, no foreign god was with him."*

Did you know that God allowed the children of Israel to experience all those stages? God works in this way with us as well. Sometimes our God casts us out. God kicks us away to remove our securities, those things that we count on so much. God must force us out of our nest. *Why would God do that? Does He not care for us?* He does care! He does that because He wants us to soar, fly high, and become what He wants us to be, what we were meant to be. *He did not make us to be chicken or turkeys, for we were made to soar His heights!*

Eagles Fly Different Than Other Birds:

Many birds flap their wings to fly with furious movements. Eagles don't do this. *They soar!* God has made them with an instinctive ability to anticipate air currents and thermals. They lock their wings to travel the thermals, the wind currents. They can soar up and down with minimal movement. Isaiah 40:29-31 states that God gives strength to the weary and increases the power of the weak. Even youths grow tired and weary, and young men stumble and fall, but those who hope in the LORD will renew their strength. They will soar on wings like eagles; they will run and not grow weary; they will walk and not be faint.

An eagle knows when a storm is drawing near long before it happens. The eagle will fly to some high spot and wait for the winds to come. When the storm hits, the eagle sets its wings for the wind to pick it up and lift it above the storm. The eagle is soaring above, while the storm is raging below. And though the eagle does not escape the storm, it uses the storm to lift it higher, for it rides on the winds that bring the storm. Isaiah compares us to eagles. He says that God blesses us and helps us to ride the winds of our storms of sickness, tragedy, failure, and disappointment in our life. Remember, it is not the burdens of life that weigh us down, but it is how we handle them. Even though the storms of life come upon us, we can still rise above them by setting our minds and faith in God. The storms must not overcome us. We must allow God's power, God's strength, to lift us above them. And though the storms of life might affect us, we can rest assured that they will help us grow in Grace and Knowledge, just like Job, Joseph, David, and many other great heroes of faith.

An Eagle Knows Its Approaching Death:

When an eagle knows his death is approaching, it will leave its nest, fly off to a rock and fasten its talons to the edge of the rock. *It will look straight into the sunset and wait there to die!* Have you ever seen an eagle die? Although I haven't seen one die, I have seen many soldiers of Christ, men and women, die. *Faithful men and women who were fastened to the Rock of Christ, for they were looking into the sun of righteousness!* I am aware that many faithful Christians have died in pain and agony throughout history but have died with the hope of eternity. *It is sad to see so many people die without Christ and the hope of eternity!*

> *"But we do not want you to be uninformed, brothers, about those who are asleep, that you may not grieve as others do who have no hope. For since we believe that Jesus died and rose again, even so, through Jesus, God will bring with him those who have fallen asleep. For this we declare to you by a word from the Lord, that we who are alive, who are left until the coming of the Lord, will not precede those who have fallen asleep. For the Lord himself will descend from heaven with a cry of command, with the voice of an archangel, and with the sound of the trumpet of God. And the dead in Christ will rise first. Then we who are alive, who are left, will be caught up together with them in the clouds to meet the Lord in the air, and so we will always be with the Lord. Therefore encourage one another with these words"* (1 Thess. 4:13-18).

II. HOW TO SOAR LIKE AN EAGLE WITH GOD:

Eagles are among the very few animals that inspire and fascinate us with awe. *Isn't it amazing, powerful, and graceful to watch these amazing creatures soar across the sky! It is awe-inspiring!* Moses compared God to an eagle in his final words to the Israelites.

> *"He found him in a desert land, and in the howling waste of the wilderness; he encircled him, he cared for him, he kept him as the apple of his eye. Like an eagle that stirs up its nest, that flutters over its young, spreading out its wings, catching them, bearing them on its pinions, the Lord alone guided him, no foreign god was with him"* (Deuteronomy 32:10-12).

While many focus on the eagle's strength and power, Moses focuses on its gentleness. *There is more to the eagle than meets the eye!* Eagles can easily serve as a metaphor for God's love. Eagles are characterized by their strength, tenacity, a keen sense of vision, swiftness of flight, intelligence, loyalty, and many other amazing attributes. But what is special about these birds of prey is the tenderness they show their young. Eagle parents nurture, and vigilantly watch over their young. During incubation, one parent always remains in the nest to provide warmth and protection for their baby eaglets. The other parent hunts, supplies food, and keeps a watchful eye, a pattern that continues even after the eaglet hatches. Notice what the Scriptures say about God and the eagle.

> *"Like a parent eagle tenderly meeting every need, so the Lord of hosts hovers over his people, protects us* (Isaiah 31:5), *provides for our every need* (Phil. 4:19), *and never, ever leaves or forsakes us* (Deut. 31:6)."

When God brought His people from Egyptian bondage, He showed His power. God sent plagues of judgment on the Egyptians to devastate them. *Imagine how the mighty world power of that time was brought to its knees as God's plagues began to destroy them!* They even lost their precious jewels and gold. God spoke to His people at Mt. Sinai saying, *"You have seen what I did to the Egyptians, and how I bore you on eagles' wings and brought you unto Myself"* (Ex. 19:4). Of course, they were not plucked by an eagle to deliver them from bondage, but with God's help, they certainly fly out of that land, as on the wings of a majestic eagle. Moses taught Israel to sing a song to God for their deliverance from Egyptian slavery. The song describes the way the eagles taught the young eagles to fly. The older eagles drifted away from their nest, encouraging the eagles to leave the safety of their nest. *"Like an eagle that stirs up its nest, that flutters over its young, spreading out its wings, catching them, bearing them on its pinions"* (Deut. 32:11). The way the young eagles learn to soar is also the way God deals with us. His eyes are over us, and His ears are wide open to listen to our prayers.

God knows our needs even before we make them known to Him. He has promised to answer our fervent prayers when we approach Hi throne. As the eagle takes its young and places them on its back, so our God carries us. He has promised those who wait on Him to renew their strength, mount up with wings like eagles, run and never be weary, walk and not faint. *"Even the youths shall faint and be weary, and the young men shall utterly fall. But those who wait on the Lord shall renew their strength; they shall mount up with wings like eagles, they shall run and not be weary, they shall walk and not faint"* (Isaiah 40:30-31). The conclusion of chapter 40 is one of the most encouraging Scriptures in the Old Testament. Consider some important points from these verses.

God Reminds us of Our Need for Him By Humbling Us:

We must be humble to let God lift us. *"Humble yourselves before the Lord, and He will lift you up"* (James 4:10). Just as lift results from air pressure changes, God lifts us by changing our perspective in the storm and reversing the dynamics of our circumstances for good. We must trust in God, who is all-powerful and greater, rather than allow the pressures of our problems crush us. With God on our side, His love and strength, we can renew our hope and courage, rising even when everything seems so hopeless and dark. We must be humble to allow God to sustain us. *"Surely God is my help; the Lord is the one who sustains me"* (Psalm 54:4). In the same way that an eagle needs the assistance of air currents and winds to maintain altitude, we need God's help to continue soaring His heights. With the wind of His Spirit in us and the warmth of His love surrounding us, we can rise above everything and soar the heights with Him. In times of war, the young soldier must use his physical strength to win. He will have to face times of disappointment, heartache, faint-heartedness, fear, and temptation. *Will he arise or soar to the challenge of his faith?* And though at times we, like the soldier, feel as if God has abandoned us, we must still put on the armor of God that He provides to win our spiritual battle (Eph. 6:10-17).

When we depend on our own knowledge and strength, we will be flapping just to stay on top of things. Instead of scraping, scrambling, and struggling, Christians have the blessing of flying high with God. God wants to release us from our struggles, something that unbelievers cannot have. Jesus urges us saying, *"Do not be anxious then, saying, 'What shall we eat?' or 'What shall we drink?' or 'With what shall we clothe ourselves?' For all these things the Gentiles eagerly seek"* (Matthew 6:31-32). *The unbelievers are always exhausted and frustrated!* In the Parable of the Sower, Jesus said that things such as worry, the deceitfulness of wealth, and the desires for other things would be detrimental to our spiritual growth (Mark 4:19). Yet, men often forget that those things that affect their spiritual growth will also affect their physical and emotional health. Worry, fear, and sin, in general, will take their toll. But God's children will find spiritual strength, enthusiasm, optimism, and joy to endure.

We Must Acknowledge That God Is All-Powerful:

God gives strength to the weak and is there to help! (Isa. 40:29). He will provide strength in our hour of temptation. He will provide endurance for our trials. He will provide steadfastness for the faint-hearted. His help is continuously available for us, for He *"neither faints nor is weary"* (Isa.40:28). *There is no God like Him! "The Lord is the everlasting God!" We wear out, but God does not!* God gives power to the faint. He gives strength to those who have no might. Even those who think they have power and strength, such as the young, wear out and fall exhausted. *God does not wear out, for He is always at work!* We must stop working when we are weary. The Lord is the everlasting

God, for He is not bound by time. We live for right now. But God does not. He will do His work as He sees fit when it is convenient for Him. *Thus, we are in no position to argue or counsel God, for He is the everlasting and all mighty One!* The weak and faint are those in verse 27, who think that God does not see or care about their circumstances. And though Israel was going into exile, God still cared deeply for them and their circumstances. God acted on behalf of the nation of Israel, and He cares for us as well. Human strength is not the power we need, for human strength fails and becomes weak. *But God does not get weary or weak!*

God Has Promised to give us Strength and Help Us:

Strength is available to all but can only be accessed by those who desire it. God offers strength only to those who seek after Him. They will mount up with wings like eagles (Isa. 40:31). The higher we soar, the less weary we will feel, for we shall run and not be weary. *We will feel "young" again! Although we may have hills to climb, rivers to ford and daily obligations to attend to, our God has promised to be there to help us!* Eagles are defenders. The eagle builds its nest nearby and defends its nest from a potential predator. The Bible teaches us that the LORD is our Defender (Psalm 46:1). He is our rock and our salvation (2 Samuel 22:3-4). We can take comfort in knowing that He will always protect and help us. Our faith is like flight for an eagle, for it is essential to survive and thrive. The Word of God teaches us that those who hope in Him will soar on wings like eagles (Isaiah 40:31). For us, this is more than a promise of strength and renewal, it is a testimony of God's compassion and love for us. He is a mighty God who knows our names and will never forsake us. *Thus, we must wait upon him in prayer and in meditation on His Word!*

We find a beautiful promise in verse 31. "*But they who wait for the LORD shall renew their strength; they shall mount up with wings like eagles; they shall run and not be weary; they shall walk and not faint.*" We are called to wait upon the promises of God to be fulfilled. We must wait for the LORD to accomplish His purposes. This is how our strength is renewed. God will do as He has said, for He has the power to fulfill His purpose. Nothing can stop Him. So, we must wait for the LORD to find the strength to soar on wings like eagles and run and not be weary or grow faint. We must find strength and hope in the LORD so that we do not grow weary. *God's understanding is limitless!* We must live by His promises and submit to Him in faith rather than trying to figure God out. God can only give strength to those who wait for Him to fulfill His promises. *Waiting is what faith does until God's answer arrives!*

When we are committed to following the LORD and doing what He says to do, we "*shall mount up with wings like an eagle.*" Those who wait on the LORD shall be made new and strengthened in their spiritual life. They will be able to endure and do greater things for the LORD, which will provide more meaning for their life. Although the eagles can soar for long periods of time, they still need to rest to soar again. This is a parallel thought to waiting on the LORD. We must find rest in the LORD to be renewed and strengthened to mount up and soar again. Eagles take time to preen their feathers while they're perched and resting. They must make sure that all the feathers on their wings are in place and ready to go at any moment. In the letter to the Corinthians, Paul writes about being ready to run and box so that he may win and not be disqualified.

> "*Do you not know that those who run in a race all run, but only one receives the prize? Run in such a way that you may win. And everyone who competes in the games exercises self-control in all things. They then do it to receive a perishable wreath, but we an imperishable [prize]. Therefore, I run in such a way, as not without aim; I box in such a way, as not beating the air; but I buffet my body and make it my*

slave, lest possibly, after I have preached to others, I myself should be disqualified" (1 Cor 9:24-27).

Satan and the world will try at all cost to discourage us from winning, but we must preen ourselves, exercising self-control, and buffeting our bodies to soar the heights of God. *Wouldn't it be wonderful to run and not grow weary?* God wants us to run or soar like an eagle and not grow weary. *With God's help and strength, we can soar with the wings of an eagle to new levels!*

CONCLUSION:

God's care for His creation is amazing! Take for instance, His care for the birds and His clothing of the lily as described in the Sermon on the Mount. In that sermon, Jesus spoke of God's care for the birds who don't sow and reap, yet God is still very much involved in their lives. God has shown us all this to help us understand Him and His providential care for us. Just take a look at the eagles that God created. In Proverbs 30:19, we are told that there are things which surpass our ability to comprehend. One of those things mentioned is the way of an eagle in the air. Imagine how men have watched birds soaring in the air for thousands of years, yet man began to fly just a hundred years ago. *Isn't the majesty of the eagle remarkable! Isn't Isaiah 40:28-31 a refreshing thought for us! When I contemplate the power that we have as His children, it is mind-blowing to me! Although we might grow weary, God never does. What a powerful truth!* God is all-powerful, and He never gets tired. *He never gives up on delivering the righteous or punishing the wicked!* Nothing can stop His purposes. *"Oh, the depth of the riches and wisdom and knowledge of God! How unsearchable are his judgments and how inscrutable his ways!"* (Romans 11:33). *God cannot be out-argued or out-planned. There is no room for loopholes!*

Our LORD has intended for us to soar above the heights. He wants His children to see everything from a higher perspective. We must soar the heights and depths of His everlasting peace. We soar His heights when we diligently seek God and His ways, allowing Him to mold us into His image. We soar high when we keep our eyes fixed on Him and heaven, forgetting the pleasures of this earth. We soar when we willingly trust in His rich goodness. We soar when we allow our hearts to be restored by Him. We must make it our main ambition to do better, live better, always learn, and seek a better path. We must soar like the eagles, who dare to soar higher without being concerned about the approval of men. *Our goal must be higher than the goals of the majority!* As His children, we cannot afford to be like chickens who peck at the ground with eyes fixed on the earth and earthly things, being satisfied with a life that merely focuses on scratching in the dirt. The only way we will soar God's heights is by seeking His wisdom and understanding. We must live a life based on His foundation. In doing this, we will soar like eagles, basking in the light of His Truth that shines like the sun high above the clouds. We can rise to such heights only when we eat from the table He has laid for us: His table of forgiveness, love, the perfection of our souls, healing, restoration, gentleness, and the meekness of His Spirit. *A table set for us for eternity!*

Sadly, we fall to earth and get hurt when we reject God's bountiful and divine table. Only at this table can we be nourished well enough to soar the heights of God. When we focus on man's approval, it will turn us away from God's higher plans for us because we forget that there is hard work, discipline, dying to self and complete trust to catch God's powerful thermals. *Did you know that eagles do not fear heights?* They soar courageously, trusting in God's power to be under their wings. They know they will not fall to earth while they are relying on God. There, high above the clouds of glory, we find freedom in doing God's ways. A freedom that makes our hearts thrill to God's peace. A peace that is vast and deeper than the ocean. But there is one thing we must always remember. Soaring in

God's freedom is not meant to be momentary but eternal. Otherwise, the fall will be a quick fall to the ground.

We can soar above our problems and be content because we know that there is much more to life than the things of this world (2 Corinthians 4:16-18). We can soar because we know that God is behind the scenes, working for us. He has the power to turn any hardship or adversity into success (Romans 8:28). We can soar because we know that life's trials will only bring stronger character and refine our faith. *Our future lies on the other side of any trial!* (Romans 5:3-5). We soar the heights of God because we know that God is in control and can depend on Him completely. We don't need to rely on our own cleverness and wisdom. We can soar with God because His goodness and mercy follow us (Psalm 23:6). We can soar confidently because we know that our past sins have been forgiven and don't have the power to take all our joy (Psalm 103:3-5). We can soar high because, with God on our side, nothing is as bad and hopeless as it might seem (Romans 11:2-5). We can soar because we know that God is looking out for us and protecting us (Romans 8:31). We can run and not get tired, for we know that our efforts in the Lord are not in vain (1 Corinthians 15:58). The more we are involved in God's work, spreading the Gospel, the stronger we become. And though our outer man may wear out and get old, our inner man is renewed day by day (2 Corinthians 4:16). Thus, we can soar when we are much older because we are getting closer to heaven, so we must motivate the young to be fruitful and have the character that makes them rejoice.

Therefore, we must wait on the LORD and rest in the LORD. We must walk in the Spirit to soar with Him. We are not on this journey alone, for we have the church who are all on the same quest. May we fellowship and work together to *"consider how to stir up one another to love and good works"* (Hebrews 10:24). So, let's run together so that we can mount up on wings like eagles and serve God faithfully.

With this in mind, let's never forget that Jesus died to break the chains of sin and darkness that would prevent us from soaring the heights of God. We must follow the example of the eagles, who always look above and see how high they can soar, because they know and are confident that they are not bound to the earth, pecking like chickens. *We are commanded to soar higher!* It is God's intention. *So, since the chains of sin and darkness are broken through our Lord Jesus, let us start soaring the heights of God today!*

> *"Is it at your command that the eagle mounts up, and makes his nest on high?"* (Job 39:27).

May we always remember that our Lord Jesus died to break the chains of sin and darkness so that we could soar His heights. May we always purpose in our hearts to soar higher to find freedom from sin and have everlasting life with Him.

**Saints, Lift Your Voices
(On Wings of Flight)**
By Donald M. Alexander

There is none like Him;
None can compare;
No god His equal,
No Prince His heir!

Have no not known Him?
Have you not heard?
God is Creator of all the earth.

Some will grow weary,
Sin they'll pursue.
Servants of God,
their pow'r He'll renew.

Chorus,

Saints, lift your voices, though dark your days!
Lift up your spirits, sing out His praise!
Upward the calling, brighter the light!
Soaring like eagles on wings of flight!

Habakkuk: In God's Providential Hands

[NOTE: There are a couple of news stories mentioned at the beginning of this article that were current events at the time of writing. Even though a few years have passed, the importance of this message is the same.]

> *"For though the fig-tree shall not flourish, Neither shall fruit be in the vines; The labor of the olive shall fail, And the fields shall yield no food; The flock shall be cut off from the fold, And there shall be no herd in the stalls: Yet I will rejoice in Jehovah, I will joy in the God of my salvation. Jehovah, the Lord, is my strength; And he maketh my feet like hinds' feet, And will make me to walk upon my high places."*
> Habakkuk 3:17-19

I am reposting this discussion because of the recent shootings at San Bernardino, California, which once again remind us that there are powerful forces at play that we cannot stop without the providential hand of God. Our message from the prophet Habakkuk reminds us of how important it is that we rest in God's confidence to fix all the evil forces of this earth through His world government. *He is King of kings and Lord of lords, and He reigns forever!*

Habakkuk is one of those prophecies that give panoramic insight into how God governs the kingdoms of men. His words are medicine for our troubled souls. Let us see if we can make a practical application of the message to our times.

The brutal Paris bombings and slaughter and now the new slaughter at San Bernardino, CA, reminded me that the Enemy is at work with an unbridled rage, putting many stumbling blocks in the path of world evangelism, the furthering of the glorious Gospel of Christ. Those bloody images tell us that the world needs us to proclaim the Gospel of the Grace of our Lord Jesus more than ever. We must pray for our leaders and their political adversaries that they might humbly seek and make wise decisions in the days to come to promote justice and peace rather than revenge. I pray that we as Christians can reach out to those affected (families, friends, and neighbors) by this horrible massacre and help them to rebuild their lives but mostly to come to know the Gospel of our Lord Jesus Christ. Although the Muslim peoples perform indiscriminate acts of revenge that lead to much worse and threatening violence, my prayer is that the Gospel of Grace might reach out to them in kindness with a message of peace.

Many Muslims do not identify with these outrageous acts committed in the name of Islam. Some of them, by the Grace of God, have been drawn to faith in Jesus Christ. Evil exists. It abounds in the face of inconceivable and indiscriminate violence. And that is why we must proclaim the Gospel of the Grace of our Lord Jesus Christ more than ever.

As I look at our nation and our world, I feel a heavyweight in my heart. *It afflicts me!* Every long-standing foundation seems to be collapsing. Everyone is turning away from their faith, questioning the efficacy of the Scriptures more than ever. Many are expressing doubts, even unbelief. Many just simply say there is no God and won't bother seeking the Truth. They think chance put the world together. They don't bother to know God, who made us and governs our universe. They are blind to the working of God in the affairs of men. That was exactly what afflicted the prophet Habakkuk. He was puzzled by God's silence. And in his ignorance, the prophet cried out to God for an answer as to why He was apparently unaware and not concerned about the unrighteousness of men. What he did not know and found out later is that in God's time, the unrighteous (the wicked) will be judged, and the righteous (the faithful) will be vindicated (Hab. 2:4).

Like Habakkuk, some call into question God's sovereignty, justice, and holiness. The apparent inactivity of God in the face of wickedness (lawlessness and unrighteousness) troubles those who struggle to do what is right. Some become bewildered and angered by God's supposed unwillingness to intervene on behalf of the righteous and judge the unrighteous. We become anxious and discouraged because of God's lack of attention to our present situation. Let us take heed lest we sin and be judged by the Almighty because of our lack of faith in His righteous government of the world.

We live in a world where evil seems to prevail. We see a broad range of injustices:

- Abortion.
- Oppressive governments.
- Terrorism and so on.

So, what can the faithful do when wrongs are not corrected?

Theodicy (the vindication of divine goodness and providence given the existence of evil) has never been more crucial since the infamous 9/11 terrorist attack on our nation (the World Trade Center). Some wondered:

- *Where was God?*
- *Why did He allow such an atrocity to happen?*
- *Was it His will or an act of His judgment?*

Sadly, both skeptics and ignorant Christians asked these questions. Habakkuk experienced the same anxiety. I sometimes wonder if our worries are not even worse than those of the prophet. Our expectations of God do not match those of God's plan. We are telling God when and how He should act. *How dare we do such a thing!* At times, the church portrays God as the *"big butler in the sky,"* waiting to attend to all our carnal and capricious impulses. This theology suggests that God is bound to give us what we ask if we ask Him in faith. We often respond the way Habakkuk did. *Why?* Because when we pray that God may judge men's wickedness (correcting the injustices) without getting an immediate answer, we respond with a wavering doubting faith. We start to question God's goodness and sovereignty over His creation, as in Habakkuk's case. There are many truths in Habakkuk that can be applied to the church today.

I am perplexed to see the reaction of many Christians on Facebook and other social media. Some express how they feel without using wisdom and common sense. *They love to talk politics!* If I were to recollect all their comments, links, comics, and memes on Facebook, it would sound like this:

1. *"America is a Christian nation."*
2. *"We have lost our moral influence."*
3. *"Political liberals are to blame."*
4. *"But if the American people were to elect the right politically conservative (or libertarian) candidate, they would restore America's power, respect, success, and leadership. Perhaps come to another great awakening."*

Let us be wise and not put stumbling blocks before the Gospel of Christ.

Let us remember that we Christians must never render to Caesar what is owed to God alone. *Why?* Because we must reject the false Gospel of American exceptionalism: the belief that America is special and unique. A concept that can be useful but also problematic. To place our hope in any human government is at odds with the Gospel of Christ. American exceptionalism is a characteristic of civil religion whose primary purpose is to unite citizens with a common cause. It is presumptuous to say that our nation is God's chosen people like ancient Israel. Civil religion must never be combined with revealed religion (God's sovereign plan) lest it be used to corrupt the Gospel. The most appropriate form of patriotism rejoices in our nation's strengths, acknowledging her shortcomings without conflicting with Christ's teaching.

Therefore, we must reject all idolatrous forms of exceptionalism as false Gospel, especially when they appear to be religious. Exceptionalism must be righteous and committed to the full authority of the revealed Scriptures and the transforming power of the Gospel of the Grace of Jesus Christ.

I encourage you to put your trust in God's providential hands. Let us not lean on our flesh, our human resources. They are not strong enough to hold us. Only God is our Rock. Only He is strong enough to help us bear our heavy burdens and traumas. He is our Rock of strength from everlasting to everlasting.

Let us focus for a moment on the faith of a man called Habakkuk. A man who learned to take every problem to God in prayer and who rejoiced despite the evil around him. He, like Jeremiah, was disturbed and distraught over the sins of his people.

The name Habakkuk means "embrace or embracer." It is to me a book of comfort when I need it. It deepens my faith, understanding, and prayer, helping me find joy and strength in our Almighty God.

I. The Theme of the Book

The book of Habakkuk begins by addressing the subject of God's righteousness in the face of man's unrighteousness. This prophet struggled to understand God's lack of immediate judgment over sin. His affliction blinded him to God's long-suffering. Habakkuk thought it was a sign of injustice that contradicted God's goodness, holiness, and righteousness. He believed that God's silence encouraged continued sin and weakened all law and justice (Habakkuk 1:3-4;13).

As we read this short book, we cannot help but notice how Habakkuk moves from burden to blessing. From worry to worship. From restlessness to rest. From wrongly focusing on God being the problem to a focus on the Person of God. And finally, from a complaint to a consolation. In the end, the prophet acknowledged that God could turn sighing into singing. But we must be willing to wait on Him with constant prayer and meditation on His Word.

Habakkuk presents to us a conversation and prayer between the prophet and Jehovah God. As the book opens, he asks God when He will respond to Judah's oppression of its poor. Notice that the Law of Moses was no longer practiced regarding protection for the poor and the weak. Because of this, the prophet cried out to God saying,

> "O Jehovah, how long shall I cry, and thou wilt not hear? I cry out unto thee of violence, and thou wilt not save. Why dost thou show me iniquity, and look upon perverseness? for destruction and violence are before me; and there is strife, and contention riseth up" (Habakkuk 1:1-3).

Then the LORD responds, explaining to Habakkuk that He has a plan. He will raise up the Chaldeans (Babylonians):

> *"For, lo, I raise up the Chaldeans, that bitter and hasty nation, that march through the breadth of the earth, to possess dwelling-places that are not theirs. They are terrible and dreadful; their judgment and their dignity proceed from themselves"* (Habakkuk 1:6-7).

When Habakkuk heard God's answer, he was shocked. No matter how bad Judah had become, Babylon was undoubtedly worse. God told Habakkuk that justice would prevail for the wicked of both Judah and Babylon in His time. God would use the Babylonians ("terrible and dreadful") to reprimand the evil of His chosen people. Judah would not get away with her sin. Habakkuk struggled to understand how a just and righteous God could use such a wicked nation as Babylon to accomplish His will.

- The Babylonians (Chaldeans) were full of pride (Hab. 1:9-11; 2:4; Jer. 50:29-31).
- They worshiped the god of might (Hab. 1:10-11).
- A nation who killed, conquered, and plundered other nations for *"evil gain"* (Hab. 2:9).

The prophet acknowledged that God has *"ordained him (Babylon) for judgment and has established him for correction"* (Hab. 1:12). God answered the prophet by explaining His sovereign power and control over the kingdoms of men and all His creation. In Habakkuk 2:18-19, God explicitly warned Habakkuk about the man-made idols that His people were still trusting in. Through Habakkuk, God continued to reveal Himself and His Laws to His chosen people.

The question remains: *Can a righteous God use a more wicked people to judge a people that is more righteous than their enemies?* (Hab. 1:3). It seems to make more sense that Judah (a less wicked nation) should be the one to be used by God to punish a more wicked people (the Babylonians) and not vice versa.

Habakkuk saw God's plan as a conflict with His holiness and righteousness. He thought it unjust (Hab. 1:13). However, God reassured Him that Babylon would also be judged and punished for her sins only after He had used them as His vessel of punishment of Judah for her sins (Hab. 2:6-19). All of God's creation is at His disposal to punish the wicked and his lawlessness, but He is a just God who rewards the faithful. The righteous who live by faith will be rewarded.

> "And Jehovah answered me, and said, Write the vision, and make it plain upon tablets, that he may run that readeth it. For the vision is yet for the appointed time, and it hasteth toward the end, and shall not lie: though it tarry, wait for it; because it will surely come, it will not delay. Behold, his soul is puffed up, it is not upright in him; but the righteous shall live by his faith" (Hab. 2:2-4).

The purpose of the prophecy is to prove God's sovereignty and wisdom in His judgment and mercy in history. That purpose is perceived only by those who walk in faith. *God's holiness and righteousness (justice) must not be questioned!*

II. The Righteous Shall Live by Faith

Toward the end of the chapter, Habakkuk understood God's plan as well as His holiness and righteousness. That understanding led him to compose a beautiful psalm of faith because of God's justice and what He had done in the past for His people. The final chapter of Habakkuk (Ch. 3) is his prayer to God. Habakkuk's conversation with God was profitable. As a result of his fervent prayer to God, he began to understand God's sovereignty and His care for the righteous. He acknowledged that God's will was to destroy Judah's wickedness using a nation whose wickedness was much greater than theirs. His conclusion is one of great faith. Despite the approaching tribulation coming to God's chosen people, Habakkuk concluded with confidence, knowing that God would keep His word and demonstrate His righteousness as He had foretold.

> *"I heard, and my body trembled, My lips quivered at the voice; Rottenness entereth into my bones, and I tremble in my place; Because I must wait quietly for the day of trouble, For the coming up of the people that invadeth us. For though the fig-tree shall not flourish, Neither shall fruit be in the vines; The labor of the olive shall fail, And the fields shall yield no food; The flock shall be cut off from the fold, And there shall be no herd in the stalls: Yet I will rejoice in Jehovah, I will joy in the God of my salvation. Jehovah, the Lord, is my strength; And he maketh my feet like hinds' feet, And will make me to walk upon my high places"* (Hab. 3:16-19).

How comforting is this passage to me in that it proves over and over God's everlasting promises, keeping us afloat in this wicked and godless world that we live in! So, let the righteous today *"live by his faith"* and hope on God's eternal promises (Hab. 2:4). The strength of our faith is through Jesus, our Lord (Phil. 4:13). Lest we forget, God is aware of all unrighteousness (injustices) and will judge in His time and in His way all lawlessness of the wicked. He has shown us in history that He will demonstrate His justice in all the nations. The wicked will never go unpunished. *The righteous will be vindicated and rewarded!*

So, when you find yourself discouraged and your faith seems to be wavering, carry your struggles before the throne of the Almighty God as Habakkuk did. And no matter how awful things appear, we must rejoice in the God of our salvation with hope. *Why not have the courage to approach God with your doubt and confusion as well as your unbelief? Why not seek our Heavenly Father in faith and understanding of His Word?* It is the faithful who dare to come near the throne of God in prayer for answers when their faith is weakened. Let us not make the terrible mistake of keeping them to ourselves because Satan will take advantage of our doubt. Let us not put our understanding of the Word of God in a box. His words help us in our times of distress, confusion, doubt, and calamity. Therefore, let us trust in God and not in any systematic theology that we have invented about Him. The danger is that it will lead us to misunderstand Him. Speculative theology leads to error. *I assure you that if we do all this, you and I will come out victorious!*

Consider how we can overcome our doubts, deepen our understanding, our faith, prayer, and find joy and hope in our Almighty God amid our distress, confusion, doubt, and calamity.

1. All Christians must wrestle with the problem of evil:

One of the most common questions among skeptics and even Christians is the problem of evil. Indeed, we live in a world where crime, war, disease, and terror seem to rule. Some have mistakenly concluded that since we live in an imperfect world, there is nothing supreme and intelligent in the universe. Otherwise, if there is a supreme and divine being out there, He would not be indifferent to good and evil. Therefore, God lacks goodness and power over His creation. They don't realize that they are making a god of their own understanding of what God should be. Some want a grandfather in heaven whose purpose is to see all His creation enjoy themselves without any consequence whatsoever.

Atheists have not failed to make known this problem either. Some go so far as to say, the problem of evil proves that God does not exist. They say that if something is right and good, that does not prove the existence of God.

- *So, how is it that when things go wrong, that proves that God does not exist, but then if something goes right, that also proves there is no God?*

- *So, if there is no God, why is there so much good?*
- *If there is a God, why is there so much evil?*

The question is not philosophical. It is moral. Read Psalm 14.

> *"The fool says in his heart, 'There is no God.' They are corrupt, they do abominable deeds; there is none who does good. The Lord looks down from heaven on the children of man, to see if there are any who understand, who seek after God. They have all turned aside; together they have become corrupt; there is none who does good, not even one. Have they no knowledge, all the evildoers who eat up my people as they eat bread and do not call upon the LORD? There they are in great terror, for God is with the generation of the righteous. You would shame the plans of the poor, but the LORD is his refuge. Oh, that salvation for Israel would come out of Zion! When the LORD restores the fortunes of his people, let Jacob rejoice, let Israel be glad.'"*

Psalm 73 also wrestles with this problem of evil. The Psalmist raises the question: *If there is a righteous and powerful God in heaven, why do evil men seem to prosper, but the godly suffer?* We see this portrayed in the New Testament with John the Baptist and Stephen.

Other skeptics outrageously say,

> *"If God is all powerful and loving, He would put a stop to evil and suffering. Evil has not stopped. Therefore, either God is not all powerful or He is not loving."*

It is vital to know God accurately through His Word to understand the problem of evil. Many make the mistake of assuming that God is obligated to explain all that He does. They expect to know God without examining the Scriptures carefully. In Proverbs 25:2, we read that *"It is the glory of God to conceal a thing; But the glory of kings is to search out a matter."* Again, in Isaiah 55:8-9, we are told, *"For my thoughts are not your thoughts, neither are your ways my ways, saith Jehovah. For as the heavens are higher than the earth, so are my ways higher than your ways, and my thoughts than your thoughts."*

Indeed, it is hard to grasp all of God's ways. There will be times when circumstances will not make sense to us and are hard to comprehend. It is common to question God when we experience evil and suffering. Job felt this agony in Job 23:2-9. David also did (Psalm 13:1; Psalm 77:7-8). Even our Lord Jesus felt this anguish on the cross (Mark 15:35). Most of us have experienced some grief in our lives. When evil or hardship afflicts us, we feel as if God has let us down. *I have!* But it is then that we must be careful not to allow Satan to take advantage of the moment to discourage us and make us abandon our trust in God. It is crucial to recognize that trials, evil, and suffering are all part of the human experience. The Bible is full of examples of heroes of the faith who underwent similar hardships. Jesus told His disciples that even they should anticipate suffering in John 16:33. The apostle Peter asserts this in I Peter 4:12-13.

When God created the universe, He acted freely and without compulsion. We did not deserve to be created in His image. Creation was an act of God's own free will. We know this from Genesis 2:7. God provided life and a lush garden for man. Likewise, God provided a special tree that offered eternal communion in His presence (Genesis 2:9). He entrusted man with the care of His garden (Genesis 1:28-30). He also gave man free will to choose between good and evil when He placed the forbidden tree in the middle of the garden. He was not to eat from the tree of knowledge of good and evil (Gen. 2:17). God sees value in choice. It gives us the freedom to express our love for God that we may have a relationship with Him. God does not want to force us to love Him.

Now, there is a risk when we are given the power to choose. We can choose the desire of the eyes, the desire of the flesh, and the pride of life over a fellowship with God. In other words, God will not prevent us from choosing evil (Romans 1:18-32). When man rebels against God, he brings upon himself the wrath of God (Gen, 3:15-19; Romans 5:12l I Cor. 15:22). Adam and Eve rejected God's offer of communion when they asserted moral independence. When God acts against sin, even the innocent suffer. In Gen. 3 we see Satan as an evil alien force in God's creation. He, Satan, is always opposing and frustrating God's purposes. He seeks to destroy God's harmony with His creation. Therefore, there is always a contest over the hearts of men.

It is Satan who inflicts us with evil and suffering (Luke 13:16; Acts 10:38). But God limits and controls his power. Therefore, we must always pray that He not lead us into temptation and that He may keep us from all evil (Matt. 6:13). Moreover, the Word of God teaches us that God's righteousness and holiness cannot commune with evil (Psalm 54). *God is faithful to His promises and warnings!*

2. Use your struggles along with the problem of evil to go deeper in your understanding of God rather than withdrawing from Him.

Let us learn from Habakkuk's example. He learned to take his questions and complaints to God through prayer, waiting on God to answer. We must proceed with caution when we are faced with doubts and the problem of evil. Many often withdraw from God and His people in depression and with a pouting expression. Others prefer to be angry with God going back to the world, convincing themselves that God does not exist because if He did, He wouldn't allow evil to happen. Others hang on to their faith without going to God in prayer to help them solve their doubts and disturbing questions. We must learn to live according to God's Word and let it work through our difficulties with prayer and hope in Him. That is what Habakkuk did. He kept crying out to God in prayer for an answer. When God's answer came, he said,

> *"I will stand upon my watch, and set me upon the tower, and will look forth to see what he will speak with me, and what I shall answer concerning my complaint"* (Hab. 2:1).

Moreover, God's second response included the famous verse, *"the righteous shall live by his faith"* (Hab. 2:4). When Habakkuk reaches his final prayer of joy (Hab. 3:1-19), he still does not have all the answers, yet he rejoiced since he had grown in his understanding, faith, and prayer, acknowledging that God was his salvation and strength. Let us always remember that our struggles will lead us to victory if we trust in God and His eternal Word. *There is a lot to gain from our struggles and calamities!*

3. God is Sovereign over all evil, and He uses evil to accomplish His purposes while holding the wicked accountable for their sins.

God's purposes are higher than any human being and our problems. God explicitly told Habakkuk that He was raising up the Chaldeans and bringing Judah to judgment because of her sins. He is the God of history, who raises up kings and peoples, taking them down again and again according to His sovereign purposes.

I know that it is easy to lose our bearings when facing hardship, evil, pain, and suffering. It was difficult for Habakkuk to grasp this when the Chaldeans were destroying the nation of Judah, leveling the city of Jerusalem and the

Temple, and slaughtering his nation. The Babylonians had deported by force many of his people as slaves leaving behind a weak remnant in the land to care for it. But he and the rest (the godly remnant) learned that they had to submit to God's greater purpose in kingdom history. Likewise, we must view our lives within God's bigger picture and purpose in history.

4. God is aware of all evil, and no evil person or nation will escape His judgment.

In answer to the prophet's second question (*How could God use an evil people like the Chaldeans to punish His people?*), God shows the prophet that the Chaldean's victims could take up a taunt song against them (Hab. 2:6). There are five woes against the wicked that demonstrate that God is aware of their evil and that He will judge them for it. Consider those woes:

1. Woes against illegal gain (Hab. 2:6-8).
2. Woes against trusting in illegal gain for security (Hab. 2:9-11).
3. Woes against violence (Hab. 2:12-14).
4. Woes against seduction and rape (Hab. 2:15-17).
5. Woes against idolatry (Hab. 2:18-20).

Take note that verse 20 says, "*But Jehovah is in his holy temple: let all the earth keep silence before him.*" In His time, God will trample all evil nations and save His people (Hab. 3:12-13). Therefore, let this be our confidence and not fear all evildoers since they cannot escape God's judgment and justice. *They will not!*

5. No evil person or wicked nation can thwart God's plans. Rather God will use them to fulfill His plans is His time.

Habakkuk states,

"Art not thou from everlasting, O Jehovah my God, my Holy One? We shall not die. O Jehovah, thou hast ordained him for judgment; and thou, O Rock, hast established him for correction" (Hab. 1:12).

Also,

"For the vision is yet for the appointed time, and it hasteth toward the end, and shall not lie: though it tarry, wait for it; because it will surely come, it will not delay" (Hab. 2:3).

Let us keep in mind that God has directed all history to bring His purpose to fruition in judging all nations and evil. We must trust Him in our troubling current events, even if these events have adverse consequences in our lives and the lives of our loved ones.

6. Even though God can use evil people and nations in His plans, He is completely apart from evil, and He is not responsible for it.

As Habakkuk 2:14 expresses it well, *"For the earth shall be filled with the knowledge of the glory of Jehovah, as the waters cover the sea."* He shows in his prayer (Hab. 3:14-15) how God was going to *"woundest the head out of the house of the wicked man, Laying bare the foundation even unto the neck."* Dig deeply into this thought!

The point of the matter is that although we must wrestle with the problem of evil, we must go deeper in our understanding of God's Word, His ways and thoughts as revealed in the Scriptures.

7. We must pray in faith whenever we cannot understand evil. We will find joy in God.

Although Habakkuk could not comprehend why God would use the Chaldeans against His people, he submitted to God's will by faith (Hab. 2:4,20). His faith is expressed in joyful prayer in Hab. 3:1-19. There are three lessons we can learn from all this.

Faith is vital to have communion with God.

> "Behold, his soul is puffed up, it is not upright in him; but the righteous shall live by his faith" (Hab. 2:4).

The Chaldeans were proud. Their pride led them to their downfall. But the faithful or righteous will always live by their faith. This statement is quoted three times in the New Testament (Rom. 1:17; Gal. 3:11; Heb. 10:38). Paul uses this statement to show that God justifies sinners through faith in His Son. The Hebrew word "emunah" is otherwise translated as "faithfulness." To be justified is to be made righteous by God. No one is righteous before God since all have sinned and need the blood of Christ. When we obey the Gospel of Christ (repenting, confessing, and baptized), God forgives us and reconciles us back to Him. To commune with God, we must live according to the teaching of His Son (1 John 1:7), remaining faithful even when evil things happen to us. If we trust God completely and submit to His Son's Lordship and rule, He will reward us and bring punishment upon the wicked, if not in this life, in eternity.

Faith and prayer are essential and helpful, but our strong emotions remain.

Habakkuk heeded God's words and submitted to them by faith. He never prayed saying, "I see, LORD. You are going to use these wicked terrorists to destroy our nation. So be it!" Instead, his prayer was "according to Shigionioth" (literally to fall back or stagger) (Hab. 3:1) even though he prayed in an emotionally poetic form. Habakkuk affirms that when *"I heard, and my body trembled, My lips quivered at the voice; Rottenness entereth into my bones, and I tremble in my place; Because I must wait quietly for the day of trouble, For the coming up of the people that invadeth us"* (Hab. 3:16). Therefore he prays, *"O Jehovah, I have heard the report of thee, and am afraid: O Jehovah, revive thy work in the midst of the years; In the midst of the years make it known; In wrath remember mercy"* (Hab. 3:2).

It is easy to see that the prophet was in terror. Nevertheless, he put his trust in the Almighty. He honestly poured out all his strong emotions, along with his fears, before the throne of God. He humbly and submissively trusted in God. Nowhere do we see the prophet railing in anger against God. He acknowledged that God is faithful and just, even when He is pouring out His wrath on the sinning people. At the same time, he pled for God to revive his work and remember mercy in His wrath (Hab. 3:2). He still trembled with fear about what was going to happen, even though he was trusting in God. *What is the application for us today?* That even when we go through calamities and severe trials, we can confidently approach God's throne with our struggles and intense emotions and still be submissive, trusting all His excellent ways.

We must find joy in the LORD despite current circumstances or events. It is this joy that reflects the truth of our faith.

Habakkuk had resolved to say, *"Yet I will rejoice in Jehovah, I will joy in the God of my salvation. Jehovah, the Lord, is my strength; And he maketh my feet like hinds' feet, And will make me to walk upon my high places"* (Hab. 3:18-19). This reminds me of Paul's triumphant words in the closing words of Romans 8:24-39. Paul affirms that absolutely nothing would separate us from the love of God in Christ Jesus, our Lord (including evil, or death itself). *Such comforting words of hope!*

Habakkuk has just rehearsed for us how God has acted in history. This book helps us to understand God's hand in history. God shows us *that "all history was hastening to a conclusion that was certain as it was satisfying."* God was working behind the scenes as He has always been. He was raising up a nation (the Chaldeans or Babylonians) to punish (judge) Judah for her sins. Take note that God is not unaware of our circumstances nor of what is happening around us. He is fully conscious of them and is always working to bring everything to a conclusion that fulfills His divine purpose. And although we do not know what He has in store for us in the future, we know for sure that He will bring everything to a satisfying end where He and His faithful ones will triumph.

Habakkuk recites all the events that happened before the exodus of God's people.

- The plagues (Hab. 3:5).
- The crossing of the wilderness (Hab. 3:6).
- The crossing of the Red Sea and the Jordan River (Hab. 3:8-10) and
- Joshua's long day when the moon and the sun stood still (Hab. 3:11).

The prophet looked back to the exodus' events and the conquest, remembering how God took part in past victories and exploits. Habakkuk could not help but see God's providential hand in all history.

Therefore, he resolved to trust God confidently to act again in his day like He had done in the past with Israel. It is a great lesson for us today in the church, our nation, and our lives. We too can have confidence in God's sovereignty and goodness. Remember that God's ways and thoughts and timing are not the same as ours. *Did you know that the theme of the book of Revelation is the same: victory for those who trust in God and leave it to Him to avenge them?*

Our present is uncertain and scary, but we must also trust in our God Almighty. Looking back at the past, we have the assurance that He will show His sovereignty and righteousness and bring all nations under His feet. We know this because we read it in His beloved Book. I am fully confident that those who follow Him, walking in righteousness, will be vindicated, and the unrighteous will be judged. *Don't lose hope! Wait on the God of our salvation!* We must remember that when doubts cloud our minds and hearts because of hardship, tragedies, pain, suffering and so on, we must go back to the truth of how God has worked in history. His greatest work was in the life, death, and resurrection of our Lord and Savior. When we stand on the God of our salvation, we can firmly stand, for He is our Rock and hiding place.

Let us unite our voices of joy with Paul as he sang in prison surrounded by enemies everywhere (Christians and non-Christians), but still could say,

> *"Rejoice in the Lord always: again I will say, Rejoice. Let your forbearance be known unto all men. The Lord is at hand. In nothing be anxious; but in everything by prayer and supplication with thanksgiving let your requests be made known unto God. And the peace of God, which passeth all understanding, shall guard your hearts and your thoughts in Christ Jesus."* (Phil. 4:4-7)

Let these words sink deeply into your hearts!

CONCLUSION

Habakkuk's journey was not just one man's journey. Many before him had walked that path as they still do today. It is a journey that we must walk at some point in our lives. Like Habakkuk, we can be confident that our God will keep His promises as well as His warnings. Our God can shake nations and destroy kingdoms. He is sovereign and almighty. God has shown us this pattern throughout history. He is all-wise, and He knows what He is doing, and we must understand this.

The book of Habakkuk highlights God's omnipotence, sovereignty, and righteousness for us. All nations are under His control. We are at His disposal. We must be still in faith and know that He is at work. We can rest assured that He will judge the wicked along with their lawlessness. And even if we cannot see it now, He is still on the throne of this universe and will eventually do so. He will defend His holiness and righteousness His way and in His own time.

We must face all the evil in the world, adversities, calamities, pain, suffering, etc. with deep faith and hope in Him. Both are vital to our walk and communion with Him. A man of faith does not live by human reasoning. Let us be wise and not get trapped into thinking the way the world thinks. It is not our job as the church to put political pressure on this nation's leaders and those of the world to enforce righteousness. Christians do not force righteousness on anybody. They preach the Gospel and persuade men to submit to the will of Christ. It is God's job to raise up national leaders and tear down the evil ones.

When one depends on human forces to bring justice and peace, it is wrong. The Word of God does not teach us to do that. Look at how different are the heroes of the faith that we read about in the book of Hebrews. They changed the world because they endured as seeing one who is invisible. Their hope was not in man but God. They waited patiently for God to work or act, and He always did the work right. As God worked, things began to change. History is a witness of how He worked, how He amazingly worked through men and women, how He stopped the mouths of lions, subdued kingdoms, overthrew thrones, won empires, and finally changed the course of history by faith.

Habakkuk 3:2 and 3:16-29, are one of the most beautiful and poetic passages in Scriptures for me.

> *"O Jehovah, I have heard the report of thee, and am afraid: O Jehovah, revive thy work in the midst of the years; In the midst of the years make it known; In wrath remember mercy."*

I encourage you to read them to see how God acts and how He worked in the past. I believe, with all my heart, Habakkuk 3:2 is what changed and convinced the prophet's heart. He could rest because the events that had occurred in the past were governed by God's providential hand. History, as acts of God, cannot be questioned, shaken, or taken away. The truth is that God has already moved in human history, and our faith must rest on this assurance. We walk by faith and not by sight (2 Cor. 5:7). We have a supreme and almighty God who has acted righteously in time and space. He has recorded His will in the history of all human events.

We must always focus on Habakkuk 3:16-19,

> *"I heard, and my body trembled, My lips quivered at the voice; Rottenness entereth into my bones, and I tremble in my place; Because I must wait quietly for the day of trouble, For the coming up of the people that invadeth us. For though the fig-tree shall not flourish, Neither shall fruit be in the vines; The labor of the olive shall fail, And the fields shall yield no food; The flock shall be cut off from the fold, And there shall be no herd in the stalls: Yet I will rejoice in Jehovah, I will joy in the God of my salvation. Jehovah, the Lord, is my strength; And he maketh my feet like hinds' feet, And will make me to walk upon my high places."*

Oh, how I love this passage! It calms my soul with trust in God, allowing me to go to the heights of God.

- Where He takes us to higher places with Him.
- Where we are set apart from the world's suffering, adversities, tragedies, and sorrow.
- Where we can rest with confidence and trust in our almighty God and finally,
- Where we can develop into what He wants us to be.

Like Habakkuk, we must find our strength in God through His Word and prayer to understand His ways. And though we can approach God's mighty throne in prayer, it does not mean that our problems will go away. Jesus declared that the problems would remain. Let us walk like Habakkuk and all those who walked before him and after him with faith, prayer, and joy in the Almighty God of all.

> *"These things I have spoken to you so that in Me you may have peace. In the world you have tribulation, but take courage; I have overcome the world."*
> John 16:33

This world of evil, distress, difficulties, suffering, and pain is not our home, for we are just passing through. We, Christians must keep our eyes fixed on our final destination (Romans 8:18; 2 Cor. 4:17). This world is just our training and preparation for eternity.

May we always trust in God with all our heart, soul, and strength since He has shown us through His revealed Word that He is the God of history. May He help us to lift our eyes to Him alone, rejoicing amid our trials, problems, calamities, pain, and suffering. May we always remember that He is the God of our salvation and strength, the God, who *"maketh my feet like hinds' feet, And will make me to walk upon my high places."*

Praying At All Times

"Praying at all times in the Spirit, with all prayer and supplication. To that end keep alert with all perseverance, making supplication for all the saints."
Ephesians 6:18

I am so grateful for the recent help that God has offered me in answer to my prayers and the prayers of many others. This year has been fraught with numberless trials and terrifying moments, but the strength of God has been there for us and continues to bring us life and hope, and peace. Let me share this study on the power of prayer and the need to pray at all times.

We live out our lives in the presence of an infinitely powerful God who offers to help us in our frailties and failures, and we don't even pause briefly to ask His help. I needed this fresh consideration of prayer. I hope I can encourage us to pray at all times and not faint.

Prayer is very dear to my heart because, through it, God has brought me to safety, preserved me, delivered me, and protected me. Through prayer, He has given me strength, endurance, and long-suffering during the darkest, emptiest, and most desperate moments of my life. I must also add the faithless and hopeless moments in my life countless times. It is then that prayer has rescued me and brought me back to my Father, His Son, and His kingdom from the clouds of doubt, despair, and sorrow.

Through prayer, God began to rescue me even before I found the Lord's church. God heard my prayers and came to my rescue. *He delivered me!* I began praying in my own way to find the Truth, the only Truth that would set me free from sin and all the confusion of religious error. *I prayed and prayed and prayed to find that Truth!* By the Grace of God, He sent someone to teach me the good news, the Gospel. When I heard it, I received it with a merry heart and was baptized the same day for the remission of my sins. *What a joy to be white as snow and be welcomed into the Kingdom of my Lord Jesus Christ!*

At the beginning of my walk with the Lord, prayer rescued me and brought me back to my faith, even when Satan tried to discourage me. He tried to force me to abandon my faith. Because of prayer, my faith grew stronger each time. Prayer has been my weapon for survival. God protects us from the evil one through the power of prayer. *Every battle we face as Christians is waged in prayer!* Prayer is part of the actual battle.

My prayer is that I may be able to encourage each of us to become people, who although small in many ways, yet offering big prayers. Praying with excellence. Praying with persistence. Praying with faith. We must follow Jesus' example of constant prayer (1 Cor. 11:1; 1 John 2:6; 1 Peter 2:21-22).

I. THE IMPORTANCE OF PRAYER IN OUR DAILY WALK:

Responsibility to Pray:

Commandments:

There is no subject more important in the Bible than prayer. Yet, too many ignore and neglect it, becoming indifferent to prayer. Prayer is both a privilege and a command from God. We seem to ignore the Lord's command and our responsibility to pray.

"Be anxious for nothing, but in everything by prayer and supplication with thanksgiving let your requests be made known to God" (Phil. 4:6).

"Brethren, pray for us" (1 Thess. 5:25).

"With all prayer and petition pray at all times in the Spirit, and with this in view, be on the alert with all perseverance and petition for all the saints" (Eph. 6:18).

"Devote yourselves to prayer, keeping alert in it with an attitude of thanksgiving" (Col. 4:2).

"Pray without ceasing; in everything give thanks; for this is God's will for you in Christ Jesus" (1 Thess. 5:17-18).

"Rejoicing in hope, persevering in tribulation, devoted to prayer" (Romans 12:12).

"First of all, then, I urge that entreaties and prayers, petitions and thanksgivings, be made on behalf of all men, for kings and all who are in authority, so that we may lead a tranquil and quiet life in all godliness and dignity. This is good and acceptable in the sight of God our Savior" (1 Tim. 2:1-3).

You see, our Lord has given us responsibilities, and prayer is one of them. In James 5:13, he highlights those duties both in good and bad times. The problem is that many of us are not dependable, lacking faith. *Why do I say that?* Because we allow God out of our box only when we need Him. Sadly, He becomes our *"emergency button"* when adversity strikes. We have no problem with falling to our knees, but only in times of distress or need. We neglect to praise our God and give Him thanks for all the great, awesome things He has given us and done in our lives. *This ought not to be!* We must change our perspective. Often, we cease to pray when things overtake us. And in doing this, we miss out on the Lord's blessings of comfort as He stands and aids us even while we endure hardship.

The Parable of the Persistent Widow:

> **"Now He was telling them a parable to show that at all times they ought to pray and not to lose heart,** saying, 'In a certain city there was a judge who did not fear God and did not respect man. There was a widow in that city, and she kept coming to him, saying, 'Give me legal protection from my opponent.' For a while he was unwilling; but afterward he said to himself, 'Even though I do not fear God nor respect man, yet because this widow bothers me, I will give her legal protection, otherwise by continually coming she will wear me out.' And the Lord said, 'Hear what the unrighteous judge said; now, will not God bring about justice for His elect who cry to Him day and night, and will He delay long over them? I tell you that He will bring about justice for them quickly. However, when the Son of Man comes, will He find faith on the earth?'"* (Luke 18:1-8)

In this parable, we are first introduced to *"a judge who did not fear God and did not respect man."* The Law of Moses demanded that judges administer impartial justice in every city (Exo. 18:21; Deut. 16:18). *Obviously, this man was not qualified to be a judge at all!* He had no reverence for God and no respect for mankind. He was very unrighteous (Luke 18:4). *He was an enemy of God!*

Next, we are introduced to the widow who is begging saying, *"Give me legal protection from my opponent."* This widow knew well this was the proper thing to do since she had no other options (Deut. 27:19). And since this wicked judge did not seek justice for the poor woman at first, and she was unable to offer a bribe, she was without any influence. Thus, she had little hope from this wicked judge.

Since the widow kept coming for justice, the judge agreed to avenge her lest she wear him out. This judge did not, in any way, care about justice. He wanted to stop her from bothering him and get rid of this bothersome widow.

So, what is the purpose of the parable? The judge symbolizes what God is not, and the widow represents us. Widowhood is symbolic of defenselessness. Without God, mankind is defenseless and without hope. Those who have obeyed the Gospel of Christ are God's "elect" who need to rely on God for justice (Rom. 12:19). It is a mistake to think that God would want to be symbolized as a wicked judge. This parable is an argument to contrast a wicked judge (who eventually rendered justice because one is persistently coming); and a righteous and loving God who avenges His children who cry out to Him for help persistently, coming to Him as this poor widow. *This is too beautiful for words!*

This parable compels us to pray always without losing heart. It implies that some may get tired of praying. Perhaps, this is so because of circumstances and the failure to receive desired answers. It should not stop us from praying without ceasing during both good and bad times (1 Thess. 5:17; Rom. 12:2). Our prayers are an indicator of our faith.

And though our God is always there for us, that does not necessarily mean that He will answer us even when we kick His door with persistence. Thus, we shall call upon Him for deliverance with confidence (1 Peter 3:12: 1 John 3:22). We must understand that God does not always answer us the way we want, expect, or in the time frame we desire. But we have the assurance that He will do what is best to aid us.

"And will He delay long over them?" Indeed, this is a crucial point in this parable. *Why?* Because from our earthly perspective, it often seems that God does not hear our cries for justice. It seems as if they are falling on deaf ears. We must understand that just as God is patient with all our flaws, shortcomings, and failures, He also is bearing with our adversaries. He may delay executing justice, vengeance upon our adversaries because He is all longsuffering, not wanting anyone to perish (2 Peter 3:9). *What a merciful and loving God we serve!* You see, our God gives the wicked a second chance, enough time to repent so that he may be saved. In doing this, the righteous often lose heart when tried. We start thinking that God does not care or has just forgotten us (Gal. 6:9; Matt. 24:12-13).

And though we serve a God who is longsuffering, He will not delay avenging us, the righteous, forever (Rev. 6:10). Remember that when He decides to deliver justice, He will do it "speedily;" in a quick manner. We must learn to trust our righteous Judge. He will bring swift destruction on those who practice lawlessness and refuse to obey the Gospel of His Son at His second coming. That same God who destroyed the whole world with a flood. The same God who destroyed the city of Sodom. May we learn to be patient in prayer until He returns.

We Communicate With God Through Prayer:

To Offer Praises of Thanksgiving:

If we are indeed grateful to God, we must tell it to God through prayer.

> *"Through Him then,* **let us continually offer up a sacrifice of praise to God, that is, the fruit of lips that give thanks to His name.** *And do not neglect doing good and sharing, for with such sacrifices God is pleased"* (Heb. 13:15-16).

For Our Anxious and Troubled Heart:

"Be anxious for nothing, but in everything by prayer and supplication with thanksgiving *let your requests be made known to God."* (Phil. 4:6)

Prayer is the remedy for anxiety since we can talk to the only One who cares, our God.

During our Seasons of Distress and Grief:

The song *"Sweet Hour of Prayer"* is a call to take time to pray. Taking time to pray is not something that we can take for granted. We cannot afford to give it up. *Why?* Because this world is filled with cares that constantly besiege us. Prayer helps us cast all our cares on God, for He cares for us (I Peter 5:7). God cares about all our heavy burdens. He will sustain us through His Word and prayer.

What a privilege we have to approach God's throne in prayer, making known all our wants and wishes to Him! (Matt. 6:9; 1 Peter 1:17). *We can freely go to Him in prayer for anything!* (of course, it must be according to His will, James 4:2-3; 1 John 5:14-15).

1. Prayer helps our souls find relief from our seasons of distress and grief.
2. It calms our troubled hearts and helps us face whatever adversity may come our way (James 5:13).
3. It rescues us when we are tempted to sin. I can assure you that when you are facing temptation and spiritual danger, praying fervently will make it easier to resist.

Our prayers ascend to heaven through our Lord and Savior (John 14:13-14). He is our Mediator (Ephesians 2:18; Heb.

4:25; Heb. 7:25). But our prayers must be asked in faith (James 1:5-8). *So why not cast all our cares, letting our God know about each one? Why not rely on Him without giving up on prayer?* Remember, God's timing is not like ours (Luke 18:7-8). *Prayer gives us so much comfort!* (Phil 4:7; Heb. 13:5-6). So, pray, pray as long as you are alive on this earth. *"Pray without ceasing"* (1 Thess. 5:17). We must pray as long as there is breath in us. There will be a day soon when we no longer cherish the sweetness of our prayers. In place of prayer, we will meet with our Creator face to face. *What a day that will be!* This ought to comfort us and give us hope.

Christians Have Access to God's Throne:

What a privilege it is to have access to God's throne in heaven! Through His beloved Son, we receive mercy and find grace in time of need (Heb. 4:16).

In James 5:13-18, we find great confidence in the power of prayer:

> *"Is anyone among you suffering? Then he must pray. Is anyone cheerful? He is to sing praises. Is anyone among you sick? Then he must call for the elders of the church and they are to pray over him, anointing him with oil in the name of the Lord; and the prayer offered in faith will restore the one who is sick, and the Lord will raise him up, and if he has committed sins, they will be forgiven him. Therefore, confess your sins to one another, and pray for one another so that you may be healed. The effective prayer of a righteous man can accomplish much. Elijah was a man with a nature like ours, and he prayed earnestly that it would not rain, and it did not rain on the earth for three years and six months. Then he prayed again, and the sky poured rain and the earth produced its fruit."*

James highlights an excellent point. Prayer must be vital in our walk with God (James 5:14-15).

1. We must pray for ourselves and others (our brethren, the lost).
2. Pray for those who are sick physically and spiritually.
3. Pray for forgiveness of sins committed.
4. Pray for spiritual strength.
5. Pray for encouragement to lift those who need it.

There are so many things that we need to pray for. Prayer is the only (and most effective) way of communication with our Father. Indeed, Satan will stop at nothing to keep us off our knees, to keep us from lifting our petitions toward our Father in heaven.

Another point that James draws our attention to is found in James 5:16.

> "Therefore, **confess your sins to one another, and pray for one another so that you may be healed.** The effective prayer of a righteous man can accomplish much."

Do we do this as Christians? We should! We all need faithful Christians to whom we may confess our sins in confidence, and thus to have them pray for us.

Why do we need to confess our sins to each other?

1. To be forgiven and be healed spiritually.
2. To be better equipped to pray properly for each other's weaknesses.

Of course, when we sin against someone, we must repent and confess that sin to the one that we have wronged and to

God (1 John 1:7-9). In failing to do so, we are running the risk of not being forgiven by our Father in heaven. *Does confessing our sins to one another require that we do it publicly in the church?* I don't think it is wise. If someone has sinned against a brother in Christ and seeks repentance, he should confess his sin to the one offended and to the Lord to be restored. There is no need to confess such sin publicly. The matter has been resolved among three parties: God, the one who sinned, and the offended one. But if the one who sinned refuses to repent, then according to Matt. 18:15-18, other Christians must be involved in the effort to save his soul. When one sins and is known publicly, then the right thing to do is to publicly confess such sin to save and restore the one who sinned.

James 5:16 ends by saying,

> *"The effective prayer of a **righteous man** can accomplish much."*

Do you believe in the power of a righteous man's prayer? You should! To pray fervently means to petition God repeatedly, pleading before Him. *Begging Him for help! Do we all do this in our prayers? We must!*

This passage highlights the importance and power of prayer. Prayer must be active and fervent.

James goes on to say in verses 17-18,

> *"Elijah was a man with a nature like ours, and he prayed earnestly that it would not rain, and it did not rain on the earth for three years and six months. Then he prayed again, and the sky poured rain and the earth produced its fruit."*

So, what do you think was the source of Elijah's power? Prayer! Elijah prayed fervently, and it did not rain. His prayers involved daily living. He looked upward toward God's throne and nothing or no one else. God listened to Elijah. God will listen to us if we are walking with Him in righteousness. God also heard Hannah when she prayed for a son (1 Samuel 1:11). And God blessed her with a son, Samuel, and other children. Hezekiah also prayed to God to live. God answered and added another 15 years to his life (Isaiah 38:2-5). *Yes!* God answers the prayers of every faithful Christian. We must trust God's answer, whether we like it or not. Therefore, cease not to pray. If the answer delays, wait. God will come in His perfect timing. *And He can never come too late!*

Thus, we can be assured that God will hear us also if we are righteous and pray without ceasing, according to His will, and without doubting.

As Christians, we find so much comfort for our trials through prayer. So, we ought to pray for one another, confessing our faults to one another. *The fervent prayers of the one who keeps God's commandments is powerful!*

Prayer Helps us in Our Relationship With Our Brethren:

Prayer Builds Closeness and Unity:

> "They were continually devoting themselves to the apostles' teaching and to fellowship, to the breaking of bread and to prayer." (Acts 2:42)

Imagine what would happen if we all prayed together as a church for a whole hour or more? Imagine what would happen if each one of us was continually devoted to prayer? Imagine if each one of us prayed daily to restore the one who is spiritually weak or has fallen into sin? That means you and me, we, every member of the congregation praying.

Paul kept close to Philemon by continued prayer even though he was far away.

> *"because I hear of your love and of the faith which you have toward the Lord Jesus and toward all the saints; and I pray that the fellowship of your faith may become effective through the knowledge of every good thing which is in you for Christ's sake. For I have come to have much joy and comfort in your love, because the hearts of the saints have been refreshed through you, brother."* (Philemon 5-7)

Likewise, Paul's love for the Corinthian brethren was able to remain stronger and steady because of his prayers.

> *"The grace of the Lord Jesus be with you. 24 My love be with you all in Christ Jesus. Amen."* (1 Cor. 16:23-24)

We Share Each Other's Burdens Through Prayer:

We need to pray for our brethren when they are distressed with many heavy burdens and dangers.

Take, for example:

1. When Paul and Barnabas were in jail, they prayed and sang together, Acts 16:24-25. And so, should we when in distress.
2. When facing dangers, traveling back to Jerusalem with the returning exiles, Ezra proclaimed a time of prayer and fasting, Ezra 8:21-23.
3. When Judah prayed as a nation for deliverance, 2 Chron. 20:14.
4. When Esther risked her life to save her people, she called on everyone to join her in prayers, Esther 4:14-17.

5. When the Sanhedrin Council was threatening Peter and John, their first response was to join the other apostles in prayer, Acts 4:23-31.

6. When Peter was in prison, many saints gathered to pray for him, Acts 12:2.

Prayer Is Both a Group Activity And a Private Individual Activity:

Everyone must be praying together in the family of God. Each and every one participating in the prayers of the church, *"Now I appeal to you, brothers, through our Lord Jesus Christ and the love of the Spirit, to join with me in **fervent prayers to God on my behalf"** (Romans 15:30-32; 2 Cor. 1:8-11). Likewise, we must trust in God to hear us even if we are praying alone (1 Kings 8:38-39).

II. ASK, SEEK, KNOCK:

Jesus in His famous Sermon on the Mount stated,

> *"Ask, and it will be given to you; seek, and you will find; knock, and it will be opened to you. For everyone who asks receives, and he who seeks finds, and to him who knocks it will be opened. Or what man is there among you who, when his son asks for a loaf, will give him a stone? Or if he asks for a fish, he will not give him a snake, will he? If you then, being evil, know how to give good gifts to your children, how much more will your Father who is in heaven give what is good to those who ask Him!"* (Matt. 7:7-11).

Our Lord is teaching us something about prayer. To ask is to make a request with our own voice. To seek is to pursue someone or something. To knock is to try to open and get through an obstacle. All these three verbs are unending in the Greek (present tense continuous action). That is, one must continue to ask, seek, and knock. They all communicate the same idea effectively.

When one prays to the Father in heaven, he must do it sincerely and not vainly. Prayer is not to be an empty ritual. We must faithfully "knock" and "seek" to pray correctly rather than to "ask" for blessings. Prayer is not just an open door to ask whatever requests we want to make. These are not requests for things one is unwilling to undertake or that he is too lazy to pray for sincerely.

God is pleased with prayers that are offered from a sincere and zealous heart. When there is little heart or devotion in our prayers, we cannot expect God to answer them with much heart either. We must continue to ask, seek, and knock according to God's will. It is only then that He can bless us. It is His promise to us. *And He will faithfully keep His Word!* The Bible is full of instructions on the mechanics of how, when, and for what we ought to pray (Matt. 6:1-13; 6:14-15; Mark 1:35-37; Ps. 5:3; Mark 14:22-24; Acts 27:35; Acts 16:25; Acts 12:5,12; 1 Thess. 5:17; Luke 18:1-8; Mark 14:35-36; Matt. 26:39; Matt. 26:53-56; 1 Tim. 2:1-3; Col. 3:17; Heb. 7:25; 1 John 5:14-16; James 1:6-7; 4:3; 1 Peter 3:7; 1 John 3:22; 5:14).

In Matthew 7:9-10, Jesus speaks of "bread" and "fish." He is comparing earthly parents (who are "evil") with God Almighty, who is perfectly good and righteous in every way. God's love for us is greater than even the love of our earthly parents. Although we may offer petitions before His throne and such are not answered as we want them to be, we must remember that God knows what's best for us and that He has our best interests in mind regardless of how He answers us. *Our God gives us good and perfect gifts!* James 1:17.

> *"Now to Him who is able to do far more abundantly beyond all that we ask or think, according to the power that works within us, 21 to Him be the glory*

*in the church and in Christ Jesus to all generations
forever and ever. Amen."* (Eph. 3:20-21)

So, our prayers must be addressed to God, acknowledging
Who He is. They must be offered in reverence and not in vain.
God knows our requests, so ask simply. They must be offered
with praise and thanksgiving and, in the name of Jesus, our
mediator with the Father.

III. HOW TO PRAY AND HOW NOT TO PRAY:

In the New Testament, many passages stress the importance and the need for prayer in the life of all Christians.
However, in Matthew 6:5-8, Jesus addresses prayer in more
depth, giving us practical counsel on how we ought to pray
and how not to pray. Consider those basic principles Jesus set
for us.

> *"And when you pray, you must not be like the hyp-
> ocrites. For they love to stand and pray in the syna-
> gogues and at the street corners, that they may be
> seen by others. Truly, I say to you, they have re-
> ceived their reward. But when you pray, go into
> your room and shut the door and pray to your Fa-
> ther who is in secret. And your Father who sees in
> secret will reward you. And when you pray, do not
> heap up empty phrases as the Gentiles do, for they
> think that they will be heard for their many words.
> Do not be like them, for your Father knows what you
> need before you ask him."*

Jesus, our Lord, expects His disciples to pray. We see this
clearly emphasized when He used the word "when" not "if."
He said,

"When you pray, you must not be like the hypocrites" (Verse 5).
Jesus stresses the need to be sincere in prayer. Those who pray

218 | Be Still My Soul

and want their charitable deeds to be seen of men have no reward from our heavenly Father. They are hypocrites or pre-
tenders who merely want to exercise their "religiousness" in
the most obvious way to receive the praise of others. Such persons are full of pride and vanity and are lovers of themselves.
They do not please the Lord (Luke 18:10-14; Matt. 23; James
4:6; 2 Tim. 3:2ff).

> *"But when you pray, go into your room and shut
> the door and pray to your Father who is in
> secret"* (Verse 6).

Here Jesus is stressing the benefit of solitude in prayer.
When one prays privately, he develops sincerity in prayer.
There are fewer distractions and disturbances in the closet.
One can easily control what surrounds him when he is isolated
from others and all distractions. The focus of our prayer must
be to seek God. One can seek Him out effectively when he is in
solitude since there is no temptation to pray to be seen of men.
God is a rewarder of those who seek Him in prayer with the
proper attitude of heart and spirit. He will grant their requests
if they're according to His will (1 John 5:14-15).

With this in mind, let us not conclude that Jesus prohibits
public prayer. In the New Testament, Christians are autho-
rized to engage in public prayer (Acts 2:42; 1 Tim. 2:8; James
5:16) even though Christ seemed to pray more often when He
was alone (Matt. 14:23; 26;36ff; Mark 1:35; Luke 5:16; 6:12;
9:18).

> *"And when you pray, do not heap up empty phras-
> es"* (Verse 7).

Our Lord emphasizes the need for simplicity in prayer. *"Be
not rash with your mouth, nor let your heart be hasty to utter a word
before God, for God is in heaven and you are on earth. Therefore, let
your words be few"* (Ecc. 5:2). He wants us to avoid using emp-

ty, careless, lifeless phrases. The pagans were guilty of this (1 Kings 18:26; Acts 19:34). Jesus doesn't condemn repetition in prayer but vain repetitions. A prayer can be repetitive and still be meaningful or substantial. *"So, leaving them again, he went away and prayed for the third time, saying the same words again"* (Matt. 26:44).

The same principle is applied to offering thanks for food in that it can turn into vain repetitions. But when one offers thanksgiving with a grateful heart to God, the One who gives all things, then it is not vain repetition.

The beauty of our Lord's model prayer is its simplicity. It is composed of only 60 words in Greek. When one follows Christ's example of prayer, public prayer becomes shorter, and our private prayers become longer.

> *"Your Father knows what you need before you ask him"* (Verse 8).

When one has God as his Father, he has the security (anchor) of knowing that his prayers will be heard. Thus, vain repetition is useless. As a matter of fact, one's petitions are known even before he utters the first petition. *Isn't it amazing! And some wonder why it is so necessary to pray?!* Our God is not ignorant of our needs, nor is He reluctant in any way to be persuaded. Our Father imparts His gifts as a response to our eagerness (desire) to receive them (Luke 11:5-13; James 4:2). And even if this were not true, we must pray simply because He commands us to do so.

In 1 Thessalonians 5:17, we are commanded to *"pray without ceasing."* That is, God expects His children to have a disposition (frame of mind) always to seek Him, have a harmonizing relationship with Him. "Praying without ceasing" is what we must always do (in every day's decisions and every compartment of our life) with a mindset so that we may do His will and respect His Lordship. It also is our way of communicating with Him privately and closely (informally) throughout our daily walk (praises, thanksgivings, confessing one's sins, shortcomings, and expressing our petitions). These prayers must be brief and offered tirelessly or frequently in our daily life. *Don't get me wrong!* I'm not recommending that our prayers be brief and with hidden thoughts. On the contrary, I think it is wise to offer in-depth prayers at various times of the day. Notice the excellent example of Daniel (Dan. 6:10).

So, when one approaches God's throne through prayer, he must do it with confidence, not doubting (Heb. 4:6). Even if one feels incapable of expressing himself completely before God, he has the assurance that God knows his heart (Rom. 8:26-27).

Our prayers must be offered with patience and persistence (Luke 18:1-8). Remember that our Father is *"is able to do far more abundantly than all that we ask or think, according to the power at work within us."* (Eph. 3:20)

Furthermore, Jesus presented for the disciples, and for us as well, an example (model) of prayer to consider and learn. Consider that example:

> *"Pray, then, in this way: 'Our Father who is in heaven, Hallowed be Your name. 'Your kingdom come. Your will be done, On earth as it is in heaven. 'Give us this day our daily bread. 'And forgive us our debts, as we also have forgiven our debtors. 'And do not lead us into temptation, but deliver us from evil. For Yours is the kingdom and the power and the glory forever. Amen.'"* (Matt. 6:9-13)

Notice that every time Jesus our Lord prayed, He always addressed our heavenly Father. He did it reverently: *"Our Father who is in heaven, Hallowed be Your name"* (cf, Psalm 145:1).

The word "hallow" means sacred. God's name is holy and sacred. Thus, it must be regarded as "holy." It is an honor or a privilege to address Him. His name must not be treated commonly and lightly. When one is addressing the Father in prayer, he must do it with reverence, and respectfully. *One must remember that he is not just speaking to anybody but to the Almighty One, the only true and living God!* If one honors his earthly father, *how much more must he give honor and reverence to our Heavenly Father?! He is the only one worthy of all praise and honor!*

"Your kingdom come" (Verse 10). This verse refers to past, present, and future petitions. We don't pray any longer for the kingdom to come since this prayer was answered in Acts 2 on the Day of Pentecost. Indeed, the kingdom of God has already come. Christ is now reigning as Lord of lords and King of kings in His kingdom (Col. 1:13; 1 Cor. 15:24-25). He rules in heaven and earth. *He is in control!* In place of praying for the kingdom to come, one should pray for the furthering of the kingdom. *Are we kingdom-minded when we pray? Or are we our own little kingdom who wants what we want and right now?! Do our prayers carry this kind of tone sometimes? Think about it!*

"Your will be done on earth as it is in heaven." This is a petition for the present. It is a prayer for the furthering of the Gospel as well as obedience to Jesus' rule. We must pray that God's will be done everywhere, at all times, and by everyone. To offer such a prayer, one must submit to the will of God and all His counsel. This is true also when we are teaching God's will to others, that they might be encouraged to submit to Him only.

"Give us this day our daily bread" (Verse 11). This petition or prayer is not for just milk and honey (symbols of luxury). Rather, we must ask for enough bread as our daily provision or needs. We want to ask God for just enough to get us through this day. He wants us to deal with today first. And as

long as it is today, one has no need of tomorrow's bread (Ex. 16:12-31). God, in His loving-kindness, will provide us with all that is necessary for our daily needs. That is if one is diligently seeking Him and His kingdom of righteousness first (Matt. 6:25-33; cf. Phil. 4:19). One must acknowledge that there is a big difference between his wants and needs. Therefore, let us be careful not to allow our prosperity to hinder our thanksgiving for daily needs (Proverbs 30:8-9).

> "And forgive us our debts, as we also have forgiven our debtors" (Verse 12).

In this passage, Jesus is using the word "debts" in a spiritual sense. Our debts are spiritual debts to God (Matt. 18:21-35). Literally, this is saying: "God forgive me as I have forgiven other people." That must concern us greatly since we are not always the most forgiving people. Often, we carry grudges that impede us from forgiving. And it must never be the case if we truly want to submit to God's will. Remember, God will forgive our trespasses if we also forgive men's trespasses (Matt. 6:14-15). How about you?

> "And do not lead us into temptation" (Verse 13).

Considering James 1:13, this request may seem a little bit troublesome for some. Why would one pray that the Father not lead him/her into temptation; since God does not tempt anyone, to begin with? Well, that phrase can easily be translated as: Do not lead us into trials. Christians face plenty of trials in life from the evil one. Don't you think we have enough reasons to pray that we might be able to escape severe temptations that Satan might present to us? We need to pray that God would keep temptation far from us! Remember that Jesus Himself made this request of keeping temptation away from Him.

The second half of verse 13 says, "but deliver us from evil" or keep us from evil (Luke 22:31-32). This is a prayer that is seldom heard publicly. Often, we pray for forgiveness of sins but neglect to pray to be delivered from the evil one, the hindrance of sin; to escape from Satan's stern and severe temptations, he puts in our way to make us stumble.

> *"For Yours is the kingdom and the power and the glory forever, Amen"* (Verse 13).

This is the prayer and life that praises God.

There are parallel accounts of Jesus' model prayer, Matt. 6:1-13, and Luke 11:1-4. Jesus' disciples asked Him to teach them to pray. Jesus then uttered a prayer. The fact that Jesus replied to His disciples' request implies that we can learn how to pray correctly. It is not a gift but rather a talent that one can develop and improve. It is one of those areas where we desperately must grow. We must learn to pray with excellence. In doing this, we will learn greater dependence on God. By the same token, it will cause us to be more thoughtful and reflective. *So how is your prayer life? Do you know that our God wants us to be prayerful, sincere, secure people in the prayers we offer to Him?* May we always be mindful of beauty and simplicity when we approach God's throne to talk to Him. May we always appreciate the benefits of seclusion.

IV. THE ONE WHO PRAYS:

Must Believe in Prayer:

Without a doubt, faith is the foundation of Christians. We must have faith that is pleasing to God. We must believe that God rewards His seekers (Heb. 11:6). Our faith helps us to press on and not fall back (Heb. 10:38-39). God is attentive to the prayers of His faithful children (Psa. 35:15). He has given us the promise that He will hear the supplications of His righteous ones. *Do you sincerely believe God's promise of listening to us in prayer?*

We have been given every assurance, so there is no need to doubt. The prayer of God's righteous children avails much (James 5:16-18). God is able to do exceedingly more than we think or ask (Eph. 3:20-21; Matt. 21:20).

God is Attentive to The Prayers of The Righteous:

The Christian (who is walking righteously), not the sinner (the willfully disobedient), has the confidence that God hears his prayers. The ungodly and rebellious must not expect from God an affirmative answer or dare to ask Him for His blessings. Sin hinders our prayers (1 Peter 3:7). *Our prayers are affected by sin in our life!* "*The face of the Lord is against those who do evil, to cut off the memory of them from the earth*" (Psalm 34:16). "*For the eyes of the Lord are on the righteous, and his ears are open to their prayer. But the face of the Lord is against those who do evil*" (1 Peter 3:12). God is not inclined to grant our supplications if we are defiant children and continue in rebellion against His will. Though God blesses sinners sometimes as well (Matt. 5:43-45; Acts 14:15-16). God causes the rain to fall on all, regardless of their faithfulness. God also hears those who are seeking after Him with a sincere heart. *I was one of them when I was searching for the Truth! Because He heard my pleas, I was able to find Him and His Truth!* (Acts 10:1-4).

It is so tragic when Christians doubt that God will fulfill His promise to hear their prayers. I hear them say, "*I prayed for such and such to happen, but God did not hear my prayer.*" What they actually are saying is that God did not jump immediately to give them what they wanted. However, to conclude that God does not hear our prayers because He did not answer quickly and positively shows a critical lack of understanding. *Take heed!*

The truth is that God hears all prayers, but He does not necessarily answer them all in a way that is noticeable to us immediately. We must distinguish between God's way of hearing and answering our prayers. He is aware of each of our prayers (including those prayers that unbelievers and believers utter). However, it is not reasonable to think that God must answer according to each petition one makes simply because He hears all prayers. *The Bible does not teach such absurdity!*

Mankind is in no position to demand anything from God. All we can do is to approach Him humbly as beggars with our pleas, requests, and petitions (supplications, Phil. 4:6). To believe that God is obliged or indebted to us to respond as we wish reflects ignorance and foolishness of heart. Those who think and behave this way are imposing their limitations, inabilities, and all such factors on God. *Why not be aware that God responds to our prayers in many different ways according to His unfathomable wisdom and omniscience? Why not be thankful to God that He is willing to answer our prayers His way?*

God's Responses to Our Prayer: Problems in Prayers:

Sometimes God answers our prayers with an instantaneous "YES."

Consider some examples:

- Hannah was not able to conceive but prayed earnestly to bear a son. God answered with a quick "yes" when He gave her Samuel and other children (1 Sam. 1-2).
- Elijah was a righteous man who prayed earnestly that it would not rain on the land for three years and six months. He prayed again, and the heavens gave rain (James 5:17-18). His prayers were answered positively and powerfully.
- We have numerous accounts where God demonstrated His grace and wisdom when responding rapidly and affirmatively to the supplications of

His righteous ones (2 Kings 20:1-7; Daniel 2:23; Ezra 8:21-23; Luke 1:13, etc.).

In the past, God used miracles as signs to confirm the words of the prophets. Today the Word of God is already confirmed or established, and God has no further use for such signs (1 Cor. 13:8ff; Eph. 4:7ff). Nevertheless, God still urges us to pray, making petitions, asking for His help for a wide variety of purposes. *There is power in prayer!* To deny the power of prayer is to deny God's willingness to intervene in human affairs. In Acts 17:27-29, Paul answered that question, *"for in Him we live and move and exist."* There is nothing wrong with praying to God when someone is sick or a loved one is dying, that God may be with the doctors who are caring for them and that He may heal and strengthen them during recovery. *Who am I to say what God will or will not do?* Of course, He will not do that which is against His will. God certainly can work in His own providential way. He is able to do exceedingly abundantly above all that we ask or think (Eph. 3:20). He is mindful of His righteous ones and answers their prayers according to His will. Therefore, we must pray with full confidence (assurance) that He will hear our pleas if it is in our best interest.

Sometimes He answers our prayers with an absolute "NO."

Such is perhaps the case of the unrighteous or unfaithful ones (Proverbs 28:9). Such is also the case of His righteous ones whose pleas are not made according to His will. If our requests are not in agreement with His will, His answer will be a "no." Likewise, if our prayers are filled with selfish and impure motives, the answer might be a negative one (James 4:3).

Paul was a righteous man who prayed to have his *"thorn in the flesh"* removed (2 Cor. 12:8). However, the Lord did not answer positively. He did not remove the thorn. Perhaps, the Lord wanted to remind Paul of his weaknesses, lest he be exalted above measure. God answered Paul according to his spiritual welfare with a *"my grace is sufficient for you."* Today we may encounter the same answer.

Jesus also offered prayers and supplications with loud crying and many tears in Gethsemane. Indeed, His Father heard Him (Heb. 5:7). However, the Father did not find it necessary to answer with a "yes" but rather a "no" to our Lord's prayers on this occasion. Mankind's redemption would have been impossible if He had answered with a "yes." Therefore, we must always follow our Lord's selfless example in His time of agonizing prayers. *"And going a little farther he fell on his face and prayed, saying, "My Father, if it be possible, let this cup pass from me; nevertheless, not as I will, but as you will"* (Matt. 26:39). Our God knew very well that there was no other way but the cross.

God alone knows what is best for us. He knows all the factors that will affect us today and years down the road in giving us what we ask in prayer. So, if God answers our prayers with a "no," trust Him with a humble, submissive, and thankful heart. Don't be discouraged if it seems that the Lord is giving you a "no" as His answer. *Even His "no" responses are blessings!*

Sometimes God answers our prayers with a "wait a while."

Sometimes we deceive ourselves, thinking that God is answering with a "no." When He is actually delaying with a positive response, "yes," to our prayers. *I have learned this well! Many times, I have to sit still and wait for His answer for a long time!*

Take, for instance, the Israelites who cried out to God for deliverance from Egyptian bondage for several generations. I am sure that many of them thought that God's answer was simply a "no." However, His reply was, "wait a while." It is not time yet. We must understand God's delay. It is all in His frame of time.

Another example of God's delay is seen in Revelation 6:9-11. John saw the souls of those who have been martyred for their faithfulness to God's Word. He described their prayers:

> *"They cried out with a loud voice, 'O Sovereign Lord, holy and true, how long before you will judge and avenge our blood on those who dwell on the earth?' Then they were each given a white robe and told to rest a little longer, until the number of their fellow servants and their brothers should be complete, who were to be killed as they themselves had been."*

Notice what verse 11 says, *"Then they were each given a white robe and told to rest a little longer."* You see, God was not refusing to hear their plea. He simply said that it was not time yet and that they had to wait patiently.

If God does not give us what we ask Him immediately, there is no reason to doubt, even though we might not be able to see it. God is teaching us patience. We must not grow weary and lose heart (Luke 18:1; 1 Thess. 5:17).

Sometimes God answers our prayers by saying "maybe" or "it all depends."

God sometimes responds with a "maybe," when the righteous pray and even when they pray according to the will of God. Let me explain. God made us with a free will. It means that He will not force us to do His will in His realm. Thus, when we pray for things that pertain to the choices of others, God's response will be a "maybe." He will not supersede someone else's free will to grant our request.

We have an excellent example of God's unconditional response in Abraham's six intercessory prayers for Sodom (Gen. 18:23ff). The fate of Sodom was dependent on the morality and choices of their men. Notice that God replied to Abraham repeatedly: *"Yes, but it all depends."*

When we pray for our rulers *"that we may lead a quiet and peaceable life in all godliness and reverence"* (1 Timothy 2:2), the effect of such prayers rests not only with God but with the choices that the rulers make. Likewise, when we pray for sinners to come to know the Lord and be saved, it involves more than God's love for them (1 Tim. 2:4), my earnest and frequent prayers, or my devotion to God. *Why?* Because if the sinner does not want to repent and obey the Truth, there is nothing that God can do to grant my request. God does not and will not force anyone to be saved. He cannot save the disobedient, Heb. 5:9. Again, God's response to such a prayer is *"it all depends."*

The same applies to any prayer that involves the behavior of others (parents' prayers that their children will remain faithful; prayer for abortion to be abolished, prayer for national and world leaders to rule wisely and so on).

The same is true of those who have forsaken the Lord's Way; those who have shipwrecked their faith; those who are bent on destroying the church. God can only answer: *"It all depends."* It is as if God is asking: *Will they repent? Will they submit to my Son's Lordship through His Word? Will they begin teaching my Truth and refute all error?* If so, then, God's answer is "yes." Otherwise, it is a "no." God can't answer any prayer with an affirmative "yes" that requires Him to override man's free will.

V. CONCLUSION:

The study of prayer has always fascinated me. Prayer is one of the most powerful tools any Christian can possess. Sadly, it is one of the most overlooked and underused tools God has given us. All Christians must pray and never lose heart. Prayer has the power to comfort us in our times of trials and distress.

Our prayer life is the barometer of our relationship with God. We either pray without ceasing or we perish. We have no other choice. The early church was a praying church (Acts 2:42; Acts 4:23-31). For a church to grow spiritually, she must be a praying church without fear. Prayer is vital in our walk with God. Jesus, who was God in the flesh, is our excellent example of prayer. We read numerous times in the Gospel accounts of Jesus praying to His Father. One of those occasions was at His baptism (Luke 3:21); the night before He chose the twelve apostles (Luke 6:12-16); before and after feeding the 5,000 (Mark 6:41, 46); on the mount of transfiguration (Luke 9:28); as He raised Lazarus from the dead (John 11:41-42); for Peter before his denial (Luke 24:30); before His betrayal and arrest at Gethsemane (Matt. 26; Mark 14; Luke 22, John 17); on the cross (Mark 15:34); and after His resurrection (Luke 24:30). *So, if Jesus, the Son of God, needed to take time to pray alone with His Father, how much more do we need to pray today?* If we indeed want to imitate Christ, we must not overlook the importance and the need for regular prayer in our life.

Jesus prayed at least for two significant reasons: for strength not to give into the temptation of vanity and for the preaching ministry, He was to embark upon (Mark 1:39). Jesus taught us that we must keep on praying even when it seems there is no result because prayer does work (Luke 18:1-7). If we pray in faith and according to His will, we have the assurance that He will hear us. He is our perfect example of praying in times of trouble and despair.

The apostle Paul is another great example of prayer. He often prayed with the elders and with the churches in Ephesus, Colossae, Philippi (Acts 20:36-38; Acts 21:3-5; Eph. 1:15-23; Col. 1:9-18; Phil 1:3-11). Paul always prayed for the brethren for knowledge, wisdom, understanding, strength, and thanksgiving. He prayed regularly for them to be faithful, to share the gospel, and that they might increase in love. And just as Paul prayed for them, he likewise asked the brethren to pray for him. He also asked the Roman brethren to pray for his safety, the success of the gospel, and for his safe travels (Romans 15:30-32). Moreover, Paul told the Corinthian brethren to pray for his deliverance from persecution, to accomplish much for the furthering of the Gospel, and to give thanks (2 Cor. 1:8-11). To the Colossians, he asked them to be devoted to prayer, alert and thankful, for the success of the Gospel, and for him to be bold despite the many difficulties. So, the question is: *Can we not, or should we not pray for the same things with the same earnestness? What hinders us?*

Prayer is also the foundation on which the church must be built on. We must be Christians who love to pray to their Creator. We must become warriors of prayer. We must pray for strength.

It grieves me to see so many souls, some sincere, naive, and struggling because they don't know the Lord and His Truth to guide them to righteousness and holiness. God gives us power in prayer to do something about it. And we must pray for them that they may come to the knowledge of the Truth. The world around us is in desperate need of a Savior. We Christians must pray without ceasing as long as we are here. Prayer is God's weapon for Christians here on earth. Just think of how many things do not happen or will not take place because we are not praying for them. Likewise, we must take the burdens of others to our Lord so that He can intercede on their behalf. Every day we face powerful storms that come our way; storms that shake us to our core. But through prayer and

God's Word, I can assure you we can be built upon the Rock, standing firm to survive the storms that threaten our faith and hope.

Let us always remember that one of the keys to heaven is prayer and supplication. I don't see any other way. With sincere hearts, let us always approach the throne of our Heavenly Father in prayer and supplication, asking Him for peace toward those who despise us. Let us ask our heavenly Father through prayer for understanding, wisdom, and real knowledge. Let us ask Him for sanctification and godliness, to walk in a manner worthy of Him. Let us pray for mercy to spread the Word to deliver men from the kingdom of darkness. We must pray to find those souls that are sincere, hungry, and thirsty to find the Tuth. Let us pray for those who minister in the Gospel. Let us ask with faith and not doubt, for a good conscience; to be watchful and alert against the adversary; for humility; for the saints; to remove bitterness and wrath, replacing it with kindness and mercy; for correction, reproof, righteousness, hardship, unity, suffering, sickness; for those who have gone astray from the Truth to bring them back to Him; for one another, for our families, our homes, and yes, yes for those who are in authority, our President, so that we may live a tranquil and quiet life in all godliness and dignity. This is good and acceptable before God. Instead of ridiculing, putting down, and many times crossing the line God has placed there, we must pray for them. Our Father wants all men to be saved and to come to the knowledge of the Truth. Let's give thanks to our Lord Jesus, who died for us so that through Him, we all can have redemption.

Let's follow the examples of those mighty men and women who prayed without ceasing to glorify God: Abraham, Gen. 20:17; Moses, Numbers 11:2; Hannah, I Samuel 1:10; Elisha, 2 Kings 4:33; Hezekiah, 2Kings 19:15; Job 42:10; Jeremiah 32:16; Daniel 6:10, 9:4 (my favorite one is Daniel); Jonah 2:1. Let's follow the prayer of our Lord Jesus in John 17:1-26.

What about your prayer life? Is it what the Lord expects it to be? Our Father wants us to be prayerful and sincere children. He wants us to find security and assurance when we offer our prayers to Him. For our prayers to be effective, we must have faith (1 John 5:14-15; Mark 11:24).

So, when you feel desperate, clueless, in doubt, suffering and persecuted without hope, get on your knees, and pray to the Almighty for safety, protection, wisdom, understanding, and deliverance.

Become acquainted with the Psalms. They take us deeper not only into the revealed Word of God but also into a profound relationship with our Creator, which is vital for every Christian. They help us to improve our prayers. They also help us to reach out to God in prayer for guidance and deeper growth in our walk with Him. The Psalms become friends and companions when we need to find refuge and strength through prayer. We must learn to love the Psalms. They strengthen the prayers that we desperately need for the battlefield. Prayers help us greatly in our spiritual war. They strengthen us in our weaknesses and in the fears that freeze us sometimes. They quiet our discontent and complaining and build up our faith.

I also want to encourage us to make a prayer list or journal as our tool to help us become more disciplined and reflective in our prayer journey. Begin by writing all your blessings (both physical and spiritual) and for which you are thankful. Include another section for the people in your life (those whom you are trying to bring to Christ). Pray for the Lord's blessings for specific needs you and others have. Make a list of personal petitions and for God's will to be done in your life. Write another list of God's attributes to praise Him. Finally, create a list of the weaknesses, flaws, and failures you are trying to overcome and the sins you need to confess and repent of. These lists are just a good starting place. Pray in secret through the entire list and update the list as you go. This will help you see how our Lord is working in your life. I hope you benefit from my humble suggestions.

May we pray fervently, persistently, and frequently as those who love their God. May we never abandon prayer because we have grown weary and have lost heart. May we always approach our God in prayer for thanksgiving, to confess our sins, to make supplication for our needs, and to intercede on behalf of others. May we always strive to recognize God's awesome nature in our prayers and His will for our lives. May we always treasure His providence in our lives, which sustains us in our daily walk. Finally, may we always be mindful of the beauty of simplicity when we talk to Him in prayer.

I want to leave you with the words of this beautiful song to encourage us to pray:

Did You Think to Pray?

Ere you left your room this morning,
Did you think to pray?
In the name of Christ our Savior,
Did you sue for loving favor,
As a shield today?

Refrain:
Oh, how praying rests the weary!
Prayer will change the night to day;
So when life seems dark and dreary,
Don't forget to pray.

When you met with great temptation,
Did you think to pray?
By His dying love and merit,
Did you claim the Holy Spirit
As your guide and stay? [Refrain]

When your heart was filled with anger,
Did you think to pray?
Did you plead for grace, my brother,
That you might forgive another
Who had crossed your way? [Refrain]

When sore trials came upon you,
Did you think to pray?
When your soul was bowed in sorrow,
Balm of Gilead did you borrow
At the gates of day? [Refrain]

Overcoming Evil
with Good

"Bless those who persecute you; bless and do not curse them. Repay no one evil for evil, but give thought to do what is honorable in the sight of all. If possible, so far as it depends on you, live peaceably with all. Beloved, never avenge yourselves, but leave it to the wrath of God, for it is written, 'Vengeance is mine, I will repay, says the Lord.' To the contrary, 'if your enemy is hungry, feed him; if he is thirsty, give him something to drink; for by so doing you will heap burning coals on his head. Do not be overcome by evil, but overcome evil with good." Romans 12:14, 17-21*

Today in June of 2020, everyone seems to be talking about their grievances. Many are nursing grudges of injustice both recent and past. As each one thinks about the slights, insults, and apparent prejudice of others against himself or against those they love, they become angrier and angrier. Wars and bloodshed often spill out of such injured feelings that turn dark descending into the depths of hatred and deep resentment that refuses to heal. Jesus has a better way. He came to the earth, born in a stable, but announced as the Prince of peace. Jesus teaches us to overcome evil with good. Let us drink deeply of the healing waters of Jesus' counsel.

One of the deadliest sins in the world is hate, whether it is in our nation, the community, the home, or yes even the church. So, the question at stake is: *How should we overcome our enemies? How should we overcome hatred? Indeed, handling our enemies is no easy piece of cake! How should we treat those who mistreat and abuse us? How should Christians relate to the evil world around them?* Our Lord Jesus teaches us to love our enemies (Matthew 5:44). *Do you find it difficult to love and be around your enemies, even your persecutors? Jesus commands us to love them! What should we do when we Christians encounter opposition and hate?* Jesus commands us to endure ridicule when we're attacked because of our faith. *Is it easy or even possible to overcome our enemies through our Lord's wisdom and comfort?*

Sadly, we live in a world where evil and evil doers seem to rule, and as long as we remain on earth, we must continue to live in it, whether we want it or not. It is part of living in this world of darkness without God. Living in a world where evil and hatred seem so strong, one finds it hard to find peace. God is the giver of peace. He is the God of peace that will soon crush Satan and his kingdom of darkness (Rom. 16:20). God has brought peace through His beloved Son. Thus, He commands us to have peace with all men (Rom. 14:19; Heb. 12:14).

We, children of Light, are commanded to live peaceably, promote peace, and be at peace with others. Thus, we must try to strive for peace and do what we must do to be at peace with believers and unbelievers. The Gospel of our Lord Jesus Christ is a Gospel of peace. Consider some Scriptures that teach us how we must deal with evil and hatred and treat those who mistreat and abuse us.

I. OVERCOMING OUR ENEMIES:

Romans 12:14, 17-21 provides us with some fundamental principles about how children of Light, Christians, must handle evil and the evildoers around us. The Word of God instructs us to be careful with our words and our actions to adorn the Gospel Message. We must be Christ-like even amid evil and persecution. We must not take vengeance on our enemies, but rather we must choose to love them, forgive them, and go the extra mile to be a blessing to them. In doing this, we may rest assured we will overcome evil with good.

Repay No Evil For Evil: (Romans 12:17)

God has commanded us not to take revenge on those who hurt or mistreat us. To the contrary, He wants us to bless and not curse them. *Indeed, that is difficult to do when we are hurt and badly treated!* But two wrongs don't make a right. To fight back, even to death, is the way of the animal kingdom. To hit, kick or bite back is the way of small children. To "fight fire with fire" is the way of the unbelievers, those who are worldly-minded. The world's thinking is, *"I am just giving him a dose of his own medicine."* The world reviles in return when they are reviled. But Jesus teaches a different standard. He gives us other measures to take. When He was reviled, he did not revile in return (1 Peter 2:23). Yes, it is easy and tempting to yell back when others yell at us; speak hateful words right back at those who hate us and return evil for evil. But God does not want His children to stoop to that level of repaying evil for evil.

As Much As Possible, Live Peaceably With Evildoers: (Romans 12:18)

God is the Giver of peace. Peace can be found in Him alone. Peace does not come through diplomacy or compromise. Because of our sins, we were separated from God. We lived in hostility toward Him. But God brought peace when Jesus conquered death, He tore down the dividing wall of hostility, the law of the commandments, and brought us reconciliation to Himself. Peace was brought to this world through Jesus and His victory over sin and death. Because of this, we can find peace with God (Eph. 2:13-17).

God commands us to have peace with others (Romans 14:18, Heb. 12:14). God calls us to live peaceably, promote peace, and be at peace with everyone. God wants us to strive for peace and do what we can do to bring about peace. He wants peace not only among believers but also with the unbelievers, the lost. *We must not suppress the Gospel of peace!* We must live godly to have peace with all men. Also, we must seek and maintain peace with others to get along with one another. We must do all that is in our power to live in peace with everyone, even evildoers.

> *"I am for peace, but when I speak, they are for war!"* (Psalm 120:7)

Living in a world of hatred, everybody seems to lack peace. They find it easier to blame others for the strife and conflicts that arise. It is foolish to demand that others do things our way, for it causes a great amount of strife. We cause strife and discord when we insist that others are wrong and we are right, demanding that they do everything our way. Jesus said,

> *"Blessed are the peacemakers because they will be called sons of God"* (Matt. 5:9).

We must think before we utter any inflammatory words that might cause anger instead of peace. We must promote harmony and peace in our relationships to have unity with one another. *Do you know that when we contribute to strife and discord, it is not the other person's fault but ours as well?* So, we must take responsibility to restore peace and be peacemakers. It means that we must take the first steps to reconciliation. We must refuse to wait for an apology and forgive, for we must act first.

Remember the words of Jesus,

"If your brother sins against you, go and tell him his fault, between you and him alone. If he listens to you, you have gained your brother" (Matt. 18:15).

Jesus commands us to not think of ourselves as the victims and the ones offended but instead, He wants us to go to those who have wronged us or who are against us. As Jesus' faithful disciples, we must swallow our pride and practice humility. We cannot restore peace when we are waiting for others to apologize. We must overlook the faults of others and seek harmony in all our relationships. We must learn to say *"I'm sorry"* when we are tempted to make excuses for our behavior. We must make right the wrongs we have committed against others. Indeed, we all have our bad, upset, and frustrating days, but that does not free us from keeping harmony as best we can, confessing that we're wrong when we are.

Each one of us must be a teacher of peace, for we must follow Jesus' footsteps. We must be teaching this world of darkness to seek peace in their lives and stop fighting God. Peace is not weakness or cowardice. It imitates the Son of God whose life was the embodiment of strength and courage.

Do Not Avenge Yourselves: (Romans 12:19)

When we take revenge into our own hands, we are usurping the role of God, for we are not in His place. He knows the motives and intentions of the human heart, not us. He alone is the one we must trust to act with perfect justice and mercy. To take the responsibility of vengeance on ourselves is to claim or take the place of God. *It is wrong! We, Christians, must acknowledge the most fundamental principle that God is God, and we are not! Presumption can keep us out of heaven!*

1. *How easy it is to take vengeance on those who falsely charge us, mistreat us, speak evil of us, and try to destroy us!*

2. *How easy it is to repay them with the same evil with which they're afflicting us!* It is so easy to repay evil for evil to those who do injustice against us.
3. *How easy it is to burn with anger and act foolishly!*
4. *How desirous we can be for retribution! But God wants His children to call on His 'anger, not on our own!* And though it is true that the wrong done against us is the cause for anger, we must know that our Lord is also angry at what is happening.

Thus, we must plead to God for action out of God's anger and not from our own. *It will indeed demand a lot of self-control!* God's children must not take vengeance for themselves. As those who walk in the Light of God, we must not under any circumstances take matters into our own hands when we have been wronged, sinned against while being innocent.

1. In Romans 12:14 we are instructed to *"Bless those who persecute you; bless and do not curse them."*
2. Romans 12:17 says, *"Repay no one evil for evil, but give thought to do what is honorable in the sight of all."*
3. Romans 12:19 says, *"Beloved, never avenge yourselves, but leave room for the wrath of God, for it is written, Vengeance is mine, I will repay, says the Lord."* Vengeance belongs to the Lord.
4. Romans 12:21 says, *"Do not be overcome by evil, but overcome evil with good."*

Thus, we must not retaliate but instead leave room for God's judgment and trust in His righteous measurement of judgment, leaving everything in His hands. *God will judge evildoers!* We must realize that judgment must come upon all. But before we call on God for His judgment upon our enemies, we must first look at ourselves and make sure that we are able to endure God's judgment upon us. *How easy it is to demand that God take vengeance on others, but how difficult it is for us to accept judgment ourselves! No, we must be ready to be judged!* We must compare our actions to theirs for God to vindicate us. *Do we dare ask God to judge when we fail to have integrity in our own lives? Should we be ready for God's judgment?* So, we must take a good look at ourselves and make changes before demanding God's judgment on others. *Think about it!*

We Must Treat Our Enemies With Human Decency: (Romans 12:20).

Although at times our emotions take over and bring out the worst in us and we get so frustrated, agitated, and angry, we must rule and bring under control such negative emotions. *Why?* It will be a stumbling block thrown our way to make us sin and bring reproach on ourselves and of course on our Lord and Savior. Jesus commands us to love our enemies (Matt. 5:44). So often, we are inclined to say, *"Okay, I'll try, but just from a distance."* But the Lord commands us to provide food and drink to our enemies that need it (Rom. 12:20). *Do you know what's that called?* Simply, "human decency." Jesus declared that even sinners do good to those who do good to them. *But we Christians must rise to a higher plain!* (Luke 6:31-35).

Do Not Be Overcome By Evil But Overcome Evil With Good: (Romans 12:21).

Here in this verse, we find the second part of our principle. We must not do evil to others even when they have done evil to us and have wronged us. In doing so, we become just like them and have allowed them to rule and control us. *Why?* Simply because we have allowed their sinful behavior to overcome us and make us respond to them in an ungodly manner. So, we have been *"overcome by evil."* But our Lord has set a much higher standard for His children. He says that instead of being *"overcome by evil,"* we must *"overcome evil with good."* It means that we must not allow the wrongdoings of others to make us stumble and cause us to do evil to them in return. *No!*

We must fight and rise above our flesh by doing good to them. *Indeed, it is not easy! Why?* Because we are in a spiritual warfare and we must fight against the wiles of Satan, holding firm to higher ground to not give in or give up on the battlefield of our souls. Our battle is not against flesh and blood but against the spiritual forces of evil (Eph. 6:12).

We must take the offensive. The defensive fail to have victory over anger, fear, and self-centeredness. They allow the world to defeat them, for they are carnal minded. Sadly, many are merely succumbers instead of overcomers. *Wouldn't it be better to overlook another's fault, Prov. 19:11? So why not choose to be better rather than bitter, sour, and unforgiving? Why not choose to overflow with love, kindness, longsuffering, righteousness, hope, joy, and faith?* Those who overflow with the fruits of the Spirit can replace that which is negative with righteousness, godliness, faith, love, and peace. *It is so distressing to see so much evil and hatred in all its diverse forms!* And though there will always be evil in this world of darkness, we still must overcome evil with good. Remember He Who is in us is greater than he that is in the world (1 John 4:4).

CONCLUSION:

Our Lord wants us to walk on a higher plain than the world. Romans 12:17-21 is very clear about how we must conduct ourselves in the face of evil or mistreatment. God expects no less of His children. It doesn't matter how others (non-believers) respond to evil: what God says to do is right. The Lord expects us to not repay evil for evil. Instead, He wants us to live peaceably with others and do that which is good for the wellbeing of the other (1 Thes. 5:15).

God commands us to be at peace with others (Rom. 14:19; Heb. 12:14). He commands us to be peacemakers. That means we must take the initiative toward reconciliation with others, those who offend us (Matt. 18:15).

Jesus says that if we only love those who love us and do good things for us, it will do us no good. Jesus wants us to be the Light of this world and be different than them. He commands us not just to love those who love us but also love our enemies. He wants us to do good even to those who hate us, don't like us, and don't appreciate us. Jesus commands that we do good to all men and bless those who curse us. He even wants us to pray for those who mistreat and abuse us. Those who treat us with cruelty. Indeed, it is not easy, but we must do it if we want to go to heaven and be with Him. He wants us to apply the golden rule to everyone.

> "So whatever you wish that others would do to you, do also to them, for this is the Law and the Prophets" (Matthew 7:12).

Since our heavenly Father has been loving, kind, and merciful to us, He expects us to do the same thing for others. He wants us to do to others as we would have them do to us. God's kindness and mercy must lead us to be kind and merciful to others. Many have heard of the golden rule, of doing to others as we would have them do to us. Yet it is rarely put into practice. Think for a moment what our world would be if everyone around us did for others what they would want others to do for them. *Can you picture in your mind what this world would look like? It would be amazing! Don't you think? How radically different this world of ours would be if everyone were to follow just this command given by our Lord Jesus! So why don't we do it? Why doesn't everyone practice it?* You may rest assured it would change all of us. *But the problem is we are just too selfish and self-centered!* We don't care and we refuse to think of others, but only of ourselves. *Why?* Simply because we are self-consumed. We do not want to think about others but only of ourselves and how others affect us. *Amazing!*

You see, when we think only about ourselves, we hurt others. Our culture is unable to see this. *Oh, how wonderful it would be to do for others as we would want them to do for us!* There would be an end to the hurt that others inflict on us and of course on everyone else. And though most everyone knows to do to others as we would have them do to us, yet no one practices this fundamental principle. *Why not?* Because it is not rooted in our way of reasoning. *Why should I do for others as I would want them to do for me?* The common alternative is for us to selfishly manipulate others to get out of them what we want. How often do we try this tactic! We do something expecting kindness in return. But when that kindness is not reciprocated, we immediately get angry and try to hurt the other person. *It is just sad!* This is the reason why marriages experience trouble. They use the same selfish manipulation instead of being selfless, giving what is needed to the other person.

God's kindness and steadfast love must motivate us to love others. It is foolish to do for others so they will do for us. *That is not what Jesus taught!* Jesus' command must compel us to deal with others by beginning with ourselves. It means that we must not determine how to treat others by looking at them, asking if they deserve it. Rather, we start with ourselves and ask what would we want and need and do for the other person. Jesus wants us to treat others graciously.

"For this is the Law and the Prophets."

This is the very heart of the Law and the Prophets. This command is the heart of the kingdom and the very heart of God. It is precisely what the Law of Moses and the prophets were trying to teach and preach to the people (God said, *"Love your neighbor as yourself"* in Leviticus 19:18). It has always been God's message. Now the cross amplifies this message in our hearts. Through Jesus' cross, God draws us to Him. We can approach His mighty throne to ask of Him, expecting to receive because He is a loving, heavenly Father. *It is beautiful beyond words!* He is the powerful God who gives good gifts to His children. *So, now let us do the same!* Let us give good gifts (blessings) to others. Let us change this world of darkness by being the light. Let us do for others what we would want them to do for us. *Let this sink deeply into your hearts!*

God's love compels us to overcome our enemies and love them. We are called to display God's love to others. In all circumstances, we are commanded by our Lord to treat others the same way that we want them to treat us. Whether they are our friends or our enemies. I am aware that it is much easier to love those who love us and do good to us. But it takes a lot of courage and strength along with humility to love those who hate us and be good to them. Nevertheless, God's children are ruled by a higher standard and we must shine our light amid those who desire to do evil, mistreat us, and afflict us.

Those who do not love God do not know God, for God is love (1 John 8). Hating those who mistreat and abuse us will rob us of our joy and happiness. It will make us miserable, for hate and misery dwell in the same hearts. You see, heaven is not for haters. It is for those who walk in love and follow in the footsteps of Jesus. Thus, let us pursue the way of love, not hatred. God's faithful children must overflow with the fruits of the Spirit: love, joy, peace, patience, kindness, goodness, gentleness, faithfulness, and self-control.

The Lord commands us to deny ourselves, take up our cross, and follow Him. We must empty ourselves of the desires of the flesh that resist doing the will of God. Pride is often the root of problems among us. It causes conflict with no way out. *There is no room for the proud heart in the kingdom of heaven!* The kingdom of Christ is only for the poor in spirit who will humbly bow before Him and say, *"I am only an unprofitable or unworthy servant, for I have done that which is my duty (Luke 17:7). Your will be done in me."* The contentious desires of our hearts cause nothing but conflicts, hatred, malice, arguing, bitterness, divisions, and strife. They are evil and foolish (James 4:1-3). Our duty before God is to live peaceably with all men.

He does not want us to repay evil for evil but do that which is honorable in His sight and in the sight of all men (Rom. 12:17-18). *I don't see any other way to heaven!*

We must treat all people, even our enemies, with righteousness, respect, and dignity. We must not let our carnal emotions defeat the Spirit of Christ living in us. It will bring reproach on us and His kingdom of righteousness. *So, we must choose to love our enemies, for this pleases our Father in heaven!* (Matt. 5:44).

Therefore, our faith must rise above our flesh (Luke 6:31-35). We must fight against the wiles of the devil (Eph. 6:10-13) that we not be overcome by evil but rather overcome evil with good. As soldiers of Christ, we must put on the whole armor of God to fight the enemy and live a life of godliness and good works (Matt. 5:16). Moreover, we must teach and live that righteous path of life. The only way to overcome evil in this world is by living a righteous life. God demands that we do right, even in the face of so much evil and mistreatment.

May God help us to put these principles of righteousness into practice in our lives, that we may live peaceably with all men and not cause anyone to stumble, for this pleases our Father in heaven.

Overcoming Discouragement and Disappointment

"Therefore encourage one another and build each other up as you are already doing... And we exhort you, brothers: warn those who are irresponsible, comfort the discouraged, help the weak, be patient with everyone." 1 Thessalonians 5:11-14

Discouragement is like a brick wall. It stops the best of us in midstride at the moment of doing wonderful things. The Lord shows us the secrets of success over this darkness. He has raised up great men to show us how they faced their own disappointments, got back on their feet, and returned to active duty. There is too much to do and too little time to do it for us to waste our time looking back. Let us study together God's recommendations to His saints who fall into disillusionment and inaction.

We all get discouraged sometimes. Disappointments are inevitable in our life. No Christian is exempt from the dark clouds in their lives. They can debilitate us in our walk with the Lord. Great men of God like David, Job, Jeremiah, Elijah, and even Jesus experienced discouragement in their lives. It can manifest in many ways and be caused by many things. The way we view and respond to disappointments will determine how we press on and persevere with joy. God's Grace equips us with all that we need to respond adequately. Disappointment is often the result of our expectations. We seem to have no choice or control.

According to Webster's dictionary, the word discouragement means deprivation of confidence, hope, or spirit. Its antonyms are encouragement, edification, and exhortation. *How can one be deprived of confidence, hope, or spirit?* The answer to this question will enable us to understand how to defeat discouragement.

A person may be discouraged because of sin and Satan's influence in his life (Matt. 13:39; Acts 10:38). You see, sin causes us to feel guilty and be discouraged for doing such things (Romans 3:19). This is God's way of helping us deal with sin and pursue the right course of action. Sadly, many don't take the appropriate course when it comes to their sinful lifestyle. They choose to ease their conscience through psychotherapy or psychology methods, which often fail to do the right thing. They need to confront and eliminate their sinful behavior. These psychotherapies can temporarily help to deal with discouragement but eventually cannot provide the right solution (Isaiah 5:20). The good news is that they can repent and accept God's standards for behavior and have a much happier life (Acts 26:18-20; Hebrews 10:22).

1. Some become discouraged when their coping mechanisms are not strong enough to support the demands of life.
2. Others lose their focus on what's important in their life (the kingdom of God and His principles of righteousness).
3. Some refuse to go on because they feel robbed of life's meaning.
4. Parents can become discouraged because of constant worry over their children.
5. Illness can be another source of anxiety as well as financial insecurity.

6. As Elijah said, "It is enough." I will be discussing him later in my study.
7. Some choose to abandon the Lord and pursue false religion or even return to the world.
8. *Many just give up and quit!*

Truly, disappointments can cause many unwelcome and harmful emotions in us and in those around us: anger, unforgiveness, frustration, bitterness, etc. It can also cause us to feel hopeless, helpless, weary, depressed, lacking enthusiasm, pessimistic, bored, and half-hearted. Discouragement affects our worship to God since we lack enthusiasm or interest. Our worship becomes duty. Our light becomes darkness. In a few words, there is not much of the Spirit of God in times of discouragement. It is then that we must approach God's throne for help. Discouragement is one of the most powerful weapons in Satan's arsenal.

> *"Your eye is the lamp of your body.* **When your eye is healthy, your whole body is full of light, but when it is bad, your body is full of darkness.** *Therefore be careful lest the light in you be darkness. If then your whole body is full of light, having no part dark, it will be* **wholly bright, as when a lamp with its rays gives you light."** (Luke 11:34-46)

Indeed, life is hard. We are constantly reminded of disasters, tragedies, heartaches, the failing economy, the decline of moral principles, lawlessness, family struggles, etc. These troublesome times make us pessimistic rather than optimistic. Many fixate on things that are tragic and negative. We must learn to see the big picture and be able to be of good cheer. No matter how bad things might appear, we Christians know that God loves us and will be there for us in our time of need. I can assure you that it will lift you up during your difficult times if you believe this with all your heart. But you must focus on God Almighty and what He can do for you. We Christians must learn to rejoice always because we have the hope of heaven as our home. Our God is there to strengthen us in our time of need. So, let us draw nearer to God in prayer, addressing all our worries, fears, pessimism, and problems to Him alone. I assure you that He will answer our prayers according to His kindness and mercy.

I. LEADING CAUSES OF DISCOURAGEMENT:

The Heart is Still in the World:

For some, the world tempts them and weighs them down with its music, entertainment, media, coworkers, peer pressure, and many other sinful things that come our way to make us stumble. The world (those who live according to the flesh) sets *"their minds on the things of the flesh"* (Romans 8:5). Undoubtedly, the battle between the flesh and the spirit can cause discouragement since the flesh seems to be always winning. Weaknesses such as alcohol, drugs, immorality, dishonesty, apathy, and laziness can be the cause of discouragement.

Pressure to Conform:

Many cannot resist peer pressure. They talk, think, and act like the world. They refuse to be different. They want to be accepted, included, and belong. They get discouraged when they feel left out, ignored, and overlooked. They claim, *"but everyone does it."* They forget why Christians must not do it! (Romans 12:1; 1 Peter 4:4; Luke 6:23)

Double-Mindedness:

The world overwhelms many and moves on them. They neglect to purify their hearts (James 4:8). Their heart is divided. Their loyalty is divided, causing great discouragement and unhappiness. Many return to the old man of sinful habits when they become discouraged. They behave in the same way the Israelites did when they left Egypt (Numbers 21:4; 14:3). They serve two masters (Matt. 6:24).

Opposition, Persecutions, Criticism, and an Antagonist Environment: Standing Alone

Some get discouraged when the vast majority (even Christians) opposes, excludes, and persecutes them for standing for God and Christ. So few faithful followers stand with them through difficult times. This can be overwhelming and discouraging, but it should not keep us from taking a stand. They are a minority who take a stand for Christ and God (God's highest standards of morality and purity). They get discouraged when, more and more, our society puts pressure on them because they will not conform to this world.

Indeed, in our times, most choose to follow their own path. Their hearts are their only guide. This leads them to reject God and His principles of righteousness as their guide. Likewise, we live in a world of materialism, secularism, skepticism, pessimism, degeneracy, and hypocrisy. There is often very little encouragement for the furthering of the Gospel. In the days of Jesus, the apostles, and the early church, this was also a problem. Remember that both Jews and Gentiles were exceedingly sinful (Romans 1:18-32; 2:1,17-24;3:9-10; Eph. 2:1-3). Their people were ignorant and vile. The rulers were bigoted and politically motivated. Their priests were oppressive and unmerciful. Not to mention, it was the skepticism, traditionalism, and hypocrisy that reigned. Yet amidst such terrible, troublesome, and abominable conditions, Jesus and the apostles began and continued their work. They refused to be discouraged in their efforts. Persecutions are certain to those who desire to live godly in Christ (2 Timothy 3:12). And though each Christian must be aware of this fact, they still must stand for Christ amid a perverse generation and persuade others to come to the obedience of the Gospel.

Fear:

Sadly, many are persuaded to back off a little by their friends or family. They are afraid to be excluded, rejected, and left out because of their faith and convictions. When Jesus walked this earth, many feared that they would be excluded by others and would not confess Him, despite the irrefutable evidence. Some of the rulers would not confess Him for the same reason (John 12:42-43). Today, many do not confess Christ because of a lack of faith in God (Deut. 31:6; Deut. 1:21, 28; 20; 1 Samuel 17:32; Mark 6:49-50).

Spiritual Matters:

Some get discouraged when their convictions for the Truth cause them to be in conflict with relatives or friends. Others get discouraged because of the hypocrisy, carnality, or apostasy of preachers, elders, or other influential Christians. Spiritual discouragement may result from the church's failure to further the Gospel, convert the lost, and edify the members. Faithfulness to God and His Word is not enough guarantee for one not to become discouraged. In fact, the more a Christian is involved in the Lord's work (locally), the greater the possibilities of getting discouraged. So often, those who strive to live godly and teach God's Truth are faced with many discouragements. *What faithful Christian, teacher, and preacher has not come face to face at one time or another with the question, 'What's the use?'" — when his efforts to live godly and teach others seem to accomplish nothing and be unappreciated?*

We must remember that many before us have traveled that same road of discouragement and disappointment. Think of Jeremiah, who encountered extraordinary disappointments and discouragements (Jer. 9:2). Yet, he stood tall and was faithful to God even to the last. Amid opposition, trials, and weary years, he longed to leave. Jesus and the apostles are also examples of those who faced discouragements. There is no sin in feeling discouraged at times. And while one might feel he is losing courage and confidence, it may be because of real problems. The real and hopeless issues of life are too broad to pretend that nothing is ever bad for heartaches and tears.

Physical Affliction:

Fatigue, loss of sleep, illness, and even some medicines can cause us to feel discouraged. The truth is that we must learn to focus on what we have, what we can do instead of focusing on what we cannot do (2 Cor. 4:16, 12:7-12; Prov. 18:14). Paul said, *"there was given me a thorn in the flesh, a messenger of Satan to torment me—to keep me from exalting myself! Concerning this I implored the Lord three times that it might leave me. And He has said to me, 'My grace is sufficient for you, for power is perfected in weakness'"* (2 Cor. 12:7-9). *What was Paul's conclusion? "Therefore I am well content with weaknesses, with insults, with distresses, with persecutions, with difficulties, for Christ's sake; for when I am weak, then I am strong."* So, *"tribulation brings about perseverance;4 and perseverance, proven character; and proven character, hope"* (Romans 5:3-4).

Unsolved Problems:

Some refuse to find the solution for every problem through the Scriptures. They reject the Scriptural solution. They would rather fight, sue, and go to court, divorce, or divide the church. Few want to do things God's way (the Scriptural solution). For example, if a brother has something against you (Matt. 5:23-24), go to him (Matt. 18:15). He sins against you, go to him. This is the Lord's way, the right way.

> *"All Scripture is inspired by God and profitable for teaching, for reproof, for correction, for training in righteousness; so that the man of God may be adequate, equipped for every good work."* (2 Tim. 3:16-17)

All our problems in the home, in the church, and in the world around us, must be resolved with the Scriptures. Some prefer not to solve their problems and instead are contentious troublemakers, stirring up controversy and causing misery. They complain saying, *"They hurt my feelings," "they mistreated me,"* or *"they were very unfair to me."* But at the same time, they don't seek the solution to their problem, as stated in Matthew 5:23-24; 18:15-17. Instead, they choose to get discouraged and quit. The Bible has the solution to all of life's problems.

Decreased Interest Because of The Perception of Failure:

When things are going our way (interest and enthusiasm are high and growing), we feel elated and very happy. But when our expectations are not met, our interest and enthusiasm lags and decreases. Some will ask, *"what's the use?"* They don't realize that Jesus, the Son of God, experienced discouragement and disappointment because of the lack of interest shown by those He was teaching. When He began His ministry, large crowds followed Him, but they considered His teachings as being *"too hard,"* so they abandoned Him and lost interest. Only a handful of His hearers remained at the end of His three years of ministry. Our Lord did not quit or allow His discouragement to control Him. Instead, He continued His ministry to bring it to fruition because He loved the souls of mankind. He knew one soul was worth more than all the riches of this world (Matt. 16:26).

Many get discouraged when their personal work is not fruitful, and no one seems to be interested.

- *Is it our fault, perhaps?*
- *Do you continue in your studies more eagerly to be a more effective teacher, perhaps?*
- *Do you have the proper attitude when you approach your hearers?*
- *Do you try your best to work at it?*

- *Or do you just quit and give up altogether?*

Remember that our work in the Lord is never in vain (1 Cor. 15:58), and we must do it with all long-suffering, in season and out of season (1 Timothy 4:2). Likewise, keep in mind that God is the one who gives the increase, though you're planting the seed (1 Cor. 3:6). We cannot force the seed to sprout. *Why not simply sow the seed, cultivate, and water it to grow effectively?* God's Word never returns to Him void. It will always accomplish what God wants it to be (Isa. 55:11). So, let us not grow weary because *"in due time we will reap"* (Gal. 6:9).

Cares of This Life:

> "But watch yourselves lest your hearts be **weighed down** with dissipation and drunkenness and **cares of this life**, and that day come upon you suddenly like a trap." (Luke 21:34)

Jesus replaced the cares of this life, dissipation (carousing) and drunkenness! All the worries of this life: materialism, debt, ambitions, evil desire can destroy us (1 Timothy 6:9). In other words, our lifestyle: wanting more and more and better and better and never satisfied with what we have. We tend to put our personal desires before the Truth (John 11:47-50; Matt. 12:22-24). *Why not get busy in the Lord's business, spreading the Gospel, helping others? Think about that!*

II. GREAT MEN OF GOD WHO HAD TO OVERCOME DISCOURAGEMENT:

Consider some great examples of discouragement and disappointment that some great men of God had to endure and let us see what we can learn from them.

Joseph:

Joseph's discouragement and disappointment could have brought about very real emotions. Discouragement affects the heart (Proverbs 13:12). It can result in bitterness, a hardness of heart, callousness, and an unforgiving spirit.

In Genesis 42:21, we read of Joseph's anguish of heart. His soul was anguished. Throughout the Scriptures, we read of anguished souls. Jesus was the most excellent example, as He prepared to die on the cross for our sins. And though we can trust God amid our discouragements and disappointments, that does not prevent us from experiencing anguish.

Throughout Joseph's disappointments, he never complained. *That is remarkable!* He was a man of quiet and mature character. He trusted in God, knowing that He was in control. We must have this heart when we are discouraged and disappointed. We must realize that our disappointments serve a purpose in our lives.

Though Joseph experienced profound disappointment in his relationship with his brothers, he focused on honoring God in every circumstance of his life (Genesis 39:2-3; 39:21-23). In Genesis 39:6-13, Joseph:

1. Resisted the temptations of Potiphar's wife because he was unwilling to sin against God.
2. He trusted in God even though he was beaten with disappointment.
3. He trusted God at every turn.
4. Joseph chose not to worry about that which he could not control.
5. Though he experienced disappointment, he didn't become absorbed with life's worries: those things that were beyond his control.

6. He acknowledged that no matter what might happen, God was going to be glorified through him.
7. He likewise bloomed in every situation. He chose to bloom where he was planted. Even in prison, he trusted in God in the hope that *"all things work together for good to those who love God"* (Romans 8:28).

You see, Joseph's disappointments carried out God's providential plan to save both him and his family. God used disappointment to change Joseph's character. Remember Joseph's brothers did not appreciate his attitude. As a young man, Joseph's conduct was not the best. Remember, he *"tattled"* on his brothers and boasted about his position and dreams. It looks like he lacked humility, wisdom, and sensitivity. You see, pride and insensitivity produce jealousy and hatred in others. And as God looked upon Joseph, He knew he could mold and shape him into a great man and used him in a mighty way. Joseph's disappointments resulted in him becoming humble and sensitive to others. *What is the lesson here?* That we must learn to lose before we can win. We must trust in God no matter our disappointments. We must stay on the right course and allow God to work in our lives. We must learn to train ourselves to rejoice when we are disappointed and appreciate the disguised blessings that come with it. We must learn not to see our disappointments as disappointments but rather as an opportunity to bloom wherever we are found and to fulfill God's will in our lives. We cannot do that without being humble.

God can use disappointments to shape our character but also to change our circumstances. Joseph's events in life led him in the right direction, into the arms of God. God saved many lives by using Joseph, a man who trusted in God through many disappointments.

Moses:

Moses was overwhelmed and discouraged because he had been given great responsibility for God's people. All they wanted to do was complain. *Moses was at his wit's end!* He was so discouraged at one point that he wanted God to end his life if nothing changed (Numbers 11:11).

Some in Moses' shoes would have given up and walked away or taken their own life. *But Moses did not do this!* He instead went to God in prayer when he felt overwhelmed (Numbers 11:16). We can rest assured that if we pray to God, He will provide relief. In Moses' case, God allowed 70 men to share Moses' responsibility. We must learn to share some of the responsibilities with others when we feel overwhelmed and when there is more than we can handle.

David:

When David was still a young man (a shepherd), the army of Israel was afraid. He came to the battlefield, not as a participant, but to visit his brothers and bring a report to his father. While he was there, he heard the mockery and the insults of Goliath. He began to wonder why no one was answering. Sadly, the entire army was acting cowardly (1 Samuel 17:11, 24). *But David was not afraid!* He dared to go after this giant alone. He trusted in God rather than his military strength or tactics (1 Samuel 17:37, 45-46). *And though he used his sling, he still trusted in God!*

Today we need to remember that God is with us! So, when we feel discouraged, let us not forget that we are not standing alone. God is with us as He has promised it (Heb. 13:5). *He will never leave us!* With God, there is no need to fear since we are standing with Him (Romans 8:31, 35-39). So, let us not be discouraged or lose heart. Let us stand with courage, knowing that God is with us as He was with David. *Through Him, we will gain victory!*

Joshua:

When Joshua was fighting against the small city of Ai, he expected an easy win. To his surprise, it did not happen. He starts blaming God for their defeat. *Does that sound familiar when we are disappointed and discouraged because things go wrong?* We refuse to acknowledge there is something else to blame. Joshua found this out when he prayed to God. God told him the real problem (Joshua 7:10-12). *So what kept them from defeating Ai? Sin!* As soon as they took care of their sin, they were able to defeat Ai. So, let us not blame God when troubling times strike us. Instead, let us acknowledge that God is there to help us succeed so that we may rejoice in Him. Sin in our life is often the cause of our problem, and we must take care of it.

Elijah:

A unique and successful man of God in many ways. He found himself (unexpectedly) floundering in a big well of discouragement. When he killed all the false prophets of Baal, he found himself in trouble. When Jezebel was after him, he felt alone and discouraged (1 Kings 19:4).

His troubles began when a new king, Ahab, ascended to Israel's throne (1 Kings 16:30). This king was a corrupt ruler. He had a wife, Jezebel, who was very wicked. *"Ahab did more to provoke the LORD, the God of Israel, to anger than all the kings of Israel who were before him"* (1 Kings 16:33).

Discouragement often begins when there is a change in the power structure, a change that seems to conflict with our principles of righteousness. Every change in the power structure can result in frustration that one must cope with. Discouragement is in the wind when you feel like you have done your very best, and yet it seems like the world is just passing you by.

While Ahab and Jezebel were on the throne, they made new rules for the kingdom of Israel and its religion, changing everything, even the elders' job. They were murdering all those who stood up to them (Naboth, for example, who wouldn't sell Jezebel his vineyard). Anyone who would stand up to them in God's name would have to have enormous courage. *No half-hearted person would do!*

Elijah was one of the greatest men who ever walked this earth. When Elijah told Ahab and Jezebel that it would not rain in Israel until they repented of their wicked ways, Ahab didn't like it, especially when it came true. Jezebel put a price on the prophet's head. Elijah hid and was fed at first by ravens in the wilderness. Then he was hosted in the home of a poor widow in Zarephath.

After three years in the wilderness, Elijah was told by God to show himself one more time to Ahab so that rain could come to the parched land of Israel. Ahab accused Elijah of bringing all this trouble upon Israel (1 Kings 18:18). *Isn't it something how defensive people lay blame on others who are trying to find a solution for their problems? Sometimes they are covering up their sin!* They unjustly, and unfairly accuse us all because one dares to tell it like it is. *That in itself is plenty cause for discouragement and disappointment!*

When Elijah went to the people, he did not beat around the bush. He said, *"How long will you go limping between two different opinions? If the Lord is God, follow him; but if Baal, then follow him."* And the people did not answer him a word (1 Kings 18:21). *There is no political double talk here!* He simply said: *we have been compromising our morals long enough.*

In response to Elijah's demand, the people did not say a word. Maybe they were afraid. Perhaps they believed their opinions did not count since they had been silenced for so long. Sadly, this pattern is seen in the church at times. Those often in authority silence members so that they lose their voices. When they feel silenced and with no hope for change, they feel helpless and become discouraged.

How do you suppose Elijah felt when he asked the assembled congregation for a decision, and all he got was silence? When he asked for action and all he got were blank stares? Whatever his re-action was, it did not stop him (1 Kings 18:22). Elijah proposed a contest: he set up two altars on Mount Carmel, two sacrificial bulls, and wood for two fires. He let each group perform their rituals but without lifting a match. *Let's see whose altar the true and living God chooses to set aflame!*

The fire of the LORD fell upon Elijah's altar and consumed the sacrifice, the wood, and everything. The people fell on their faces and worshiped God. The crowd then fell on the 450 false prophets with swords, killing them. You see, it was a success for Elijah. The people came around, and shortly it begins to rain in the land after a 3-year drought.

Elijah runs away to Beersheba and asks to die when he should have been rejoicing as the faithful prophet he was. *He brought the people of Israel back to God! So what does he do instead?* He sat under a tree and deeply discouraged, said, *"It is enough, O Lord, Take my life... !"*

He ran away when Ahab told Jezebel about the killing of her false priests. She sent a message to Elijah, stating that he would be killed. But think for a moment. There was a price on his head for the previous three years that did not break his spirit. *So, what is the difference now?*

First, Elijah had gone through some traumatic events.

1. He stood up to the King, face to face, making his case clearly.
2. He gathered the people and presented the case before them.
3. He challenged them to claim their identity and dignity as followers of the true and living God.
4. And after all was said and done, he got no response for his efforts.

I am sure Elijah's feelings were hurting! How many times have you felt like Elijah, thinking you were standing alone with your problems, and no one seemed to care? And though he felt this way, he was not alone because God was right there with him (1 Kings 19:15).

Second, Elijah's other traumatic events:

1. The great contest.
2. The fireball from heaven.
3. The massacre of the priests.

Don't you think that was plenty of trauma to handle? It must be processed and might short circuit our emotions. *Stress plus adrenaline!*

Elijah was overworked and worried and overcome by fear and fatigue. That would be enough to bring on depression and discouragement. *Don't you think? Wait, that's not all!* Elijah seems to have gotten a bit *"stuck on himself"* too. He said, *"I have been very jealous for the Lord, the God of hosts. For the people of Israel have forsaken your covenant, thrown down your altars, and killed your prophets with the sword, and I, even I only, am left, and they seek my life, to take it away"* (1 Kings 19:14). *Me, me, all alone, only me!*

The truth is, he was not alone. God was with him. It was evident to everyone except for Elijah himself. Furthermore, there were 100 others hidden in the caves of Samaria thanks to Obadiah, an officer of high rank in the court of Ahab (1 Kings 18:3). Toward the end of chapter 19, we find out that God knew of 7,000 others that shared His cause: *"Yet I will leave seven thousand in Israel, all the knees that have not bowed to Baal, and every mouth that has not kissed him"* (1 Kings 19:18). *Isn't that remarkable!*

Elijah had miscalculated big time when he thought he was the only faithful one left. He was 7,000 times mistaken. Never deceive yourself, believing you are doing all on your own. It gets lonely, standing up for righteousness. When God is working along with us, we've got all the help we need. *And though His help is invisible, you can rest assured that His help is real!* Let us learn from Elijah to take it one day at a time, keep pressing on, stay involved in the Lord's work, even when things seem too hard. It is not the right moment to run away when righteousness is at stake. Let us join the fabric of the faithful, and don't try to do it all on your own. You don't have to. We are in this together. We are part of God's kingdom.

So, let's not allow pessimism and discouragement to defeat us. I know it is tempting to fall prey to discouragement and pessimism like Elijah did. It is easy to be a pessimist rather than an optimist in a culture full of so much darkness and unbelief. Likewise, it is easier to feel depressed, discouraged, and pessimistic when divisiveness, apathy, indifference, compromise with sin, or religious error seem to reign. Modern mass media is not off the hook either. They appear to be focused on the despicable, glorifying all kinds of lawlessness, belittling, and ridiculing the righteous. Let us not run away in fear like Elijah, feeling sorry for ourselves. Instead, let us be courageous, trusting in our God, and getting busy in His vineyard.

Even though many things are not what they must be, there is still hope in the Lord and His Gospel to change and mold the hearts of men. There are still many precious and faithful souls who have not bowed down to Baal (the wickedness of the world). Let this be our motivator when we are tempted to be discouraged and be a pessimist. Perhaps this was a crash course for Elijah and us to rid us of discouragement and disappointment. Elijah needed to listen to that *"still, small voice"* to get his life back on track. Therefore, let us take courage and take a stand and take it one day at a time without running away; leaving some empty spaces in our day, for the Lord's *"still, small voice"* of wise counsel, to give us a word of encouragement that we might not drown in self-pity, but continue living for God in all holiness and righteousness.

Good cheer is something we must exercise and train ourselves in. If we perish for serving God, then so be it. But let us never surrender to discouragement or depression over negative circumstances that are beyond our control. *Remember, we are not alone, and all is not lost!*

Jeremiah:

Jeremiah was well acquainted with discouragement and sorrow in his life. He is known as the *"weeping prophet."* He was given the responsibility of preaching to God's people just before the Babylonian invasion. His message of repentance and God's judgment upon them was not well received by God's people. Despite his pleas and cries for their repentance, they did not turn from their wicked ways.

The prophet Jeremiah was overwhelmed with discouragement and despair. He began to curse the day he was born and wondered why he did not die before birth inside the womb. He said, *"Why did I ever come forth from the womb to look on trouble and sorrow so that my days have been spent in shame?"* (Jeremiah 20:18). *Do you think this is an exaggeration? Not at all!* We read in chapter 20 that the chief officer had him beaten (the Law allowed 40 lashes) then placed him in stocks.

Possibly, he was tortured with such a device that caused his body to bend double.

Imagine this happening after he was beaten! Why did he suffer this? Was he guilty of any crime? Absolutely not! He had simply declared the Word of God. He did what was right, but in return, he received punishment. His once-trusted friends mocked him, throwing his own words back at him, calling him the name that God by prophecy had given to Pashur, the priest, Magor-Missabib, meaning *"terror on every side." That hurt him, no?* His prayers were full of loneliness and complaints: *"O LORD, Thou hast deceived me and I was deceived; Thou hast overcome me and prevailed. I have become a laughingstock all day long; everyone mocks me.... for me the word of the LORD has resulted in reproach and derision all day long"* (Jeremiah 20:7-8).

His constant loneliness and rejection caused him to be discouraged. Jeremiah was emotionally spent, even to the point of doubting God (Jeremiah 15:18), but God was not done with him. He felt alone, useless, and discouraged, lacking faith (Jeremiah 15:19).

From his life, we can find comfort in knowing that even great prophets of God, like Jeremiah, experienced rejection, discouragement, and disappointment as they walked with the God. This is a normal part of growing spiritually.

We can surely see a discouraged man in despair and anguish. *Have you ever felt this way when you were tried, tested and low, feeling as low as you can get, sunk in the mud?* Yet Jeremiah obeyed because of his great faith, humbleness, compassion, courage, and perseverance. He remained faithful even when he stood alone (like Noah, Joseph, Daniel, and many others) amid so much turmoil. *He rose above discouragement!*

Paul:

Paul, who always said to rejoice (Philippians 4:4), must have been discouraged when he said he had *"become the scum of the world, the dregs of all things"* (1 Cor. 4:13). Jesus told Paul to take courage when he was in prison. *"But on the night immediately following, the Lord stood at his side and said, 'Take courage; for as you have solemnly witnessed to My cause at Jerusalem, so you must witness at Rome also'"* (Acts 23:11).

He learned to see the positive side of everything, all the good things that could come from imprisonment (Philippians 1:12). Paul trusted in God despite his antagonistic environment and the circumstances he found himself in. He knew God was with him (Acts 27:25). Paul always knew how to listen to the voice of God (Acts 27:23, 24). Indeed, he received a lot of encouragement to keep his spirits up. He trusted in the Word of God that helped him to be encouraged (Acts 27:33-36).

III. WHAT NOT TO DO WHEN DISCOURAGED AND DISAPPOINTED:

Don't Quit Attending Church:

Some neglect to attend all the meetings of the church. They say, *"I am going to stop coming only for a time to reexamine my life, and then I will be back."* But Hebrews 10:25 says, *"not neglecting to meet together, as is the habit of some, but encouraging one another…"* *"On the first day of the week, when we were gathered together to break bread"* (Acts 20:7).

They don't realize that they are forsaking the assembly altogether, they are failing to participate in the Lord's Supper, and failing to contribute (1 Corinthians 16:2). *Have you ever noticed how some make up the contribution they didn't give for the time they neglected to come?* Sometimes it has been for two or more years. Likewise, they neglect to sing and worship God in songs, *"teaching and exhorting each other"* (Ephesians 5:19). Since they are not nurturing their soul with the Word of God, their souls grow weaker for lack of nourishment.

Don't Blame Others:

Why not be honest and blame ourselves? Because the real problem lies within us! It is our fault for our loss of interest and faith. *"You are the man!"* (2 Samuel 12:7). Blaming others is a very common tactic many use to cope with discouragement and disappointment. Others blame God for everything, even their discouragement, apathy, and disappointment. In the Bible, we have many examples of great men who underwent disappointments and got discouraged but never blamed God. One of them is Job. Blaming others sometimes works (Acts 6:1-5) but worsens the circumstances most of the time (2 Kings 6:30-31).

For their discouragement, they blame someone who:

1. Doesn't greet them.
2. Didn't visit them when they were supposed to.
3. Hurt their feelings.
4. Didn't care about them,
5. Did not miss them when they didn't come.
6. Preached an offensive sermon.
7. Is too boring (preachers, song leaders, Bible class teachers), and
8. Does not please them.

The tragic thing is that they plunge back into the world. Their attitude is negative. They say, "What's the use?" "I might as well eat, drink and be merry." The danger with this negative attitude of heart is that it will be much harder for them to repent and return to the Lord. God sees it as *"The dog returns to its own vomit, and the sow, after washing herself, returns to wallow in the mire."* (2 Peter 2:22)

IV. WHAT TO DO WHEN DISCOURAGED AND DISAPPOINTED:

Discouragement and disappointment demand our immediate attention. *"Neither God nor man can use a discouraged person."* Indeed, this is a true statement. Discouragement and disappointment affect our faith and renders us unprofitable. It can infect others. It is one of the weapons in Satan's arsenal. He will try at all costs to deceive us and devour us if we give him the opportunity and open the door for him (2 Cor. 2:11). So we must understand that discouragement and disappointment are one of his devices, but if we take action before it is too late, we can have victory. We cannot allow him to drag us down.

In times of discouragement, God will be there to help us. But we must determine not to remain discouraged or disappointed. Consider what to do when dealing with discouragement and the lack of encouragement.

Determine Not to Remain Discouraged:

We must determine not to stay down. We must use mental discipline. The Bible speaks a lot of physical discipline and self-control. It also encourages us to use mental discipline (Proverbs 23:7; 2 Cor. 10:5). So we must determine not to be discouraged. God has given us His will and His Word to help us overcome discouragement and disappointment.

Insist on Finding the Good in Every Circumstance:

This is crucial to defeating discouragement. David said, *"It is good for me that I was afflicted, that I might learn your* statutes" (Psalm 119:7). Sometimes affliction in our life causes us to turn our hearts back to the Word of God.

Set Realistic Goals:

Setting achievable goals helps us deal with discouragement and disappointment. Often, those who become discouraged and disappointed find out that they have set their goals so high that they will never reach them. On the other hand, if we set our goals too low, knowing in our heart, we can do more, discouragement and disappointment may still set it in. So let's not set our goals too high or too low. God knows our hearts and abilities, and He can make us become more than we can imagine. One passage of Scripture that might help us to set realistic goals is found in Matt. 25. We read about a five talent man, a two talent man, and one talent man. All three had abilities. Let us follow Him both diligently and faithfully and become more excellent servants of God. This should help us and comfort us in setting realistic goals that we can achieve. So if we use our abilities in the Lord's service, this will bless us and bring comfort to us (Mark 14:3).

Cultivating a Positive Outlook on Life Helps Us with Discouragement:

Some Christians' outlook on life is so pessimist, gloom, and doom that they allow themselves to feel discouraged and disappointed all the time. They forget to acknowledge that they are serving a living God who is all-knowing, all-powerful. He has promised us He will make all things work together for our good. *So how in the world can a Christian go around with a pessimist attitude?!* As children of God, we must be more optimistic. Our outlook determines our outcome.

Observe God's Dealings with His Children and Be Thankful:

That is, count your many blessings and see what the Lord has done for you. When we observe how God has dealt with us, it should encourage us. When we think about how much mercy and love God has bestowed on us, it must help us not be discouraged and lose heart. God stands on all His promises, and He will not forsake us (Psalm 37:25, John 10:29). So observing how God has never failed us should help us to overcome discouragement in our life.

Use Difficult Times to Strengthen Your Faith:

It is a fact that we all will have difficult times in our life. We will use them to destroy or weaken our faith, or on the other hand, they will strengthen our faith. Think of Paul and Job, who faced difficult times throughout their lives but did not let their difficulties overwhelm them (Job 14:1; 2 Tim. 2:3). Therefore, as soldiers of Christ is His army, let us endure hardship, learn, and grow from them, grow in our faith.

Resist the Devil:

As I said earlier, discouragement and disappointment are one of Satan's wiles. So let us learn to resist him (James 4:7; 1 Peter 5:9). We must resist Satan by being steadfast in our faith. Through God's Word, we have the assurance that if we resist the devil in whatever he throws at us, he will flee from us. It should encourage us to know that our brethren are experiencing the same difficulties we are, and do not allow Satan to discourage them. If they can overcome their discouragement, we can too.

Avoid Self-Pity at All Cost:

This is where we get into trouble so many times. We must understand that discouragement and disappointment are universal and that our brethren have experienced the same things that we are (1 Peter 5:9). So when you start thinking and feeling sorry for yourself, thinking you have it so bad, think of what our Lord Jesus had to endure for you and me on this earth, all of His sufferings (Hebrews 12:1).

Get Involved in The Lord's Work So That You Can Overcome Discouragement:

It is no surprise that Satan overwhelms us at times, simply because we are too stagnant and idle, making it easier for him to discourage us. Get involved in His work and be about His business, and don't be idle. The more work we do for God, the more focused we will be on Him, and the fewer times we will be discouraged (Acts 26:20).

Encourage Others:

This is another good way to defeat discouragement. *It helps a lot!* Encouragement is the best weapon to combat discouragement. So encourage one another and learn to be more like Barnabas. He was a great encourager to the apostles. His name literally means son of encouragement (Acts 4:36). Another great example is Timothy (1 Thess. 3:1-3). He encouraged the Thessalonians tremendously to remain faithful to God through their many afflictions. Thus, let us be encouragers like Timothy and Barnabas.

Make Prayer a Daily Habit:

Surrender yourself to prayers. Let us make prayer a daily habit to overcome discouragement (Luke 18:1). We lose heart when we don't pray the way we must. And that is exactly what discouragement is, losing heart. I assure you that if you pray and study the Word of God when you are discouraged, you will not lose heart. I have noticed this in my life. So pray, pray, and don't faint. Take it to the feet of Jesus. He will rescue you. Remember that Jesus spent a lot of time in prayer, and we should too. In fact, Jesus advised His apostles to do the same.

Escape The Past:

Take heed to what Paul said, *"Brethren, I do not regard my-self as having laid hold of it yet; but one thing I do: forgetting what lies behind and reaching forward to what lies ahead"* (Philippians 3:13).

Paul is urging us not to hang on to the past. We must put our past behind and not allow it to drag us down. Likewise, we must be continually growing and reaching forward to the goal that is set before us, heaven.

As Christians, we must be hungering and thirsting for righteousness always (Matt. 5:6). We live by every Word that proceeds from the mouth of God (Matt. 4:4). We must esteem God's Word more than our earthly needs (Job 23:12). When one is pressing forward,

1. He will devote himself to learning more and more about God's will and ways.
2. He will do his best to follow Christ's footsteps.
3. He will faithfully strive to please God and not him-self.
4. He will have a strong desire for his goal, heaven. Nothing will impede him from this goal.

Therefore, let us always look forward to heaven and keep pressing on to reach it and not allow our past to discourage us and rob us of our goal.

Nurture a Patient Spirit Within Yourself with The Emphasis on Yourself!

As we grow in Christ, we must realize that this is a process that will not happen in 1 or 2 days. It is a lifetime commitment of devotion to the Lord. So don't become discouraged, thinking that you're not growing as fast as you should. Remember that as long as you're striving hard to grow, that is all that matters to God. Thus, try to be patient with yourself and with others as well. It will leave no room for discouragement and disappointment (1 Thess. 5:14; Ezra 10:13).

Take Life One Day at a Time (Matt. 6:34):

Often, we allow ourselves to be discouraged and disappointed because we are constantly thinking about tomorrow. The Bible tells us to redeem the time for the days are evil (Eph. 5:16). We must grasp this to focus on what really matters. Today we have enough problems to distract us, so let us not drag in tomorrow's problems.

Study Your Bible to Find Encouragement (Lam. 3:22; Micah 7:8; 2 Thess. 6:16-17):

It is healthy food for our souls. Have Bible studies in your homes, even if there are no visitors. Go more frequently to Gospel meetings to be edified and be with brethren of the same precious faith. *"From the end of the earth I call to you when my heart is faint. Lead me to the rock that is higher than I"* (Psalm 62:1).

Surround Yourself with Positive and Godly People:

When Job was undergoing moments of grief and loss, his friends offered prayers and comfort. They also tried to convince Job that the reason for his suffering was sin. In their efforts to try to help Job, they ended up pulling him away from God. *Can this be us at times?* The advice of our friends or family may take us further from the Lord. On the other hand, what really helps and edifies us is the company of positive and godly people when we are low or discouraged (2 Cor. 7:6). It is such a blessing to have the company of those who love the Lord and are bound to frequently pray and love the Word of God with all their heart. This is priceless and of great help to the faint-hearted. It can be a well of strength, comfort, and re-freshment to the discouraged and disheartened soul.

CONCLUSION:

Discouragement and disappointment are a reality that every Christian must deal with and embrace. With God's help, we can overcome both. We can choose to mope, groan, and laze around, or we can opt to be positive and seek God for help.

Jesus is our perfect example of conduct and attitudes. We must imitate Him (1 Cor. 11:1). While Jesus was here on earth, He also had to face discouragement but did not give up. He recognized that the key to His circumstances was in Him, not in the obstacles. *And He faced it!* Discouragement is a condition of the mind and not of one's circumstances. Happiness does not depend on our circumstances but on us. Keeping a good spirit is the solution to discouragement. Jesus saw things from God's viewpoint, and that viewpoint is not discouraging. He urged His disciples to have the same perspective. In John 4:35, He told them to *"lift up your eyes."* So, no matter what happens in our lives, everything will turn out positively and well if we are faithful in doing God's will. All things will work out for good to all faithful Christians (Romans 8:28). Jesus kept work-ing when He found obstacles in every direction. He always tried to find the solution to all His obstacles. Nothing was left for Him to do but to die. He went to the cross, willingly and confidently.

Learn to deal with your emotions (anger, resentment, frus-tration, bitterness, hopelessness, and depression). They can cause many unwanted and harmful things. Don't blame others for your discouragement and disappointment. Don't allow room for the spirit of blame in your life. Understand why you are discouraged. Discouragement does not depend on others but us (Phil. 4:11). Learn to see things from God's viewpoint and in light of eternity. *How will it look in view of heaven or hell on Judgment Day?* Remember that we must cast all our anxieties on Him in times of discouragement and disappointment because He cares for us (1 Peter 5:7).

Though things may not turn out the way we have planned or would have wanted them to be, look to Jesus, and follow His example. You may feel so discouraged and disappointed that you want to quit or give up, look to Jesus, and follow His example. Keep doing your best to reach your goal, heaven, and keep doing God's will with all your might. So, pray and pray and do not faint. Pray like Jesus always did. When faced with discouragement and disappointments, pray, and don't give up (1 Thess. 5:17).

Our Lord Jesus will be there in times of discouragement and disappointments to calm us. Take courage, knowing that our God is with us. Even amid discouragement and threats, we can still be examples of holiness and righteousness. So do not despair. Know that our God and our brethren can help us through our difficult times. Do not let discouragement, disappointment, doubt, and worry, pull you away from God. It is very dangerous to let yourself be discouraged because of problems. So, when the world says give up, God whispers, "try it one more time and don't give up, I am with you." *Why not trust in God and pray to Him?* He can see us through anything. He is our Rock that will lift us up when we are down. We can confidently *"pant"* for Him as a deer pants for the cool refreshing water. Therefore, do not be weary in well-doing; for in due season we shall reap if we faint not (Gal. 6:9).

May we rest in the Lord's unfailing love when overtaken by discouragement. May we turn the eyes of our hearts to our tender and loving Savior who does not break the reed that is already bruised. And may we be sustained by God's strength to overcome our distresses.

The following is a beautiful Psalm for the discouraged. God cares and can help us overcome doubt and discouragement. He will give us the strength to overcome our discouragement and disappointments. He will command His lovingkindness on us to heal our hearts.

Why Are You Cast Down, O My Soul?
(Psalm 42)

As a deer pants for flowing streams,
  so pants my soul for you, O God.
My soul thirsts for God,
  for the living God.
When shall I come and appear before God?

My tears have been my food
  day and night,
while they say to me all the day long,
  "Where is your God?"

These things I remember,
  as I pour out my soul:
how I would go with the throng
  and lead them in procession to the house of
  God
with glad shouts and songs of praise,
  a multitude keeping festival.

Why are you cast down, O my soul,
  and why are you in turmoil within me?
Hope in God; for I shall again praise him,
  my salvation and my God.
My soul is cast down within me;
  therefore I remember you
from the land of Jordan and of Hermon,
  from Mount Mizar.

Deep calls to deep
    at the roar of your waterfalls;
all your breakers and your waves
    have gone over me.

By day the Lord commands his steadfast love,
    and at night his song is with me,
    a prayer to the God of my life.

I say to God, my rock:
    "Why have you forgotten me?
Why do I go mourning
    because of the oppression of the enemy?"

As with a deadly wound in my bones,
    my adversaries taunt me,
while they say to me all the day long,
    "Where is your God?"

Why are you cast down, O my soul,
    and why are you in turmoil within me?
Hope in God; for I shall again praise him,
    my salvation and my God.

Called to Thankfulness

"Therefore, as you received Christ Jesus the Lord, so walk in him, rooted and built up in him and established in the faith, just as you were taught, abounding in thanksgiving." Colossians 2:6-7

If you had a good mother, she taught you early in life to say please and thank you. Such small courtesies are great indications of culture and refinement. In this way, children learn that they are not gods, and the people around them are not their servants. Above all, we teach them that only God in heaven is worthy of worship, and we owe Him our gratitude for every good thing that we receive.

Thanksgiving is one of the noblest and most non-controversial holidays of the year. The giving of thanks is fundamental to the worship and honor that we offer to the Father of lights from whom all blessings flow. It is a good time for us to meditate on some of the good reasons we have for giving thanks every day of our lives on this earth. It is my hope that we Christians may be thankful to our Almighty God every day of our lives, and not just on Thanksgiving Day. As grateful children of God, our gratitude must be perpetual, choosing to be grateful each day and not waiting until the end of November to do so. We have so much to be thankful for, even when it seems there is much to complain about. We must praise God and be always mindful of the many blessings our loving God showers down upon all of us. When the church first began in Acts 2:46, the disciples broke bread daily from house to house and ate their food with gladness. They were so thankful to be partakers of God's family that they ate together with joy (gladness and sincerity of heart). I have prepared some thoughts based on Psalm 138, for it offers thanksgiving for the LORD's lovingkindness toward us. I love the Psalms because they praise God for His lovingkindness and mercy. They help our hearts find deep appreciation and gratitude toward the God of heaven and earth. I hope this study is edifying to your walk with our Lord and Savior, Jesus Christ.

Thanksgiving Day is a day of reflection where we're supposed to stop, meditate, and be thankful for all that God has done for us. Unfortunately, we live in a world of convenience and materialism in which greed rules over thankfulness and contentment. Rather than being happy with what they have, our society is becoming more materialistic and greedy. *Why?* Because they don't include God in the picture. They forget God and all that He has given to us. They take all God's blessings for granted. God wants our hearts to be grateful and full of joy. *Is that too much for God to ask for? Are we so ungrateful that we forget to be thankful toward our Creator, where all blessings come from?* In Colossians 2:6-7, the apostle Paul exhorts us to walk, abounding in thanksgiving. Sadly, our thanksgiving is often focused on the physical things of this earth, for we tend to be physical people. So, we thank God only for those physical things that our eyes can see. Indeed, we are grateful for our jobs, our families, our material riches, and many other material things such as these. *But, are we forgetting what God wants us to be thankful for? Why not turn your hearts to Psalm 138 to open the eyes of your hearts to learn what we must be thankful for?* I invite you to walk through this amazing Psalm with me.

I. THANKSGIVING FOR GOD'S LOVINGKINDNESS:

Psalm 138 is one of a group of eight psalms ascribed to King David. It recognizes the existence of God and His authority over His creation. It shows reverence and respect to God and His holiness. It praises and glorifies God, for He is our

God to whom we owe everything. He protects His children in a world of lawlessness and darkness. Thus, we must be thankful and give Him praise and honor. Jesus said we must be lights that shine brightly in so much darkness that others might see our good works and glorify our Father in heaven. Paul likewise said we must shine as lights amid a dark and crooked world. Darkness is sin and evil. So we must shine in contrast to those around us who live in darkness. We must show the love of God, His longsuffering and mercy in our daily lives to others that perhaps they might come to the Light and be transformed into His likeness.

Giving Thanks Wholeheartedly (138:1):

> "I will give thee thanks with my whole heart: Before
> the gods will I sing praises unto thee."

The Psalmist starts out by offering praises of thanksgiving to God with all his heart. *When was the last time we offered praises of thanksgiving to God with all our heart? When was the last time we poured out our thanks to God with our whole being? When was the last time we passionately proclaimed praises of thanksgiving without holding back, reservation, or regard?* Verse 1 shows us a beautiful picture of a heart that abounds in praises of thankfulness to God.

> "I will give thee thanks with my whole heart."

It is indeed a heart that yearns to sing praises of thankfulness to God in the presence of the heavenly court. The Psalmist sings praises before the gods, the heavenly assembly of spiritual beings, the heavenly hosts. The gods in our context can also be rulers, magistrates, and earthly authorities. He is not speaking of idols. He sings praises because of his thankful heart, and so must we, all the days of our lives. Our singing is not just an act of worship every Sunday as we have been commanded, but rather an act that we do every moment in our lives with all our heart and being. God is delighted when we offer praises of thanksgiving to Him from our hearts. *Have we forgotten that part of our daily worship to God our Creator originates from a thankful heart? Where do you suppose our singing and prayers must come from?* From a heart that overflows with thanksgiving and gratitude. A halfhearted person finds it difficult to offer worship and praise from the depths of his heart. A singing heart overflows with thanksgiving, for the words we sing pluck our hearts as we praise God with our whole being. This is precisely what the Psalmist is portraying for us. He offers praises of thanksgiving with his whole heart to God before all who can hear him. *What do you think the Psalmist is praising God for?* Let us take a look at the following verses of this beautiful Psalm.

Giving Thanks to God for His Steadfast Love and Faithfulness (138:2-3):

> *"I will worship toward thy holy temple, And give thanks unto thy name for thy lovingkindness and for thy truth: For thou hast magnified thy word above all thy name. In the day that I called thou answeredst me, Thou didst encourage me with strength in my soul."*

The Psalmist is referring to the Tabernacle. He bows down toward God's holy temple. Bowing down toward the temple is a call of repentance (1 Kings 8). This is portrayed in verse 2. The Psalmist thanks God for His steadfast love and faithfulness. He is thankful for God's salvation, forgiveness, and restoration. *It is beautiful beyond words how faithful God is toward us!* He is faithful to us through our valleys of difficulties and trials. He is faithful to us even amid our sinfulness. Knowing God's faithfulness and steadfast love toward us, *Do we reflect on how faithful our God has been to us even amid our difficulties, pains, and trials? Do we pause to acknowledge God's steadfast love toward us even amid our many failures and sinfulness? How often has He forgiven us throughout our walk with Him?* As I read verse 3, *I cannot help but see that this is true in my life!*

> *"In the day that I called thou answeredst me, Thou didst encourage me with strength in my soul."*

I cannot help but think of the many, many times I have called on my God, and He has answered me with His steadfast love and kindness!

1. I think about the many times I've been in the pit of life or on the mountaintop of glory and how my God has answered my prayers.
2. I think about the times my heart has been weak and overwhelmed with life's anxieties and difficulties and how my God has given me the strength to endure those dark times.
3. I think about all the times He has rescued and sheltered me when I thought all hope was lost.
4. I think about all the times I have been broken and crushed, but my God has been there to strengthen my soul and give me encouragement and support.
5. *For all those trying times and God's lovingkindness and faithfulness toward me, my heart will always sing praises of thanksgiving to Him!*

The Psalmist focuses his prayer on verse 2. He gives thanks writing,

> *"And give thanks unto thy name for thy lovingkindness and for thy truth: For thou hast magnified thy word above all thy name."*

In Exodus, *"the name"* represents a person's character, for it reflects who the person is. The Psalmist praises God as he exalts His name and Word above all things. Think about what we know about the name of the LORD. Exodus 34 gives us the answer about what God's name reveals. Here are God's words.

> *"And Jehovah descended in the cloud, and stood with him there, and proclaimed the name of Jehovah. And Jehovah passed by before him, and proclaimed, Jehovah, Jehovah, a God merciful and gracious, slow to anger, and abundant in lovingkindness and truth; keeping lovingkindness for thousands, forgiving iniquity and transgression and sin; and that will by no means clear the guilty, visiting the iniquity of the fathers upon the children, and upon the children's children, upon the third and upon the fourth generation"* (Exodus 34:5-7).

What a wonderful grace it is to us, God's exalted name and Word! His name reveals His mercy, grace, patience, steadfast love, and faithfulness. His name reveals His love, forgiveness, and righteousness (His justice). God's glory is good and righteous. Thus, we must always praise God's righteous and holy character. We must praise God, not only for what we have received from Him but also for who He is. Because of God's holy and righteous character, we have life, hope, and confidence. God strengthens our soul when we call on Him because of who He is.

Calling All People To Give Thanks to God (138:4-6):

> *"All the kings of the earth shall give thee thanks, O Jehovah, For they have heard the words of thy mouth. Yea, they shall sing of the ways of Jehovah; For great is the glory of Jehovah. For though Jehovah is high, yet hath he respect unto the lowly; But the haughty he knoweth from afar."*

The Psalmist calls for the rulers of the earth to give thanks to God. Our text can be read two ways. One way one could understand the Hebrew text would be prophetic. The Psalmist states, *"All the kings of the earth shall give thee thanks, O Jehovah."* According to the Psalmist, the kings of the earth will one day give thanks to God. That will be possible because the Scriptures declare that one day, every knee will bow before the Lord (Philippians 2:10). The other possibility would be that the Psalmist is calling on the kings of the earth to give thanks to God. My understanding of this passage is that this is a call to all people (even kings of the earth) to praise and give thanks to God. All people of the earth are compelled to hear God's decrees and offer praises of thanksgiving to Him alone. They are obliged to sing of His greatness.

> *"For though Jehovah is high, yet hath he respect unto the lowly; But the haughty he knoweth from afar."*

Although God is high and exalted with all glory, He is merciful to the lowly and looks kindly on them. He draws the lowly to Him. But the arrogant and haughty, He knows from afar. God abhors the proud and keeps His distance from them. Though He is great and awesome, He cares for the humble. *How sad it is when rulers refuse to honor and praise God with praises of thanksgiving!* They are blind and arrogant, for they refuse to acknowledge that the reason why they rule is God's will. God has given them that position to rule (cf. Romans 13:1; John 19:11; Daniel 4:32). The prouder rulers become, refusing to give thanks and praise to God for putting them in the position of rule and authority, the worse they rule, and the further they fall from God. No one can escape from God, for He knows man's heart (the lowly and the arrogant). And though He knows man's heart, He delights in the lowly in heart and is near them but keeps the arrogant in heart afar off. *Isn't that amazing! Why?* Because although God's glory is amazing and great, He gives grace and draws nearer to the humble. He does not keep His distance from them. He keeps His distance from the proud. Our God is worthy of our praise and our thanksgiving, for He draws nearer to the humble, though He is high in exalting glory. Thus, we must praise Him and offer praises of thanksgiving, for He has drawn near to us, the lowly in heart.

Giving Thanks For Our Lives (138:7):

> *"Though I walk in the midst of trouble, thou wilt revive me; Thou wilt stretch forth thy hand against the wrath of mine enemies, And thy right hand will save me."*

God protects, delivers, and keeps us safe even amid our troubles, shortcomings, and failures in life. His steadfast love is always there for us. *Isn't that amazing! Such love is beyond words!* With God's steadfast love, we are confident in our walk, whatever may come our way, for we know He will be faithful to His faithful children till the end. *God is for us! How sad it is to fail to realize that the power that sustains our life is God's power and Word!* We're shortsighted when we fail to think of life this way. Nothing and no one is outside of God's will, for He controls everything. Thus, we must be grateful and thank Him for keeping us alive and providing for us day in and day out so faithfully. *How sad it is to take for granted all of God's provisions and care!* We fail so often to acknowledge that it is by His will that we live and move and that nothing is accomplished without His will. We deceive ourselves, assuming that tomorrow we will still have all we need, and we will live on this earth forever. So we act as if we were in control of everything without God's will in the picture.

1. We must wake up and start thanking God for all that He has done, is doing, and will be doing in our lives and never take any of His blessings, care, and love for granted.
2. We must wake up and become better stewards of the blessings that God provides for us from His

mighty and providential hands: our spouse, our children, our brethren, our families.

3. We must wake up and start being more grateful to God that He has given them to us yet another day.

4. *Do you not know that these things, these blessings are not promised to us?*

5. *Do we not acknowledge that life is not promised to us?*

6. *Do we not know that the only thing that is promised to us is death and judgment, not life?*

7. So, we must wake up and start appreciating everything, and be more thankful for what God has done and still does for us, far more than we deserve, for we do not deserve anything from God's mighty and providential hands.

Giving Thanks to God For Accomplishing His Purposes in Us (138:8):

> "*Jehovah will perfect that which concerneth me: Thy lovingkindness, O Jehovah, endureth for ever; Forsake not the works of thine own hands.*"

The Psalmist ends this mighty Psalm giving thanks to God for "*Jehovah will perfect that which concerneth me.*" God's will is done on earth and heaven, for He always accomplishes His purposes or that which concerns Him that we do for Him. God accomplishes His purposes in us and through us, for we are part of His mighty plans. We are His instruments that must be at work in His kingdom. Thus, we must pray to Him to use us and make us the servants that He wants us to be to accomplish His purposes. *How beautiful it is to be God's servant and the work of His hands! How beautiful it is to be changed and molded into His image for His purposes! How beautiful it is to be useful servants in His kingdom of righteousness!* We must be grateful and rejoice for Him to use us as His vessels of righteousness to His glory. We must be thankful to God that He has called us from death to life, to present our bodies as instruments of righteousness

(Romans 6:13). *Why not listen to the words of the beautiful and amazing picture that is portrayed in 1 Peter 2:4-5?*

> *"Unto whom coming, a living stone, rejected indeed of men, but with God elect, precious, ye also, as living stones, are built up a spiritual house, to be a holy priesthood, to offer up spiritual sacrifices, acceptable to God through Jesus Christ."*

What an amazing and beautiful picture of God's children! Though we are God's living stones, we still have rough edges and bad cuts because of our sins and shortcomings. We're still terrible stones that, at times, are not useful for building anything. But thanks to God's lovingkindness, He patiently helps us by cutting off those terrible and rough edges, refining you and me to become living stones built into Jesus' spiritual house. A house that He patiently is building for Himself. *It is beautiful beyond what words can describe!* I believe that is the message that the Psalmist is proclaiming toward the end of this amazing Psalm in verse 8.

> *"Thy lovingkindness, O Jehovah, endureth for ever;*
> *Forsake not the works of thine own hands."*

O how wonderful it is for our God to work in our lives for His glory and purposes! O how wonderful it is for God to never give up on us! He keeps refining us, molding us, cutting us, and changing us into what He wants us to be for His glorious purposes! O how wonderful it is to know that God will fulfill His purposes in us, for we are His instruments of righteousness! O how wonderful it is to know that His faithful love endures forever! For these reasons and many more, we must cry out to God in prayer, knowing that He will not abandon the work of His hands and that He is patiently and lovingly shaping us and changing us into what He wants us to be for His glory. May He never stop shaping us and changing us into His likeness. May we always be thankful for His steadfast love and for not abandoning the work of His mighty hands. May we always trust in God with full confidence, knowing that His marvelous promises will indeed be fulfilled.

CONCLUSION:

We have so many reasons to be thankful. We have an abundance of blessings bestowed on us, for which we must be thankful. Consider some of the many blessings: Our families, our good health, our freedom to worship God. We have the Gospel of Christ, the Word of God, our redemption, our hope of eternal life, our many freedoms like being able to home educate our children. We have air to breathe, water to drink, food to eat, and most of all, our Lord and Savior who redeemed us, who cares for us, who sympathizes with our weaknesses, and who has sworn never to forsake us. Therefore, we are more than rich since we have all these abundant blessings. Being grateful is the key to spiritual victory. Joy is the result of a grateful heart. A thankful heart is the product of a person who always chooses to give thanks no matter what the circumstances may be. It is the person who never compares himself to other people but always to Christ. It is the heart that realizes he is rich beyond measure because he is a child of God and that in Him, he finds His portion. It is the heart that is always looking for reasons to be content and give thanks.

Therefore, we must learn to appreciate and be thankful for God's steadfast love and lovingkindness. Notice what David once said:

> *"Blessed be the Lord, For He has made marvelous His lovingkindness to me in a besieged city"* (Psalm 31:2).

There is nothing more critical than finding oneself in a besieged city. It is as bad as one's circumstances can get. Yet David acknowledges God's steadfast love and lovingkindness toward him. God heard his cry for deliverance. He made David aware of His love and compassion for him. *Are we aware, and do we acknowledge God's steadfast love and lovingkindness toward us? Can we fathom the depth of His steadfast love toward us? Have we forgotten the message of Romans 8:38-39?*

Despair is the opposite of a faithful and thankful heart. When our affections are on earthly things and not on God, we are in danger. We tend to cling to our immediate circumstances rather than to God. It makes us not only anxious but also insecure. Only God can fill our hearts with His peace. We have so much to give thanks for. It is not so much for material things but for God's love in sending His only begotten Son to die for our sins so that through Him, we could be redeemed and have access to eternal life. We have all we need in Christ. He is the fullness that fills all in all. *Why not take a moment to give honor and offer praises of thanksgiving to God for His goodness and lovingkindness? Why not praise and bless our God? Why not look beyond all the material blessings we have received? Why not look beyond the pleasures of this life and meditate on all that God has done for us, the undeserving? Why not give thanks to God wholeheartedly for His faithfulness toward us during our trials, sufferings, failures, and yes, even sins? Why not give thanks to Him with all our heart and being, for answering our prayers and carrying us through our valleys of suffering, hardship, and trouble? Why not give thanks wholeheartedly to God for drawing near to us, though He is high and exalted? Why not give thanks to God wholeheartedly for keeping us safe and preserving our lives yet another day? Why not give thanks to our God with all our hearts, for what He is accomplishing and will accomplish in us for His purposes? Why not give thanks to God for using us as His instruments of righteousness to accomplish His will in us? Why not give thanks to God for shaping, molding, and changing us into His living stones built into a great spiritual house for Him?*

May we always have grateful hearts for God's lovingkindness and steadfast love toward us. May our Lord help us to give thanks always, no matter what our circumstances may be. May we live in His peace, trusting in Him with all our hearts, minds, and souls. May we always have a thankful and grateful heart that we may see the power of God and our faith in Him working in us to accomplish His purposes. May we never forget that God is the Giver of all good gifts. May we keep calm and know that He cares for us. May we never forget that He is near. To Him be the glory. Amen!

Are You an Unhappy Child of God?

"Rejoice in the Lord always; again I will say, rejoice. Let your reasonableness be known to everyone. The Lord is at hand; do not be anxious about anything, but in everything by prayer and supplication with thanksgiving let your requests be made known to God. And the peace of God, which surpasses all understanding, will guard your hearts and your minds in Christ Jesus. Finally, brothers, whatever is true, whatever is honorable, whatever is just, whatever is pure, whatever is lovely, whatever is commendable, if there is any excellence, if there is anything worthy of praise, think about these things. What you have learned and received and heard and seen in me — practice these things, and the God of peace will be with you." Philippians 4:4-9

How is it possible that some people seem to be happy and cheerful even when they live in undesirable circumstances, but others who have substantial advantages appear to be sour, bitter, and unhappy? The apostle Paul wrote about a peace that is incomprehensible to those who do not know Christ and His Gospel. The key to understanding how to live and to have what the Gospel calls life is found in doing exactly what Jesus prescribes and thinking the way that God wants us to think. Let us examine some of the ways that He teaches us to be filled with joy inexpressible.

One of the major reasons why Jesus our Lord came to earth and died a cruel death on the cross on Calvary was because both the Father and Jesus the Son wanted us to be happy and full of joy (Philippians 4:4-8). The secret to true happiness, joy, and strength is totally rooted in knowing and believing in Jesus.

> *"I know how to be brought low, and I know how to abound. In any and every circumstance, I have learned the secret of facing plenty and hunger, abundance and need. I can do all things through him who strengthens me"* (Philippians 4:12-13).

Paul's happiness did not depend on his circumstances or situations, expecting or waiting on others to make him happy, and events to make him truly happy. Paul's life was not easy and a bed of roses but learned the secret of contentment through knowing Jesus and His promises. When we focus on the externals, the things of the world, we will never find inner peace and joy, for these things will let us down. Inner peace and joy are rooted and grounded in Jesus and all that He has promised to those who would love and follow Him. When we walk by the Spirit, it will be impossible to satisfy the desires of the flesh, because such desires move us to act contrary to the teachings of the Spirit. The laws of the Spirit oppose many fleshly desires, which keep us from doing those things that are righteous and holy before God. Joy is one of the fruits of the Spirit. It shows our spiritual maturity (Galatian 5:22-26). Our people deceive themselves when they think that they will be happier if they get what they want. They run from where they are to some other place, or they become someone different from who they are, someone without God in the picture. They crave for the wrong things of this life and find themselves unhappy, looking to get something else. They run away from their problems, deceiving themselves, thinking that things will be better somewhere else. But that happiness accorded to them is but for a short time, for they cannot escape their own negative attitudes of their heart. Jesus came to give us abundant life, and to have it to the full. Without Jesus as the Lord and Master in our life, it is impossible to find the happiness and joy that our souls are craving. Faith in Jesus and His promises is the key to contentment, happiness, and peace. Jesus made these great blessings and happiness available to us when He died on the cross for us.

God's Word has all the answers for positive mental health. We Christians must rid ourselves of all the layers of unhappiness and move swiftly in the opposite direction. The purpose of the present study is to encourage us, by considering what we must not do if we wish to stay happy. At the same time, we must acknowledge God's eternal wisdom and His principles of righteousness to remain happy or content, for God has commanded that we be content. So, let us consider some ways in which we run the risk of remaining unhappy or not content. It is our choice to be happy and rejoice in the Lord for what He has provided for us. It is our choice to choose to be happy, have joy and have a more positive mental state and ask God for help to help us overcome whatever it is that hinders our joy or contentment (happiness). It is our choice to become wiser and happier people. *Why not meditate on God's wisdom?* In wisdom, we can say like Paul,

> "I have learned the secret of facing plenty and hunger, abundance and need. I can do all things through him who strengthens me" (Philippians 4:12-13).

I. HOW TO REMAIN UNHAPPY:

Are you a happy and joyful Christian? What is your state of mind? Consider the following ways which can keep us unhappy, lacking joy or contentment.

Dwell on The Past:

Some people like to dwell on things that happened in the past. They ignore that everybody makes mistakes. They destroy their present by remaining in the past with all their failures and mistakes rather than moving on the best they can. The cure for this is found in Philippians 3:13-14. We must choose to forget those things which are behind us, reaching forward to those things which are ahead, heaven, our crown of life and glory.

Be Obsessed With the Future:

Some love to dwell on all those things that might happen to them in the future: job, health, bills, death, and many other things that, when we worry about them too much, they rob us of our joy. They're always saying, *"What if... what if... what if...?"* They ignore what Jesus said in Matthew 6:31-34 about those things that make us anxious and that the unbelievers seek after. God wants us to seek Him first and His kingdom of righteousness. He will add all that we need according to His will. Therefore, we must choose to not worry about tomorrow, for tomorrow will bring its own things and troubles.

Complain About Our Problems or Circumstances:

We may choose to complain about every little thing and grumble or feeling sorry for ourselves. Complaining is always easier than choosing to fix our problems, taking the necessary steps to resolve them. *But what do complaining and grumbling accomplish? Nothing!* So, we must choose to do all things without complaining or arguing (Philippians 2:14).

Fear and Resist Change:

Isn't it something how some resist progress and fight against it! It is futile! Change is intrinsically neutral. The change that we must fear is the one that leads to doing evil. *So, we must resist it!* However, some changes are good for us, especially when one acknowledges his need for the Lord, choosing to submit to Him in obedience to the Gospel (Acts 3:19). *That kind of change must never be resisted!*

Condemn Ourselves for Not Achieving Perfection:

Some condemn themselves even when they're working hard and doing their best because they fail to meet their own expectations. And, though some struggle with pride and the vanity of thinking too highly of themselves, others tear themselves down when they don't achieve perfection (Col. 3:23; Matthew 22:39).

Associate With Those Who Belittle Us:

Some people seem to enjoy tearing others down. The more time we spend with this kind of people, the more they will affect our state of mind. Hanging out with those who belittle us does not encourage us to have a healthy state of mind (Phil. 4:8).

Keep Doing the Same Thing Over and Over Again; Never Learning Anything New:

One can lose focus when he gets in a rut for *"What has been will be again, what has been done will be done again; there is nothing new under the sun"* (Eccl. 1:9). Although schedules and habits are good for us, changing and learning things is also good, for they help us keep things anew or fresh, reminding us of life's purpose (Eccl. 12:13-14).

> *"Fear God and keep his commandments, for this is the duty of all mankind. For God will bring every deed into judgment, including every hidden thing, whether it is good or evil."*

Be Lazy, Following the Path of Least Resistance:

God created us to work and be fruitful. Laziness does not lead to good and healthy mental health. In the book of Proverbs, we find many exhortations against being lazy and its terrible consequence.

> "Lazy hands make for poverty, but diligent hands bring wealth" (Proverbs 10:14).

> "The way of the lazy is as a hedge of thorns, But the path of the upright is a highway" (Proverbs 15:19).

> "The soul of a lazy man desires, and has nothing; But the soul of the diligent shall be made rich" (Prov. 10:14).

Hold on to Anger and Resist Forgiveness:

Some hold on to anger for weeks, months and even years! But God demands that we do otherwise, for it is not good to be angry and let the sun go down on our anger or wrath. So we must take care of that problem today before it is ever too late! We must refuse to give the devil any opportunity to make us sin (Eph. 4:26-27).

Always Insist That One is Right And Never Wrong:

Those who are proud and are unwilling to admit their failures, shortcomings, and mistakes can never find real joy or happiness. They are always right in their own eyes and never let anyone else be more right than them. The Bible warns us that God hates the sin of pride and will discipline the proud! Let us not see ourselves as "wise in our own eyes" but let us be humble and willing to learn from God and others! Jesus is our ultimate example of selflessness who gave Himself on the cross for us!

"But he gives more grace. Therefore it says, "God opposes the proud but gives grace to the humble" (James 4:6).

"When pride comes, then comes disgrace, but with humility comes wisdom" (Prov. 11:2).

"Where there is strife, there is pride, but wisdom is found in those who take advice" (Prov. 13:10).

Comparing Ourselves to Others:

When we compare ourselves negatively or unfavorably to others who are more successful or more blessed than we are, it is not productive or fruitful. It doesn't glorify God, and it brings reproach on us. It opens the door to envy, jealousy, and complaint. We must use our talents faithfully to the glory of God. In Matthew 25, in the parable of the talents, we notice that the servant who received two talents did not complain against the servant who received five talents. Instead, he went out and used the talent that he had faithfully without complaint, envy, or jealousy. *This is an excellent lesson for us to learn!*

Allow Small Problems or Issues To Escalate and Become Big Problems:

It is foolish to ignore the small problems, hoping it will go away by itself. Take for instance, when one offends somebody, it is our obligation to go to the offended person and correct the problem or wrongdoing while it is still small and there is hope of resolving it (cf. Matt. 5:23-24). It is foolish to wait in solving problems when the sooner they are addressed, the easier it will be to resolve them. It is wise to solve them right away rather than later, whether they be spiritual problems or physical ones.

Refuse to Take Responsibility For Our Own Wrongdoings and Actions:

It is not wise but foolish to refuse to take or accept responsibility for our actions, blaming everyone except ourselves. Take for instance, Adam. He blamed Eve, his wife for eating of the tree that God had commanded them not to eat. Adam shifted the blame to Eve saying, *"The woman whom thou gavest to be with me, she gave me of the tree, and I did eat."* Eve did the same thing when God questioned her for disobeying Him. *"And Jehovah God said unto the woman, What is this thou hast done? And the woman said, The serpent beguiled me, and I did eat"* (Genesis 3:11-13). Even though Adam had received Eve, his wife, as a great gift from God, he after a short time, accused Eve, God's gift. What Adam did not realize was that he was accusing God himself for the wrong that he had done. Both Adam and Eve failed to take responsibility for their actions. *It is amazing!*

Refuse to Let Anyone to Help us:

Many refuse to let others help them because they are too proud. They won't accept help from someone else and will refuse to ask for help even when they really need it. *It is foolish!* God has commanded us to bear each other's burdens, for this is the fulfillment of the Law of Christ (Galatians 6:2).

Quit When The Going Gets Tough:

We sometimes give up or stop working hard when things are challenging, wasting our potential, failing to endure until the end. Some will be discouraged and will be deceived, giving up their faith and their hope. But Jesus has taught us to endure to the end to be saved and receive our crown of life, righteousness and glory (Matt. 10:22; 1 Cor 9:25; Ph. 4:1; 1 Thess. 2:19;2 Tim. 4:8;1 Pet. 5:4;Jas. 1:12; Rev. 2:10).

Refuse to Rest for Overall Health:

Some refuse to rest, for they don't expect to get tired. They think they can do it all. The human body needs enough rest to maintain strength and good health. But, it is possible to go to the other extreme and become lazy and unprofitable (Prov. 6:9).

Say "Yes" to Everyone and Everything:

Although it is always good to be busy and productive, it is wise not to fill our plate with demands or commitments all the time, overwhelming ourselves to the point of neglecting what must be the most crucial thing in our lives, seeking and serving God and His kingdom of righteousness (Mark 6:31).

Striving to Be Everyone's Friend:

It is good to try to be everyone's friend, but it is not so good when they hinder our walk with Jesus. *No one can be a friend to everyone!* Jesus had many enemies. So many that they crucified Him. The Bible warns us saying, *"Woe to you when all men speak well of you, for so did their fathers to their false prophets"* (Lk. 6:26).

Refuse to Spend Time Alone to Meditate:

It is wise and good to spend time alone, decompress sometimes, for life can be stressful. Find quiet time to be alone, meditate on God's Word and pray alone with God. That is what we need. Jesus stressed this in Matthew 6:6: *"But when you pray, go into your room and shut the door and pray to your Father who is in secret. And your Father who sees in secret will reward you."*

Avoid Helping Others Unless We Have to:

Indeed, doing the things that would benefit us is pure self-centeredness and a sure way for unhappiness. Jesus gives us the remedy to self-centeredness in Philippians 2:3-4. *"Do nothing from selfish ambition or conceit, but in humility count others more significant than yourselves. Let each of you look not only to his own interests, but also to the interests of others."*

Hang Out With Those Who Complain and Whine All The Time:

Do you want to be unhappy, just hang out with whiners and complainers, for it will affect your heart tremendously! Spending too much time with them will sourpuss you and make you into one like them. Be careful and do not be deceived about choosing your friends, for they will corrupt your good habits and righteousness (1 Cor. 15:33).

Having a Negative Outlook Toward Life, Refusing to be a Cheerful Person:

Some people take life and everything too seriously, for they want to be solemn. There is nothing wrong with smiling and laughing when it is appropriate. *It makes life better!* Those who laugh and enjoy life live longer. *A merry heart or broken spirit is a choice!* A joyful, loving, thankful, peaceful, forgiving, and full of praise heart will be a blessing to others. On the other hand, a negative person with a negative attitude always finds something wrong in his everyday life (Pr. 15:15). Contentment and joy are choices, and we must choose well. *"A merry heart doeth good like a medicine: but a broken spirit drieth the bones"* (Prov. 17:22).

Performing a Job That You Hate and Are Not Passionate About:

Spending most of your God-giving time on a career field that you do not enjoy can indeed make you very unhappy. *Why not pursue another line of work or career that makes you happy and productive?*

Focusing on Our Problems, Struggles, and Bad Things:

We all have our share of blessings and struggles that we must deal with every day, but we must choose to have a positive mental focus. Focusing on the good in life will make us more optimistic and productive. Focusing on the bad things that happen to us in life, will bring us down quickly and will make us unhappy. *"As a man thinks in his heart, so he is"* (Prov. 23:7).

Thinking Always About the Things We Don't Have:

Focusing always on the things that we don't have will make us unhappy and rob us of our joy. We must learn to count our blessings and name them one by one. *It will surprise you all that God has done for us!* Paul is our greatest example of joy and contentment, for he learned to be content in all things and circumstances (Phil. 4:11-13).

Setting Goals too High, Lofty:

Setting goals that are unreasonably lofty is foolish, for it will hinder us from accomplishing them and will make us unhappy. We must learn to use discipline and continued effort to achieve our goals, for doing it this way will help our mental health significantly.

Refuse to Take Care of Our Physical Body to Stay Healthy:

Lack of exercise and self-control at the table will harm our bodies, the temple of the Holy Spirit. God cannot use us if we neglect our temples, our bodies, for they will get sick and become fruitless, unprofitable for God's things (1 Tim. 4:8).

Set Our Hearts on Material Things and Money:

Although money is not bad, it can become a stumbling block in serving God and His kingdom of righteousness faithfully. Focusing our lives on money and material riches can make us selfish. When our money is directed toward self and family, it becomes a significant problem. *Why?* Because God expects us to do good and bless others with our resources. God commands us not to put our trust on material riches but on Him alone, for He blesses us richly in all things to enjoy and share them with others. He wants us to be rich in good works and ready to give and be generous, willing to share with those who are needy (1 Tim. 6:17-19).

Spend More Than We Earn, Accumulating Financial Debt:

Racking up lots of debt will surely bring unnecessary stress and sorrow to our lives. We must discipline ourselves to live within our income, even when others are not. The Word of God commands us not to owe anything to anyone except to love one another (Rom. 13:10).

Make Empty Promises We Cannot Keep:

We must learn to do what we say we will do. There are times when we may say *"yes"* and times when we must say *"no."* Thus we must always do what we promise or commit ourselves to do. We must avoid at all costs, making promises which we are not serious about keeping. *"Better not to vow than to vow and not pay"* (Eccl. 5:5).

Frown All the Time:

Although it takes effort to smile, we must, for it is worth it! We have so many reasons to be joyful. God has blessed us and given us more than we deserve. *"Rejoice in the Lord always; again I will say, rejoice!"* (Phil. 4:4). *"Be glad in the LORD and rejoice, you righteous ones; And shout for joy, all you who are upright in heart"* (Psalm 32:11). *"And you shall rejoice in all the good that the Lord your God has given to you"* (Deut. 26:11).

Always Keeping Everything to Ourselves and Not Asking Others For Counsel or Advice:

Communication is essential to strong and healthy relationships which can, in the long run, bear much joy in our lives. One way to stay unhappy is to never tell anyone how we feel or what we're thinking.

Do All Things to Impress Someone Else:

When our focus is primarily on pleasing others and seeking their approval, we will fail, accomplish nothing and be unhappy. *The One we must focus on exclusively and please is the Lord, for we are His servants!* In Galatians 1:10 Paul declared, *"For am I now seeking the approval of man, or of God? Or am I trying to please man? If I were still trying to please man, I would not be a servant of Christ."*

Waste Time Watching TV And Online Every Moment:

This seems to be an escape for many, but it wastes away our God-given precious time when in fact we ought to be doing other more important things to His glory, things of eternal value. Spending too much time on social media and personal entertainment like watching TV and many other things such as these allows our heart to be filled with filth, both in mind and heart (Phil. 4:8).

Always Working and Not Taking Time Off:

It is wise to take time off for recreation, rest, recharging or refreshing. It will add quality to our life. God made us and knows what is best for a healthy state of mind. In the Old Testament God told His people to rest on the Sabbath Day. Although we're not under the Sabbath Law today, it is wise to take time off to rest from our daily burdens and cares (Exo. 20:8-11).

Let Our Close Relationships Deteriorate:

When we stop nurturing and investing in our relationships with others, especially our spouses, they will wither. To love our spouse the way God demands, must be the primary relationship we work on (Eph. 5:22ff).

Never Finish What We Start:

Nothing will make us more unhappy than to start a project and then stop. *"Whatever your hand finds to do, do it with your might"* (Colossians 3:23). It is not very fulfilling to dabble a little bit here and there. So we must work hard with our might to finish what we start (Eccl. 9:10).

Take Everything Personally:

We will never be happy if we expect others to tolerate and be patient with us without reciprocating. *We must not tolerate in ourselves a persecution complex!* Ours is to give and not to receive. *"Therefore, whatever you want men to do to you, do also to them, for this is the Law and the Prophets"* (Matt. 7:12).

Never Apologize, Ask Forgiveness or Say, "I'm Sorry, or I Love You."

We must humble ourselves when we make a mistake, do wrong or sin against each other. We must be willing to apologize, ask forgiveness and say the most important phrases in any language (*I'm sorry, and I love you*). *Are we saying them enough?*

Rely on Others to Do Everything for Us:

The truth is we are not entitled to anything, for every blessing is a gift from God (James 1:17). Although it is not bad to rely on others sometimes, it is not wise and healthy to rely on everyone for everything. It is pure immaturity and selfishness when one refuses to do anything for himself. It will not lead to a joyful state of mind.

Destroy Our Bodies and Minds With Illegal Drugs and Alcohol:

Many do these things to escape from their daily burdens and cares, but they never bring real happiness. *"Wine is a mocker, strong drink a brawler and whoever is lead astray by it is not wise"* (Prov. 20:1).

Procrastinate and Refuse Making Decisions:

When we are indecisive, we allow our God-given life and opportunities to pass us by. Since we are promised only today and live on this earth only once, we must choose to do it right according to God's will (Heb. 9:27).

Always Belittle and Disregard Others' Opinions and Advice:

Disregarding other people's opinions and suggestions will bring us ruin and unhappiness. Those who refuse the counsel of others often fall and find no safety (Prov. 11:14). To grow in wisdom, we must allow wise counsel to correct us, replacing our thoughts and opinions with their wise counsel. This is a hard choice to make, for it is hard to be criticized and correct-ed. To receive the wise counsel of others, we must learn to crush our pride and subject our ideas and plans to the analysis and examination of others. By choosing godly and successful people as our counselors, we can instantly raise the quality and results of our decisions. *This will indeed bring happiness to our life!*

II. WHY ARE SO MANY CHRISTIANS UNHAPPY? WHAT IS THE PROBLEM?

Solomon wrote,

> *"As a man thinketh in his heart, so is he"* (Prov. 23:7).

As I mentioned earlier in my study, happiness is a state of mind, for it is all in our head. Too often we are guilty of think-ing wrong and not according to God's ways. We deceive our-selves thinking that we will be happier if we get what we want or escape to someplace else or try to look like or become someone different than we are. Consider the parable of the great banquet where a certain man goes out of his way to pre-pare a feast, inviting his friends and neighbors, to come and enjoy it with him.

> *"When one of those who reclined at table with him heard these things, he said to him, 'Blessed is every-one who will eat bread in the kingdom of God!' But he said to him, "A man once gave a great banquet and invited many. And at the time for the banquet he sent his servant to say to those who had been in-vited, 'Come, for everything is now ready.' But they all alike began to make excuses. The first said to him, 'I have bought a field, and I must go out and see it. Please have me excused.' And another said, 'I have bought five yoke of oxen, and I go to examine them.*

Please have me excused.' And another said, 'I have married a wife, and therefore I cannot come.' So the servant came and reported these things to his master. Then the master of the house became angry and said to his servant, 'Go out quickly to the streets and lanes of the city, and bring in the poor and crippled and blind and lame.' And the servant said, 'Sir, what you commanded has been done, and still there is room.' And the master said to the servant, 'Go out to the highways and hedges and compel people to come in, that my house may be filled. For I tell you, none of those men who were invited shall taste my banquet'" (Luke 14:15-24).

In this parable, none of the guests that were initially invited came to this feast, for they all made up various excuses as to why they couldn't attend. When the servants of the master reported this to him, he became very angry. The master was hurt most likely because of all the preparations, expense and trouble he had to go through to show these guests how special they were by throwing a big banquet for them but they preferred to do something else, refusing to show up. We all can relate to this one way or another. *Wouldn't it hurt you and be upsetting if you had put so much effort into showing hospitality to others and no one showed up?* In this story, the master didn't give up but sent his servants to find any or everyone he could find, even if they were strangers to him, to come to this big feast. I believe God is trying to tell us something in this parable. He is telling us how He feels when we refuse to take advantage of His great blessings that He has provided for us. *God has provided us with so many blessings!* He has offered us abundant life, joy, peace, and an excellent inheritance equal to that of His beloved Son, Jesus our Lord. Yet so many Christians seem to be blind or forget those blessings and promises made by God. And just like the man in this story was disappointed, I believe our God is disappointed when we choose to be unhappy, miserable, sad, depressed, whining and complaining despite all the many blessings He bestows on us. We come up with all kinds of excuses as to why we don't want to take advantage of what He is offering us (all His precious and magnificent promises to become partakers of His divine nature). Here is a wise reminder for us.

> *"His divine power has granted to us all things that pertain to life and godliness, through the knowledge of him who called us to his own glory and excellence, by which he has granted to us his precious and very great promises, so that through them you may become partakers of the divine nature, having escaped from the corruption that is in the world because of sinful desire"* (2 Peter 1:3-4).

Because of God's glory, excellence, and love for us, He has given us great and precious promises to help us share or be partakers of His divine nature and escape the corruption of this world. When we put on Christ, we also put on God. Another great promise given to us is found in Romans 6:23. *"For the wages of sin is death, but the free gift of God is eternal life in Christ Jesus our Lord."*

1. God has promised us, His faithful children, that He will be with us and not leave us orphans (John 14:15-19).
2. In Philippians 4:7, we are told that God will guard our heart and mind in Christ Jesus when we have the peace of God which surpasses all understanding.
3. In Romans 8:35, God has promised His faithful children that nothing will separate them from the love of Christ (Romans 8:35).
4. In 1 Corinthians 10:13, God has promised that He will not let us be tried or tempted beyond what we can endure.

5. In Romans 8:28, He has promised that all things work together for our good.
6. In 2 Corinthians 9:8, we are told that God is able to make Grace abound to us so that all our needs are met, for we are in God's favor.
7. We are promised an amazing inheritance, Eph. 1:14; Col. 1:12.
8. We are promised that we can approach God with freedom and confidence, Eph. 3:12.
9. In Hebrews 2:18, Jesus has promised to help us when we are being tempted.
10. God has promised to give us wisdom if we ask Him for it, James 1:15.
11. He has promised that if we draw near to Him, He will draw near to us as well, James 4:8.
12. God will continue to forgive and cleanse us of new sin, if we confess those sins to Him, 1 John 1:9.
13. We have been promised that we will be like Jesus when He reappears, for we will be made like Him, 1 John 3:2.
14. We are promised new heavens and new earth in which righteousness dwells, 2 Peter 3:13.
15. God has promised us eternal life through His Son, Matt. 7:13-14; John 3:16; Rev. 3:5-9; 1 John 5:11-14.

These are just a few of the many promises or blessings given to all faithful Christians. So, we have a choice to make. We can choose to be happy, content and rejoice because of who we are in Christ, God's sons and daughters and because He has set heavenly glory to richly bless us in our daily walk with Him. On the other hand, we can choose to be miserable, unhappy, sad, angry, depressed, feel sorry for ourselves, whine and complain about every little thing in life. The choice is ours to make, *"as a man thinketh in his heart, so is he."* One way leads to abundant life with God. The other way leads to destruction, for it is a sad and unhappy way of life. The key is what we believe, think and ultimately it is our faith in God. So we must examine our hearts and start making up our minds, choosing to rejoice in the Lord every day for what He has done and provided for us. *Why not pray to God to help you be a more positive and happier person? Why not acknowledge and thank God for His love and the abundant promises He has made to bless you?* Reflect on this with all your heart and mind and one day you will be able to join Paul's voice and say,

> "*I have learned the secret of being content in any and every situation, whether well fed or hungry, whether living in plenty or in want. I can do all this through him who gives me strength*" (Phil. 4:12-13).

CONCLUSION:

In the "Beatitudes of Christ," we find the most condensed collection of wisdom ever given about human joy. In Matthew 5:3-12 Jesus declared,

> "**Blessed** *are the poor in spirit, for theirs is the kingdom of heaven.* **Blessed** *are those who mourn, for they shall be comforted.* **Blessed** *are the meek, for they shall inherit the earth.* **Blessed** *are those who hunger and thirst for righteousness, for they shall be satisfied.* **Blessed** *are the merciful, for they shall receive mercy.* **Blessed** *are the pure in heart, for they shall see God.* **Blessed** *are the peacemakers, for they shall be called sons of God.* **Blessed** *are those who are persecuted for righteousness' sake, for theirs is the kingdom of heaven.* **Blessed** *are you when others revile you and persecute you and utter all kinds of evil against you falsely on my account.* **Rejoice and be glad**, *for your reward is great in heaven, for so they persecuted the prophets who were before you.*"

Jesus is giving us here a formula for real and lasting joy! To learn real and lasting joy, we must be humble and empty ourselves of all pride and self-sufficiency and become more *"poor in spirit"* as we mourn for our sinfulness before a Holy and Righteous God. In doing this, we can rest assured that it will be easier to submit to God and His rule completely and become strong (i.e., "me") under His control. Those who are meek and submit to God and His rule completely will naturally *"hunger and thirst after righteousness,"* for they acknowledge that without God and His spiritual nourishment, they are destitute. For one to be "merciful," he must strongly desire to do righteousness because God is so merciful to him. One must strongly desire to be righteous, *"hunger and thirst after righteousness"* to be pure in heart. A "peacemaker" strongly desires to do what is right to be full of mercy and is devoted to being completely pure. However, those who possess all these attributes of true joy will be hated by those who reject the righteousness of God. The righteous of God will suffer as they are *"persecuted for righteousness' sake." Nonetheless, such persecution does not weaken or dampen the spirits of those who "hunger and thirst after righteousness," for they know their reward is not on earth but in heaven!*

So Christian, do you consider yourself to be happy and full of joy? How much time do you have left to be really happy and full of joy? Are you aware that the Father sent His Son Jesus into this world to die for you and me on that cruel cross of Calvary so that you and I could have joy, and rejoice in the Lord always, Phil. 4:4-7? Let these thoughts sink deeply into your hearts!

May we find our joy, inner peace, and strength, rooted in knowing and believing in Jesus, for He will never let us down. May we trust our Lord Jesus and all that He has promised to those who love and follow Him. May we get rid of our negative attitudes to please God and find the joy that our souls crave. May we have faith in Jesus and all His promises to us so that we can unlock the key to real happiness. May we take advantage of God's great blessings, the blessings that our God has made available to us so that we can have joy and peace.

And may we hunger and thirst after righteousness, acknowledging that without God and His spiritual nourishment, we are bankrupt, needy, and poor.

> *"But the fruit of the Spirit is love, joy, peace, patience, kindness, goodness, faithfulness, gentlenesses, self-control; against such things, there is no law. And those who belong to Christ Jesus have crucified the flesh with its passions and desires"* (Galatians 5:22-24).

Do Not Be Anxious About Anything

"Do not be anxious about anything, but in every-thing by prayer and supplication with thanksgiving let your requests be made known to God. And the peace of God, which surpasses all understanding, will guard your hearts and your minds in Christ Jesus." Philippians 4:6-7

Martha was distracted with much serving. Jesus gently rearranged her priorities saying, *"Martha, Martha, you are anxious and troubled about many things, but one thing is necessary. Mary has chosen the good portion, which will not be taken away from her."* The Lord might say the same to you and me when we are distracted by the many things that trouble us. Only one thing is necessary, and we must choose that good portion.

Jesus' kingdom is not of this world, and though His disciples live in the world, they still must do God's will and not be anxious about earthly things, for they harm and destroy our souls. They quickly become our master and steal our faith, our heavenly treasures, and our service to our true Master. Jesus does not want us to worry and be anxious about the things of this earth. He wants all our hearts. Our faith is weakened when we become anxious about the material things of this world. Anxiety prevents us from seeking the kingdom of God and His righteousness. Jesus commands us to not be anxious. He wants us to devote our care to seeking Him and His right-eousness. Although we will have cares, worries and anxieties here on earth, we still must pursue His heavenly treasures and serve Him with all our heart, soul, and mind.

You see, when our hearts doubt God's provisions (Matthew 6:31), we fall into deep anxiety. When we worry and fear for the future, stress takes over, and we become anxious, and our focus is no longer on heavenly things, and God's kingdom but on earthly things, those things that we think will calm our fears and anxieties.

We must get rid of all layers of distractions and worries about careers, school, health, government, the economy, financial security, retirement, and many things such as these that draw our hearts away from God and His kingdom. We run the danger of becoming the thorny ground of Matthew 13:22, where *"the cares of the world and the deceitfulness of riches choke the word, and it proves unfruitful."* We deceive ourselves thinking that the answer to our fears and worries is found in our own strength or the earthly things of this life. Our anxieties become so powerful that they threaten to take control of our lives, leaving us no escape. Although Jesus understands our anxieties, He still commands us not to be anxious over earthly or physical things but His heavenly things. He proceeds with a question.

> *"Is not life more than food, and the body more than clothing?"* (Matthew 6:25)

I. REASONS NOT TO BE ANXIOUS:

> *"Therefore I tell you, do not be anxious about your life, what you will eat or what you will drink, nor about your body, what you will put on. Is not life more than food, and the body more than clothing? Look at the birds of the air: they neither sow nor reap nor gather into barns, and yet your heavenly Father feeds them. Are you not of more value than they?*

> *And which of you by being anxious can add a single hour to his span of life? And why are you anxious about clothing? Consider the lilies of the field, how they grow: they neither toil nor spin, yet I tell you, even Solomon in all his glory was not arrayed like one of these. But if God so clothes the grass of the field, which today is alive and tomorrow is thrown into the oven, will he not much more clothe you, O you of little faith? Therefore do not be anxious, saying, 'What shall we eat?' or 'What shall we drink?' or 'What shall we wear?' For the Gentiles seek after all these things, and your heavenly Father knows that you need them all"* (Matthew 6:25-32).

In verses 26, 28-30, Jesus gives us four reasons why worry is pointless since the Father provides what we need.

The first reason Jesus gives us comes from nature: (verses 26-30).

Jesus asks us to consider the birds. Birds do not sow, reap, or gather into barns or refrigerators, and yet God always feeds them. In verses 28-30. Jesus asks us to consider the flowers. They do zero work, yet God clothes them more beautifully than the richest of kings. God has made man to sow, reap, and gather. He has made us in His image and more valuable than all plants and animals. Our heavenly Father has provided an abundance of plants, animals, and humans for thousands of years. Knowing all this, *do you doubt that our Father in heaven will not also provide what we need? Do we dare to doubt His consistent and continuing provision for us? Do we dare to doubt that God will give us what we need? He did not create us to abandon us and watch us die! He created us to live!* So, He will provide. Jesus stresses that worry is a matter of faith and trust, for our Father in heaven is in control of what we need.

Jesus' second reason for not worrying is found in verse 27:

> *"And which of you by being anxious can add a single hour to his span of life?"*

Worry and anxiety accomplish nothing! Worry doesn't fix our problems, but it can make us sick. We cannot add one hour to the span of our lives, no matter how intensely we worry. This ought to free us from our cares and worries. We have little power to control our future. Worry shows our lack of faith (verse 30).

Jesus' third reason is a grave reminder of the dangers of anxiety:

Jesus labels those who are always anxious as people of little faith. Anxiety is a lack of trust. *Why?* Because when we worry about God's providential care, we doubt His love, care, and power in our lives. Worry is an affront to God. *What good does it do to wear the name of Christ, and defend our faith fiercely if we allow worry and anxiety to plague our life?* Our faith means very little, for we refuse to put it into practice when we worry and do not have trusting faith in our Father in heaven.

Jesus' fourth reason is that worry or anxiety makes us look like the world: (verses 31-32).

> *"Therefore do not be anxious, saying, 'What shall we eat?' or 'What shall we drink?' or 'What shall we wear?' For the Gentiles seek after all these things, and your heavenly Father knows that you need them all."*

Seeking after food, drink, and clothing is what Gentiles do. Their lives are consumed with the cares of this world. *What else does a godless person live for? They believe in nothing else but to seek food, drink, and clothing!* For the godless (Gentiles), having no food, drink, and clothing means death and no meaning in life. Christians have learned that life has more meaning and purpose, for they are God's children. But when we Christians worry, we are telling God that we do not trust Him, and thus our faith is small. When our minds are set on earthly things, our purpose in life is not in God and His kingdom of right-eousness but in empty and carnal pleasures. *Worry and anxiety is for those who are without Christ!* Our faith and our trust in God makes us shine our light. *Worry and anxiety take away our trust in our heavenly Father and make us look like the world, for they have not God!*

Tomorrow Will Be Anxious For Itself:

> *"Therefore do not be anxious about tomorrow, for tomorrow will be anxious for itself. Sufficient for the day is its own trouble"* (Matthew 6:34).

The final instruction that helps us to fight and eliminate worry and anxiety is found in verse 34. *What an excellent way to close the book of our worries and anxieties!* But you might say, *"You don't understand! I have so much to do tomorrow! Tomorrow is Monday! I have this and that..."* Jesus tells us to lay our con-cerns about tomorrow or any day afterward to rest, for we cannot control what tomorrow might bring. *If we run out of bread tomorrow, then we will deal with that tomorrow! We cannot solve tomorrow's problems today!*

We must compel our minds to do what we must focus on today and let God take care of the rest. Since we have only to-day, we are commanded by God to seek His kingdom and righteousness. It will be impossible to seek God today when our hearts and minds are so full of tomorrow's worries and anxieties. We must focus on what is important, not the future things of this world that seem urgent. *Jesus urges us not to be anxious about tomorrow because tomorrow is tomorrow, and it is not today! We have what we need for today! Let tomorrow worry about tomorrow! Today has enough trouble!* So we must learn to deal with today and live for today, taking advantage of today and being grateful for what God has given us today. *We cannot fix tomorrow, for worry will not change tomorrow!* Remember, God is in control of tomorrow. And we must handle what God has given us today by faith. *Anything could happen tomorrow, but nothing might happen tomorrow!*

The Teacher of Ecclesiastes exhorts us, saying that life is just the same tomorrow as it was today. *So why must we worry? Tomorrow might be different than today, and there is nothing you and I can do to change it!* So we must not worry about what is beyond our reach. Instead, we must put our hope and trust in God for today and for whatever comes our way, good or bad. *Why not choose to trust our Father in heaven instead of being anxious, worried, and frightened, for we are His children whom He loves and cares for?* That ought to give us hope, for God shows His steadfast love and will not forsake us if we faithfully seek after Him and His kingdom of righteousness.

So we must choose to serve Him and be devoted to Him, for everything in this life belongs to Him. Everything we do must be done for Him, according to His will. He will provide for our needs. He is all-powerful and can help us overcome all our struggles, fears, and hardships. So we must examine our hearts and choose to commit our life to Him and not this world. God will establish us, putting us on His winning team. We don't dare to bargain with God under any circumstances but commit to serving Him faithfully by drawing nearer to Him (James 4:8). Remember that a life that pleases God is a life that is empty of materialism and worry, for we must store up treasures in heaven and not on earth (Matthew 6:19-24).

But Seek First The Kingdom of God:

> *"But seek first the kingdom of God and his right-eousness, and all these things will be added to you"* (Matthew 6:33).

In verse 25, Jesus stresses that life is more than food and clothing, our basic needs. Worrying about these basic needs distracts our hearts from what life is truly about. Worrying about life's basic needs puts our primary focus on earthly things and distracts us from God's purpose in life for us, seeking Him and His kingdom of righteousness. You see, the urgency of our worries and anxieties hinders us from seeking the kingdom of God and the pursuit of righteousness. Our lives were created to seek the kingdom of God and His righteousness. *It is what matters the most in this life!* We must not make our worries and anxieties more important than the real food God gives us. We must be filled with and clothed with His Words of righteousness. When we seek the kingdom of God and His righteousness, all of life's basic needs will be added to us. Jesus has promised to provide for our physical needs when we seek what is most important, Him and His kingdom.

So why be so consumed with worry and anxiety? Jesus chips away our worry, anxiety, and fear, for the Father will provide what we need to focus on what is more important in life. So, we must worry and be anxious about the things of God, the heavenly things in His kingdom of righteousness. We must seek righteousness instead of earthly things. The pursuit of righteousness is seen throughout the Sermon on the Mount in Christ's teaching, as expressed in the beatitudes. Jesus stresses the need for us to hunger and thirst after righteousness. One who is truly hungry longs for and craves food. When we crave for righteousness, we will be driven to be holy. It will rule our thoughts, reading, and actions. When we seek after righteousness, we will be merciful, for righteousness compels us to treat others with mercy. Mercy is an attitude that springs from the heart of a renewed person who has experienced God's mercy and wants to show it even to his enemies. Christians are blessed when they seek purity of heart. So, we must seek to become the light of the world and love our enemies.

When we seek after righteousness, we will not have time for worry and anxiety, for our hearts will be filled with thoughts of righteousness. There won't be any need to worry because we know the Lord will provide what we need. So, we must free our hearts from the layers of worry, anxiety, and fear and focus more on the essential things, the things of God's kingdom. We must meditate more on His Word, show mercy in our words, fill our lives with spiritual things, not earthly things. We must meditate on what God has done for us through His Son. Worry and anxiety spring from a faithless heart that's filled with the things of this world. We must choose to win over worry and anxiety, allowing our heart to stand firm, trusting the Lord. God can carry us through our difficult and trying times. He will give us hope for today. When we seek God and His righteousness, we can rest assured that He will provide for our needs. *We will never find righteousness in the worries, anxieties, and uncertainties of this world! We will find the Lord's provision when we seek after His kingdom!*

CONCLUSION:

Jesus stresses why we must not be anxious and worried but instead have faith and trust that God will take care of us. He wants this to be our focal point in life. Worry does not trust God. When we don't trust God, having faith, we're in danger of taking all matters into our own hands. Thus, we become anxious and worried about what we must do to find the solutions to our problems. The most popular solution is, *"don't worry, be happy," "keep calm and play volleyball"* or something else. So, it is met with a response, *"I can't keep calm; I have anxiety!" So how do we overcome anxiety, fear, and worry?* Not by focusing on the things of this world. *It will not work! How can we find peace, remove all layers of distraction that clutter our souls from the peace of God, the peace that frees us from all the cares and anxieties of this world?*

We must first accept that life is more than the empty things of this earth (Matthew 6:25). *That is materialistic and shallow! How sad and vain to pursue these things!* "Man does not live on bread alone" (Matthew 4:4). *We must not live by food alone but depend on God for life and breath!* We must remind ourselves always that our Heavenly Father cares for us (Matthew 6:26). It is the only way to defeat worry and anxiety.

Jesus used the birds to illustrate this great truth. Birds do not store up treasures in barns and houses and yet are fed by our Father in heaven. *So if our gracious Father feeds these tiny creatures, will He not care for us?! Are we not more valuable than the birds?! So how much more will our Father in heaven care for us! He cares and provides for all His awesome creation, but we must develop faith, trusting that God will also care for us! If we believe that our heavenly Father cares for us, why do we worry and get anxious? We must learn to trust in Him and faithfully put our lives in His hands!* We must trust in God and refuse to worry and be anxious, for it does not do any good for us. It hurts us (Matthew 6:27).

Worry is pointless and does not solve our problems. Worry and anxiety cannot solve the past or change the future. Jesus doesn't want us to worry and become anxious (Matt. 6:25). We must combat worry and anxiety and start acknowledging that our God will take care of us (Matt. 6:28-30). We must consider the flowers of the fields. They do not sow or reap or clothe themselves. *Yet they are beautiful and splendid, for God covers them! So, if our gracious God adorns the flowers and the grass, will He not do the same to His faithful children?* In Matthew 6:30, Jesus exhorts us saying,

> "But if God so clothes the grass of the field, which today is alive and tomorrow is thrown into the oven, will he not much more clothe you, O you of little faith?"

Indeed, this is a true fact! Worrying and becoming anxious shows a lack of faith in God. *God is our heavenly Father, and there is nothing to worry and be anxious about!*

One thing that will keep us from worrying is acknowledging that our heavenly Father knows what we need (Matthew 6:32). *It is a test of our faith! God knows what we need tomorrow, so there is nothing to worry about tomorrow!* We must fight worry and anxiety to have a much higher perspective or goal, for we must first seek the kingdom of God and His righteousness above everything else (Matt. 6:33). *God alone is worthy of our total devotion and service!*

We must trust God and have faith rather than being anxious about tomorrow because tomorrow is tomorrow, for it is not today. *We have what we need for today! Let tomorrow worry about tomorrow, for today has enough trouble!* We must handle what God has given us today by faith. *So why must we worry and be anxious about what is beyond our reach? Why not put our trust and hope in God alone, come what may?*

Sadly, many become anxious when things are tough, and life is difficult. They lose heart and become discouraged. In those dark moments, they find it hard to understand the purpose of their trials. They become anxious about the unknown. *They are overwhelmed!* Despair is the opposite of true thanksgiving. It makes us not only anxious but also insecure. When our affections are on earthly things and not on God, we are in danger. We tend to cling to our immediate circumstances rather than to God. Only God can fill our hearts with His peace.

> *"Rejoice in the Lord always; again I will say, rejoice! Let your forbearing spirit be known to all men. The Lord is near."* Philippians 4:5-6

We must always remember that God is in control. God is already in the future because He stands outside of time. Let's never forget His beautiful and faithful promises we find in Matthew 6:28-34. Our God wants us to live in His peace.

> *"And the peace of God, which surpasses all compre-hension, shall guard your hearts and your minds in Christ Jesus."* Philippians 4:7

He doesn't want us to become weary and anxious. He wants us to let go of the bondage of anxiety. It doesn't mean that we will escape feeling sorrow or stress, but we will find a satisfying deep calm in our hearts. Such tranquility can only come from trusting God with all our hearts. We must have the disposition to give thanks to God no matter our circumstances. Yes, we must have a heart of thanksgiving even in death, in life, in sickness, in health, in abundance, and poverty. God expects us to be grateful in all circumstances.

A muscle is strengthened with a lot of exercise. In the same way, our spiritual strength is developed by a lot of practice enabling us to defeat anxiety. We cannot let Satan lie to our minds and emotions. *This surely will drive us crazy!* We can't afford to walk his pathway of lies and anxiety. Anxiety is just that—a great, big lie.

> *"For even though they knew God, they did not honor Him as God, or give thanks; but they became futile in their speculations, and their foolish heart was darkened."* Romans 1:21

Let's remember that God is not a God of chaos and anxiety.

> *"For God has not given us a spirit of timidity, but of power and love and discipline."* 2 Timothy 1:7

Anxiety is not of God but rather the work of Satan. Satan uses this as a weapon against us to distract us from the peace of God. The only way to defeat him is by dwelling in God's Truth, fixing our eyes on Him. Dwelling in lies, trusting that we are in control and not God, is of Satan. Let us always remember that God holds us in His hands and that He is the author of time. Let us remember that we are here temporarily and that He is in control. So, my question is, *what is there to become anxious about?*

May we find that peace and rest that our souls need so much through our Lord Jesus. May we seek His kingdom and His righteousness and trust in His promises. May we live in His peace, trusting Him with all our hearts, minds, and souls. May we keep calm and know that He cares for us. May we never forget that He is near. To Him be the glory.

But One Thing I Do!
Pressing Onward

"Not that I have already obtained, or am already made perfect: but I press on, if so be that I may lay hold on that for which also I was laid hold on by Christ Jesus. Brethren, I count not myself yet to have laid hold: **but one thing I do**, *forgetting the things which are behind, and stretching forward to the things which are before,* **I press on toward the goal** *unto the prize of the high calling of God in Christ Jesus."* Philippians 3:12-14

When a cowboy mounts his horse, he does not ride off in ten directions at once. I sometimes feel that is how we live our lives. We are all very busy working very hard for many good reasons, but *what is our focus?* Let's take a moment and think about this inspiring challenge from the apostle Paul.

I have been thinking a lot about this beautiful and encouraging passage. As I began meditating on each word, I remembered my early walk with Christ, when I acknowledged and accepted that I had to focus on just one thing: to do what was necessary to enter the kingdom of God and His righteousness. It would in no way be an easy task. It would require a lot of letting go, dying to self and even pain in the journey. It would not be easy to crucify the old man with his sinful habits. I knew I had to consider myself dead to sin but alive to Christ, as one that was brought from death to life to become an instrument of righteousness. As in the sentiments expressed by

John the Baptist, *"He must increase but I must decrease"* (John 3:30).

I knew well that the cost of following my Lord would be very high. But I considered the high price He had paid for my sins. It made my journey easier, my steps lighter, and brought me much joy as I walked with my Master. Yes, I knew even then that I had to let go of the past and stretch forward to the future, living for Jesus, my Lord. I had to learn that my life is a race to be won, a course to be completed, and a life to be lived in righteousness brought to fruition. It would require me to set heavenly goals rather than earthly ones. It would demand lots of discipline, like the training of an athlete or soldier, so that I could press on, reaching forward to win the prize, the crown of righteousness, glory, and life. There was no room to give up and quit regardless of my circumstances. *It was going to be a continual battle, but Heaven is worth it all!* There would be times for climbing mountains peaks and times for crossing deep valleys. Periods of sweet rest, then more troubles to come. Times of discouragement and opportunities to revive or refresh my soul.

I learned early on that apart from Jesus and His principles of righteousness, there is no way of salvation. He is the only way to heaven (the ultimate prize). So, I needed to fix my eyes only on Him and not men. I needed to walk with an unfeigned faith and a living hope to fight the good fight of faith and finish the race victoriously. It would demand all my life, energy, and enthusiasm. *Heaven is not for quitters. It is for winners!* But we must keep pressing on toward our goal until our last breath of life. *Victory is just around the corner!*

Many people set high goals for physical things, forgetting the most significant ones in the spiritual realm. We can learn a lot from the apostle Paul about disciplining ourselves to press on toward the right goals, those that pertain to the kingdom of Christ and His righteousness.

There was once a man who lived for things that seemed to him more praiseworthy. Notice what he declares in Philippians 3:4-6 concerning the external things that he possessed to a high degree.

> *"Though I myself might have confidence even in the flesh: if any other man thinketh to have confidence in the flesh, I yet more: circumcised the eighth day, of the stock of Israel, of the tribe of Benjamin, a Hebrew of Hebrews; as touching the law, a Pharisee; as touching zeal, persecuting the church; as touching the righteousness which is in the law, found blameless. Howbeit what things were gain to me, these have I counted loss for Christ."*

Indeed, Paul surpassed many of his contemporaries, Galatians 1:14. He had a lot to boast about his flesh, his externals. However, he declared that there was no virtue whatsoever in the things of the flesh. All those things mentioned in Philippians 3:4-6 in which many of his fellow Jews still trusted. Paul acknowledged that to trust in the flesh would give too much importance to the list of things mentioned before. He then said in verse 7 that *"what things were gain to me, these have I counted loss for Christ."* Things such as honor and distinction, illustrious ancestors, higher education, leadership among those of the strictest sect, and the great respect and honor of his contemporaries. Notice that in verse 7, Paul used the language of accounting. He put all these things under the category of *"jettisoned cargo"* and not under *"essential to survive."* We are all in one way or another "accountants." The word "loss" in the Greek "zemian" is used in Acts 27:10, 21 (to save the crew, sailors, and soldiers). Many things in the ship and cargo were cast into the ocean. Significant "loss" is suffered with great joy when contemplating the lives that were saved.

We are all in one way or another "accountants." Every day we must judge the worth of many things: a good education, wealth, prestige, skills, or talents, and so on. *But are these things really "gain" or "loss"?* It all depends on how one uses them. They can indeed be great "gain" if they are employed to glorify our Lord, or they can be a significant "loss" and destroy our soul.

> *"For what will it profit a man if he gains the whole world and forfeits his soul? Or what shall a man give in return for his soul?"* (Matthew 16:26).

Paul learned that apart from Jesus, everything he lived for was mere rubbish. Indeed, Paul cast many things into the sea to save his spiritual ship, Hebrews 10:32-34. Paul's primary goal was to gain Christ, becoming like Him in His death and resurrection. Paul viewed his life as a race to be won, a life to be lived in righteousness, and a course to be completed or brought to fruition. Although he acknowledged that he had already run a lot, fought a lot, and had won great victories for Christ, he had not yet reached the ultimate goal for the prize. He recognized that though now he was an old man who had done great things for Christ, he was not free from the dangers of sin (I Cor. 9:27).

If Paul, who excelled in love, zeal, self-denial and complete devotion to Christ, thought it necessary to speak this way, *how much more should we who have not even begun to sacrifice like he did?!* Even though Paul knew, without a doubt, he was on the right path, the Way (John 14:6; Mat. 7:13-14; Acts 24:14), he never believed that he could not fall (I Cor. 9:27; 10:13). He has taught us that we must run our race well until the battle is over. Yes, Paul, who was so faithful and endured so much for the Lord's sake, could not "rest," *how much less we!*

The word "perfect" the way Paul uses it in this text, means that absolute perfection of *"the spirits of the righteous made perfect"* (Heb. 12:23). This is accomplished when one finishes the race. In Philippians 3:15, the word "perfect" is used in the sense of maturity (Philippians 3:8-11).

Consider what Paul had to do to keep pressing on toward the goal: to *"gain Christ."*

I. HE HAD TO FORGET THE PAST:

> *"Forgetting the things which are behind"* (Phil. 3:13).

The key word here is "forgetting."

- *Forgetting what?*
- *Leaving behind what?*
- *How can we leave behind all our past failures, regrets, and disappointments?*
- *Those who have let us down.*
- *Sins of the past.*
- *Wounds, wrongdoings, and betrayals left by those who intended to hurt us.*
- *How do we let go of the past's ugliness and sorrows?*
- *Slandering and gossip.*
- *How can we leave behind honor or recognition, material gains, or pleasures?*
- *How can we prevent our past from destroying our future even as it pollutes our present?*
- *How can we do that?*

Paul gives us his attitude of heart and the answers found in God's revealed Word. Few can rival the apostle Paul for reasons to have regrets. Remember, he had persecuted the church and had Stephen stoned to death. He dedicated all his energy, time, and his greatness to chasing down Christians, throwing them into jail. He tortured them and compelled them to blaspheme. In his own words, he was the *"chief"* of all sinners.

Paul chose to "forget" his past and move forward. He did not try to dwell on all the heinous or wicked acts he had committed when he persecuted Christ and His church (I Timothy 1:13). He could not afford to allow success to puff him up. Not the greatness of his past, nor his great achievements, or his severe sacrifices or even the surpassing greatness of the revelations he received (2 Cor. 11:24-28; 12:7). He was resolved not to let anything distract him. Paul refused to live in the past. He focused on the future and moving forward. *The highest prize was still ahead, at the goal line!*

Perhaps, Paul in Philippians 3:13 is referring to all of the advantages or benefits he had in Judaism (verses 4-5); but it could well encompass anything concerning his past life that might have kept him from running and finishing his race in Christ. Impediments such as discouragement, sorrow, persecution, and success. Paul forgot about all those things he could have trusted in. He also had to forget all that could have discouraged him or distracted him.

So, Paul was forced to forget everything. If he didn't, it would have been like the Israelites who kept longing for and remembering all they had left behind in Egypt (Numbers 11:5-6).

We, too, must forget all that we have left behind, our forgiven sins (Hebrews 8:12). God, in His infinite mercy, has forgiven us of our sins. Therefore, we must forgive ourselves. We must not continue afflicting ourselves all the time for having committed them. Sadly, many Christians have not stopped grieving. They don't want to. Their memories are still very alive in their heart and mind. Their guilt and remorse prevent them from moving forward. They cannot win the spiritual race and the prize that God has set before them. *We must move on and not get stuck in the past!* Let us correct what can be rectified and leave the past behind. It is not good for our souls. Our goal must be the future. Our prize is future, and we have not yet reached it. The past is the past and we must forget it and leave it behind. *It is the only way to heaven!*

Moreover, we must forget past offenses. We must forgive others so that our Father in heaven can forgive us. A grudge does not edify the soul, nor does bitterness and anger (Ephesians 4:31-32). We cannot forgive someone as if we were doing them a big favor. Because in doing this and having that negative attitude of heart, the forgiven person is still indebted to us. *And it must not be this way among us!*

In like manner, we must forget our past sufferings. Some are obsessed with them. We must not allow the memory of our suffering to dominate our thoughts and hearts. Instead, we must focus on the kingdom of righteousness, where Christ is seated and ruling. Even our present suffering should not be the focal point. Sadly, many Christians do not speak of anything but their sufferings, regrets, failures, disappointments, afflictions, and trials. It is a mistake to seek sympathy and feel sorry for self. It is the desire of the flesh that does not need to be satisfied.

I realize that each of us has his fair share of suffering, both mental and physical, but we Christians must be careful not to unload our sufferings on others all the time, apparently being obsessed with them. Follow Paul's example. He turned all his sufferings, trials, and problems into opportunities when he said,

> *"I want you to know, brothers, that what has happened to me has really served to advance the gospel, so that it has become known throughout the whole imperial guard and to all the rest that my imprisonment is for Christ. And most of the brothers, having become confident in the Lord by my imprisonment, are much more bold to speak the word without fear"* (Philippians 1:12-14).

So, why not have this attitude of heart like Paul did?

II. REACHING FORWARD TO THE FUTURE:

> *"Stretching forward to the things which are be-fore."* (Philippians 3:13)

Paul redirected his focus by moving forward with the work he had at hand to do. We are either moving forward, standing still, or falling behind. Paul believed in moving forward, and we must use all the forces God has given us to move on and not get stuck in the past. We must meet all the challenges that God has for us. We must accept this challenge and make a difference. The difference must come as we live rooted and grounded in the Word of God.

- Accept and embrace the challenge to move forward in evangelizing even if many are not open to the Gospel.
- The challenge of leadership.
- The challenge of obeying God's Word.
- The challenge of praying more.
- The challenge of rejoicing more and being content rather than being anxious.
- The challenge of moving the Lord's church forward into the future, but that involves every member. It is the only way to bring souls to the foot of the cross.

Life is too short to get stuck in the past, not moving forward for the glory of God. Life is too short to neglect the opportunity to move forward with joy, doing good for others, enriching them spiritually as we speak to them about our Savior and His plan of redemption. Let us not get stuck in self-pity. Let us move forward and let go of whatever impedes us from doing it.

Paul knew he could not afford to get stuck in the past and fail to move forward. There was strenuous work to do. He did what was in front of him to accomplish his highest goal. Getting ourselves busy helps us with so many afflictions of the flesh: depression, valleys of suffering, and problems. We must leave behind the negative conversation within our hearts because it will not amount to anything and never get the job done. It dooms us and keeps us in the past. But we must get down on our knees to press on toward the goal, *"to finish the race and complete the task the Lord Jesus has given me"* (Acts 20:24). It is all about our journey, forgetting what lies behind and stretching forward, always pressing on toward our goal.

In this same letter, Paul speaks with a singular voice, *"Rejoice in the Lord always; again I will say, rejoice."* There is nothing to be anxious. Worries choke the Word (Luke 8:14) and are incompatible with peace (Phi. 4:7). So, let us resolve our worries and anxieties with joy and gentleness, casting all our fears and anxieties on Him because He cares and loves us immensely. Let us be careful and grateful about our circumstances. Every suffering, affliction, and heavy burden has a Bible solution (2 Timothy 3:16-17). And let us fix our eyes only on Jesus rather than men. Our Lord and Savior is the "goal," and nothing else. Let us not be moved from our hope. Let us draw near to God and He will draw near to us. Therefore, let us be successful athletes who play to win (I Cor. 9:27). But strong desire and motivation are vital to reaching forward to those things which are ahead (Phil. 3:13).

So, let us find true contentment (Phil. 4:11-13). Let us change how we react to all our problems and sufferings. No tranquilizer can alleviate even one of life's problems or the anguish of heart we feel. Pills cannot change our circumstances. We must find our strength in Christ. It is all about our attitude of heart. Paul did not become bitter, angry, anxious, or worried but chose to say,

"To the present hour we hunger and thirst, we are poorly dressed and buffeted and homeless, and we labor, working with our own hands. When reviled, we bless; when persecuted, we endure; when slandered, we entreat. We have become, and are still, like the scum of the world, the refuse of all things" (1 Cor. 4:11-13).

"Not that I am speaking of being in need, for I have learned in whatever situation I am to be content. I know how to be brought low, and I know how to abound. In any and every circumstance, I have learned the secret of facing plenty and hunger, abundance and need. I can do all things through him who strengthens me" (Philippians 4:11-13).

Oh, how I love to read these passages when my heart is overwhelmed with the heavy burdens of this world. It fills my soul with joy and hope!

III. HAVING OUR HEARTS FIXED ON THE GOAL:

"I press on toward the goal unto the prize of the high calling of God in Christ Jesus." (Philippians 3:14)

The Greek word for "press toward" is a stronger word than the one in verse 13 translated "reaching forward." "Reaching forward" implies the direction one is headed toward the goal. On the other hand, "pressing forward" indicates using pressure to advance toward that goal. Likewise, it conveys the idea of intense endeavor.

The word "goal" refers to the "target," which is the primary objective (target, goal) reached by the one who is running. Now, the "prize" is the reward given by the Author and Finisher of the victorious race, that is, the "crown of righteousness" (1 Cor. 9:24; 2 Tim. 4:8); the "crown of life" (Revelation 2:10), the "unfading crown of life" (1 Peter 5:4).

Regarding this race, Paul exhorts us saying,

> *"Do you not know that those who run in a race all run, but only one receives the prize? Run in such a way that you may win"* (1 Cor. 9:24).

So, what is the final goal or target? The final meeting with our Lord Jesus, either when one dies (1:23) or at *"the appearing of the glory of our great God and Savior Jesus Christ"* (Titus 2:13). Paul's primary focus in life was the future glory that was to be revealed (Romans 8:18). Paul is our greatest example of heavenly perspective. Heaven was his primary target. He would obey God with all his might, pressing on toward his final goal of heaven. He pressed on as a faithful Christian to receive the crown of life. *What a motivator this is for us!*

Paul was not controlled by his past but rather looked with anticipation toward the future. *No wonder he had so much joy!* He knew his life did not depend on those things of the world, but on the eternal principles of righteousness found in our Lord and Savior, Jesus Christ.

We must concentrate on just one thing.

- *"But one thing I do"* (Phi. 1:13).
- *"But one thing is necessary"* (Luke 10:42),
- *"One thing I do know"* (John 9:25).

Our prize cannot be obtained without both effort and focus. Remember that the runner presses on and finishes the race because he does not give up. He is focusing on the reward or keeping the prize in mind. Therefore, he is unwilling to quit, even for a second, despite his pain, agony, or exhaustion. That is what we must also do. Even during persecution, tragedy, pain, suffering, etc., he keeps his faith.

The winners of the contest will be rewarded! The winner will receive an imperishable crown.

1. *So, how are you running your race?*
2. *Is heaven your goal?*
3. *Are you motivated and dedicated enough to achieving it at any cost?*
4. *If you are not putting Christ and His kingdom of righteousness first, I don't see how you can have heaven as your primary goal or target!*
5. *Are you making significant sacrifices for God according to His Word?*
6. *Are you pressing toward the goal, the prize, eternal life, or are you just dreaming about it, and living as you please?*

Think about it! Don't let go of your prize!

Therefore,

1. Let us set our *"minds on things that are above, not on things that are on earth"* (Col. 3:2).
2. Let us not get entangled in the affairs of this life (2 Tim. 2:4).
3. Let us walk like Paul and Christ, who walked faithfully (1 Cor. 11:1).
4. And let us walk after the pattern we see in the New Testament that we may win the race and receive the prize.

IV. THERE MUST BE A FERVENT DESIRE TO WIN THE PRIZE:

"For that is far better" (Phil. 1:23).

There must be:

- A *"hunger and thirst for righteousness"* (Matt. 5:6).
- A thirst for the living God (Psalm 42:2).
- A desire for a *"better country, that is, a heavenly one"* (Heb. 11:16).
- A desire *"to strive to enter through the narrow door"* (Luke 13:24).

VI. THE HOPE OF SALVATION IS VITAL TO RUN THE RACE WELL:

We must run our race with the full confidence of winning. Otherwise, we will not reach the goal.

> *"For in hope we have been saved, but hope that is seen is not hope; for who hopes for what he already sees?"* (Romans 8:24).

> *"But since we are of the day, let us be sober, having put on the breastplate of faith and love, and as a helmet, the hope of salvation"* (1 Thess. 5:8).

Therefore, all athletes who enroll must contend to win. They must play with the real hope of winning. *It is of great importance!* Revelation 21, 22, and Matthew 25:34 must be our top motivators to victory in heaven, where we will receive our crown of righteousness, glory, and life. *Our hope is so strong that we can almost taste it!*

CONCLUSION:

Sometimes our past is our worst enemy. We struggle with our past (mistakes, disappointments, failures, wrongdoing, wounds, past sins, accomplishments, achievements, traditions, etc.), finding it almost impossible to forget and move on. It is easier to remember than to forget.

The apostle Paul exhorts us through the revealed Word to forget what lies behind and reach forward to what lies ahead. Paul was able to get beyond his own past mistakes and outstanding accomplishments by forgetting the past and reaching forward to the future for the prize of the upward calling of Jesus our Lord. And though Paul had won many spiritual battles, extending the Gospel of Jesus to the Gentiles in Asia Minor, he did not claim to have attained spiritual maturity (the state of completion as a Christian). Thus, he pressed on, pursuing consistently with all deliberate speed to obtain the prize that Christ had in store for him. He seized Christ just as Christ seized him (on the road to Damascus, changing his life forever). Paul wanted to take hold of Christ, know, and love Him as much as Jesus had taken hold of him.

In other words, Paul pursued the goal of being like Christ. He did so with the enthusiasm and perseverance of a runner like those who participated in the Greek games. He conformed to the image of Christ. He knew but one thing: *"forgetting the things which are behind, and stretching forward to the things which are before, I press on toward the goal unto the prize of the high calling of God in Christ Jesus."*

Indeed, Paul ran focusing on those things that matter the most, the spiritual ones and not the things of the flesh which are only temporary. He focused on his citizenship, heaven and not earth. We must be of the same mind as Paul, who kept reaching forward and pressing on toward the goal of eternal life in heaven. It is where we belong.

Sadly, for many, their affections are not on heavenly things. They become distracted by this world (materialism, entertainment, recreation, lusts, pleasures, etc.). They are willing to lose their souls for earthly pursuits. *Are you?* May we always seek first the kingdom of God and His righteousness (Matt. 6:33).

As Christians, we must move forward with the right attitude of heart, accepting our challenges by focusing and being rooted in the Word of God. But to move forward, we must fight with tooth and claw the enemies of ignorance, unbelief, apathy, and sin. We cannot afford to lose the battle and our race. We must run and fight well to win our prize.

We must fix our eyes on Jesus and not man to reach our goal. Likewise, we must have an intense hunger and thirst for righteousness and for the living God to reach the goal. We must strive to enter the narrow gate. But one thing we must do, one thing is needful, one thing I know: *"reaching forward to those things which are ahead."*

The hope of salvation is vital to run and finish the race victoriously. We must run with the hope of winning the race to win the prize.

Therefore, let us not allow ourselves to become distracted by the past and be discouraged. On that final day, the faithful will be given incorruptible, glorious, and heavenly bodies. They will be with the Lord for eternity. *Such hope is worth fighting for!*

May we continue to press on toward our goal, heaven where our citizenship is. May we never allow ourselves to become distracted by the things of this world and give up our heavenly citizenship. May we gain Christ for this is indeed gain. May we compete according to the rules, as real athletes, to win the prize. And finally, may we fight the good fight, finish the race, and keep the faith and receive our reward, the crown of righteousness.

Will Your Anchor Hold in the Storms of Life?

"Wherein God, being minded to show more abundantly unto the heirs of the promise the immutability of his counsel, interposed with an oath; that by two immutable things, in which it is impossible for God to lie, we may have a strong encouragement, who have fled for refuge to lay hold of the hope set before us: which we have as an anchor of the soul, a hope both sure and steadfast and entering into that which is within the veil..." Hebrews 6:17-19

The past few weeks have been tough for me with my father's passing and getting sick with COVID-19. It has been four weeks, and by the Grace of God, we have recovered and are feeling much better. Our prayers have been answered. Our second COVID-19 test has come back negative, and we are not contagious anymore. Out next step will be to donate plasma (our antibodies) for the treatment of others who are suffering in the hospitals due to COVID-19. May God be praised for His goodness and mercy toward us through your prayers. My family, both here and in Florida, also got sick. They also have recovered except for my sister, who is fighting the virus and will remain in the hospital for at least a few more days. We continue to hope that the new treatment with antibodies (plasma) will give her a complete recovery according to the Grace of God.

With these things in mind, let us think for a while about what God provides for us as an anchor for our souls during the stormy seasons of our lives through His Son, our Lord Jesus.

In all this, I have learned that no matter how righteous a Christian might be, he is not exempt from suffering, and we must learn to accept our trials and sufferings with joy. All our trials and sufferings refine our faith and mold us into what God wants us to be that we might be faithful to Him until we die. In all our sufferings, our Lord Jesus Christ is honored. And no matter what happens in our life, our Lord and Savior must be honored, for He is worthy of all honor and praise. We must continue with joy and confidence in our eternal home. Our faith must remain strong, that we not become bitter, sour, and ungrateful.

Our pain and suffering grow our faith. Our faith helps us to endure all of life's sufferings and difficulties. God uses our afflictions to perfect our faith for our good. Indeed, it is difficult to have a positive and peaceful mindset when we go through trials and pain. But there are so many disguised blessings when we endure our pain and struggles to survive and keep afloat! When we are suffering, our expectations are debilitated and shattered. We forget what God can accomplish through our pain. Our trials and sufferings must not hinder our fervent love for Christ. Often, in our grief, we stop reading and studying our Bibles. We stop praying and singing songs of praise to God. Our desire to honor Christ must compel us to pray, praise, study, and have fellowship with Him and one another during the days of suffering. God allows suffering for a reason. It is for His glory. Suffering with hope and praise honors Christ, for He alone is our solid Rock in Whom we find refuge and strength.

Suffering and pain are good for us. No matter how intense our affliction may be, God will find a way to provide what we need to comfort us. *I am happy to be sharing in the sufferings of my Lord Jesus!* Through pain and suffering, I have come to know the power of God. Suffering grows our faith in Christ, for it compels us to rely on His power and not our own. Though we might find ourselves utterly burdened beyond strength, God is able to deliver us. But we must depend on Him for deliverance. God can strengthen and comfort us so that we might endure our afflictions. God's comfort is not intended to make us comfortable but rather to make us comforters to others. Our pain and trials must be used to help others who are enduring similar trials. May we learn to comfort those who are suffering and be the means of God's comfort to them (2 Cor. 1:3-4).

The Psalms have become my best and most loyal companions when I descend into the valleys of despair. I go to them for guidance, comfort, refreshment, and healing. They teach me to trust in God despite my circumstances. When my heart is overwhelmed and my world is upside down, they guide me and force me to discern and accept that God's ways are not my ways and that I must hold on to Him even when it seems like He is not holding on to me. The Psalms help me understand God more and more. As I read and meditate on them, I see that I must walk with Him faithfully in a real world of pain and suffering. They teach me to trust in Him, for He is working behind the scenes and behind the real screen of the great unknown. He is with us even when the hopeless mist of struggles clouds our mind and heart.

Singing songs of praise helps me to trust in Him even when I cannot see His obvious works, His great deliverance. Singing songs of praise strengthens me when my spirit is flagging. *O, how I long to immerse myself in His Word and sing songs of praise when my heart is distressed!* It is the only antidote that can heal my crushed heart. Such songs help me face tragedy, for they keep me focused on the unseen and lead me to acknowledge God (trust Him, His Word, and His providence).

The Gospel gives us hope despite the troubled world that roars all around us. Let's think about what our Lord has provided to anchor our souls and bring us calm amid the storms.

I. OUR HOPE AS AN ANCHOR IN TROUBLED TIMES:

I have selected the song "We Have An Anchor" because it pictures our hope as an anchor of the soul, both sure and steadfast. This song also reminds us of the anchor provided to our souls by our hope in our Lord and Savior, Jesus Christ. This anchor provided by our Lord keeps us from drifting. When a storm buffets a ship, it needs an anchor to provide security and safety (Acts 27:29). And just as ships are often faced with storms, so it is that we must face storms in this life. The clouds unfold wings of strife when we are faced with various trials and tribulations (James 1:2-3). Thus, we must have an anchor fastened to something steadfast that we not drift (Hebrews 2:1). *Will your anchor drift or firm remain?*

The Christian's Hope:

1. *What is the meaning of hope to the Christian?*
2. *How does the Bible define hope?*

Hope is crucial to the Christian. The hope that the Bible speaks of is not an *"I-hope-so,"* but rather an *"I-know-so."* It does not wish for the best. It is not waiting to see what happens and hope that it turns out well. Hope is not a feeling or emotion. Hope is the knowledge of facts. The Bible defines hope as the sure anchor of the soul. Human hope is insignificant in comparison to the hope of the Bible.

Our hope allows us to desire and expect what God has in store for us.

> *"Wherein God, being minded to show more abundantly unto the heirs of the promise the immutability of his*

counsel, interposed with an oath; that by two immutable things, in which it is impossible for God to lie, we may have a strong encouragement, who have fled for refuge to lay hold of the hope set before us: which we have as an anchor of the soul, a hope both sure and steadfast and entering into that which is within the veil; whither as a forerunner Jesus entered for us, having become a high priest forever after the order of Melchizedek." (Hebrews 6:17-20)

The hope we have as Christians is based on *"two immutable things, in which it is impossible for God to lie."* Consider them:

- God's promise.
- God's oath.

So, what is this promise, and what is this oath? The promise is the one given to Abraham that his seed should be blessed, and in this seed should all nations of the earth be blessed. The questions are:

- *To whom was the promise made?*
- *Who are the "seed"?*

The Seed is our Lord Jesus, through whom all nations are blessed. This promise was made not according to the flesh but according to the Spirit. We Christians are the seed of Abraham since our Father is the God of the faithful. Therefore, God's promise is established securely for all who are faithful to Him as Abraham, who was faithful to Him. Abraham believed God's promises and walked in the steps of faith as an example to us. All who are faithful to Christ Himself will be blessed as sons of Abraham.

So, what is the oath? It is the oath that the Lord swore to Abraham after he had offered his son Isaac as a sacrifice to Him. It is the oath of His priesthood. Our Lord Jesus is our

Priest, who has finished His sacrificial work and has already gone within the veil and is now seated at the right hand of God, the Father forever. *His priesthood is abiding in eternal efficacy!*

What a blessed anchor to the soul it is to know our Lord and Savior is within the veil! Our King of righteousness and peace is now seated before the throne of our Father in heaven, interceding for us. Therefore, I have that hope of assurance and security in Him.

1. *What better Anchor can the faithful have?*
2. *What a consolation that we can be heirs of such a promise!*
3. *What hope it is for His faithful ones to rely on His oath and promise!*

Our Anchor, Jesus, is drawing us home to Himself, not downward beneath raging and devouring waves, but upward to blissful joys. *Our hope is nearer than when we first believed! It is near to its fruition!* We are anchored to heaven's precious promises.

> *"So that by two unchangeable things, in which it is impossible for God to lie, we who have fled for refuge might have strong encouragement to hold fast to the hope set before us"* (Hebrews 6:18).

And the foundation of our hope, our joy, and our peace is our confidence in the unfailing promises of God. His promises are evident in His Word.

> *"For when God made a promise to Abraham, since he had no one greater by whom to swear, he swore by himself, saying, "Surely I will bless you and multiply you." And thus Abraham, having patiently waited, obtained the promise"* (Hebrews 6:13-15).

The Christian's definition of hope is far superior to that of the world. A Christian knows that his hope is based on solid, concrete evidence because it is grounded in the Word of God, and we know that God cannot lie (Heb 6:18; Num 23:19). The Christian has a faith that is *"the assurance of things hoped for, the conviction of things not seen"* (Heb 11:1). It is the hope of faith that will not be shaken or moved by circumstances or what the eyes see because an unseen God is seen in His faithfulness.

In Romans 8:24-25, Paul tells us the following.

> *"For in hope were we saved: but hope that is seen is not hope: for who hopeth for that which he seeth? But if we hope for that which we see not, then do we with patience wait for it."*

> *"And hope does not disappoint, because the love of God has been poured out within our hearts through the Holy Spirit who was given to us."* (Romans 5:5)

It is the hope of resurrection. *"The hope and resurrection of the dead."*

> *"Now when Paul perceived that one part were Sadducees and the other Pharisees, he cried out in the council, 'Brothers, I am a Pharisee, a son of Pharisees. It is with respect to the hope and the resurrection of the dead that I am on trial.' And when he had said this, a dissension arose between the Pharisees and the Sadducees, and the assembly was divided. 8 For the Sadducees say that there is no resurrection, nor angel, nor spirit, but the Pharisees acknowledge them all."* (Acts 23:6-10)

> *"So also is the resurrection of the dead. It is sown in corruption; it is raised in incorruption: it is sown in dishonor; it is raised in glory: it is sown in weak-*

ness; it is raised in power: it is sown a natural body; it is raised a spiritual body. If there is a natural body, there is also a spiritual body." (1 Cor. 15:42-43)

We all long to be with our Lord in His heavenly Jerusalem. However, we must pass through the storms of life before we arrive at our destination. Yet, our Lord helps us to achieve our goal by keeping us pressing onward, knowing that in this hope, *"We have an anchor."*

Our God has provided us an anchor to our souls through our Lord Jesus Christ to hold us fast lest we be shipwrecked, unhappy, unstable, useless, and hopeless. Jesus, our Lord, is God's perfect provision for us. *He is our City of Refuge!* The true Anchor holds because,

1. Our Father in Heaven has provided us with hope (Heb. 6:19).
2. We have a home, and our anchor is secured in heaven, in the Holy of Holies since Jesus is there as our High Priest (Heb. 6:19-22; Heb. 9:11-12).
3. Our anchor is set firmly in the regions above, and every step of our journey is bringing us closer to our heavenly destination.
4. We are anchored to heaven's peerless Priest (Heb. 6:20).
5. Our peerless Priest has proceeded to heaven before us and is our *"forerunner"* (Heb. 6:19-20).
6. Heaven's peerless Priest has perfected us by redeeming us and is sitting at the right hand of God's throne interceding for us (Heb. 10:12-14).
7. Heaven's peerless Priest is preparing for us a place (Heb. 6:20).
8. Our anchor holds since it is anchored to the Solid Rock, Jesus Christ, the one whose name is above all names.

When our hope is in Christ, we are safely moored because our anchor will be well-secured by our Savior's mighty hand. This anchor secures us to our Savior (Lk. 2:11). It is as if cables were passing from our Savior's heart to ours. But this can only be true when we are devoted to Him and love Him with all our hearts (Mark 12:30). Through these spiritual cables, we are able to defy the blast, for we will be strengthened with power through His Spirit in our inner being (Eph. 3:16-17). The anchor that Jesus provides to us by our hope in Him will guide us in the straits of fear. As we sail life's seas, we will be faced with situations that will produce fear. But God has not given us a spirit of fear but of power, love, and self-control (2 Tim. 1:7). And though the tempest might rave fiercely all around us, there is nothing to fear, for God has promised to be with us to calm the storm (Heb. 13:5-6). With God on our side, we can rest assured that no angry wave shall our bark overflow. Perfect love casts out all fear (1 John 4:18).

The anchor provided by our Lord Jesus will sustain us in the floods of death. When we, Christians, pass through the floods of death, our eyes can behold that city of gold (Rev. 21:1-2). Although many debate where the soul actually goes after we die, whether it is heaven or not, we, Christians, must agree that the righteous who die in the Lord are in a state of bliss because they are near that shore where the pure river of the water of life flows (Rev. 22.1-2). Here, they are resting from their labors, and their storms are all past, for God has promised that there will be no more death, sorrow, crying, or pain to bring about those storms (Rev. 21:3-4). We may rest assured that one day, we all must pass through the floods of death (Heb. 9:27). However, in Christ, we have a steadfast anchor, and that can never fail. Such hope will result in our salvation (Rom. 8:24-25). Such an anchor can never fail because it reaches and fastens to that which is within the veil, our Lord Jesus Christ (Heb. 10:19-20). *The anchor will bring us to the golden harbor of heaven!*

CONCLUSION:

All faithful Christians must be ready for hardships, diffi-culties, discomfort, and afflictions. Satan uses our afflictions to move us away from God. His goal is for us to give up. He de-lights in striking us from every angle so that we give up on God. Satan wants to hear us say, *"It's too much, and it is too hard!"* He wants to wreck our lives. And it does not matter if we lose everything in this life, for we must learn to live for God, honor, serve, and worship Him. We must surrender to Him whatever He gives us in life. We must trust God while suffering (1 Peter 4:19). Our suffering demonstrates our gen-uine faith and must continue to do good. In doing this, we will defend the hope we have in Christ and help others. We moti-vate unbelievers and believers by the way we behave in the face of suffering. When we continue steadfast in our service to God in the face of suffering, we are opening doors for unbe-lievers to come to Jesus. Honoring Jesus is rejoicing even in our massive trials. We must be like Job, who said, *"Shall we receive good from God, and shall we not receive adversity"* (Job 2:10)."*The LORD gave and the LORD has taken away, blessed be the name of the LORD"* (Job 1:21). *Amen to that!*

Therefore, I am resolved not to be moved by my afflictions. We must be ready to suffer and carry Jesus' cross no matter what may come our way in this life. We must be ready for tri-als and suffering. We must take joy in Christ, who gives us the strength necessary to bear all of life's pain and trials. He is our Comforter and the Father of all mercies who comforts us in all our afflictions (2 Cor. 1:4). Pain and suffering teach us to share the comfort of God with those who are afflicted and need it most. God's comfort does not end with us. God teaches us through our suffering to comfort others with the same comfort that we receive from Him. He comforts us in our afflictions that we may be His conduits of comfort to others who are also suffering. You see, our suffering has a divine purpose. God's purpose is that we may understand compassion toward one another. Suffering is not a competition about who has suffered the most. I often hear those who are suffering say that their pain is so much worse than anyone else's. *This is naïve!* It hinders us from being a channel of real comfort and blessing. *We must not wallow in self-pity seeking others' attention, but rather lift our eyes and see the ways we can comfort others even while we are suffering!*

We often plant ourselves in shifting sand, leaving our ship adrift and in danger of sinking. You see, people are desperately trying to fasten themselves to an insecure world, forgetting the true anchor that is secure, grounded in the deep. Indeed, this world, like a restless sea, can be a cruel and dangerous place filled with storms, tribulations, trials, and pain.

We all have stormy seasons that rage fiercely, turning everything upside down. They are:

1. The storms of doubt, discouragement, despair, and defeat as well as the winds of temptation, trials, and sorrows that tear at our sails.
2. The seas of sin, sorrow, and sickness leave us wounded and discouraged.
3. Our barriers of fear, frustration, and failures can cause us to lose our joy, hope, and peace as well.

Thus, we start to wonder if we are going to make it or not. *Will your anchor hold steadfastly or drift away when adversities touch your life? Will your faith survive?*

Jesus, our Anchor, will steady our ship when we anchor our lives to Him. He will calm the storms of our life that batter our ship and set it adrift in the violent seas. He will hold fast our ship and keep it from drifting as He sees us safely home. He is our anchor of hope, our daily motivation, and encouragement when we place our faith in Him.

Our hope is our anchor. The hope of the Bible is compared to a ship on the sea that is threatened by raging storms that drive the ship from its intended course. As the ship's anchor reaches down to the seafloor, out of sight, so the Christian's anchor rises out of sight into heaven. *When it strikes solid ground there, it is fixed!*

The purpose of the anchor is to hold us fast to our God. Our hope gives us stability in stormy times.

May we make sure our anchor holds and grips the Solid Rock, Jesus our Lord. May we be fastened to the Solid Rock that *"keeps the soul steadfast and sure while the billows roll."* May our anchor hold to the Rock, which *"cannot move, grounded firm and deep in the Savior's love." Our only hope!* May the Lord be our Anchor, as our soul's refuge, in times of trouble and *"stormy seas."* May God's Word, prayer, and songs of praise be our anchors in all our troubled times. May we hold fast to our true Anchor lest we drift away. May we all be encouraged by the hope that is set before us, which we have as an anchor of the soul.

Read with me the words of this beautiful song. It is one of my all-time favorite songs. I hope the words of this lovely song stir your soul the way it does mine.

Will Your Anchor Hold?

"Will your anchor hold in the storms of life,
When the clouds unfold their wings of strife?
When the strong tides lift, and the cables strain,
Will your anchor drift or firm remain?"

"It is safely moored, 'twill the storm withstand,
For 'tis well-secured by the Savior's hand;
And the cables passed from His heart to mine
Can defy the blast through strength divine."

"It will firmly hold in the straits of fear,
When the breakers have told the reef is near;
Though the tempests rave and the wild winds
      blow,
Not an angry wave shall our bark o'erflow."

"It will surely hold in the floods of death,
When the waters cold chill our latest breath;
On the rising tide it can never fail,
While our hopes abide within the veil."

"When our eyes behold through the gathering
      night
The city of gold, our harbor bright,
We shall anchor fast by the heavenly shore,
With the storms all past forevermore."

Chorus,
"We have an anchor that keeps the soul
Steadfast and sure while the billows roll,
Fastened to the Rock which cannot move,
Grounded firm and deep in the Savior's love."

It Is Well With My Soul

"Blessed be the God and Father of our Lord Jesus Christ, the Father of mercies and God of all comfort, who comforts us in all our affliction, so that we may be able to comfort those who are in any affliction, with the comfort with which we ourselves are comforted by God. For as we share abundantly in Christ's sufferings, so through Christ we share abundantly in comfort too. If we are afflicted, it is for your comfort and salvation; and if we are comforted, it is for your comfort, which you experience when you patiently endure the same sufferings that we suffer. Our hope for you is unshaken, for we know that as you share in our sufferings, you will also share in our comfort." 2 Corinthians 1:3-7

Most of us are familiar with the hymn, *"It Is Well with My Soul."* I love it, not only for its beautiful message but because of the history behind it. Horatio Gates Spafford wrote it. Horatio and his wife lived in Chicago with their five children. He always maintained his faith despite financial success. He was a businessman who lost almost all his sizable investments in the Great Fire of Chicago in 1871. At about that same time, his four years old son died of scarlet fever.

Two years later, in 1873, after he had lost his business, Spafford was advised by his doctor to take a rest. And then, to make things worse, a little while after that, his wife had health problems due to their son's loss. He planned a trip for her to help her emotionally. He was going to take his family to England, but due to unexpected, last-minute business, he had to remain in Chicago and sent his wife and their four daughters ahead of him. His family sailed on a French steamer without him. The ship sank in the middle of the Atlantic Ocean when it was struck by the Loch Earn, an iron sailing vessel. He lost his four daughters, all his family except for his wife, Anna Spafford. *What a tragedy!*

It is believed that he wrote a poem shortly after that as an expression of his faith in God. The poem began with the following words.

> *"When peace, like a river, attendeth my way,*
> *When sorrows like sea billows roll;*
> *Whatever my lot, Thou has taught me to say,*
> *It is well, with my soul."*

Three years later, in 1876, Spafford gave the poem to Ira David Sankey.

The song *"It Is Well with My Soul"* is a beautiful and moving song that gives us hope amid life's fiery trials and reminds us that God will redeem our souls from the power of the grave and receive us into His heavenly portals. Let us consider the hope that we have as an anchor of our soul. An anchor that reassures us of our hope and that helps us to say with confidence,

> *"It Is Well with My Soul."*

I. THE PEACE OF GOD AMID OUR FIERY TRIALS:

> *"When peace, like a river, attendeth my way,*
> *When sorrows like sea billows roll;*
> *Whatever my lot, Thou hast taught me to say,*
> *It is well, it is well with my soul."*

The poem's first stanza describes the peace that God extends to us like a river amid our fiery trials (Isa. 66:12). Those who trust in God can have the peace that keeps their souls when sorrows and anxiety come our way. God does not want us to be anxious about anything. He wants us to make known our needs by supplication and prayer to Him with thanksgiving. He promised to give us His peace and guard our hearts and minds (Phil. 4:6-7). *We must believe that His peace is available to us when sorrows cause us anxiety and despair!* We must learn to be content whatever our lot, knowing that God is with us all the way. He has promised not to leave us nor forsake us. We can assuredly say,

> *"The Lord is my helper; I will not fear; what can man do to me?"* (Heb. 13:5-6).

II. THE ASSURANCE OF REDEMPTION IN OUR TRIALS:

> *"Though Satan should buffet, though trials should*
> *come,*
> *Let this blest assurance control,*
> *That Christ hath regarded my helpless estate,*
> *And hath shed His own blood for my soul."*

The second stanza gives us the assurance of redemption in our time of trials. Although Satan might buffet us through the fiery trials of life, God's faithful children, those whose hearts are right with Him, can rest assured that God cares and is aware of what is happening to us. As faithful Christians, we must rejoice and be glad, for we are sharing in Christ's sufferings (1 Peter 4:12-13).

Thus, *"we can draw near with a true heart in full assurance of faith, with our hearts sprinkled clean from an evil conscience and our bodies washed with pure water"* (Hebrews 10:22). Our full assurance is based on Christ's own blood that was shed for us.

"For this is my blood of the covenant, which is poured out for many for the forgiveness of sins" (Matt. 26:28).

III. FORGIVENESS OF SINS IN CHRIST:

"My sin, oh the bliss of this glorious thought!
My sin, not in part but the whole,
Is nailed to His (or the) cross, and I bear it no more,
Praise the Lord, praise the Lord, O my soul!"

The third stanza describes the forgiveness of sins through Christ's blood. Since we all have sinned and have fallen short of the glory of God, we need the blood of Jesus to redeem us (Romans 3:23). Jesus, our Lord, bore our sins when He gave His body on the tree as a sacrifice for us that through Him we might be forgiven of our sins and rise up in newness of life to righteousness.

"He himself bore our sins in his body on the tree,
that we might die to sin and live to righteousness.
By his wounds you have been healed" (1 Peter 2:24).

Thus, through His precious blood, we have redemption, the forgiveness of our sins (Eph. 1:7).

IV. WE HAVE LIFE IN CHRIST:

"For me, be it Christ, be it Christ hence to live:
If Jordan above me shall roll,
No pain (or pang) shall be mine, for in death as in life
Thou wilt whisper Thy peace to my soul."

The fourth stanza (not in HFWR) declares that we have life in Christ, and He lives in us. Since we have been crucified with

Christ in the waters of baptism, we must cease the practice of sin, for He lives in us.

> *"I have been crucified with Christ. It is no longer I who live, but Christ who lives in me. And the life I now live in the flesh I live by faith in the Son of God, who loved me and gave himself for me"* (Gal. 2:20).

In our stanza, *"Jordan"* symbolizes the time of death (Heb. 9:27). As those who have been redeemed by the precious blood of Jesus, we must magnify, honor the Lord both in life and death (Phil. 1:20).

V. WE MUST PRESS ON TOWARD OUR GOAL:

> *"But Lord, 'tis for Thee, for Thy coming we wait,*
> *The sky, not the grave, is our goal;*
> *Oh, trump of the angel! Oh, voice of the Lord!*
> *Blessed hope, blessed rest of my soul."*

The fifth stanza (also not in HFWR) tells us that we have a goal to press on toward and that we must patiently wait for the Lord's coming (1 Thess. 1:9-10). This promise should motivate us to keep ourselves pressing on toward our goal, our prize.

> *"Brothers, I do not consider that I have made it my own. But one thing I do: forgetting what lies behind and straining forward to what lies ahead, 14 I press on toward the goal for the prize of the upward call of God in Christ Jesus"* (Phil. 3:13-14).

Thus, we must look forward to hearing His voice (John 5:28-29).

VI. OUR EXPECTATION OF CHRIST'S COMING:

> *"And Lord haste the day, when the faith shall be*
> *sight,*
> *The clouds be rolled back as a scroll;*
> *The trump shall resound, and the Lord shall de-*
> *scend,*
> *Even so, it is well with my soul."*

The sixth stanza speaks of our expectation that Christ will come as He has promised. We don't know, and we are not told when that day will be, but we do know that someday the trumpet will sound. Then the Lord, as He has promised, will descend in the same way as He went to heaven (Acts 1:11).

> *"Behold! I tell you a mystery. We shall not all sleep,*
> *but we shall all be changed, 52 in a moment, in the*
> *twinkling of an eye, at the last trumpet. For the*
> *trumpet will sound, and the dead will be raised im-*
> *perishable, and we shall be changed"* (1 Cor. 15:51-
> 52).

> *"And said, 'Men of Galilee, why do you stand look-*
> *ing into heaven? This Jesus, who was taken up from*
> *you into heaven, will come in the same way as you*
> *saw him go into heaven'"* (Acts 1:11).

Thus, we must live faithfully and live with this expectation, eagerly waiting for His coming.

> *"Even so, come, Lord Jesus"* (Rev. 22:20).

CONCLUSION:

Maybe, you and I have not lost our children, but some have. Tragedies like this often rob us of our peace. It may be debilitating health, death, significant financial losses, rebellious children, unbearable conflicts in our marriage, brethren or many other things that are thrown our way to rob us of our peace. The list may be extensive, but we must remember to turn our hearts toward the Lord, as Horatio did, to find true peace. *Divine peace that surpasses our terrible circumstances in life, and that so often passes our own understanding!*

> *"And the peace of God, which surpasses all comprehension, will guard your hearts and your minds in Christ Jesus"* (Philippians 4:7).

Divine peace can only be found in God. He has told us how to think.

> *"Finally, brethren, whatever is true, whatever is honorable, whatever is right, whatever is pure, whatever is lovely, whatever is of good repute, if there is any excellence and if anything worthy of praise, dwell on these things. The things you have learned and received and heard and seen in me, practice these things, and the God of peace will be with you"* (Philippians 4:8-9).

Jesus, our Lord, puts tranquility in our hearts, no matter our circumstances, no matter the severe storms in our lives that rage furiously all around us. Trusting in Him will lead us to perfect, divine peace and an abundant thankfulness. It will help us to learn more about the greatness of our Lord God Almighty.

This beautiful song expresses in the chorus the wellbeing of the soul who trusts in the Lord.

> *It is well (it is well),*
> *With my soul (with my soul),*
> *It is well,*
> *It is well with my soul.*

This song gives us hope in heaven. We have an anchor of hope that reassures us, and that will help us to say with confidence,

> *"It Is Well with My Soul."*

> *"So when God desired to show more convincingly to the heirs of the promise the unchangeable character of his purpose, he guaranteed it with an oath, so that by two unchangeable things, in which it is impossible for God to lie, we who have fled for refuge might have strong encouragement to hold fast to the hope set before us. We have this as a sure and steadfast anchor of the soul, a hope that enters into the inner place behind the curtain, where Jesus has gone as a forerunner on our behalf, having become a high priest forever after the order of Melchizedek"* (Hebrews 6:17-20).

Whether difficult or not, may our circumstances not rob us or keep us from holding fast and drawing nearer to our Father in heaven. He is our everlasting hope. *In Him, we have that peace like a river that attendeth our way!*

Be Ye Steadfast and Immovable

"Therefore, my beloved brethren, be steadfast, immovable, always abounding in the work of the Lord, knowing that your toil is not in vain in the Lord." 1 Corinthians 15:58

Our lives are constantly changing. The waves and tides on the sea come and go. The branches of a tree blow back and forth in the wind. Like large rocks and mountains, some things in life are constant and show no signs of movement. Jesus' faithful followers must be immovable in their faith. They must stand on His teachings, live in purity, and trust in Him just like the large rocks of the sea. They show no sign of movement despite the fierce winds that blow, for they are steadfast. Jesus' faithful disciples must be steadfast, just like these rocks.

"Therefore, my beloved brethren, be steadfast, immovable, always abounding in the work of the Lord, knowing that your labor is not in vain in the Lord" (1Corinthians 15:58).

In 1 Corinthians 15:58, we are urged to be steadfast and immovable, always abounding in the Lord's work, knowing that our labor in the Lord is not in vain. Let us consider each of these admonitions.

I. STEADFAST AND IMMOVABLE:

We must be steadfast since Jesus our Lord has promised that He will return to resurrect the dead and judge both the living and the dead. The word "steadfast" literally means "firm" and implies an unwavering commitment to Christ and His rule (His will and commandments). And though we must be firm or steadfast, that does not mean that we won't have our ups and downs, a few storms now and then, tossing great waves into our lives. But we must resolve in our hearts to hold fast to the rope that is tied to our anchor (hope), refusing to let go until Christ calms the furious waves of our lives.

> *"This hope we have as an anchor of the soul, a hope both sure and steadfast and one which enters within the veil"* (Hebrews 6:19).

Firm (Steadfast and Immovable) In Our Faith:

Many begin their journey as faithful Christians but lose their faith easily. *It is tragic!* Without faith in Jesus, there is no hope. In John 6:66-69, we find some hard words Jesus said to His disciples.

> *"From that time many of His disciples went back and walked with Him no more. Then Jesus said to the twelve, 'Do you also want to go away?' But Simon Peter answered Him, 'Lord, to whom shall we go? You have the words of eternal life. Also we have come to believe and know that You are the Christ, the Son of the living God.'"*

You see, Jesus has the words of eternal life. Without faith in Jesus, we have nothing. Abraham is an excellent example of faith.

> *"He (Abraham) did not waver at the promise of God through unbelief, but was strengthened in faith, giving glory to God, and being fully convinced that what He had promised He was also able to perform. And therefore 'it was accounted to him for righteousness'"* (Romans 4:20-22).

Thus, we must be like Abraham, who did not waver through unbelief but was strengthened in faith. We must be steadfast and immovable.

> *"Watch, stand fast in the faith, be brave, be strong"* (1 Corinthians 16:13).

All Christians must stand firm on the teachings of salvation and righteousness without wavering.

> *"That we should no longer be children, tossed to and fro and carried about with every wind of doctrine, by the trickery of men, in the cunning craftiness of deceitful plotting"* (Ephesians 4:14).

We must constantly be learning and growing in the Truth that we might recognize false teaching, reject it, and take a stand for the Truth. When we accept false teaching, we run the risk of being blown away by it. In 2 Thessalonians 2:15, the apostle Paul urged us saying,

> *"Therefore, brethren, stand fast and hold the traditions which you were taught, whether by word or our epistle."*

Since we have been given the hope and assurance of a glorious, righteous resurrection and an eternity in heaven (within the veil), we must be unwavering in our commitment to the Lord, keeping a steadfast hold on our anchor.

Firm (Steadfast and Immovable) in Righteous Living:

All Christians must stand fast or be firm in living a righteous and holy life despite temptations. We must not allow sin to rule our lives, but rather we must give up all pleasures of sin for salvation's sake. In 2 Peter 3:17-18, we have an admonition.

> *"You therefore, beloved, since you know this beforehand, beware lest you also fall from your own steadfastness, being led away with the error of the wicked; but grow in the grace and knowledge of our Lord and Savior Jesus Christ."*

You see, Esau, the brother of Jacob, sold his inheritance for some bread and stew. In Hebrews 12:16-17, we are given another exhortation about being steadfast and immovable.

> *"Lest there be any fornicator or profane person like Esau, who for one morsel of food sold his birthright. For you know that afterward, when he wanted to inherit the blessing, he was rejected, for he found no place for repentance, though he sought it diligently with tears."*

We must not, under any circumstances, sell our salvation for the pleasures of sin. We must remain firm and immovable in our faith.

The word *"immovable"* is used in the New Testament only once, and its meaning is similar to *"steadfast."* It means to be firmly planted and unwilling to budge from our position or run away from it. *While we are standing firmly in the Lord and fighting for righteousness against the fierce attacks of the devil, we must be "always abounding in the Lord's work!"* We must be fighting tooth and nail for God's kingdom of righteousness, abounding in His work.

Today, many believe that all we have to do is believe in Jesus to be eternally safe and secure. *Is that right? No, and No! Being faithful Christians demands hard work!* It demands great effort to serve the Lord faithfully in righteousness and resist Satan's allurements. We can rest assured that if we are steadfast, immovable, and always abounding in the Lord's work, He will always be with us to help us remain faithful.

> *"So then, my beloved, just as you have always obeyed, not as in my presence only, but now much more in my absence, work out your salvation with fear and trembling; for it is God who is at work in you, both to will and to work for His good pleasure"* (Philippians 2:12).

As long as we remain faithful to God, fighting the good fight of our faith, He will never leave us alone in our struggles! We have so much to fight for in light of Christ's glorious return!

The apostle Peter also spoke about the coming of Christ to motivate us to serve Him faithfully and live our lives in righteous devotion to Him.

> *"Since all these things are to be destroyed in this way, what sort of people ought you to be in holy conduct and godliness"* (2 Peter 3:11).

Amen to that!

Nothing this world has to offer us is worth losing heaven over!

Thus, stay steadfast and unmovable!

II. ALWAYS ABOUNDING IN THE WORK OF THE LORD:

Besides being steadfast and immovable, we are also commanded to abound in the work of the Lord always.

"For by grace you have been saved through faith, and that not of yourselves; it is the gift of God, not of works, lest anyone should boast. For we are His workmanship, created in Christ Jesus for good works, which God prepared beforehand that we should walk in them" (Ephesians 2:8-10).

Since we were saved by grace through faith and were also created in Jesus for good works, we are urged to abound in the work of the Lord always. Since the Lord has promised that He will return and destroy the works of Satan, and sin and death will be swallowed up in righteousness and victory, we must make our calling and election sure, being on the right side with the sheep when the parting occurs (Matthew 25:31-33).

"When the Son of Man comes in his glory, and all the angels with him, then he will sit on his glorious throne. Before him will be gathered all the nations, and he will separate people one from another as a shepherd separates the sheep from the goats. And he will place the sheep on his right, but the goats on the left."

Since we are awaiting a resurrection, let us not drink and be merry (I Cor. 15:32; Luke 12:19). But rather, let us be steadfast and immovable and always abounding in the work of the Lord. In doing this, we can rest assured that we will receive all that God has promised us. *Our labor in the Lord will never be in vain!*

"For God is not unjust to forget your work and labor of love which you have shown toward His name, in that you have ministered to the saints, and do minister. And we desire that each one of you show the same diligence to the full assurance of hope until the end, that you do not become slug-

gish, but imitate those who through faith and patience inherit the promises" (Hebrews 6:10-12).

As we walk our path of faith, we must become aware that
we must work hard for the Lord. The work that the Lord has
entrusted to us must be done by all the brethren.

> "Therefore, my beloved brethren, be steadfast,
> immovable, always abounding in the work of the
> Lord, knowing that your labor is not in vain in
> the Lord" (1 Corinthians 15:58).

Although this command was given to "the church of God,
which is at Corinth" (1 Corinthians 1:2), it applies to us today
as well. His children must do the work that Jesus wants us to
do. God's children are those who have been baptized into
Christ.

> "For you are all sons of God through faith in
> Christ Jesus. For as many of you as were baptized
> into Christ have put on Christ" (Galatians 3:26-
> 27).

The work of the Lord cannot be done by some government
organization or by the denominations of the world. One must
be "in Christ" to do the work of the Lord. Otherwise, our labor
is in vain. The message is clear.

> "Unless the Lord builds the house, They labor in
> vain who build it; Unless the Lord guards the
> city, The watchman stays awake in vain" (Psalm
> 127:1).

The work that the Lord has commanded Christians to do
involves evangelism, edification, and benevolence. What a privilege it is for God's children to spend time and bear good fruit in the
work of His kingdom, saving souls! Jesus said,

"Go ye into all the world, and preach the gospel to every creature. He that believeth and is baptized shall be saved; but he that believeth not shall be damned" (Mark 16:15-16).

The work that our Lord wants Christians to do for His kingdom is to edify and build others up. Paul wrote,

"From whom the whole body, joined and knit together by what every joint supplies, according to the effective working by which every part does its share, causes growth of the body for the edifying of itself in love" (Ephesians 4:16).

The work of the Lord is to be involved in benevolence.

"Therefore, as we have opportunity, let us do good to all, especially to those who are of the household of faith" (Galatians 6:10).

All Christians must study, pray, worship, and work to the glory of God. We must be faithful about everything we do or say because it is *"the work of the Lord." All the work that we do for the Lord helps us to stay faithful!* So, let us be like *"Tryphena and Tryphosa, who have labored in the Lord."* Let us be like, *"the beloved Persis, who labored much in the Lord"* (Romans 16:12).

The work of the Lord must be done by Christians who are strong spiritually (1 Corinthians 15:58). God demands that we Christians be steadfast and involved in the Lord's work. Each member of each local church must be faithful and busy in the Lord's work. God's children must be *"immovable, always abounding in the work of the Lord."* Each Christian must be steadfast and have a strong desire to do the work of the Lord with all their heart, soul, mind, and strength without complaining.

When Jesus gave Himself for our sins, He died to purchase a people *"zealous of good works"* (Titus 2:14). As faithful disciples of our Lord and Savior, we must always abound in the work of the Lord. We must not be *"on and off"* in the Lord's work. *We must be working with all our might for the Lord daily!* The early church was steadfast, faithful, and abounding in the work of the Lord, even amid persecution and hard times.

> *"And daily in the temple, and in every house, they did not cease teaching and preaching Jesus as the Christ"* (Acts 5:42).

Those who are steadfast, immovable, and always abounding in the work of the Lord, will receive their reward, for God has promised saying,

> *"Your labor is not in vain in the Lord"* (1 Corinthians 15:58).

CONCLUSION:

The one who conquers and endures until the end will not be hurt by the second death (Matthew 16:24-26; Revelation 2:10-11). As faithful Christians, we must endure, keep going, keep working, stay with it, and move forward despite life's hardships and difficulties. We are commanded to be courageous and not resign. It does not matter if everything collapses, we must keep working hard, be steadfast, and abound in the Lord's work. We must be careful not to be carried away by this world's lawlessness, darkness and lose our own stability or steadfastness.

> *"You therefore, beloved, knowing this beforehand, take care that you are not carried away with the error of lawless people and lose your own stability."* (2 Peter 3:17)

We must remain on our heavenly call and be abounding, making progress always. And though hard times and various trials might come (James 1:2-4; 12), we must choose to remain steadfast and immovable, acknowledging the purpose behind it all. Our faithfulness, stability, steadfastness or firmness praises, honors, and glorifies our Lord.

> *"His divine power has granted to us all things that pertain to life and godliness, through the knowledge of him who called us to his own glory and excellence, by which he has granted to us his precious and very great promises, so that through them you may become partakers of the divine nature, having escaped from the corruption that is in the world because of sinful desire. For this very reason, make every effort to supplement your faith with virtue, and virtue with knowledge, and knowledge with self-control, and self-control with steadfastness, and steadfastness with godliness, and godliness with brotherly affection, and brotherly affection with love."* (2 Peter 1:3-7)

So, we must prepare our minds for action and remember that we were ransomed with the precious blood of Jesus (1 Peter 1:13-19). Let us choose to put our faith and hope in God and nothing else.

> *"He was foreknown before the foundation of the world but was made manifest in the last times for the sake of you who through him are believers in God, who raised him from the dead and gave him glory, so that your faith and hope are in God."* (1 Peter 1:20-21)

Although there are times in life when we find ourselves in a season of frustration, suffering, challenges, discouragement, and confusion where everything seems to be falling apart, we must be steadfast and immovable. God demands that we be steadfast and immovable, always abounding in His work. *We must do God's will!*

Can we tell God that He is wrong for demanding that we be steadfast and immovable? Can we dare to question the depth of His wisdom? It is God's purpose that we stay steadfast and immovable to grow us and mold us to His glory. You see, when we are not steadfast, we run the risk of not growing in God and cutting His work short.

The apostle Paul declared,

> *"For I am confident of this very thing, that He who began a good work in you will perfect it until the day of Christ Jesus"* (Philippians 1:6).

Remember, God has begun a good work in us and expects us to bring it to fruition! Through His Grace, He will make sure that we finish the work He has purposed for us despite our circumstances. He will lead us toward confidence. He will reassure us. He wants us to not lose our confidence despite our circumstances. Momentary unhappiness is not a reason to lose our confidence. God tells us not to. He demands that we be steadfast and immovable to do His will.

Notice that the word steadfastness means firmly fixed in place, not subject to change, firm in belief, determination, or adherence. The Hebrew word for steadfastness is *"chessed"* (steadfast kindness, love, reliability). It is in our steadfastness that we can show the right attitude toward God and glorify Him. It is then, in our steadfastness, that we can show our love and faithfulness to God. The same way He shows His love and faithfulness to us.

The Lord has promised us that He will bring the work He began in us to completion at the day of Jesus Christ. So, my question is, *"should we not stay steadfast and immovable until God has completed His work through us?"* Let us be wise and not become blind. Let us not build walls of blindness that would prevent us from seeing the possibilities of what God can do through us. We must trust God as our long-term eyes. He can see the long-term goals for us and others. God wants us to stay steadfast and immovable, shining our light.

Maybe, He wants to refine us; grow us in wisdom; grow us in our relationships with others that are difficult to deal with in a godly way. It is in all this that He is growing us into His image and less like the world. God wants us to be steadfast, reflecting His righteousness to others, even amid our difficult times and trying circumstances. Yet when we behave in a way that is just like the world, we do not allow God to grow us in our steadfastness. We are not allowing Him to shine through us. *What if we are the only ones who can show Him and His kingdom of righteousness to others right where we are, in our steadfastness?!*

So, let us trust God with all our soul, heart, and mind in our trials, sufferings, frustrations, difficulties, fears, and whatever it is that we want to move away from. Let us remain unmovable and steadfast in our faith and godly living. Let us not cut God's work short but rather let us abound in His work and finish the work He has planned for us to bring to completion. *Thus, let us be steadfast and immovable!* It is the only way we can move on confidently, knowing that we have finished what He has purposed for us to do. Even amid our difficulties and trying circumstances, God is growing us and molding us in His likeness. *He is revealing Himself to us and others and leading us all the way!* However, we must remain steadfast and unmovable. We can be confident when the work He purposed for us is finished, that is, abounding in the work of the Lord, that our work is never in vain (I Corinthians 15:58).

Consider that nothing is ever wasted when it is done with steadfastness for the Lord. God's eyes see the quiet things, our thoughts, and the unseen. But He demands that we be steadfast. He is steadfast for us and has always been. Remember, Christ was steadfast when He went to die on the cross for us. *He was not afraid, nor did He cut His work short. He finished it! And what did we get as a gift from God? Salvation and the hope of eternal life!* Our steadfastness will help us to grow in Christ, be fruitful in His work (abounding), find peace, and have eternal life with Him.

May we learn to be steadfast and immovable to grow in our daily walk with our Lord and receive our reward. May our Father in heaven give us the strength to complete what He has purposed for us to finish. May He give us steadfastness in our faith and our daily walk with Him, trusting His plans for us with confidence and joy. To Him be the glory. Amen.

This World Is Not My Home

"Do not lay up for yourselves treasures on earth, where moth and rust destroy and where thieves break in and steal, but lay up for yourselves treasures in heaven, where neither moth nor rust destroys and where thieves do not break in and steal." Matthew 6:19-20

Our lovely song, *"This World Is Not My Home,"* has a very special place in my heart. It speaks of the faith that we must have in God's promises. Our song expresses how this earth filled with worldly cares is not our home, for we are just pilgrims on a journey. The Lord has commanded us not to dwell on the things of this world but to set our minds on eternal things, our eternal home, which is heaven. Likewise, our song urges us to lay up treasures in heaven, not on earth. Let us consider God's point of view about our earthly treasures.

In Matthew 6:19-20, the Lord declared,

"Do not lay up for yourselves treasures on earth, where moth and rust destroy and where thieves break in and steal, but lay up for yourselves treasures in heaven, where neither moth nor rust destroys and where thieves do not break in and steal."

Our hearts reveal our thoughts and our treasures. If our thoughts dwell on the treasures of this earth, they will constantly be there. But if our hearts dwell on our eternal home, our thoughts and actions will be directed toward heavenly things, God's promises, and doing God's will to please Him. In Matthew 6:21, we have a reminder.

> *"For where your treasure is, there your heart will be also."*

Although it is wonderful to enjoy the things that God has blessed us with here on this earth, we Christians must acknowledge that our focus must not be on the things of this world but the things of heaven. If our focus is only on earthly things, we must examine our hearts and make sure that we put it in the right place. Since God is the author of our blessings, we must purpose in our hearts to give Him the glory, remain humble, and focus only on Him and our heavenly home with Him one day.

I. WE MUST NOT REGARD THIS WORLD AS OUR HOME:

In 1 Peter 2:11, we are described as pilgrims and sojourners here on this earth.

> *"Beloved, I urge you as sojourners and exiles to abstain from the passions of the flesh, which wage war against your soul."*

Our song answers why the pilgrim Christian must not look upon this world as his final home.

Hebrews 11:13 tells us that God's faithful followers understood this truth, and faithfully lived their lives without receiving God's promises. They lived by faith, for they were looking for something better beyond this life.

"These all died in faith, not having received the things promised, but having seen them and greeted them from afar, and having acknowledged that they were strangers and exiles on the earth."

Jesus wants us to lay up treasures in heaven.

"And Jesus, looking at him, loved him, and said to him, 'You lack one thing: go, sell all that you have and give to the poor, and you will have treasure in heaven; and come, follow me.'" (Mk. 10:21)

"As for the rich in this present age, charge them not to be haughty, nor to set their hopes on the uncertainty of riches, but on God, who richly provides us with everything to enjoy. They are to do good, to be rich in good works, to be generous and ready to share, thus storing up treasure for themselves as a good foundation for the future, so that they may take hold of that which is truly life." (1 Tim. 6:17-19)

Jesus wants His followers not to lay up treasures on this earth but instead lay them up in heaven with the assurance that nothing will destroy them.

"Do not lay up for yourselves treasures on earth, where moth and rust destroy and where thieves break in and steal, but lay up for yourselves treasures in heaven, where neither moth nor rust destroys and where thieves do not break in and steal. For where your treasure is, there your heart will be also. 'The eye is the lamp of the body. So, if your eye is healthy, your whole body will be full of light, but if your eye is bad, your whole body will be full of darkness. If then the light in you is darkness, how great is the darkness!'" (Matthew 6:19-23)

We must not lay treasures on earth and make this world our final home! The pursuits of this life must not be our priority. *Why do many Christians reject this truth?* They sing *"This World Is Not My Home"* but do not obey the principles by which it is founded. Sadly, many "Christians" have little interest in spiritual matters because they are more interested in worldly things, not the things of the Lord.

Jesus told His disciples,

> *"If anyone would come after me, let him deny himself and take up his cross and follow me. For whoever would save his life will lose it, but whoever loses his life for my sake will find it. For what will it profit a man if he gains the whole world and forfeits his soul? Or what shall a man give in return for his soul? For the Son of Man is going to come with his angels in the glory of his Father, and then he will repay each person according to what he has done."* (Matthew 16:24-27)

We must not place on hold our heavenly obligations while we pursue our worldly desires. *What is most important, heaven or earth?*

1. We must not put the Lord on hold while we pursue our desires and earthly pursuits.
2. Our desires must be the pursuit of our Lord.

Our song reminds us that our citizenship is in heaven.

> *"But our citizenship is in heaven, and from it we await a Savior, the Lord Jesus Christ, who will transform our lowly body to be like his glorious body, by the power that enables him even to subject all things to himself."* (Phil. 3:20-21)

And that we are "pilgrims," that is, "*one passing through.*"

> "*Beloved, I beg you as sojourners and pilgrims, abstain from fleshly lusts which war against the soul, having your conduct honorable among the Gentiles, that when they speak against you as evildoers, they may, by your good works which they observe, glorify God in the day of visitation.*" (1 Pet. 2:11-12)

The angels beckon us to continue on our journey toward heaven's open door to receive these treasures.

> "*Just so, I tell you, there is joy before the angels of God over one sinner who repents.*" (Lk. 15:10)

Truly, the angels rejoice when a sinner repents! They want us to go to heaven. Our song reminds us to set our affections on things above, not on things of this earth.

> "*If then you have been raised with Christ, seek the things that are above, where Christ is, seated at the right hand of God. Set your minds on things that are above, not on things that are on earth.*" (Col. 3:1-2)

II. OUR SAVIOR PARDONED US IN HEAVEN:

The phrase "*They're all expecting me*" of our second stanza refers to the redeemed of all ages. They are that great cloud of witnesses who cheer us on and sing praises to God in the spiritual realm.

> "*Therefore, since we are surrounded by so great a cloud of witnesses, let us also lay aside every weight, and sin which clings so closely, and let us run with endurance the race that is set before us, looking to Jesus, the founder and perfecter of our faith, who for the joy that was set before him endured the cross,*

despising the shame, and is seated at the right hand of the throne of God." (Heb. 12:1-2)

"After this I looked, and behold, a great multitude that no one could number, from every nation, from all tribes and peoples and languages, standing before the throne and before the Lamb, clothed in white robes, with palm branches in their hands, and crying out with a loud voice, 'Salvation belongs to our God who sits on the throne, and to the Lamb!' And all the angels were standing around the throne and around the elders and the four living creatures, and they fell on their faces before the throne and worshiped God, saying, 'Amen! Blessing and glory and wisdom and thanksgiving and honor and power and might be to our God forever and ever! Amen.' Then one of the elders addressed me, saying, 'Who are these, clothed in white robes, and from where have they come?' I said to him, 'Sir, you know.' And he said to me, 'These are the ones coming out of the great tribulation. They have washed their robes and made them white in the blood of the Lamb.'" (Rev. 7:9-14)

However, there is a much greater blessing of heaven, our Savior, who has pardoned us and promised to be there waiting for us. So, we must be looking forward to heaven. You see, the faithful patriarchs of old looked forward to God's promises. They acknowledged that they were strangers and pilgrims on the earth. God is preparing for them and us, His faithful, a heavenly city.

"These all died in faith, not having received the things promised, but having seen them and greeted them from afar, and having acknowledged that they were strangers and exiles on the earth. For people who speak thus make it clear that they are seeking a homeland. If they had been thinking of that land

from which they had gone out, they would have had opportunity to return. But as it is, they desire a better country, that is, a heavenly one. Therefore God is not ashamed to be called their God, for he has prepared for them a city." (Heb. 11:13-16)

"My Savior pardoned me, and now I onward go."

My Savior pardoned ME? What about everybody else? Although Jesus' sacrifice is personal, it is also universal.

"For the grace of God has appeared, bringing salvation to all men" (Titus 2:11).

Jesus has brought salvation through His sacrifice to all men. God's Grace applies to all men and women who obey His Son's Gospel of salvation. God can pardon our sins when we obey Him and His commandments.

"Although he was a son, he learned obedience through what he suffered. And being made perfect, he became the source of eternal salvation to all who obey him" (Heb. 5:8-9).

"Enter by the narrow gate. For the gate is wide and the way is easy that leads to destruction, and those who enter by it are many. For the gate is narrow and the way is hard that leads to life, and those who find it are few" (Matt. 7:13-14).

Our Savior has promised to take us through, even though we are weak and poor and sinful, for He offers salvation, forgiveness to all men. Otherwise, there would be no hope of heaven, for all have sinned and deserve due punishment.

"For all have sinned and fall short of the glory of God" (Rom. 3:23).

> *"For the wages of sin is death, but the free gift of God is eternal life in Christ Jesus our Lord"* (Rom. 6:23).

All Christians must be working out their own salvation with fear and trembling, doing God's will even while we're pressing on toward the mark of the prize of the high calling of God.

> *"Therefore, my beloved, as you have always obeyed, so now, not only as in my presence but much more in my absence, work out your own salvation with fear and trembling, for it is God who works in you, both to will and to work for his good pleasure. Do all things without grumbling or disputing, that you may be blameless and innocent, children of God without blemish in the midst of a crooked and twisted generation, among whom you shine as lights in the world, holding fast to the word of life, so that in the day of Christ I may be proud that I did not run in vain or labor in vain"* (Phil. 2:11-16).

> *"Not that I have already obtained this or am already perfect, but I press on to make it my own, because Christ Jesus has made me his own. Brothers, I do not consider that I have made it my own. But one thing I do: forgetting what lies behind and straining forward to what lies ahead, I press on toward the goal for the prize of the upward call of God in Christ Jesus"* (Phil. 3:12-14).

III. OUR LOVED ONES WHO DIED IN THE LORD WILL BE IN HEAVEN:

Although some of our loved ones (relatives, friends, and brethren) will not be in heaven, those who died faithfully in the Lord will indeed be in heaven. *It is one of those things we Christians eagerly look forward to!*

> *"But we do not want you to be uninformed, brothers, about those who are asleep, that you may not grieve as others do who have no hope. For since we believe that Jesus died and rose again, even so, through Jesus, God will bring with him those who have fallen asleep. For this we declare to you by a word from the Lord, that we who are alive, who are left until the coming of the Lord, will not precede those who have fallen asleep. For the Lord himself will descend from heaven with a cry of command, with the voice of an archangel, and with the sound of the trumpet of God. And the dead in Christ will rise first. Then we who are alive, who are left, will be caught up together with them in the clouds to meet the Lord in the air, and so we will always be with the Lord"* (1 Thess. 4:13-17).

Those beloved saints who are in heaven make heaven a place for which we earnestly groan to be clothed with our habitation.

> *"For in this tent we groan, longing to put on our heavenly dwelling, if indeed by putting it on we may not be found naked. For while we are still in this tent, we groan, being burdened—not that we would be unclothed, but that we would be further clothed, so that what is mortal may be swallowed up by life. He who has prepared us for this very thing is God, who has given us the Spirit as a guarantee"* (2 Cor. 5:1-8).

"Waiting now for me in heaven's open door."

The phrase *"waiting now for me in heaven's open door"* raises the question of whether we can view the departed saints as being in heaven or not. I believe the souls of the righteous dead are in Paradise in the Hadean realm awaiting the second coming of Christ, a universal resurrection, and final judgment before going to heaven, the heavenly city, our habitation itself. Nevertheless, the truth is that the saints who have died have gone to be with Christ and are in some way waiting for us if we die faithfully in the Lord also.

> *"I am hard-pressed between the two. My desire is to depart and be with Christ, for that is far better"* (Phil. 1:23).

IV. ETERNAL LIFE AND VICTORY WILL BE IN HEAVEN:

"Up in glory land, we'll live eternally."

In the world to come, we shall receive eternal life.

> *"Who will not receive a hundredfold now in this time, houses and brothers and sisters and mothers and children and lands, with persecutions, and in the age to come eternal life"* (Mk. 10:30).

"Just up in glory land we'll live eternally; The saints on every hand are shouting victory!"

Victory belongs to Christ, for He has won the battle and obtained the victory. God has given us victory through Jesus. Jesus defeated sin through His sinless life and arose from the dead, destroying death's power over us. God showed victory over death through Jesus, and He gives that victory to everyone who belongs to Him.

> *"Therefore, my beloved brothers, be steadfast, immovable, always abounding in the work of the Lord, knowing that in the Lord your labor is not in vain"* (1 Corinthians 15:57).

When Jesus, our Lord, overcame sin, He took away the power that death had. *Death will be swallowed up in victory when our perishable bodies put on the imperishable!* The resurrection of the dead is pictured as the ultimate destruction of death. The hope of the resurrection must motivate us to live faithfully, for it is our main foundation for godly and righteous living. It motivates our actions and is our vital foundation for Christian living. Thus, we must be steadfast and immovable, always abounding in the work of the Lord, for we know that our work in Him is not in vain.

> *"I tell you this, brothers: flesh and blood cannot inherit the kingdom of God, nor does the perishable inherit the imperishable. Behold! I tell you a mystery. We shall not all sleep, but we shall all be changed, in a moment, in the twinkling of an eye, at the last trumpet. For the trumpet will sound, and the dead will be raised imperishable, and we shall be changed. For this perishable body must put on the imperishable, and this mortal body must put on immortality. When the perishable puts on the imperishable, and the mortal puts on immortality, then shall come to pass the saying that is written: 'Death is swallowed up in victory.' 'O death, where is your victory? O death, where is your sting?' The sting of death is sin, and the power of sin is the law. But thanks be to God, who gives us the victory through our Lord Jesus Christ. Therefore, my beloved brothers, be steadfast, immovable, always abounding in the work of the Lord, knowing that in the Lord your labor is not in vain"* (1 Cor. 15:50-58).

When Jesus returns to take us home, death will be swallowed up in victory, and all the faithful saints on every hand will be shouting victory (1 Cor. 15:50-57). *Oh, what a wonderful day that will be!*

The heart of the Gospel *"in which you stand"* is the resurrection.

1. The resurrection is what keeps us standing firm, for it gives us the strength to endure, be steady, and be faithful.
2. Our hope of the resurrection is what keeps us immovable in our trials and suffering.
3. The hope of the resurrection takes away our fear of death.
4. God will ultimately have victory over Satan, sin, and death. He proved it through His Son when He raised Him from the dead and exalted Him.

"The songs of sweetest praise drift back from heaven's shore."

The songs of sweetest praise that drift back from heaven's shore invite us to press onward and endure till the end.

> *"Then I saw in the right hand of him who was seated on the throne a scroll written within and on the back, sealed with seven seals. And I saw a mighty angel proclaiming with a loud voice, 'Who is worthy to open the scroll and break its seals?' And no one in heaven or on earth or under the earth was able to open the scroll or to look into it, and I began to weep loudly because no one was found worthy to open the scroll or to look into it. And one of the elders said to me, 'Weep no more; behold, the Lion of the tribe of Judah, the Root of David, has conquered, so that he can open the scroll and its seven seals.' And between the throne and the four living creatures and among the elders I saw a Lamb standing, as though it had been slain, with seven horns and with seven eyes, which are the seven spirits of God sent out into all the earth. And he went and took the scroll from the right hand of him who was seated on the throne. And when he had taken the*

scroll, the four living creatures and the twenty-four elders fell down before the Lamb, each holding a harp, and golden bowls full of incense, which are the prayers of the saints. And they sang a new song, saying, 'Worthy are you to take the scroll and to open its seals, for you were slain, and by your blood you ransomed people for God from every tribe and language and people and nation, and you have made them a kingdom and priests to our God, and they shall reign on the earth.' Then I looked, and I heard around the throne and the living creatures and the elders the voice of many angels, numbering myriads of myriads and thousands of thousands, saying with a loud voice, 'Worthy is the Lamb who was slain, to receive power and wealth and wisdom and might and honor and glory and blessing!' And I heard every creature in heaven and on earth and under the earth and in the sea, and all that is in them, saying, 'To him who sits on the throne and to the Lamb be blessing and honor and glory and might forever and ever!' And the four living creatures said, "Amen!" and the elders fell down and worshiped" (Rev. 5:8-14).

Therefore, we must stand in the Gospel, always abounding, that is, overflowing in the work of the Lord without any excuses, without taking any vacation from His work or without ceasing to do what we must do as His servants. There is no room to say, *"I have done my part."* We don't stop working for the Lord because of our trials or for any other reason. Nothing must stop us from abounding in the Lord's work, for if we do that, we belittle the Grace of God seen in Jesus' resurrection. Remember that our work in the Lord is not in vain or a waste of time. *The time that we invest in His work is not a waste, for it is essential and has meaning and value to Him! He is faithful and will reward us for doing a valuable and important work for Him in His vineyard!* Our reward will be heaven and eternal life.

CONCLUSION:

> *"This world is not my home, I'm just a passing thru."*

We are just passing through this life and very quickly. James 4:14 states.

> *"What is your life? For you are a mist that appears for a little time and then vanishes."*

We have been given just a short life to live on this earth. Thus, we must make heaven our home and foremost goal in life. Jesus died on the cross for us to give us a second chance to be forgiven of our sins and be with Him eternally in heaven. *He did not have to do this, and yet He did!* Because of His cruel death, He can pardon us our sins and provide us the opportunity to be with him in heaven. And though we are weak and sinful men, by God's Grace, we can be strengthened through our Savior and receive God's rich blessings in heaven as long as we remain faithful to Him, making heaven our home and not this world.

The chorus verse of this song,

> *"And I can't feel at home in this world anymore."*

The chorus reminds us to lay up treasures in heaven, set our affections on things above, and press on toward the goal for the prize of the upward call of God in Christ Jesus (Phil 3:14).

Satan is always trying to ensnare us with earthly pleasures and troubles. God wants His faithful children not to lose sight of His promise and be consumed with earthly cares. Our constant prayers and fellowship with other saints of like precious faith supply us with strength to prevent temptations. God's promise to us of an eternal home with Him must motivate us and give us peace. God's faithful saints must acknowledge that this world's cares and troubles are only temporary.

Indeed, this earth is not our "home," for we are eagerly longing and waiting for a heavenly home, our habitation. So, we must proclaim the Gospel, the good news, to those who have not obeyed the Gospel and do not have that hope of an eternal home. If we haven't met the conditions that God has revealed in the Gospel, heaven will not be our home. In His Word, God has already stated what we must do to be justified before Him in this life and receive our eternal hope of glory.

> *"For if we go on sinning deliberately after receiving the knowledge of the truth, there no longer remains a sacrifice for sins, but a fearful expectation of judgment, and a fury of fire that will consume the adversaries. Anyone who has set aside the law of Moses dies without mercy on the evidence of two or three witnesses. How much worse punishment, do you think, will be deserved by the one who has trampled underfoot the Son of God, and has profaned the blood of the covenant by which he was sanctified, and has outraged the Spirit of grace? For we know him who said, 'Vengeance is mine; I will repay.' And again, 'The Lord will judge his people.' It is a fearful thing to fall into the hands of the living God."* (Heb. 10:26-31)

Therefore, we must determine to serve Him faithfully here on earth, teaching and sharing His message to the lost to go to heaven, helping others, and doing His will in this life. But while we are preparing to go to heaven, we must acknowledge daily that *"this world is not my home."*

May each of us live every day, acknowledging that *"this world is not my home."* May we engrave those words in our hearts, remembering God's faithful promise to those who believe in Him and do His will.

> This world is not my home, I'm just a passing
> through;
> My treasures are laid up Somewhere beyond
> the blue.
> The angels beckon me from heaven's open
> door,
> And I can't feel at home in this world anymore.
>
> They're all expecting me, and that's one thing I
> know;
> My Savior pardoned me, and now I onward go.
> I know He'll take me through though I am
> weak and poor,
> And I can't feel at home in this world anymore.
>
> I have a loving mother up in glory land;
> I don't expect to stop until I shake her hand.
> She's waiting now for me in heaven's open
> door,
> And I can't feel at home in this world anymore.
>
> Just up in glory land we'll live eternally;
> The saints on every hand are shouting victory!
> Their songs of sweetest praise drift back from
> heaven's shore,
> And I can't feel at home in this world anymore.

Chorus,

O Lord, you know I have no friend like You;
If heaven's not my home then, Lord, what will I
   do?
The angels beckon me from heaven's open
   door,
And I can't feel at home in this world anymore.

The Bible Doctrine of Heaven

"Blessed be the God and Father of our Lord Jesus Christ! According to his great mercy, he has caused us to be born again to a living hope through the resurrection of Jesus Christ from the dead, to an inheritance that is imperishable, undefiled, and unfading, kept in heaven for you, who by God's power are being guarded through faith for a salvation ready to be revealed in the last time." 1 Peter 1:3-5

Our hands grow weak when our hope of heaven grows dim. *How do you envision Heaven? Is it really worth the demanding regeneration that Jesus requires? Is it really worth it all?*

Almost everyone believes in heaven, and I would imagine we all, Christ's faithful saints, long to go to that place someday. Indeed, heaven is the reward of the faithful—the eternal destiny of the righteous. Heaven is God's abode. It is the perfect dwelling of things eternal where God dwells and all other heavenly beings. The place where the saints go to be with God (Revelation 21:3). *What an amazing blessing it is for God's faithful and righteous ones, his saints, to receive heaven as their final reward and to be in His presence throughout all eternity! It is too much for me to fathom!* And though no one has ever seen God's face (John 1:8), in heaven, we will not only see His face, but God will dwell among us. Angels also dwell in heaven (Rev. 4:4, 6; 5:6). Only the saved among men will be in heaven. Thus, Heaven will be the future dwelling or abode of the resurrected saints. This abode of the saved or disembodied spirits is different from "Abraham's bosom" (Luke 16:22) or Paradise (Luke 23:43).

I. WHO WILL BE IN HEAVEN?

Take notice that Heaven is prepared only for the saved ones where they will dwell in their resurrected bodies. Our salvation is laid up for us in Heaven (Col. 1:5; 1 Pet. 1:4). The names of God's faithful and righteous ones are written in Heaven (Luke 10:20). Heaven is God's building for us (2 Cor. 5:1). Our reward and treasures are in Heaven (Matt. 5:12; 6:20; 19:21). Sinners (those who die in their sins) are excluded from entering the gates of Heaven.

> "But as for the cowardly, the faithless, the detestable, as for murderers, the sexually immoral, sorcerers, idolaters, and all liars, their portion will be in the lake that burns with fire and sulfur, which is the second death" (Rev. 21:8, 27).

God is portrayed as the "God of heaven" (2 Chronicles 36:23; Neh. 1:4-5). Thus, heaven is described as God's abode or dwelling (Isa. 57:15; 63:15; Matt. 6:9-10). Heaven is the reward of the faithful. It is where the righteous are accepted to dwell eternally in God's abode. God the Father, God the Son, and God the Holy Spirit are the occupants of heaven (2 Chron. 36:23; John 1:32; 3:13; 31; 6:33, 38, 42, 51, 58).

In Romans 2:5-8, 10 we read that God will give eternal life only "to those who by patience in well-doing seek for glory and honor and immortality, he will give eternal life." But to "those who are self-seeking and do not obey the truth, but obey unrighteousness, there will be wrath and fury (hell)." You see, God will render each one of us an entrance into either heaven or hell according to our works or deeds. He will give eternal life (heaven) only to those who do the will of God and persevere in faith and faith-ful service. Faith is not complete without active, good, and righteous works. We are justified by works and not by faith alone. *"For as the body apart from the spirit is dead, so also faith apart from works is dead"* (James 2:18-26). Modern Protestants err by making a distinction between "the faith that saves" (without obedience or "works") and the faith that obeys the Lord Jesus. But such theology is pure folly. *The Bible does not speak that way!*

The Bible stresses the need to persevere (doing good works as a result of our active faith, James 2:18) and finish well to re-ceive our crown of life (heaven), Revelations 2:10. Paul explic-itly states that those who do not obey the Gospel of Christ will suffer punishment, eternal destruction, and the wrath of God *"when the Lord Jesus is revealed from heaven with his mighty angels in flaming fire, inflicting vengeance on those who do not know God and on those who do not obey the gospel of our Lord Jesus"* (2 Thes-salonians 1:7-9).

To persevere implies a habitual conduct worthy of the Gospel of Christ, a firm and steady faith (steadfast faith), in-stead of serving God from time to time when it is convenient, along with an endless number of excuses. They put worldly matters in first place before God and His Kingdom of right-eousness. In Matthew 10:22, Jesus declared, *"and you will be hated by all for my name's sake. But the one who endures to the end will be saved."* You see, only those (the redeemed by the blood of Christ) who endure, walking in righteousness, holiness and without blemish will be saved. For Christians to receive eter-nal life, heaven as their reward (the crown of life and glory), they must be faithful unto death. There is no room here for lukewarmness or cowardice. We must be courageous and completely faithful to the Lord until the end of our lives. In Hebrews 12:1-2 we have been admonished to *"lay aside every weight, and sin which clings so closely, and let us run with en-durance the race that is set before us, looking to Jesus, the founder*

*and perfecter of our faith, who for the joy that was set before him en-
dured the cross, despising the shame, and is seated at the right hand
of the throne of God."* We, Christians, must finish our race well
with endurance, putting away all sin and lawlessness to save
our souls and receive our reward which is heaven.

Sadly, many begin the "race" as champions but soon get
tired. They become distracted, discouraged, and stop running.
They don't continue the race to the end to receive the prize
(heaven). God will render to each one according to his works.
The word "works" includes all aspects of our lives, our deeds,
our words, our thoughts, and such. *"When Christ who is your
life appears, then you also will appear with him in glory"* (Colossians 3:4). It means that we (the faithful) will be in the presence
of our Glorious God, and will be like Christ, His Son. We will
receive "immortality" because our resurrected body will not
be subject to corruption anymore. Those *"who in well-doing seek
glory"* are those who persevere in doing those righteous or
good works that glorify God. Moreover, those who have died
to sin (they have been buried with Him and raised from the
dead with Him by baptism), walking in newness of life, cruci-
fying the old self so that sin no longer reigns in them, but only
righteousness. Only they will receive eternal life, heaven as
their reward. Therefore, if sin reigns in us and not righteousness, heaven will not be our reward but eternal punishment, hell.

II. WHAT IS HEAVEN LIKE?

Both heaven and hell are described in terms that are easy
for men to understand. The Bible describes heaven as a place
of eternal bliss. It uses metaphors to describe this place. Let us
think about some figures that the Bible uses to describe heav-
en.

1. Participation in the wedding feast where the bride of Christ is the church (Matt. 22:1-14; 25:10; Eph. 5:22-23).
2. The joys of the Lord (Matt. 25:21, 23). Heaven will surely be the "joys of our Lord." Therefore, He is patiently inviting all to share these joys with Him.
3. The Lord's Kingdom as our inheritance (Matt. 25:34; cf. Acts 20:32; Eph. 1:11, 14; 1 Pet. 1:4-5). Inheriting the Lord's kingdom implies possessing it as our permanent possession. God's kingdom will endure forever, and He will reign forever in His Kingdom.
4. Everlasting life (Matt. 25:46; 7:14; 19:29). Spiritual life rather than spiritual death (the second death).
5. Sitting with Abraham, Isaac, and Jacob (Matt. 8:11) and being invited to sit at the King's table, having table fellowship with the Lord in the Kingdom of Heaven in terms of a great Messianic banquet.
6. It is where Christ will confess us before His Father (Matt. 10:32). He will confess His fellowship and friendship with those who are His faithful children.
7. It is our final reward (Matt. 5:12; 10:42; 1 Cor. 3:14; Col. 2:18; 3:24; Heb. 11:26). The faithful will be rewarded graciously for serving God with all their love, strength, mind, and heart.
8. Everlasting habitations or eternal dwellings (Luke 16:9). And though the Bible describes our earthly bodies as "tabernacles" (2 Cor. 5:1) which will be destroyed by fire, those who are the faithful will receive a building not made with hands (an incorruptible body) that will dwell in eternal habitations.
9. A home (Eccl. 12:5) where we will dwell with God the Father, our Elder Brother, our Lord and Savior, and all those faithful ones who have gone before us, forever in sweet fellowship. The word "home" is one of the most precious words in any language.

We long to be at "home" with our heavenly Father and all His faithful children. *Such a precious hope!*

10. It is where we will be reunited with our loved ones. It will be the renewal association with those saints who have gone before us. Many of us have experienced the sorrow over the passing of our loved ones. *It is so comforting to have this promise! I can't stop weeping!*

11. It is the New Jerusalem (Rev. 3:12; 2:12; 21:2, 10). It is the home of our King of kings and Lord of lords.

12. It is the Holy City (Rev. 21:22; 22:19) where spiritual sacrifices are offered.

13. It is a place where there will be no sin or lawlessness (Rev. 21:8, 27).

14. A place where all our troubles and the cares of life will end.

15. A place of eternal rest (Rev. 14:13) where all our labors, sufferings and trials will be over.

16. A place of perfect safety and protection where the gates never close (Rev. 21:15).

17. A place where God will tabernacle, dwell among men (Rev. 21:3).

18. Paradise (Rev. 2:7) as the Garden of Eden that man lost because of sin but will regain through Christ.

19. The water of life and the tree of life (Rev. 21:6; 22:1; 1:17; Rev. 2:7; 22:2. 14).

20. Finally, a place of eternal life (Mark 10:30; John 3:15-16; Rom. 2:7). It will be an eternal spiritual fellowship that will never end.

Thus, Heaven is worth it all!

III. THE BEAUTY OF HEAVEN AND THE DESTINY OF ALL MEN:

In Revelation 20-22, John received a clear revelation of God's Final Judgment and man's ultimate destiny. God has not told us the time of the end, but God has indeed shown us through His revealed Word that when that time comes, there will be two classes of men meeting their destiny: The redeemed and unredeemed (Rev. 20:11-15; 21:8; 27; 22:15). John saw the dead, small and great, standing before the throne of God in heaven, waiting for God to execute His sentence. The term "small and great" does not necessarily mean a particular group of people, but rather the dead in general. God will weigh us in His scales of judgment according to our works or deeds, which are recorded in God's books. His books contain a record of all that men have done in the flesh and His "book of life" is a register of those who are redeemed. *No one will escape God's Judgment!*

If any man's name is not found in the "book of life," his "book of works" will condemn and doom him to the *lake of fire*. On the other hand, if any man's name is found in the "book of life," he will be safe from God's Judgment (condemnation). He will be with the great body of the redeemed.

Revelation 21-22:5 speaks of the destiny of the redeemed. They will inherit the new Heaven as their abode with God throughout all eternity. He will have perfect fellowship with them, and there will be no more separation because in this new heaven and earth, "the sea is no more." John describes for us the perfect description of a beautiful city where God's redeemed will dwell with Him in perfect fellowship. This amazing city is a symbolic picture of a city with walls of jasper placed on foundations of sapphire, chalcedony, emerald, sardonyx, beryl, topaz, amethyst, etc. Each of its twelve gates is a huge pearl where its streets are made of pure gold. In that beautiful heavenly city, there is no need of any lamp since their Light is the Lamb. There is no temple either. The temple was where sacrifice and intercession were made for sin. This temple is not needed anymore in the New Jerusalem since there is no more sin to be atoned and because those who are the redeemed are in the presence of God. People of all nations inhabit this glorious city.

The Garden spoken of in Revelation 22:1-5 symbolizes the destiny of the redeemed. It is indeed a beautiful Garden with a river of crystal water which is the water of life which emerges from the throne of God and of the Lamb. On each side of this river grows the tree of life which bears its fruit twelve months out of the year. Three things are essential to sustain life: food, water, and health. This picture symbolizes all that is needed to sustain eternal life in man. In this Garden, men shall serve God forever. There will be no barriers, obstacles or impediments in Heaven and His servants shall serve Him.

Another beautiful thought is found in the expression, *"they shall see His face." Don't we all have this longing?! I do!* When this earth is passed, and we all find ourselves in the presence of our Redeemer-God, then we will all look at the face of our Lord and serve Him forever, for all eternity. *What greater joy could any human being ask for?! Could there be a better and longing than for eternal life with our Redeemer?! Could there be a better or more perfect place of fellowship, protection, provisions, and service to our God?! What a terrible contrast between the destiny of the wicked and the destiny of the redeemed!*

CONCLUSION:

Abraham, who lived some 3,500 years ago, longed to go to heaven when he died.

> *"By faith Abraham obeyed when he was called to go out to a place that he was to receive as an inheritance. And he went out, not knowing where he was going. By faith, he went to live in the land of promise, as in a foreign land, living in tents with Isaac and Jacob, heirs with him of the same promise. For he was looking forward to the city that has founda-*

tions, whose designer and builder is God" (Hebrews 11:8-10).

I am sure that Abraham caught a glimpse of that city and said,

"*Heaven is surely worth it all! Heaven is worth leaving home and loved ones. It is worth living as a stranger and pilgrim while we're here on earth. It's worth all of life's hardship and pain. Heaven is surely worth it all.*"

Peter was another one who had some insight about our inheritance, the one that awaits every faithful child of God when he said,

"*Blessed be the God and Father of our Lord Jesus Christ! According to his great mercy, he has caused us to be born again to a living hope through the resurrection of Jesus Christ from the dead, to an inheritance that is imperishable, undefiled, and unfading, kept in heaven for you, who by God's power are being guarded through faith for a salvation ready to be revealed in the last time*" (1 Pet. 1:3-5).

You see, Peter also caught a glimpse of heaven. It was as if he were saying, "*Heaven is worth a total transformation of my life. It is worth all the hardship and pain I have had to endure. It is worth more than my own life. Heaven is surely worth it all!*"

Of course, our path to Glory is not easy, but Heaven will surely be worth it all! It is worth being exiled from home, family, and friends. It is worth the loneliness, the pain, the suffering, and the high cost we have been called to pay. Heaven is worth all the pain that comes our way. It is worth the hatred and the persecution. It is worth the sorrow and the attacks. *Heaven is surely worth it all!*

Jesus, our Redeemer, is inviting all men to accept the gift that our God is offering, the gift of salvation. The Spirit invites us; the Bride invites us (the church, Rev. 19:7); each and every saint invites us. The invitation is extended to anyone who will accept the terms of redemption and salvation.

"Then I heard what seemed to be the voice of a great multitude, like the roar of many waters and like the sound of mighty peals of thunder, crying out, 'Hallelujah! For the Lord our God the Almighty reigns. Let us rejoice and exult and give him the glory, for the marriage of the Lamb has come, and his Bride has made herself ready; it was granted her to clothe herself with fine linen, bright and pure"— for the fine linen is the righteous deeds of the saints. And the angel said to me, 'Write this: Blessed are those who are invited to the marriage supper of the Lamb.' And he said to me, 'These are the true words of God.' Then I fell down at his feet to worship him, but he said to me, 'You must not do that! I am a fellow servant with you and your brothers who hold to the testimony of Jesus. Worship God.' For the testimony of Jesus is the spirit of prophecy.'" (Revelation 19:6-10)

"Then I saw a new heaven and a new earth; for the first heaven and the first earth passed away, and there is no longer any sea. And I saw the holy city, new Jerusalem, coming down out of heaven from God, made ready as a bride adorned for her husband. And I heard a loud voice from the throne, saying, "Behold, the tabernacle of God is among men, and He will dwell among them, and they shall be His people, and God Himself will be among them, and He will wipe away every tear from their eyes; and there will no longer be any death; there will no longer be any mourning, or crying, or pain; the first *things have passed away." And He who sits on the throne said, "Behold, I am making all things new." And He said, "Write, for these words are faithful and true." Then He said to me, "It is done. I am the Alpha and the Omega, the beginning and the end. I will give to the one who thirsts from the spring of the water of life without cost. He who overcomes will inherit these things, and I will be his God and he will be My son. But for the cowardly and unbelieving and abominable and murderers and immoral persons and sorcerers and idolaters and all liars, their part will be in the lake that burns with fire and brimstone, which is the second death.... and nothing unclean, and no one who practices abomination and lying, shall ever come into it, but only those whose names are written in the Lamb's book of life"* (Revelation 21).

Many years ago, when I was searching and seeking for the Truth, I began reading my Bible for the first time. I had heard my mother read it. I heard the liturgies and catechism, but never took the time to dig into the Bible. It was at that point that in my heart, I knew I had to pursue something bigger. Although she was a devout Catholic, my mother encouraged me to start walking, searching, and digging into the pathways of God because she was also searching. I don't know why, but the first book I began reading seriously was the Book of Revelation. As I read through, I was more aware that my present state was condemned before God. As I read, I began to worry that I could never be forgiven of my sins. But as I came to the end, the last chapters of the Book of Revelation, especially chapters 21-22, *I found hope!* It captured my hungry and thirsty soul. I began wishing and hoping to go to that New Jerusalem, the holy city, where the bride, the wife of the Lamb is. She came down from heaven, having all the glory of God, brilliant like a valuable and precious stone. At that time, I thought this was a prophecy of something future, but as I have learned more of the language of the New Testament, I realize that this beautiful language is meant to describe the glory of the Lord's church today.

> "But you have come to Mount Zion and to the city of the living God, the heavenly Jerusalem, and to myriads of angels, and to Jesus, the mediator of a new covenant, and to the sprinkled blood, which speaks better than the blood of Abel to the general assembly and church of the firstborn who are enrolled in heaven, and to God, the Judge of all, and to the spirits of the righteous made perfect." (Hebrews 12:22-24)

As I read the description of the New Jerusalem, this precious city, with all its majesty, splendor, and glory, I was speechless. Everything about this beautiful city was majestic. It was filled with all precious stones, the 24 pillars that were the 12 apostles and the 12 tribes of Israel. I was astounded as I read on, that there was no temple but that our Lord God Almighty and the Lamb were its temple and we, His church, are God's building, the holy Tabernacle as described in Ephesians 2:18-22, "for through Him we both have our access in one Spirit to the Father. So then you are no longer strangers and aliens, but you are fellow citizens with the saints, and are of God's household, having been built on the foundation of the apostles and prophets, Christ Jesus Himself being the corner stone, in whom the whole building, being fitted together, is growing into a holy temple in the Lord, in whom you also are being built together into a dwelling of God in the Spirit."

In the kingdom parables of Jesus as recorded in Matthew chapters 13,18,22 and 25, the church is called the kingdom of heaven. The church is the heavenly city. It became more desirable and precious in my heart as I read that it had no need of the sun or moon to shine on it because the glory of God was enough to enlighten it, having our Lamb, Jesus as the central lamp. This lamp would make all peoples walk in His light, bringing glory to it. Its gates will not be closed because they will be there to bring the glory and honor of the nations into it. *I longed to enter the gates of this city!*

As I finished reading chapters 21 and 22, I felt relief because there was hope for me, a sinner, to wash the clothes, stained by all the filth of sin, with the precious and powerful blood of the Lamb.

> *"Blessed are those who wash their robes, so that they may have the right to the tree of life, and may enter by the gates into the city."* (Revelation 22:14)

> *"The Spirit and the bride say, 'Come.' And let the one who hears say, 'Come.' And let the one who is thirsty come; let the one who wishes take the water of life without cost."* (Revelation 22:17)

I was motivated to begin seeking the Truth in the Scriptures diligently because I wanted to partake of this New Jerusalem, the holy city. I wanted to save my soul and be received by our Father and His Lamb into Their everlasting kingdom. These four chapters (Revelation 19-22) were my inspiration in seeking the Truth to set me free from sin. It took a while before I found the church of the Lamb. But God, through His everlasting Grace, put in my way someone who taught me the WAY.

I sincerely think that those hearts who are honestly and diligently seeking the LORD will find the Truth to set them free from sin. *I was one of them!* The Book of Revelation is very dear to my heart because it brought hope to my dying soul. Please, don't be afraid of this precious book. Despite all the speculation and error and difficult symbols, the message shines through to the humble seeker. It is a powerful message that gives hope to the dying and saves the soul. *It is a great shout of victory!*

"I am coming soon." Amen. Come, Lord Jesus!

May our Lord help all those good and honest hearts who seek the heavenly city, the church of the Lamb. May all men humbly accept this gift of redemption and wash their robes so that they may have the right to the tree of life and that they may enter the city by the gates. May all men thirst for the spring of the water of life without payment. May we all conquer so that we may receive our inheritance and be with God forever in Heaven. May our names be written in the Lamb's book of life.

Sing to Me of Heaven
By Ada Powell

Sing to me of Heaven, sing that song of peace,
From the toils that bind me it will bring release;
Burdens will be lifted that are pressing so,
Showers of great blessing o'er my heart will flow.

Chorus
Sing to me of Heaven, let me fondly dream,
Of its golden glory, of its pearly gleam;
Sing to me when shadows of the evening fall,
Sing to me of heaven, sweetest song of all.

Sing to me of Heaven, as I walk alone,
Dreaming of the comrades that so long have
    gone;
In a fairer region 'mong the angel throng,
They are happy as they sing that old, sweet song.

Sing to me of Heaven, tenderly and low,
Till the shadows o'er me rise and swiftly go;
When my heart is weary, when the day is long,
Sing to me of Heaven, sing that old, sweet song.

There Is a Habitation

"And he carried me away in the Spirit to a great, high mountain, and showed me the holy city Jerusalem coming down out of heaven from God, having the glory of God, its radiance like a most rare jewel, like a jasper, clear as crystal. It had a great, high wall, with twelve gates, and at the gates twelve angels, and on the gates the names of the twelve tribes of the sons of Israel were inscribed—on the east three gates, on the north three gates, on the south three gates, and on the west three gates. And the wall of the city had twelve foundations, and on them were the twelve names of the twelve apostles of the Lamb." Revelation 21:10-14

The song *"There Is A Habitation"* is such a beautiful and moving song. This song helped me so much when my mother died, and it continues to help me with the recent loss of my father, mother-in-law, and cousin. It gives us so much hope amid our troubled times and sufferings. The Bible defines hope as the sure anchor of the soul. Human hope is insignificant in comparison to the hope of the Bible. This lovely song describes the great city, the New Jerusalem, where the glory of God dwells. This precious city is filled with majesty, splendor, and glory. This majestic and glorious city is filled with all precious stones, the 24 pillars, or foundations that are the 12 apostles and the 12 tribes of Israel. In this majestic city, there is no temple, but our Lord God Almighty and the Lamb are the temple, and we, His church, are God's building, the holy Tabernacle as described in Ephesians 2:18-22.

"For through Him we both have our access in one Spirit to the Father. So then you are no longer strangers and aliens, but you are fellow citizens with the saints, and are of God's household, having been built on the foundation of the apostles and prophets, Christ Jesus Himself being the corner stone, in whom the whole building, being fitted together, is growing into a holy temple in the Lord, in whom you also are being built together into a dwelling of God in the Spirit."

I. HEAVEN IS A HABITATION BUILT BY THE LIVING GOD:

Our song describes the glories of heaven poetically. A "habitation" is a dwelling place. The church, as described in Ephesians 2:18-22, is God's habitation or dwelling place here on earth. In the kingdom parables of Jesus, as recorded in Matthew chapters 13, 18, 22, and 25, the church is called the kingdom of heaven. The church is the heavenly city. It had no need of the sun or moon to shine on it because God's glory was enough to enlighten it, having our Lamb, Jesus, as the central lamp. This lamp would make all peoples walk in His light, bringing glory to it. Its gates will not be closed because they will be there to bring the nations' glory and honor into it.

God also has built for us, His children, an eternal habitation or dwelling in heaven. A city whose only foundation is God, for He is the Principal Designer and Builder. This "habitation" is the abode for all *people "from every tribe and language and people and nation." It is a kingdom of priests to God, reigning on the earth!*

"By faith Abraham obeyed when he was called to go out to a place that he was to receive as an inheritance. And he went out, not knowing where he was going. By faith he went to live in the land of prom-

ise, as in a foreign land, living in tents with Isaac and Jacob, heirs with him of the same promise. 10 For he was looking forward to the city that has foundations, whose designer and builder is God." (Heb. 11:8-10)

"And when he had taken the scroll, the four living creatures and the twenty-four elders fell down before the Lamb, each holding a harp, and golden bowls full of incense, which are the prayers of the saints. And they sang a new song, saying, 'Worthy are you to take the scroll and to open its seals, for you were slain, and by your blood you ransomed people for God from every tribe and language and people and nation, and you have made them a kingdom and priests to our God, and they shall reign on the earth.'" (Rev. 5:8-10)

II. HEAVEN IS A CITY WITH FOUNDATIONS:

This heavenly city has foundations where there will be no wars. As I mentioned earlier in my introduction, this heavenly city, the New Jerusalem, has twelve foundations: The Lamb's twelve apostles (Revelation 21:14). These foundations are as firm and strong as God's throne. Nothing abominable or unclean will be there but God's throne and His Lamb. There will be no wars, nor desolations. Everything that is not clean, causing wars, will be excluded.

"And the wall of the city had twelve foundations, and on them were the twelve names of the twelve apostles of the Lamb." (Revelation 21:14)

"But nothing unclean will ever enter it, nor anyone who does what is detestable or false, but only those who are written in the Lamb's book of life." (Revelation 21:27)

III. THERE WILL BE NO SORROW, DEATH, OR DECAY IN HEAVEN:

There will be no night, sorrow, death, or decay in that glorious heavenly city, no yesterday or tomorrow, for there will be eternal life.

> "And its gates will never be shut by day—and there will be no night there." (Rev. 21:25)

> "And I heard a loud voice from the throne saying, 'Behold, the dwelling place of God is with man. He will dwell with them, and they will be his people, and God himself will be with them as their God. 4 He will wipe away every tear from their eyes, and death shall be no more, neither shall there be mourning, nor crying, nor pain anymore, for the former things have passed away.'" (Rev. 21:3-4)

> "And this is the promise that he made to us—eternal life." (1 John 2:25)

IV. IN HEAVEN, BOTH ANGELS AND GLORIFIED IMMORTALS WILL SING PRAISES TO THEIR KING:

In the glorious heavenly city, its "portals" are gates that have twelve gates within its high wall. At the gates, there are twelve angels, and the names of the twelve tribes of Israel. Within these portals or gates, angelic armies sing,

> "Worthy is the Lamb who was slain, to receive power and wealth and wisdom and might and honor and glory and blessing!" (Revelation 5:11-12)

In this heavenly city, the angels will join the glorified immortals, the redeemed of all ages.

"But you have come to Mount Zion and to the city of the living God, the heavenly Jerusalem, and to innumerable angels in festal gathering, and to the assembly of the firstborn who are enrolled in heaven, and to God, the judge of all, and to the spirits of the righteous made perfect, and to Jesus, the mediator of a new covenant, and to the sprinkled blood that speaks a better word than the blood of Abel." (Heb. 12:22-24)

CONCLUSION:

Although life on earth is tough for God's children, there always is heaven's hope, our "habitation." This hope strengthens us and helps us to endure when the trials are difficult and painful. Thus, whatever may come our way, we know that our reward, our prize, is waiting for us in heaven if only we will remain steadfast 'till the end. *Heaven is worth it all!*

The faithful of God have the hope of eternal life in heaven, a habitation. We Christians hope for a beautiful place called heaven, our habitation. We look forward to eternal life within its gates. We anticipate with joy entering the gates of the heavenly city, our eternal home, or habitation. This hope gives us joy and quenches our sorrows here on earth.

God's Word often speaks of heaven as God's "habitation" where He dwells (Isa. 57:15; 1 King 8:30). Heaven is also the dwelling of God's throne, where He rules in majesty over His entire creation (Ps. 103:19). Not only is heaven God's habitation, but it is also the place where His faithful saints will dwell forever. *They can rightly call heaven their eternal home, the glorious heavenly city! O Zion, Zion, I long thy gates to see; O Zion, Zion, when shall I dwell in thee?* I commend this lovely song to your thoughts.

There is a habitation,
Built by the living God,
For all of every nation
Who seek that grand abode.

A city with foundations,
Firm as th' eternal throne
Nor wars nor desolations
Shall ever move a stone.

No night is there, no sorrow,
No death, and no decay,
No yesterday, no morrow–
But one eternal day.

Within its pearly portals,
Angelic armies sing,
With glorified immortals,
The praises of its King.

The chorus

O Zion, Zion,
I long thy gates to see;
O Zion, Zion,
When shall I dwell in thee?

Walking by Faith, Not by Sight

"For we walk by faith, not by sight" 2 Corinthians 5:7

The Lord's coming will be like a thief in the night. It will be a total surprise for those who do not watch for Him. Even when we are watching, we are sometimes caught off guard by unexpected mishaps. It will often be a moment of "glory," but it might be when we are tired or weak. They are humbling experiences, but they test the metal of our character.

God is glorified in our weaknesses, and His joy is our strength. There are days, moments, and seasons in our lives when God takes us by surprise. This surprise may feel like a big blow to our dreams, hopes, and expectations. We may not even be conscious of it at that moment, but often those big surprises require us to lay ourselves at His feet and surrender to Him and the unknown. *At times, I just have to smile and shake my head!* Of course, this is God's plan and purpose for my days. It is then that I become aware that I must remove my thoughts of fear and trust Him, knowing in my heart without any hesitation, that this is His plan and the path that He has placed before me. I must conclude that God has different plans for us as the years unfold. *It demands a lot of faith!* Faith not in ourselves and our abilities, but faith in our Jesus who loves us and walks with us in the path of life, a path filled with His Grace.

Christians make a life-changing commitment to love and follow Christ but often fail to live in the fullness that God has purposed for them. On such occasions, we must recommit our faith. We must never forget that the only thing worth holding on to in our lives is our faith. We must choose to put our faith in Christ throughout our lives, trusting that He is the Author of good things and the Giver of life even when our lives are not going the way we have planned.

In Hebrews 11:1 we read,

> *"Now faith is the assurance of things hoped for, the conviction of things not seen."*

There are times in our lives when things don't look encouraging, when life is full and chaotic. *We feel inadequate!* But it is at this moment that we know and must be conscious that our faith is being put to the test even though we cannot see the purpose. It is hard to be confident in God while our path unfolds before us, and the circumstance or perhaps our mental state is bigger than we can imagine.

When the storms of life hit us, they almost always appear to be stronger to us than God's Word. *We cannot afford for a moment to allow our perceptions to control us! It can be very deceptive and damaging!* So, my question is, *what are we going to do when circumstances strike us, putting fear in our hearts? Where is our faith?* God wants us to trust Him with all our mind, soul, and heart without hesitation. It is here that we must be of good courage, knowing that we must walk by faith and not by sight (2 Corinthians 5:7). It pleases our Father in heaven.

I find myself often asking God for the faith that I will need to trust Him in my life. And then I realize I must live in a state of humility amid my humanity. *This is powerful!* God intends for us to live in fellowship with Him. He wants me to trust His Grace because His Grace is sufficient for all I am lacking.

"And He has said to me, 'My grace is sufficient for you, for power is perfected in weakness.' Most gladly, therefore, I will rather boast about my weaknesses, so that the power of Christ may dwell in me" (2 Corinthians 12:9).

Walking by faith is not the easiest road to take. It may not seem to be a road that makes any sense from the outside, but there are so many blessings filled with God's presence and faithfulness, building our faith stronger and stronger as we draw nearer and walk closer to Him, the Author of all good things.

As we walk this path of life, we must turn our hearts and fix our eyes on Him, even as we face the unseen, walking by faith alone. If we walk not by sight, our vision becomes much more focused.

"And without faith it is impossible to please Him, for he who comes to God must believe that He is, and that He is a rewarder of those who seek Him" (Hebrews 11:6).

Is God asking you to trust Him perhaps today, with the assurance of things unseen? Remember, God gave His only begotten Son so that we may boldly live our lives, trusting Him instead of what is right in front of us.

May our Lord help us to walk our path of life by faith, trusting in His goodness and His Grace with that assurance of things unseen, believing that He is and that He is a rewarder of those who diligently seek Him.

God Amid the Storm

""Now there was a day when the sons of God came to present themselves before the LORD, and Satan also came among them. 7 The LORD said to Satan, 'From where have you come?' Satan answered the LORD and said, 'From going to and fro on the earth, and from walking up and down on it.' 8 And the LORD said to Satan, 'Have you considered my servant Job, that there is none like him on the earth, a blameless and upright man, who fears God and turns away from evil?' 9 Then Satan answered the LORD and said, 'Does Job fear God for no reason? 10 Have you not put a hedge around him and his house and all that he has, on every side? You have blessed the work of his hands, and his possessions have increased in the land. 11 But stretch out your hand and touch all that he has, and he will curse you to your face.' 12 And the LORD said to Satan, 'Behold, all that he has is in your hand. Only against him do not stretch out your hand.' So Satan went out from the presence of the LORD.'" Job 1:6-12

Suffering is the universal experience of man. How do you deal with the dark days? If we don't understand what is going on the larger picture, it is easy to fall into depression and despair. The Scriptures are a gift of our Creator who truly understands. God gives us enough information to face adversity in the best possible way, even though He does not explain everything. If we will listen to the heavenly Father, we will find faith to strengthen us and hope to help us endure to the end. The following study is my attempt to explain the treasures of God's wisdom on these matters, beginning with the wisdom of Job.

I have been reading the book of Job. In its pages, I observe how Job remembers the good times (his prior blessings) before his trials struck. The first chapter ends with success. Job proves His faithfulness to God, expecting nothing in return. His faithfulness to God was not because of the many blessings God had bestowed on him. Despite Job losing his children, possessions, and wealth, he never sins, charging God with wrong (Job 1:22). Satan (the accuser) had suggested that God had put a protective hedge around Job to assure his righteous behavior. Satan attempted to cheapen God's righteousness and blessings. While it is true that some do act righteously, not out of love, to receive God's blessings or gain benefits, some will still serve God even when those physical blessings are removed. By the end of the book, we hope that God's discussion with Satan is over, but unfortunately, it is not the case.

I. HOLDING ON TO FAITH AMID SUFFERING:

God and Satan:

> "Again there was a day when the sons of God came to present themselves before the Lord, and Satan also came among them to present himself before the Lord. And the Lord said to Satan, 'From where have you come?' Satan answered the Lord and said, 'From going to and fro on the earth, and from walking up and down on it.' And the Lord said to Satan, 'Have you considered my servant Job, that there is none like him on the earth, a blameless and upright man, who fears God and turns away from evil? He still

> *holds fast his integrity, although you incited me*
> *against him to destroy him without reason.'"* Job
> 2:1-3

The first two verses of chapter 2 are almost identical to chapter one, verse six, seven, and eight.

> *"Now there was a day when the sons of God came to*
> *present themselves before the LORD, and Satan also*
> *came among them. The LORD said to Satan, 'From*
> *where have you come?' Satan answered the LORD*
> *and said, 'From going to and fro on the earth, and*
> *from walking up and down on it.' And the LORD*
> *said to Satan, 'Have you considered my servant Job,*
> *that there is none like him on the earth, a blameless*
> *and upright man, who fears God and turns away*
> *from evil?'"* Job 1:6-8

The apparent reason for this repetition is to show us that Satan was responsible for Job's afflictions. God permitted the adversary of men to afflict Job. The only difference between chapter two and chapter one is that this time God affirms Job's integrity before Satan. Satan was proven wrong, and God was vindicated. Once again, God remains blameless because He is not responsible for these temptations.

> *"Let no one say when he is tempted, 'I am being*
> *tempted by God,' for God cannot be tempted with*
> *evil, and he himself tempts no one."'* James 1:13

The first three verses of chapter 2 start with the sons of God presenting themselves before Him. But Satan is doing all in his power, going to and fro through the earth. He still does that to God's righteous children today. He is a roaring lion seeking to devour anyone.

"Be sober-minded; be watchful. Your adversary the devil prowls around like a roaring lion, seeking someone to devour." 1 Peter 5:8

As we saw in chapter 1, God is showing us the motive and purpose of Satan. God draws Satan's attention to Job again. Job is blameless, upright, fears God, and turns away from evil. In verse 3, there is only one new statement made in this discussion.

"He still holds fast his integrity, although you incited me against him to destroy him without reason."

God declared that Job was a man of integrity. He had remained blameless and did not curse God as Satan said he would do. Job did not have false motives. He was not hypocritical. He remained faithful to God despite his terrible circumstances, losing his children and possessions. But Satan is not more powerful than God. He needed permission to do what he did to Job. Not only this, but God also constrained Satan.

"And the LORD said to Satan, 'Behold, all that he has is in your hand. Only against him do not stretch out your hand.' So Satan went out from the presence of the LORD.'" Job 1:12

What Job had to endure did not happen without God's knowledge or agreement. God took responsibility for what happened in Job 2:3.

"And the Lord said to Satan, 'Have you considered my servant Job, that there is none like him on the earth, a blameless and upright man, who fears God and turns away from evil? He still holds fast his in-

tegrity, although you incited me against him to de-
stroy him without reason.'"

God never said that Satan did it (though he did). Rather,
He said that He did it Himself.

"You incited me against him to destroy him without
reason.'"

But notice that this is not the only time that God did this.

"Then all his brothers and all his sisters and all who
had known him before, came to him, and they ate
bread with him in his house; and they consoled him
and comforted him for all the adversities that the
LORD had brought on him." Job 42:11

Dark Despair:

Suffering is not God's fault. He is not responsible. Satan is
the one afflicting Job (1:12; 2:3; 42:11). Nothing that happened
to Job was because he sinned. God did not punish Job for his
sins, receiving what he deserves. His suffering is undeserved.
Suffering is part of our Christian life. No Christian is exempt
from suffering (Job 1). Even the most righteous will suffer. We
are not exempt from experiencing suffering and difficulties
just because we are Christians. Often, it is the godly and the
righteous who receive worse treatment than the world. We deceive ourselves thinking that we will be free of pain and suffering because we are righteous and faithful. The righteous
must accept that suffering is part of their path here on earth.
Job's righteousness did not insulate him from undergoing the
most traumatic of trials.

We can learn endurance that builds our faith through suffering, acknowledging that everything we have belongs to

God. It is not ours. God gives and takes away. He does not have to give at all. We are not in control if we have a miserable life from start to finish. It is naive to think that God must be compelled to meet our life expectations just because we are faithful and righteous. Instead, we must continue being faithful to God, even if we must lose everything in life. So, we must be willing to praise God no matter our suffering.

Endurance is submission to God even when we lose everything we have. Job lost so much! He lost all his possessions, and his children died. His body was afflicted with sores from the top of his head to the bottom of his feet. He sat in the ashes, grieving, and mourning while scraping the sores on his body with a broken piece of pottery. His three friends did not even recognize him. His suffering continued for many months. In his pain, shock, and grief, Job opens his mouth and breaks, saying,

> *"Shall we receive good from God and shall we not receive adversity"* (2:10).

> *"The LORD gave, and the LORD has taken away; blessed be the name of the LORD"* (1:21).

Job's circumstances were dark, for there was no light or hope. All his happiness and joy had vaporized. It disappeared. He was in so much despair and pain that he cursed the day he was born. Job did not speak to anyone, not to his friends, or even to God. He just expressed his pain. He did not curse God.

> *"After this Job opened his mouth and cursed the day of his birth. And Job said: 'Let the day perish on which I was born, and the night that said, 'A man is conceived.' Let that day be darkness! May God above not seek it, nor light shine upon it. Let gloom and deep darkness claim it. Let clouds dwell upon it; let the blackness of the day terrify it. That night—let*

thick darkness seize it! Let it not rejoice among the days of the year; let it not come into the number of the months. Behold, let that night be barren; let no joyful cry enter it. Let those curse it who curse the day, who are ready to rouse up Leviathan. Let the stars of its dawn be dark; let it hope for light, but have none, nor see the eyelids of the morning, because it did not shut the doors of my mother's womb, nor hide trouble from my eyes.'" Job 3:1-10

Job's lamentation (3:11-19) is parallel with Jeremiah 20:14-18 and Lamentations 3:1-18.

"Why did I not die at birth, come out from the womb and expire? Why did the knees receive me? Or why the breasts, that I should nurse? For then I would have lain down and been quiet; I would have slept; then I would have been at rest, with kings and counselors of the earth who rebuilt ruins for themselves, or with princes who had gold, who filled their houses with silver. Or why was I not as a hidden stillborn child, as infants who never see the light? There the wicked cease from troubling, and there the weary are at rest. There the prisoners are at ease together; they hear not the voice of the taskmaster. The small and the great are there, and the slave is free from his master." Job 3:11-19

Job is hopeless amid the darkness of his pain. Death seems to be the only solution to his suffering. He wanted peace from his suffering and pain. Because of all that he was enduring, Job thought he had lost his relationship or friendship with God. He felt like God was not with him. So, he grappled with tough questions:

1. *Is it worth it to hold on to faith when God would allow such things to happen?*

2. *Is it possible to continue to believe in a good and right-eous God in a world where righteousness is no longer rewarded?*

Job was at a loss and wanted peace from so much turmoil internally and externally. In verses 13-19, Job declared that it does not matter who we are or what status we enjoy in life, for death will bring rest to us.

So, What is The Message For us Today?

• First, faith is not two dimensional:

We are not supposed to look at Job and conclude that he suffered and trusted God. When we are suffering, there is despair and darkness. One of the most extraordinary things we learn from Job is that faith, suffering, and hopelessness are not incompatible. And though we may have faith in God, we can still feel the crushing weight of our trials and suffering that cause us to feel broken. *Walking the narrow way of Christ is not sunshine and rainbows!*

Our walk of faith is not *"put a smile on your face"* and pretend you have no pain. Stoicism is not a godly response to suffering. Often, many deceive themselves thinking that the way to handle suffering is to pretend that there is no pain. It is a fact that trials hurt us. They can hurt us so deeply that we are not able to see the light but only darkness.

Faith and despair are not incompatible. We can suffer and feel despair and still have full faith in God. There is nothing wrong with us when we feel darkness. David expressed this beautifully in Psalm 23.

> *"Even though I walk through the valley of the shadow of death, I will fear no evil, for you are with me."*

Friends, we are walking through the valley of the shadow of death sometimes. Pain and darkness are unavoidable in our lives. But the question is, *what are we going to do when we enter the darkest valley? What will our response be?*

• Second, we serve a God who allows such unfiltered questions and laments amid our despair:

God will let us cry out our pain and feelings when things are painful and difficult. God can handle it, for He does not limit our feelings or expressions of pain. Consider how many Psalms express this kind of hurt, pain, suffering, and questioning. The Psalms are wonderful to read and meditate on when we are in pain and suffering. Listen to what God wants us to do.

> *"Since then we have a great high priest who has passed through the heavens, Jesus, the Son of God, let us hold fast our confession. For we do not have a high priest who is unable to sympathize with our weaknesses, but one who in every respect has been tempted as we are, yet without sin. Let us then with confidence draw near to the throne of grace, that we may receive mercy and find grace to help in time of need."* Hebrews 4:14-16

We have Jesus as our faithful friend who can sympathize with our weaknesses, for He endured temptations and trials just like we do. Jesus was deeply distressed and troubled.

> *"And he took with him Peter and James and John, and began to be greatly distressed and troubled."* Mark 14:33

So, let us draw near to the throne of grace and receive mercy and find grace to help in our time of need. Pain is not incompatible with faith. Let us not sit in the darkness of our trials, hiding our pain, and pretending that we do not hurt. We all must enter the darkest valley. *But what will be your response?* God wants us to come to Him through His beloved Son Jesus, who is our sympathetic High Priest. He hears our cries and pain. He will give us mercy and grace. *Where could we go but to our Lord?*

II. WHAT TO DO WHEN LIFE TURNS INTO LOSS:

Job's greatest pain was believing that he had lost his relationship with God when he was God's friend.

> *"And Job again took up his discourse, and said: 'Oh, that I were as in the months of old, as in the days when God watched over me, when his lamp shone upon my head, and by his light I walked through darkness, as I was in my prime, when the friendship of God was upon my tent, when the Almighty was yet with me, when my children were all around me, when my steps were washed with butter, and the rock poured out for me streams of oil!'"* Job 29:1-6

He remembers God's presence and His blessings in his life and how God was with him through life's darkness (29:3-6). Job contrasts his present circumstances as he recalls his prior blessings and joy. Chapter 30 ends with Job's expressing his hopelessness.

> *"Yet does not one in a heap of ruins stretch out his hand, and in his disaster cry for help? Did not I weep for him whose day was hard? Was not my soul grieved for the needy? But when I hoped for good, evil came, and when I waited for light, darkness came. My inward parts are in turmoil and never still; days of affliction come to meet me. I go about darkened, but not by the sun; I stand up in the as-*

sembly and cry for help. I am a brother of jackals and a companion of ostriches. My skin turns black and falls from me, and my bones burn with heat. My lyre is turned to mourning, and my pipe to the voice of those who weep." Job 30:24-31

Job's final words are an appeal to his righteousness.

• He is morally pure (31:1-4):

"I have made a covenant with my eyes; how then could I gaze at a virgin? What would be my portion from God above and my heritage from the Almighty on high? Is not calamity for the unrighteous, and disaster for the workers of iniquity? Does not he see my ways and number all my steps?"

• He has lived in integrity (31:5-8):

"If I have walked with falsehood and my foot has hastened to deceit; (Let me be weighed in a just balance, and let God know my integrity!) if my step has turned aside from the way and my heart has gone after my eyes, and if any spot has stuck to my hands, then let me sow, and another eat, and let what grows for me be rooted out."

• He has been faithful in his marriage (31:9-12):

"If my heart has been enticed toward a woman, and I have lain in wait at my neighbor's door, then let my wife grind for another, and let others bow down on her. For that would be a heinous crime; that would be an iniquity to be punished by the judges; for that would be a fire that consumes as far as Abaddon, and it would burn to the root all my increase."

• He has shown no partiality (31:13-15):

> *"If I have rejected the cause of my manservant or my maidservant, when they brought a complaint against me, what then shall I do when God rises up? When he makes inquiry, what shall I answer him? Did not he who made me in the womb make him? And did not one fashion us in the womb?"*

• He has been charitable (31:16-23):

> *"If I have withheld anything that the poor desired, or have caused the eyes of the widow to fail, or have eaten my morsel alone, and the fatherless has not eaten of it (for from my youth the fatherless grew up with me as with a father, and from my mother's womb I guided the widow), if I have seen anyone perish for lack of clothing, or the needy without covering, if his body has not blessed me, and if he was not warmed with the fleece of my sheep, if I have raised my hand against the fatherless, because I saw my help in the gate, then let my shoulder blade fall from my shoulder, and let my arm be broken from its socket. For I was in terror of calamity from God, and I could not have faced his majesty."*

• He has been humble (31:24-28):

> *"If I have made gold my trust or called fine gold my confidence, if I have rejoiced because my wealth was abundant or because my hand had found much, if I have looked at the sun when it shone, or the moon moving in splendor, and my heart has been secretly enticed, and my mouth has kissed my hand, this also would be an iniquity to be punished by the judges, for I would have been false to God above."*

• He has shown hospitality (31:29-34):

"If I have rejoiced at the ruin of him who hated me, or exulted when evil overtook him (I have not let my mouth sin by asking for his life with a curse), if the men of my tent have not said, 'Who is there that has not been filled with his meat?' (the sojourner has not lodged in the street; I have opened my doors to the traveler), if I have concealed my transgressions as others do by hiding my iniquity in my heart, because I stood in great fear of the multitude, and the contempt of families terrified me, so that I kept silence, and did not go out of doors— "

• Job's final cry to God (31:35-40):

"Oh, that I had one to hear me! (Here is my signature! Let the Almighty answer me!) Oh, that I had the indictment written by my adversary! Surely I would carry it on my shoulder; I would bind it on me as a crown; I would give him an account of all my steps; like a prince I would approach him. "If my land has cried out against me and its furrows have wept together, if I have eaten its yield without payment and made its owners breathe their last, let thorns grow instead of wheat, and foul weeds instead of barley."

Job calls on God to tell him the charges He has against him (31:40).

1. *So, what must we learn from Job's experiences?*
2. *What must we do when life falls apart?*
3. *What must we do when life explodes?*

Indeed, we can learn many lessons in Job's final speech. Consider at least nine foundational facts that help us in our times of trials and sufferings.

- We can remain faithful and righteous while suffering immensely.

We see this portrayed throughout the book of Job. Like Job, we have Jesus as the ultimate example of righteousness who was made to suffer.

- We must continue to glorify God amid our suffering (Job 26).

The apostle Paul shared these same sentiments.

> "Not only that, but we rejoice in our sufferings, knowing that suffering produces endurance, and endurance produces character, and character produces hope, and hope does not put us to shame, because God's love has been poured into our hearts through the Holy Spirit who has been given to us."
> Romans 5:3-5

- The righteous hope in God for future justice (Job 27).

> "For this is a gracious thing, when, mindful of God, one endures sorrows while suffering unjustly. For what credit is it if, when you sin and are beaten for it, you endure? But if when you do good and suffer for it you endure, this is a gracious thing in the sight of God. For to this you have been called, because Christ also suffered for you, leaving you an example, so that you might follow in his steps. He committed no sin, neither was deceit found in his mouth. When he was reviled, he did not revile in return; when he

suffered, he did not threaten, but continued entrust-
ing himself to him who judges justly." 1 Peter 2:19–
23

- The wisdom that we need while suffering must be based on fearing the Lord (Job 28).

Even when it seems like the righteous and the wicked's fate is the same, we must know that wisdom still belongs to God. When we are suffering, we need God more, not less. So, we must draw closer to God, not move further from Him.

> *"Count it all joy, my brothers, when you meet trials*
> *of various kinds, for you know that the testing of*
> *your faith produces steadfastness. And let steadfast-*
> *ness have its full effect, that you may be perfect and*
> *complete, lacking in nothing. If any of you lacks*
> *wisdom, let him ask God, who gives generously to all*
> *without reproach, and it will be given him."* James
> 1:2-5

- Suffering does not mean we have lost our relationship with God (Job 29).

And though Job felt like his suffering meant he was God's enemy and that God had forsaken him, this is not the case, for God has given us wonderful promises.

> *"Keep your life free from the love of money, and be*
> *content with what you have, for he has said, 'I will*
> *never leave you nor forsake you.' So we can confi-*
> *dently say, "The Lord is my helper; I will not fear;*
> *what can man do to me?'"* Hebrews 13:5-6

- We must enjoy what we have now because it can be gone tomorrow (Job 30).

We must not deceive ourselves, thinking that things will always be the same today and tomorrow, for everything can change with the blink of an eye. Job, a righteous man, woke up one day and saw that everything he had was taken from him. All he had left was God. The writer of Ecclesiastes repeatedly warns us that life is just a vapor and that our circumstances are unpredictable, for they can change at one moment and then change the next. *So, we must learn to appreciate and enjoy what we have today!*

- Even while suffering, we must remain pure and holy (Job 27:3-5; 31).

Nothing would make Satan happier than turning to sin and forsaking God. After all this suffering, imagine if Job had turned to sin and rebelled against God's laws! It would have proved that Job only served God for the good he received. *Will we only serve God when life is good and smiling at us? Or will we serve God and love God faithfully, no matter our experiences in life?*

We will never get any answers to why we are suffering. It is one of the big messages of the book. And though we might think we have the answers to our whys, they are just guesses and nothing else. We will never know the why of our suffering. When Jesus' disciples found the blind man in John 9, they thought there were only two options: his parents sinned, or he sinned. Jesus said that neither of those options was correct. To say that we know the whys of our suffering is to presume that we know God's mind and intentions. *We do not know God's intentions and reasons!*

- Faith can grow through our trials (Job 3-31):

Job's faith increased from his early cries. In Job 3, we can see that as his faith grew, he defended God. So, we must consider the growth of our faith and rule our tongue through our trials and sufferings.

Thus, we must trust God to help us handle our sufferings to glorify Him. We need God to help us through trials (Job 6:14-30). We must remember that God is with us amid our trials and suffering. He loves us and will never push us beyond the strength that He supplies for us (1 Corinthians 10:13). God's purpose is not to destroy us but to save us. God allows trials to refine our faith and make us what He wants us to be. God wants us to be His children and enjoy eternal life with Him. Let us hold firm to Him through our trials and sufferings and continue to trust in Him.

III. SUFFERING IS INSTRUCTIVE:

God uses suffering instructively. God's discipline is His Grace to save us. He is merciful and desires to deliver us from going into the pit. He uses suffering to direct our steps so that we may not be destroyed.

> *"My son, do not despise the Lord's discipline or be weary of his reproof, for the Lord reproves him whom he loves, as a father the son in whom he delights."*
> Proverbs 3:11-12

> *"And have you forgotten the exhortation that addresses you as sons? 'My son, do not regard lightly the discipline of the Lord, nor be weary when reproved by him. For the Lord disciplines the one he loves, and chastises every son whom he receives.' It is for discipline that you have to endure. God is treating you as sons. For what son is there whom his father does not discipline? If you are left without discipline, in which all have participated, then you are illegitimate children and not sons. Besides this, we have had earthly fathers who disciplined us and*

we respected them. Shall we not much more be subject to the Father of spirits and live? For they disciplined us for a short time as it seemed best to them, but he disciplines us for our good, that we may share his holiness. For the moment all discipline seems painful rather than pleasant, but later it yields the peaceful fruit of righteousness to those who have been trained by it.'" Hebrews 12:5-11

God allows discipline and instruction in our lives through suffering for our good, to make us what He wants us to be. So we must rejoice in our sufferings, for God's instruction and wisdom are found in them.

"Not only that, but we rejoice in our sufferings, knowing that suffering produces endurance, and endurance produces character, and character produces hope, and hope does not put us to shame, because God's love has been poured into our hearts through the Holy Spirit who has been given to us." Romans 5:3-5

"Count it all joy, my brothers, when you meet trials of various kinds, for you know that the testing of your faith produces steadfastness. And let steadfastness have its full effect, that you may be perfect and complete, lacking in nothing." James 1:2-4

Suffering is an expression of God's grace and mercy. Suffering is good for us, for pain is instructive and will help us not fall into the pit and harm our souls eternally. We must acknowledge that God is not punishing through our suffering, but rather He is teaching us. God allows suffering in our lives to teach us to consider our ways and keep our eyes focused on Him alone. He allows suffering to refine us and make us wiser and not lose our souls. He wants us to draw closer to Him amid our suffering.

IV. LET US NOT ALLOW OUR SUFFERING AND TRIALS TO GO TO WASTE:

In Philippians 1:12-26, Paul show us how to take advantage of hardships and suffering so that what he suffered would have purpose and meaning and not be wasted. Suffering is a great challenge to the faith of our walk with God. In the book of Job, we learn that Satan uses suffering to tempt us to forfeit our faith and turn away from the Lord. No one is immune from suffering, for everyone will experience suffering, difficulties, and trials in life. Paul wrote the letter to the Philippians while he was in prison. We read about his imprisonment at the end of the book of Acts. Here we see the great apostle Paul, imprisoned for over two years in Caesarea. After a horrible journey to Rome that included a shipwreck, he is imprisoned in Rome, awaiting his trial before Caesar. Listen to what he has to say about his circumstances.

> *"I want you to know, brothers, that what has happened to me has really served to advance the gospel, so that it has become known throughout the whole imperial guard and to all the rest that my imprisonment is for Christ. And most of the brothers, having become confident in the Lord by my imprisonment, are much more bold to speak the word without fear. Some indeed preach Christ from envy and rivalry, but others from good will. The latter do it out of love, knowing that I am put here for the defense of the gospel. The former proclaim Christ out of selfish ambition, not sincerely but thinking to afflict me in my imprisonment. What then? Only that in every way, whether in pretense or in truth, Christ is proclaimed, and in that I rejoice. Yes, and I will rejoice, for I know that through your prayers and the help of the Spirit of Jesus Christ this will turn out for my deliverance, as it is my eager expectation and hope that I will not be at all ashamed, but that with full courage*

now as always Christ will be honored in my body, whether by life or by death. For to me to live is Christ, and to die is gain. If I am to live in the flesh, that means fruitful labor for me. Yet which I shall choose I cannot tell. I am hard pressed between the two. My desire is to depart and be with Christ, for that is far better. But to remain in the flesh is more necessary on your account. Convinced of this, I know that I will remain and continue with you all, for your progress and joy in the faith, so that in me you may have ample cause to glory in Christ Jesus, because of my coming to you again." Philippians 1:12-26

Paul's imprisonment turned out for good. His suffering helped to advance the Gospel. The Gospel had reached unbelievers. The whole imperial guard knew that Paul was imprisoned for the cause of Christ. The Gospel was spread in the city of Rome through Paul's suffering and imprisonment. Not only this, but the apostle Paul also declared in verse 14 that Christians were confident in proclaiming the Gospel due to his imprisonment. Other Christians have become bolder to speak because of Paul's boldness that led to his imprisonment. Paul's suffering has encouraged others to suffer, as well. *Isn't it remarkable!*

Paul was not angry, bitter, and wallowing in self-pity because of his imprisonment and his circumstances. It was not the end of the world and the worst thing that had ever happened to him. He did not shake his fist at God for his imprisonment. He was happy to be proclaiming the Gospel. He could see the positive in his circumstances. Not only this, but Paul also declared that some were preaching Christ out of envy and rivalry (Philippians 1:15-18). Even though they were teaching from wrong motives, desiring to harm him, Paul still rejoices since Christ is proclaimed. Paul turned the negative as a positive worthy of rejoicing because Christ is proclaimed.

Paul's joy is that the Gospel is proclaimed, and the message of Jesus is spread. Thus, we must examine our lives through the lens of the Gospel's progress, not by our comfort. Joy is rooted in the Gospel's proclamation, not personal circumstances, as we so often evaluate our lives. We can have joy in suffering because Christ and the Gospel are benefiting through our turmoil. As Christians, our aspirations must not be rooted in wealth, marriage, children, travel, career, retirement, or anything else that is not the Gospel's advancement. Our trials and suffering must be used for the advancing of the Gospel.

The apostle Paul seems to be quoting Job 13:16.

> *"Though he slay me, I will hope in him; yet I will argue my ways to his face. This will be my salvation, that the godless shall not come before him."*

When Job declared these words, he was also speaking about his spiritual salvation, not just his physical salvation. This makes the thrust of what Paul was saying more powerful. Paul's faith will be vindicated, no matter how his trials turn out. He knew that through the prayers of Christians and the strength from the Spirit of Jesus Christ, all would be for his spiritual salvation. Paul's point is the same point the whole New Testament makes about our trials and suffering refining our faith, molding us into what God wants us to remain faithful to the Lord till we die. Listen to Peter's words.

> *"In this you rejoice, though now for a little while, if necessary, you have been grieved by various trials, so that the tested genuineness of your faith—more precious than gold that perishes though it is tested by fire—may be found to result in praise and glory and honor at the revelation of Jesus Christ."* 1 Peter 1:6-7

No matter our suffering, Christ must be honored. No matter what happens to us, Christ must be honored. If that means living or dying, Christ must continue to be honored. Our purpose in suffering is to make Christ look excellent, honored, and worthy. *How do we make Christ look worthy and honored? By trading everything, even life, to gain Christ. Christ must be greater in life or death!*

So, we must pursue Jesus regardless of the cost, for all that matters in this life is that Christ is glorified, honored, whatever our circumstances. The value of gaining Christ is worth the loss of all things, even life itself. This is what it means to live for Christ and die to be gain. It is how we treasure Christ in our lives. Paul saw death as the fulfillment of all his labors in life and the glorious possession of Christ. Our lives must bear fruit for Christ, even amid our pain and suffering. *We must be willing to serve and honor Christ regardless of our circumstances!* When we suffer, sacrifice, and die to self, we would not waste our suffering and trials.

Therefore, let us not waste our suffering and trials.

1. Let us use our trials and suffering to honor Christ and to advance the Gospel.
2. Let us use our difficulties to encourage other Christians to be courageous in the Lord.
3. Let us use our pain to grow our faith toward the salvation of our soul.
4. Whatever our circumstances, to live is Christ and to die is gain.
5. Let us honor Jesus in all things before the world.
6. Let us allow Christ to be the center of our relationships, aspirations, desires, and self-denial.

Let us rejoice even amid our pain. When we approach our pain with strength, it is easier to spread that strength to others and strengthen their faith. *Our experiences and trials can strengthen others!* The apostle Paul didn't suffer in prison alone. He allowed others to share in his suffering. He did not keep his *"thorn in the flesh"* quiet. He taught the Corinthians what he learned from it. *We must be open about our suffering to give and receive encouragement through our healing process!*

CONCLUSION:

God puts limitations on what Satan can do to us. God is in control through Job's trials. In Job 1:12, God tells Satan.

> *"Behold, all that he has is in your hand. Only against him do not stretch out your hand."*

God tells Satan what he can and cannot do. Satan can do anything with what Job has, but nothing can be done against his body.

> *"Behold, he is in your hand; only spare his life."* Job 2:6

Satan is not God and does not operate independently of God's power. God's children need to grasp well the problem of suffering. God is in full control of Satan. Whatever Satan does is within God's constraints and rule. This knowledge gives us hope. God is in control of the circumstances. He is ruling over our trials, and nothing will happen outside His knowledge. Since God is ruling over our trials, we can be hopeful amid our trials and sufferings. God loves us. He sent His Son to save us, not to destroy us through our trials and sufferings. *So, we must look at the cross and acknowledge His amazing and sacrificial love!* Although God puts limitations on what can happen to us, our faith must be tested.

> *"Now these things occurred as examples for us, so that we might not desire evil as they did. Do not become idolaters as some of them did; as it is written, 'The people sat down to eat and drink, and they rose up to play.' We must not indulge in sexual immorality as some of them did, and twenty-three thousand fell in a single day. We must not put Christ to the test, as some of them did, and were destroyed by serpents. And do not complain as some of them did, and were destroyed by the destroyer. These things happened to them to serve as an example, and they were written down to instruct us, on whom the ends of the ages have come. So if you think you are standing, watch out that you do not fall. No testing has overtaken you that is not common to everyone. God is faithful, and he will not let you be tested beyond your strength, but with the testing he will also provide the way out so that you may be able to endure it."* 1 Corinthians 10:6-13

After speaking about these tests that Israel experienced in the wilderness and failed, the apostle Paul tells us that these tests that Israel experienced in the wilderness and failed serve as an example for us not to fall and fail God like they did (1 Cor. 10:11-12). In verse 13, we have a promise that gives us hope.

> *"No testing has overtaken you that is not common to everyone. God is faithful, and he will not let you be tested beyond your strength, but with the testing he will also provide the way out so that you may be able to endure it."*

Many translations read this as *"no temptation has overtaken you,"* but there are others like the NRSV and NET that read *"no testing"* or *"no trial."* The word that is translated "temptation" or "trial" here simply means *"to put to the test or prove."* So we must read this text as a promise regarding our trials and temptations. God is sovereign over these events in our life. God puts limits so that our testing will not press us beyond our strength. God is faithful. *He will not let us be tested beyond our strength!* Satan is limited. Satan needs permission. Satan cannot act beyond God's power and knowledge.

If Job overcame his trial, we may rest assured we can overcome ours as well. God is faithful, and He is with us amid our darkest storms. *With God's help, we can endure what has been given!*

> *"As an example of suffering and patience, brothers, take the prophets who spoke in the name of the Lord. Behold, we consider those blessed who remained steadfast. You have heard of the steadfastness of Job, and you have seen the purpose of the Lord, how the Lord is compassionate and merciful."* James 5:10-11

Often when suffering strikes us, we stop praying, praising, reading our Bibles, and meeting for worship with our brethren. A Christ-honoring attitude must compel us to pray, praise, study, and have fellowship with those of the like precious faith to help us in our suffering. *We must stop thinking from a fleshly perspective, serving self, but a heavenly perspective focused on honoring Christ!* Instead of complaining, saying, *"How can I get out of this trial?"* Why not think from a heavenly perspective, *"How can the Lord use this trial for His glory?"* Let us not miss the point of our suffering. Christ allows suffering and persecution for a reason. When we suffer with hope and praise, we honor Christ, proving that He is the solid Rock.

Paul and the apostles are our best examples of rejoicing during massive trials, persecution, empty stomachs, and imminent death. Godly joy is rooted in something other than physical circumstances. In Philippians 1:17-19, Paul rejoices because Christ is proclaimed, Christ will be honored in his body, he and the Philippians may soon die for Christ.

In Acts 5:41, Peter and the apostles rejoiced after being beaten, for they were counted worthy to suffer for Christ. And though each of these circumstances was full of pain, the apostles still rejoiced. They did not rejoice because of their physical circumstances, but instead, they rejoiced because the Lord's purposes were being accomplished. *True life and perspective change joy for us!*

> *"Indeed, I count everything as loss because of the surpassing worth of knowing Christ Jesus my Lord. For his sake I have suffered the loss of all things and count them as rubbish, in order that I may gain Christ..."* Philippians 3:8

Suffering the loss of material possessions, academic knowledge, and even family have no worth in comparison to the joy found in knowing Christ. I would rather lose everything and gain Christ and still count it as joy. *We must determine to stop placing our hope in this world!* Our happiness must not be based on our economic situations, a successful day at work, healthy bodies, or our family and friends' happiness. Trusting in all these earthly things to give us joy or happiness will lead us to a miserable life, for they will fail us at some point in our lives. There is no lasting joy when our primary focus is on these physical things to fill us.

Our priorities must be in the right places: honoring Christ and the furthering of His Gospel. When our hope is in the firm foundation of the Lord, our joy will be full. And though we may experience pain, sickness, and even death, we still can rejoice because of our hope. In John 4:32-34, Jesus said,

"I have food to eat that you do not know about... My food is to do the will of him who sent me and to accomplish his work."

May the Lord's will be accomplished through our suffering. May we rejoice amid our sufferings and trials to complete the work of the Lord.